ON FREEDOM AND
FREE ENTERPRISE

LUDWIG VON MISES

ON FREEDOM AND FREE ENTERPRISE

ESSAYS IN HONOR OF LUDWIG VON MISES

PRESENTED ON THE OCCASION OF
THE FIFTIETH ANNIVERSARY OF HIS DOCTORATE
FEBRUARY 20, 1956

Editor

MARY SENNHOLZ

CONTRIBUTORS

C. ANTONI, Italy
FAUSTINO BALLVÉ, Mexico
LOUIS BAUDIN, France
PERCY L. GREAVES, JR., U.S.A.
F. A. HARPER, U.S.A.
F. A. HAYEK, U.S.A.
HENRY HAZLITT, U.S.A.
W. H. HUTT, South Africa
BERTRAND DE JOUVENEL, France

L. M. LACHMANN, South Africa
F. MACHLUP, U.S.A.
WILLIAM H. PETERSON, U.S.A.
W. E. RAPPARD, Switzerland
LEONARD E. READ, U.S.A.
W. RÖPKE, Switzerland
MURRAY N. ROTHBARD, U.S.A.
J. RUEFF, France
HANS F. SENNHOLZ, U.S.A.

LOUIS M. SPADARO, U.S.A.

D. VAN NOSTRAND COMPANY, INC.

PRINCETON, NEW JERSEY

TORONTO

LONDON

NEW YORK

D. VAN NOSTRAND COMPANY, INC.

120 Alexander St., Princeton, New Jersey
257 Fourth Avenue, New York 10, New York
25 Hollinger Rd., Toronto 16, Canada
Macmillan & Co., Ltd., St. Martin's St., London, W.C. 2, England

*All correspondence should be addressed to the
principal office of the company at Princeton, N. J.*

A 7

PRINTED IN THE UNITED STATES OF AMERICA

Table of Contents

v

Acknowledgments

I would like to acknowledge with gratitude the generous devotion of time and effort that each of the contributors has given to this volume. Their response and cooperation have made this work possible. I am grateful to my husband for his invaluable assistance in the preparation of the manuscript. Thanks is also due to Miss Vernelia Crawford for her contribution of the index.

Professor Röpke's paper on "The Place of Economics Among the Sciences" originally appeared in the July 1953 issue of *Studium Generale*, Springer, Berlin, Göttingen, Heidelberg. Mr. Hazlitt's review of Dr. von Mises' book on *Socialism* first appeared in *The New York Times* on January 9, 1938, and his review of *Human Action* in *Newsweek* on September 19, 1949. I would like to thank their editors and publishers for the permission to reprint these papers.

M.S.

Ludwig von Mises

If Carl Menger may be called the father of the Austrian School of economic thought, Ludwig von Mises is his most famous descendant. Since the beginning of the first decade of this century, it is he who has combined and greatly developed the economic teaching of Menger, Böhm-Bawerk, and Wieser. But while his great predecessors lived and wrote at a time in which the growing forces of socialism and interventionism were just gathering to assault the capitalist social and economic order, Ludwig von Mises witnessed their offensives and triumphs. Surrounded by hostile forces and often alone, he refused to surrender. With his great courage and power of reasoning he counterattacked, always bearing the brunt of the battle. For almost half a century he has been the rallying-point for the forces of freedom and free enterprise, and for the courageous remnants of liberalism.

Ludwig von Mises was born on September 29, 1881, in Lemberg in what was then Austria-Hungary. Together with his younger brother Richard, who lived to become a great mathematician, he received a thorough education. From 1892 to 1900 he attended the "Akademische Gymnasium" in Vienna to prepare himself for the university. Upon graduation he studied law and economics at the University of Vienna. On February 20, 1906, the University conferred upon him the degree of Doctor of Law and Social Sciences, or, as the traditional Latin title goes, of Both Laws, i.e., of Roman and Canon Laws. In commemoration of this event in the life of Ludwig von Mises some of his friends and disciples have prepared this volume the title of which indicates his greatest concern: freedom and free enterprise.

After a short occupation with the administration of justice, his increasing interest in social and economic matters induced him to accept the position of economic adviser of the Austrian Chamber of Commerce. For almost thirty years he endeavored to stem the tide of interventionism and socialism from this post, until Austria became a part of the German Reich. And for more than two decades he taught the economics of free enterprise at the University of Vienna until he left for Geneva, Switzerland, to become professor of international economic relations at the Graduate Institute of International Studies.

The political and economic world changed rapidly and materially during this period. The forces of interventionism and economic nationalism gnawed at the foundation of the Austro-Hungarian monarchy which had united the smaller nations in Central Europe and on the Balkan Peninsula in peaceful coexistence and cooperation. Undermined and weakened by the ideology of interventionist dissension and conflict, the Union finally collapsed on the occasion of its military defeat in World War I. Ludwig von Mises witnessed this grave hour of his nation as a captain of the Austrian artillery.

As early as 1912 Dr. von Mises had vigorously opposed those doctrines whose application was bound to destroy Austria-Hungary and peace and prosperity in Europe. In his book on the *Theorie des Geldes und der Umlaufsmittel* he had exploded the most important economic element in the rising ideology of destruction: inflationism. His inquiry into a field which his predecessors had largely neglected drew upon it passionate attacks by the advocates of government spending and omnipotence. But the events during the ensuing decades bore out the validity of his keen criticism. His book is as revealing and significant for the student of present-day political and economic phenomena as it was more than four decades ago.

At the end of World War I collectivism triumphed in large parts of Europe. Nationalism and socialism were the accepted ideologies, and liberalism and capitalism were decried as the sources of all vice and evil. To Ludwig von Mises these notions merely constituted "a revolt against reason" and a denial of two hundred years of economic thought. In his two books, *Nation, Staat und Wirtschaft*, which is a restatement of his liberal convictions and a devastating analysis of collectivism, and in *Die Gemeinwirtschaft*, which is a comprehensive critique of socialism, he uncompromisingly attacked and rejected the prevailing ideologies and their disastrous application by governments. In nearly every respect he ran counter to the main stream of contemporary thought.

In Austria he was fighting a losing battle. In spite of his prodigious labor and relentless counterattacks, the cause of freedom and free enterprise failed to hold its ground. In 1934 he left for Geneva to occupy a chair at the Graduate Institute of International Studies. In the Swiss atmosphere of peace and serenity he observed the rise of nationalist-socialist Germany and the outbreak of World War II. It is here that Professor von Mises wrote his magnum opus, *Nationalökonomie, Theorie des Handelns und Wirtschaftens,* which is a comprehensive treatise on economics. Its revised American edition is known under the title *Human Action.* His disciples hail it as "the most uncompromising and most rigorously reasoned statement of the case for capitalism that has yet appeared." For a theoretical treatise of its size it has attained a remarkable circulation.

In 1940 Ludwig von Mises immigrated to the United States where he had spent some time twice before. In 1926 he was a visiting professor sponsored by the Lama Spellman Rockefeller Foundation, and in 1931 he attended the Congress of the International Chamber of Commerce in Washington, D.C. Now he came to stay and make America his country of choice. He continued to write and lecture. His book, *Omnipotent Government,* is a most penetrating history of the rise and fall of Germany during the last one hundred years. It analyzes the collapse of German liberalism and its substitution by the ideologies of nationalism and socialism. Since 1945 he has been lecturing as a visiting professor of economics at the Graduate School of Business Administration of New York University. It is here that his young disciples gather for discussions and seek his inspiration and guidance which his seminars have been providing for over forty years.

Ludwig von Mises' work and influence will be judged by the economic historians of future generations. His contemporaries at first were inclined to ignore or scoff at the writings of this "reactionary" Viennese professor. There was no place, no recognition for him in this era of "new economics." But he never hesitated to point out that the collectivist road chosen by modern governments was bound to lead to further economic distress and infringement upon man's liberty. Again and again he correctly anticipated the ultimate outcome of socialist and interventionist measures. While the large majority of people continued to clamor for more intervention to cure prior intervention, an ever-widening circle of scholars and writers began to recognize the cogency of his teaching. His influence on contemporary social and economic thought has been growing constantly. Today his writings are familiar to the liberal schools in various countries. He has lectured at universities and other learned institutions in Great Britain, Germany, the Netherlands, France, Italy, Mexico, and Peru. Indeed, he has been incessantly exerting his great strength and ability that the truth be known. When the nations once again prefer reason and freedom to instincts and bondage, every student cannot fail to recognize the invaluable service Ludwig von Mises has been rendering to the social sciences.

In their New York City apartment, Dr. and Mrs. von Mises, who has been his inseparable companion and indefatigable collaborator since the days of Geneva, are the frequent hosts to libertarian friends and scholars from many parts of the world. The authors of this volume sincerely hope and wish that they will be with us and further guide us through their wisdom and example for a long time to come.

MARY SENNHOLZ

Professor von Mises' Most Important Writings

Theorie des Geldes und der Umlaufsmittel, Duncker & Humboldt, München, 1912; 1924. English edition: *The Theory of Money and Credit*—translated by H. E. Batson, London, 1934; new English edition with essay on "Monetary Reconstruction," Yale University Press, New Haven, 1953. Spanish edition: *Teoria del Dinero y del Crédito*—translated by Antonio Riaño, M. Aguilar, Madrid, 1936. Japanese edition by Yonco Azuma, 1949.

Nation, Staat und Wirtschaft, Manzsche Buchhandlung, Wien, 1919.

Die Gemeinwirtschaft; Untersuchungen über den Sozialismus, Gustav Fischer, Jena, 1922; 1932. English edition: *Socialism; An Economic and Sociological Analysis*—translated by J. Kahane, Jonathan Cape, London, 1936; new English edition with epilogue, Yale University Press, New Haven, 1951. French edition: *Le Socialisme; Etude économique et sociologique*—translated by P. Bastier, A. and F. Terrasse, Librairie de Médicis, Paris, 1938.

Liberalismus, Gustav Fischer, Jena, 1927.

Geldwertstabilisierung und Konjunkturpolitik, Gustav Fischer, Jena, 1928. Italian edition: *La stabilizzazione del potere d'acquisto della moneta e la politica della congiuntura*—translated by Professor Jenny Griziotti Kretschmann, Torino, 1935.

Kritik des Interventionismus; Untersuchungen zur Wirtschaftpolitik und Wirstchaftsideologie der Gegenwart, Gustav Fischer, Jena, 1929.

Die Ursachen der Wirtschaftskrise, J. C. B. Mohr, Tübingen, 1931. Dutch edition: *De Oorzaken van de Economische Crisis*, Met een voorwoord van den vertaler Ir. A. J. Bergsma, Mouton & Co., Den Haag, 1933.

Grundprobleme der Nationalökonomie, Gustav Fischer, Jena, 1933.

"The Disintegration of the International Division of Labor" in *The World Crisis* by the Professors of the Graduate Institute of International Studies, pages 245-274, Longmans, Green & Co., London & New York, 1938. French edition: *Les illusions du protectionisme et de l'autarcie*—translated by R. Godet, Librairie de Médicis, Paris, 1938.

Nationalökonomie; Theorie des Handelns und Wirtschaften, Editions Union, Geneva, 1940.

Omnipotent Government, Yale University Press, New Haven, 1944. French edition: *Le Gouvernement Omnipotent*—translated by M. de Hulster, Librairie de Médicis, Paris, 1947. Spanish edition: *Omnipotencia Gubernamental*—translated by Pedro Elcoibar, Editorial Hermes, Mexico.

Bureaucracy, Yale University Press, New Haven, 1944. French edition: *La Bureaucratie*—translated by R. Florin & P. Barbier, Librairie de Médicis, Paris, 1946.

Human Action, Yale University Press, New Haven, 1949.

Planning for Freedom, Libertarian Press, South Holland, Illinois, 1952.

Notes on the Contributors

CARLO ANTONI

Born at Trieste in 1896. Disciple of Benedetto Croce. As commissioner for foreign cultural relations from 1944 to 1947, he re-established cultural exchange with the United States, France, and England. Member of the National Council and secretary of the council for foreign affairs from 1946 to 1947. Professor at the University of Padua and since 1946 at the University of Rome where he teaches philosophy of history. At present professor of history of modern philosophy and director of the Institute of Philosophy. Associate founder of the Mont-Pèlerin Society, member of the Accademia Nazionale dei Lincei, Einaudi Prize for philosophy, vice-president of the Italian Association for the Liberty of Culture, member of the Superior Council of Public Instruction.

Works: *Dallo storicismo alla sociologia*, 1940; *La lotta contro la ragione*, 1942; *Considerazioni su Hegel e Marx*, 1946; *Commento a Croce*, 1955.

FAUSTINO BALLVÉ

Born in Barcelona, Spain, in 1887. He studied juridical and economic science at the universities of Barcelona, Madrid, Berlin, and London. From 1915 to 1936 Dr. Ballvé practiced international and corporation law in Barcelona. Member of Parliament of the Spanish Republic. In 1939 he immigrated to France and in 1942 from there to Mexico City, where he is an attorney at law and professor of economics at the Technological Institute. Dr. Ballvé is the foremost representative of liberalism and adherent of the Austrian School of thought in Mexico. He is chairman of *Ateneo*

1

Libertad and member of the board of *Instituto de Investigaciones Sociales y Económicas.*

Among his numerous writings are: *La teoría jurídica del delito según Beling,* Madrid, 1912; *El socialismo y la guerra,* Editorial Estudio, Barcelona, 1915; *Spanien als Betätigungsfeld für Fremdenhandel und -industrie,* Baedeker, Berlin, 1924; "Spanishes Recht" in *Europabuch der Rechtsanwälte und Notare,* Salaban, Berlin, 1926; *Función de la tipicidad en la dogmática del delito,* Mexico, 1951; *Metodología Jurídica,* Ediciones Botas, Mexico, 1955; *Economía en diez lecciónes,* Instituto de Investigaciones Soc. y Económicas, Mexico, 1955; *La Crisis de la Libertad,* Mexico, 1956.

Louis Baudin

Born in Brussels, Belgium, in 1887. Doctor of Juridical Science. Professor at the Faculté de Droit and Ecole des Hautes Etudes Commerciales in Paris. Member of Conseil supérieur de l'Education Nationale; president of Association française de science économique; member of Institut de France.

Officer of the French Legion of Honour. Doctor "honoris causa" of several foreign universities.

Among his numerous writings are: *Manuel d'économie politique* in two volumes, presently in 7th edition; *Précis d'histoire des doctrines économiques,* in 4th edition; *Le Système non règlementé des relations économiques internationales,* also translated into English; *Le corporatisme,* 2nd edition; *L'aube d'un nouveau libéralisme; Le crédit-La monnaie et la formation des prix,* 2nd edition; *La monnaie,* 4th edition, also translated into Spanish and Portuguese; *Le mécanisme des prix,* also translated into Spanish; *L'empire socialiste des Incas,* 3rd edition, translated into Spanish; *La vie de François Pizarre; Les Incas du Pérou,* 3rd edition, translated into German; *La vie quotidienne au temps des derniers Incas.*

Percy L. Greaves, Jr.

Born in Brooklyn, N. Y., in 1906. Mr. Greaves received a B.S. degree in Business Administration from Syracuse University in 1929. He did graduate work in economics at Columbia University and New York University. Mr. Greaves' business experience has been largely in the advertising and public relations research field in the

United States and abroad. From 1943 to 1945 he served as associate research director with the Republican National Committee and from 1945 to 1946 as assistant to minority members of the Joint Congressional Committee Investigation of the Japanese attack on Pearl Harbor. In 1947 Mr. Greaves was committee expert for the preparation and passage of the Taft-Hartley Law. Since 1948 he has been free-lance research economist, writer, and lecturer. In 1950 he became economic adviser to the Christian Freedom Foundation and columnist for *Christian Economics*, in which capacities he is still serving. He is a member of Phi Kappa Phi, Beta Gamma Sigma, American Historical Association and the American Economic Association.

Works: *Operation Immigration*, 1947; Co-author of *Perpetual War for Perpetual Peace*, 1952. Author of many articles on economics, politics, and public affairs.

F. A. HARPER

Born in Middleville, Michigan, in 1905. He received his B.S. from Michigan State College in 1926, and his Ph.D. from Cornell University in 1932. From 1928 until 1946 Dr. Harper taught economics and marketing at Cornell University. From 1930 to 1931 he served as research field agent for the Federal Farm Board, and in 1934 as business analyst for the Farm Credit Administration. He was acting head of the Department of Agricultural Economics at the University of Puerto Rico in 1937. Since 1946 Dr. Harper has been associated with the Foundation for Economic Education as economist.

Among his numerous writings are: *Crisis of the Free Market*, 1945; *Liberty: A Path to its Recovery*, 1949; *Inflation*, 1951; *Morals and the Welfare State*, 1951; *Sequoyah: Symbol of Free Men*, 1952; *Gaining the Free Market*, 1952. Contributor of articles to professional journals.

F. A. VON HAYEK

Born in Vienna, Austria, in 1899. He acquired doctorates in law and economics at the University of Vienna. After four years in the Austrian civil service interrupted by a year of graduate study in New York, he became, in 1926, director of the new Austrian Institute of Economic Research. He also taught economics at the University of Vienna. In 1931 he was appointed Tooke professor of economic science and statistics at the University of London, where he remained until 1950, in which year he accepted the invitation to become a professor of social and moral science at the University of Chicago—a position he still holds. Professor Hayek is a British citizen and Fellow of the British Academy.

Books published: *Prices and Production*, 1931; *Monetary Theory and the Trade Cycle*, 1933 (from the German edition of 1929); *Monetary Nationalism and International Stability*, 1937; *Profits, Interest, and Investment*, 1939; *The Pure Theory of Capital*, 1941; *The Road to Serfdom*, 1944; *Individualism and Economic Order*, 1948; *John Stuart Mill and Harriet Taylor*, 1951; *The Counter-Revolution of Science*, 1952; *The Sensory Order*, 1952.

HENRY HAZLITT

Born in Philadelphia in 1894. Mr. Hazlitt started his editorial career in 1913 as a member of the staff of the *Wall Street Journal*. He became successively a financial editor, a literary editor and editorial staff writer with the *New York Evening Post*, the *New York Evening Mail*, the *New York Herald*, *The Sun*, *The Nation*, the *American Mercury*, *The New York Times* and *The Freeman*. Since 1946 Mr. Hazlitt has been associate editor of *Newsweek* and the author of the column, "Business Tides."

Works: *Thinking as a Science*, 1916; *Instead of Dictatorship*, 1933; *The Anatomy of Criticism*, 1933; *A New Constitution Now*, 1942; *Economics in One Lesson*, 1946; *Will Dollars Save the World?* 1947; *The Great Idea*, 1951.

W. H. HUTT

Born in London in 1899. He attended the London School of Economics and after graduation took employment in business. In 1928 he was appointed professor of commerce at the University of Capetown, South Africa, where he is now dean of the Faculty of Commerce. W. H. Hutt is an eminent defender of individual liberty and the market economy in South Africa. He ardently opposes the interventionist and segregational policies of his government.

Works: *The Theory of Collective Bargaining*, 1930; *Economists and the Public*, 1936; *The Theory of Idle Resources*, 1939; *Plan for Reconstruction*, 1943.

BERTRAND DE JOUVENEL

Born in Paris, France, in 1903. Mr. de Jouvenel is the descendant of a famous family which gave France noted statesmen and writers. He studied mathematics and law. After graduation he entered French politics, but he soon discovered that his heart lay with journalism. In the following years he became an active reporter on international affairs. In the latter part of World War II he took refuge in Switzerland where he completed his great work *Du Pouvoir* which is a keen analysis of present-day totalitarianism. In 1947 he was called to the University of Manchester where he lectured on society and sovereignty. He is known for his reports on the current scene to English, American, and French periodicals and as a regular columnist for *La Gazette de Lausanne*. He is now president of a bureau of economic research in Paris.

Among his many writings are: *The Crisis of American Capitalism*, 1933; *Problems of Socialist England*, 1946; *Du Pouvoir*, 1945, published in English, *On Power*, in 1948; *Ethics of Redistribution*, 1951; *The Political Good*, 1955.

L. M. LACHMANN

Born in Berlin in 1906. Dr. Lachmann studied at the University of Berlin where he graduated in 1930. He emigrated to the United Kingdom in 1933 and completed a degree of M.Sc. Econ., University of London in 1935. From 1938-1940, he held the Leon Research Fellowship of the University of London and was appointed assistant lecturer on the staff of the University College, London, in 1941. From 1943-1948 Professor Lachmann was acting head of the Department of Economics and Commerce of the University College, Hull. He was appointed as professor of economics and head of the Department of Economics and Economic History at the University of the Witwatersrand, Johannesburg, South Africa, in 1948, where he is presently teaching.

His principal works are: "Commodity Stocks and Equilibrium," in *Review of Economic Studies*, June, 1936; "Uncertainty and Liquidity Preference," *Economica*, August, 1937; "Investment and Costs of Production," *American Economic Review*, October, 1937; "On the Measurement of Capital," *Economica*, November, 1941; "The Role of Expectations in Economics as a Social Science," *Economica*, February, 1943; "Finance Capitalism?" *Economica*, May, 1944; "Complementarity and Sub-

stitution in the Theory of Capital," *Economica,* May, 1947;
"Investment Repercussions," *Quarterly Journal of Economics,*
November, 1948; "Economics as a Social Science," (Inaugural
Lecture), 1950; "The Science of Human Action," *Economica,*
November, 1951.

FRITZ MACHLUP

Born in Wiener Neustadt, Austria, in 1902. In 1923 he received
a Ph.D. degree from the University of Vienna. Dr. Machlup
lectured at the Volkshochschule in Vienna from 1929 to 1933 and
then came to the United States as a research fellow sponsored by
the Rockefeller Foundation. In 1935 he became a visiting lecturer
at Harvard University and later accepted the Frank H. Goodyear
chair in economics at the University of Buffalo, where he stayed
until 1947. In the same year he was appointed Abram G. Hutzler
professor of political economy at Johns Hopkins University where
he is still teaching. He is a member of the American Economic
Association (board of editors, 1938-41, acting managing editor,
1944-45), the Royal Economic Society, the Econometric Society, the
American Association of University Professors, Phi Beta Kappa
(hon.).

Among his many writings are: *The Stock Market, Credit and
Capital Formation,* 1940; *International Trade and the National
Income Multiplier,* 1943; *The Basing Point System,* 1949; *The
Political Economy of Monopoly,* 1952; *The Economics of
Sellers' Competition,* 1952.

WILLIAM H. PETERSON

Born in New York in 1921. Dr. Peterson studied at New York University where he received his B.S. and Ph.D., and at Columbia
University where he received his M.S. He lectured at Rutgers
University, 1948-1952, at Columbia University, 1949-1950, and at
Polytechnic Institute of Brooklyn, 1949-1953. He is presently associate professor of economics and administrative assistant at New
York University. Dr. Peterson was formerly associated with International Business Machines Corporation and Friden Calculator
Company. He is a member of the American Economic Association
and the Industrial Relations Research Association.

Works: *The Farm Problem,* 1953. Contributor to *The Commer-*

cial and Financial Chronicle, New York, and *The Freeman,* Irvington, N. Y.

WILLIAM E. RAPPARD

Born in New York in 1883. Citizen of Geneva, Switzerland. Professor Rappard studied law at the university at Geneva where he received a degree of Doctor of Juridical Science. He taught economic history, political economy and finance at the universities of Geneva and Harvard; he repeatedly was president of the University of Geneva and of the Institut Universitaire de Hautes Etudes Internationales in Geneva. Professor Rappard held leading positions with the International Bureau of Labor and organizations of the League of Nations. He headed Swiss diplomatic missions in Washington, Paris, and London and at international conferences for labor. He is now president of the Institut Universitaire de Hautes Etudes Internationales. Professor Rappard received honorary doctor degrees from the universities of Harvard, Pennsylvania, Algiers, Lyon, Princeton, and California.

Among his numerous writings are: *The Government of Switzerland,* D. Van Nostrand, N. Y., 1936; *Le nationalisme économique et la Société des Nations,* Académie de Droit International, Recueil des Cours, 1937; *The Crisis of Democracy,* University of Chicago Press, 1938; *The Quest for Peace since the World War,* Harvard University Press, Cambridge, Mass., 1940; *Cinq siècles de sécurité collective* (1291-1798), George, Genève, 1945; *Collective Security in Swiss Experience* (1291-1948), Allen & Unwin, London, 1948; *Vues rétrospectives sur la Société des Nations,* Académie de Droit International, Recueil des Cours, Paris, Sirey, 1948; *La Suisse et l'organisation de l'Europe,* La Baconnière, Neuchâtel, 1950; *A quoi tient la supériorité économique des Etats-Unis?,* Ed. de Médicis, Paris, 1954.

LEONARD E. READ

Born in Hubbardston, Michigan, in 1898. Mr. Read reveals a rare combination of entrepreneurial and scholarly abilities. In 1920 he embarked upon a business career with the Ann Arbor Produce Company. But after five years he decided to enter chamber of commerce work. He made his way from secretary of the Burlingame Chamber in 1927 to general manager of a number of chambers. He managed the large Los Angeles Chamber of Commerce from 1939 to 1945. Here he became vitally interested in the cause of freedom and free enterprise and launched a program of libertarian education among the citizens of Southern California. In 1945 he accepted the position of executive vice president with the National Industrial Conference Board, where he stayed until 1946. He then became founder and president of the Foundation for Economic Education, Irvington, New York. Since 1954 he also heads the Irvington Press which publishes *The Freeman*.

Works: *Romance of Reality*, 1937; *Pattern for Revolt*, 1945; *Students of Liberty*, 1950; *Outlook for Freedom*, 1951; *Government—An Ideal Concept*, 1954. Contributor to trade and commercial periodicals.

WILHELM RÖPKE

Born near Hamburg, Germany, in 1899. Professor Röpke taught at the universities of Jena and Marburg in Germany, Graz in Austria, and Istanbul in Turkey. From 1926 to 1927 he visited the United States as a professor sponsored by the Rockefeller Foundation. In 1933 Dr. Röpke was one of the first German professors dismissed by Hitler for his liberal convictions. In 1937 he accepted the chair for international economics at the Graduate Institute of International Studies at Geneva, which he still occupies. Professor Röpke served as economic adviser to the Brüning Government of Germany from 1930 to 1932 and has been serving the Adenauer Administration in the same capacity since 1949. In 1954 Columbia University conferred on him the degree *Doctor in litteris humanioribus honoris causa*.

Among his many writings are: *German Commercial Policy*, 1934; *Crises and Cycles*, 1936; *Explication économique du monde moderne*, 1940; *International Economic Disintegration*, 1942; *The Solution of the German Problem*, 1947; *Civitas humana*, 1948; *The Social Crisis of our Time*, 1950.

MURRAY N. ROTHBARD

Born in New York in 1926. Mr. Rothbard studied at Columbia University where he received a Bachelor's degree in mathematics and economics in 1945 and a Master's degree in 1946. He passed the oral examination for his Ph.D. in 1948. He taught economic principles and money and banking at the College of the City of New York from 1948 to 1949. He is presently completing his doctoral dissertation and writing a comprehensive treatise on economics. He is a member of Phi Beta Kappa, the American Economic Association, the Royal Economic Society, and the American Political Science Association.

Works: "Mises' *Human Action:* Comment," *American Economic Review* (March, 1951); and "Praxeology: Reply to Mr. Schuller," *ibid.* (December, 1951).

JACQUES RUEFF

Born in Paris, France, in 1896. Mr. Rueff studied at the Ecole Polytechnique in Paris. In 1927 he joined the League of Nations Secretariat as a member of the economic and financial section. In the following years he served as financial attaché to the French Embassy in London, as professor of economics at the Ecole libre des Sciences politiques, as assistant director in the Ministry of Finance, and finally, in 1936, as head of the French Treasury. From 1939 to 1940 he was vice-governor of the Bank of France. During and after World War II he successively occupied positions as president of the economic and financial delegation to the Military Mission for German and Austrian Affairs, economic advisor to Commander-in-Chief in Germany, French delegate to Reparations Commission in Moscow, president of Paris Conference on Reparations, president of Inter-allied Reparations Agency in Brussells, delegate to Peace Conference in Paris and to the first assembly of the United Nations, and member of U.N. Economic and Employment Commission. Today he is judge at the Court of Justice of the European Coal and Steel Community. Occasionally he lectures as professor of economics at the Institut des Sciences politiques in Paris.

Works: *Des Sciences physiques aux Sciences morales,* 1922; *Théorie des Phénomènes monétaires,* 1927; *L'Assurance-chômage,* 1931; *L'Ordre social,* 1945; *Epître aux dirigistes,* 1949; *Une cause du désordre mondial: l'état actuel du système des paiements internationaux.*

HANS F. SENNHOLZ

Born near Dortmund, Germany, in 1922. He studied law and political science at the universities of Marburg and Cologne from 1946 to 1949. In the same year he immigrated to the United States and studied economics at New York University. M.A., Marburg,

1948; Dr. rer. pol., Cologne, 1949; Ph.D., New York, 1955. From 1951 to 1953 he was with a brokerage house in Wall Street, and from 1954 to 1955 with Iona College, New Rochelle, N. Y., as assistant professor of economics.

Works: *How Can Europe Survive?*, D. Van Nostrand Co., Inc., N. Y., 1955; Co-translator of E. v. Böhm-Bawerk's *Capital and Interest*, Libertarian Press, South Holland, Ill., 1955. Numerous contributions to *Rundschau*, Cologne; *Deutsche Zeitung und Wirtschaftszeitung*, Stuttgart; *Staatszeitung*, New York; *The Freeman*, Irvington, New York.

LOUIS M. SPADARO

Born in Manhattan, N. Y. in 1913. Dr. Spadaro has concentrated his academic career in the major schools of his native New York. After attending the public schools, he took his undergraduate work at the College of the City of New York and pursued graduate studies at both Columbia and New York universities. He taught for some years in the New York public high schools and, in 1938, joined the faculty of the School of Business of Fordham University, where he is now associate professor of economics and assistant dean.

PART ONE

Grato Animo Beneficiique Memores

I

The Intransigence of Ludwig von Mises [1]

by JACQUES RUEFF

(from the French by George D. Huncke)

LUDWIG VON MISES is a rara avis in this twentieth century of ours, for he considers reason a valid and efficacious instrument even in the study of questions that concern economics. According to him, "any given social order was thought out and designed before it could be realized . . . any existing state of social affairs is the product of ideologies previously thought out . . . action is always directed by ideas." [2]

The very title of his great book, *Human Action*, is in and of itself both an affirmation and a denial. It indicates what, for its author, constitutes the real economic problem, which is raised by the behavior of men with respect to the things they desire—the things called wealth. And it shows that the real economic problem is completely encompassed within the study of such behavior; that it does not consist only in an analysis "of objective processes taking place quite independently of human will." [3]

Mises considers social organization to be dependent upon and in conformity with the very ideas that inspire it. It is merely a system of ways and means for attaining certain ends. He is convinced that the vast majority of people concur on the ends. Hence the economic

[1] *Le refus de Ludwig von Mises.*

[2] Ludwig von Mises, *Human Action.* Yale University Press, New Haven, 1949, p. 188.

[3] Stalin, *Les problèmes économiques du socialisme en U.S.S.R.*, Ed. Sociale, p. 4.

problem is only that of choosing the means by which men can achieve, effectively and at the lowest cost, the results desired.

This problem constitutes an object of science and is open to only two kinds of solution—those which are effective, and those which are not. Reason—and only reason—enables us to choose between them. "Man has only one tool to fight error: reason." [4] It is the task of the economist to tell the politician which system he must set up in order to give men what they want, and not the very opposite.

Such an attitude on the part of Mises sets him apart from other economists. Most of his colleagues take the social structure as a fact that cannot be changed in any respect by the will of men. The Marxists explain it as a revelation of history. The non-Marxists look upon it as the inevitable product of a technical evolution which has given rise to a capitalism of large units, and to monopolies, cartels, and trusts. Marxists and non-Marxists alike ascribe to our modern economies a rigidity which makes them almost completely immune to the price mechanism.

For both groups any doctrine basing the establishment and maintenance of economic equilibria on price movements is false, fruitless, and outdated. According to them, it is the task of the economist to discover the proper processes that guarantee economic order without resorting to spontaneous regulation. The sum total of these processes constitutes the new science of economics, which is required by the actual state of the world in which we live.

It is true—nor does Mises deny it—that our contemporary economy is more rigid than that which existed before employers' associations and labor unions had regimented a large part of the forces of production.

The essential thing, however, is that the present inelasticity of our societies is far more the result of their institutional character than it is of the nature of the techniques applied.

It is institutions established by men and wanted by them that immobilize prices, salaries, and rates of interest. It is the same institutions that lend their protection, without which the oligopolies or monopolies in their quasi-totality could never exist.

If, then, such institutions are wanted by men, it is because the economists have failed to convince them that these institutions are leading and must lead to results diametrically opposed to the ones desired and expected to be attained. In actual fact, the character-

[4] Ludwig von Mises, *Ibid.*, p. 187.

istic rigidity of most contemporary economies, and particularly of several economies, has been made possible only by the silence of the economists. Had they but shed a revealing light on the social consequences that such rigidity could not fail to bring about, and on the privations and sufferings which it was bound to engender, the rigidity could have been neither established nor maintained.

French legislation on rents, for example, has been inspired by laudable social considerations. And yet, it has been a tremendous source of unhappiness and disorder. Anybody of good faith and with the slightest knowledge of the price mechanism could have foreseen these tragic social effects. But no! The few warnings that did foretell the ill-fated consequences have always been denied by the chorus of complacent men anxious above all not to oppose the solutions wanted by public opinion and accepted by governments.

It would be cruel to insist on learning the reasons for the practically universal renunciation of thinking. Leibnitz already indicated that, "If geometry conflicted with our passions and interests as much as morality does, we would no less question and violate its laws. And this despite all the proofs offered by Euclid and Archimedes, which we would then treat as flights of fancy and believe to be full of fallacies. And in that case Joseph Scaliger, Hobbes, and others who attacked Euclid and Archimedes, would not be so bereft of supporters as they now are." [5]

What this philosopher said of morality applies with even more validity to political economy.

But though there may be but few minds in the field of economics who have remained loyal to Euclid and Archimedes, Ludwig von Mises undoubtedly is the most pronounced, the most efficient, and the most determined. With an indefatigable enthusiasm, and with courage and faith undaunted, he has never ceased to denounce the fallacious reasons and untruths offered to justify most of our new institutions. He has demonstrated—in the most literal sense of the word—that those institutions, while claiming to contribute to man's well-being, were the immediate sources of hardship and suffering and, ultimately, the causes of conflicts, war, and enslavement.

No consideration whatever can divert him in the least from the straight steep path where his cold reason guides him. In the irrationalism of our era he has remained a person of pure reason.

Those who have heard him have often been astonished at being led by the cogency of his reasoning to places whither they, in their

[5] Leibnitz, *Nouveaux Essais*, I.II.12.

all too human timorousness, had never dared to go. His person and ideas have always brought to my mind the story of Mr. Teste in which Paul Valéry personifies intelligence devoid of all weakness, and reason subject only to its absolute logic and the certainty of its own conclusions.

In the following words, one of Mr. Teste's listeners reports the sensations experienced while listening to him. "He shatters my mind with a word, and I feel like a defective vase that the potter has discarded. He is as hard, sir, as an angel. He is unaware of his own strength; he finds unexpected words that are all too true, that overwhelm people, that awaken them in the midst of great folly confronting them, all ensnared in being what they are, in the meshes of living, in foolishness. We live in comfort, each in his own absurdity, like fish in water, and we never become aware, except by chance, of how much stupidity is contained in the life of a reasonable person." [6] And the same listener goes on to say, "There is in him some appalling purity, detachment, undeniable strength and light. Never have I observed such complete absence of confusion and of doubt in an intelligence that is so deeply industrious. He is awfully quiet! There can be ascribed to him no uneasiness of soul, no shadow in his heart." [7]

If we compare the guile of economic irrationality with the imperturbable intransigence of his lucid thinking, Ludwig von Mises has safeguarded the foundations of a rational economic science, the value and effectiveness of which have been demonstrated by his works. By his teachings he has sown the seeds of a regeneration which will bear fruit as soon as men once more begin to prefer theories that are true to theories that are pleasing. When that day comes, all economists will recognize that Ludwig von Mises merits their admiration and gratitude. For it is he who, amidst the confusion of a science which tends to belie the reasons for its own existence, has indefatigably affirmed the rights of reason, its supremacy over matter, and its effectiveness in human action.

[6] Paul Valéry, *Monsieur Teste.* NR.F., p. 86.
[7] *Ibid.*, p. 104.

II

On Reading von Mises

by WILLIAM E. RAPPARD

W<small>HEN</small> I was invited to contribute an essay to a volume in honor of Ludwig von Mises, I was surprised and still more delighted. My astonishment was due to the fact that the contributors were to be chosen from the ranks of some of the most distinguished living economists, among which I have no reason to count myself. It was, on the other hand, a happy prospect to be allowed publicly to state my esteem and my affection for a very dear friend, and to be urged to spend at least some weeks in his intellectual intimacy.

That, I confess, was the main motive of my acceptance. During the all too brief years, from 1934 to 1940, during which Dr. von Mises had consented to be associated with the Institute at Geneva which I was directing with my friend Paul Mantoux, I very often and, I am afraid, very indiscreetly, enjoyed his company. All those who have ever had a like privilege realize that he is not only one of the keenest analytical minds among contemporary economists, but that he also has at his disposal a store of historical culture, the treasures of which are animated and illuminated by a form of humanity and Austrian wit rarely to be found today on the surface of this globe. In fact, I sometimes wonder, not without fear, whether our generation is not the last to be blessed with what seems to have been a monopoly of pre-war Vienna.

In reflecting upon our numerous and, to me, always very enlightening conversations, two points on which the fundamental opinion of L. von Mises never varied are most prominent.

On the one hand, he was ever insistent on the purely scientific character and functions of economics. As with all other sciences, the role of economics was solely to analyze and to explain reality, not to assess nor to improve it. It was completely *wertfrei*. Values could be assumed, posited, believed in or disbelieved, claimed or denied. They could not be known nor demonstrated. Therefore, economists who invoked the authority of their intellectual discipline to urge upon society measures calculated to reform it were imposters. Reforms could only be means to an end. Economics dealt, and could legitimately deal, only with means. The means adopted or rejected, of course, depended essentially on the ends chosen. But the choice of ends was quite beyond the discretion of our own, or of any other, science. Therefore, while economists might well advise statesmen as to the probable results of the means suggested to achieve their ends, they could not, as men of science, express any valid judgment as to the excellence of these ends. This they would leave to seers, to prophets, to metaphysicians, or to the man in the street. The visions of the latter might be admirable, but their assertions could but be the expression of their faith and never be postulates of their sole reason.

On the other hand, von Mises missed no opportunity, in private as well as in public, to proclaim his abhorrence of all forms of state intervention in the processes of economic life. Our age knows no more consistent and but very few as passionate advocates of policies of complete *laissez-faire* in an unhampered market economy.

A single personal recollection—it could be readily multiplied— may serve to illustrate my point. This recollection is drawn from a meeting of the Mont-Pèlerin Society. As is well known, this very loose association of liberal intellectuals was formed some years ago by economists, historians, and philosophers of a score of countries. What brought them together were a common love of liberty and a common apprehension that statist policies, ever more generally preached and practised the world over, would bring about an eclipse of freedom, and consequently also of prosperity. Von Mises was naturally a charter member of this organization which, from the start, was presided over by our colleague, von Hayek. It might well have been expected that the periodical gatherings of this Society could not fail to generate an atmosphere exceptionally congenial to the revered dean of twentieth-century liberals.

Well, what I am about to narrate shows that even the Mont-Pèlerin Society seemed to him dangerously infected by the virus of statism. This episode took place at a meeting held in Seelisberg, a Swiss mountain resort situated just above the Grütli, the traditional birthplace of Helvetic freedom. The topic discussed was the social policies of liberalism. What interventions of public authorities to combat unemployment and industrial destitution were to be favored, or at least tolerated? Social insurance, minimum wages guaranteed by the state, such and similar devices were rather timidly urged by some of the liberals present. None of their proposals found the slightest mercy at the hands of von Mises. "But what would you do," it was asked of him, "if you were in the position of our French colleague, Jacques Rueff," who was present at the meeting and who happened at that time to be shouldering the responsibilities of the administration of the Principality of Monaco. "Suppose that for some reason which could easily be imagined, there was in that Principality widespread unemployment and therefore famine and revolutionary discontent. Would you, could you advise the government to limit its activities to police action for the maintenance of order and the protection of private property?"

Our friend von Mises was entirely unmoved. He replied: "If the policies of non-intervention which I advocate prevailed—universal free trade, freely fluctuating nominal wages, no form of social insurance, etc.—there would be no acute unemployment. Private charity would suffice to prevent the absolute destitution of the very restricted hard core of unemployables."

It might be tempting to recall many other instances in which, in the course of private conversation or collective debate, von Mises absolutely rejected as ill-considered any form of state meddling in the operations of the free market. Tempting, but quite superfluous. No one who is apt to glance over these pages can ignore the uncompromising stand which our friend has ever taken in these matters. In fact, in spite of his many original and learned writings, which have long made of him one of the most renowned living economists, I would venture to assert that he is most widely known the world over as the staunchest, most undaunted, and most uncompromising friend of economic and social liberty of mid-twentieth century.

Now, a question has often arisen in my mind: how his stand on this major matter of policy was to be squared with his equally uncompromising banning of absolute values from the orbit of economic science, and therefore also of economic policy. Of course, there is no logically necessary inconsistency between these two mental attitudes. Psychologically, however, they are not often adopted by the same mind. Theoretical agnostics in the matter of ultimate value are apt to be somewhat reserved and cautious as advocates of policy. And enthusiastic crusaders and intolerant critics in the field of action are usually to be found in the ranks of those who feel least hesitation about proclaiming as absolutely good or evil the policies they champion or combat.

In order fully to comprehend the thought of my esteemed friend on these two fundamental issues, the invitation to take part in this intellectual symposium suggested the idea of discovering it by a careful perusal of his most recent important work, *Human Action*, published in English in 1949. I therefore resolved to forego all other avoidable work until I had given myself the full benefit of the spiritual and mental intimacy with him I anticipated from carefully reading from cover to cover this major exposition of his mature social philosophy.

•   •   •

The experience proved well worth the effort. Besides the profit and delight I derived from the many weeks devoted to this most exhilarating task, a question insistently arose in my mind: how many, before me, had found it tempting to undertake and possible to carry out the long, intellectual journey through the 880-odd pages from which I have just returned?

No one will ever be in a position to answer this question. The numbers of the copies of the book absorbed by the market offer no adequate clue. Every self-respecting periodical has doubtless reviewed the volume and no self-respecting public library has failed to purchase it. But reading a book is a very different matter from purchasing or even from reviewing it.

It is not my purpose to carry this incidental query any further. But it does concern what is to my mind one of the fundamental problems of our contemporary civilization. A learned treatise is not a dictionary one keeps for reference purposes on one's shelves. Even when it is admirably composed and adequately indexed, as in the present case, it cannot really and fairly be judged by one who is content to dip into its chapters here and there. The author has the right to expect a less cursory treatment on the part of the reader. But how can he hope to receive it in the present day when at least a thousand volumes are published for every one that appeared in the age of Adam Smith? True, among this torrential output one is not likely to find a *Wealth of Nations*. If contemporary economists find it possible to read carefully only one extensive book a year, they would not be ill-advised to select, if they have not already done so, the *Human Action* of Ludwig von Mises.

*   *   *

To revert to the main purpose of this disquisition. In his latest great work our author has very clearly confirmed what I thought I knew of his intellectual positions on the two points stated above. He makes it abundantly clear that economics, no more than any other science, can establish the absolute validity of any ultimate aims of human conduct. Furthermore I have never, in all my previous recollections of him, found him more passionately addicted to the defense of the free market economy nor more intolerant of all forms of what he likes to call "statolatry."

A few quotations will prove these two assertions. After presenting them I shall conclude by showing how they are reconciled in his social philosophy.

*   *   *

In the opening pages of *Human Action* we find a statement on the first point so clear that it renders any repetition almost superfluous. It is as follows:

. . . economics is a theoretical science and as such abstains from any judgment of value. It is not its task to tell people what ends they should aim at. It is a science of the means to be applied for the attainment of ends chosen, not, to be sure, a science of the choosing of ends. Ultimate decisions, the valuations and the choosing of ends, are beyond the scope of any science. Science never tells a man how he should act; it merely shows how a man must act if he wants to attain definite ends.[1]

To this opinion the author remains unswervingly faithful throughout his lengthy book. Its constant repetition is as a *Leitmotiv* which in various forms recurs in almost every chapter.[2]

The importance he attaches to it is shown by the following statement quoted from one of his very last pages:

While many people blame economics for its neutrality with regard to value judgments, other people blame it for its alleged indulgence in them. Some contend that economics must necessarily express judgments of value and is therefore not really scientific, as the criterion of science is its valuational indifference. Others maintain that good economics should be and could be impartial, and that only bad economists sin against this postulate.[3]

[1] *Human Action*, Yale University Press, New Haven, 1949, p. 10.
[2] *Ibid.*, pp. 10, 21, 29, 46, 87, 89, 92, 96, 148, 157, 172, 173, 179, 180, 243, 264, 292, 295-6, 617, 713, 715, 716, 717, 719, 749, 879.
[3] *Ibid.*, p. 879.

We shall revert in our conclusion to what is here indicted as "the semantic confusion" responsible for this ambiguity. Before doing so, let us turn from the consistent and insistent apologist of *Wertfreiheit* in the realm of economics to the equally consistent and insistent advocate of pure liberalism as the proper and, in fact, the only proper economic policy. We shall now see how this intransigent champion of intellectual neutrality in the field of science becomes a most bellicose gladiator when he descends into the arena of economic policy.

❖   ❖   ❖

It cannot be the purpose of this study to analyze minutely the opinions expressed by von Mises in *Human Action* on all the controversial issues which oppose his unadulterated liberalism to the various forms of state interventionism, practiced by all contemporary governments and recommended or at least condoned by the vast majority of writers on economic topics in the middle of our century.

A few quotations must suffice to show that he fully deserves his reputation as the most outspoken and least compromising advocate of a complete policy of pure *laissez-faire* in the world today.

Ludwig von Mises is an individualist but not an anarchist. Thus he writes:

The anarchists overlook the undeniable fact that some people are either too narrow-minded or too weak to adjust themselves spontaneously to the conditions of social life. . . . We may agree that he who acts antisocially should be considered mentally sick and in need of care. But as long as not all are cured, and as long as there are infants and the senile, some provision must be taken lest they jeopardize society. An anarchistic society would be exposed to the mercy of every individual. Society cannot exist if the majority is not ready to hinder, by the application or threat of violent action, minorities from destroying the social order. This power is vested in the state or government.

State or government is the social apparatus of compulsion and coercion. It has the monopoly of violent action. No individual is free to use violence or the threat of violence if the government has not accorded this right to him. The state is essentially an institution for the preservation of peaceful interhuman relations. However, for the preservation of peace it must be prepared to crush the onslaughts of peace-breakers.[4]

But, he adds, "the principle of majority rule or government by the people as recommended by liberalism"[5] has nothing in common with the statolatry as widely advocated today. This can be defined as the conception which "assumes that there exists above and beyond

[4] *Ibid.*, p. 149.
[5] *Ibid.*, p. 150.

the individual's actions an imperishable entity aiming at its own ends, different from those of mortal men, . . . the concept of a super-human being." [6]
Under this assumption,

. . . one cannot evade the question whose ends take precedence whenever an antagonism arises, those of the state or society or those of the individual. The answer to this question is already implied in the very concept of state or society as conceived by collectivism and universalism. If one postulates the existence of an entity which ex definitione is higher, nobler, and better than the in-dividuals, then there cannot be any doubt that the aims of this eminent being must tower above those of the wretched individuals. [7]

It is the prevalence of statolatry which is responsible for interna-tional tension and war.

The alternatives to the liberal and democratic principle of majority rule are the militarist principles of armed conflict and dictatorial oppression. [8]

Writing at the close of two world wars, he, of course, could not avoid considering the impact of international conflicts, present and future, on the responsibilities and functions of the state. This topic, as well it might be, is clearly distasteful to him. War, which is mainly the product of antiliberal ideas and institutions, is as brutal in its operations as it is futile in its consequences. He writes:

. . . in the long run war and the preservation of the market economy are incompatible. Capitalism is essentially a scheme for peaceful nations. [9]
Modern civilization is a product of the philosophy of laissez faire. It cannot be preserved under the ideology of government omnipotence. Statolatry owes much to the doctrines of Hegel. However, one may pass over many of Hegel's inexcusable faults, for Hegel also coined the phrase "the futility of victory" (die Ohnmacht des Sieges). To defeat the aggressors is not enough to make peace durable. The main thing is to discard the ideology that generates war. [10]

However, in spite of the obvious logical and historical links be-tween economic liberalism and international peace on the one hand, and statolatry and war on the other, the necessities of na-tional defense are no valid excuse for the extent and forms of state intervention practiced by all belligerent nations in the most recent armed conflicts. This is how our author deals with this topic, ob-viously one of the most embarrassing for all advocates of eco-nomic liberalism:

[6] *Ibid.*, p. 151.
[7] *Ibid.*, p. 151.
[8] *Ibid.*, p. 152.
[9] *Ibid.*, p. 824.
[10] *Ibid.*, p. 828.

The market economy, say the socialists and the interventionists, is at best a system that may be tolerated in peacetime. But when war comes, such indulgence is impermissible. It would jeopardize the vital interests of the nation for the sole benefit of the selfish concerns of capitalists and entrepreneurs. War, and in any case modern total war, peremptorily requires government control of business.

Hardly anybody has been bold enough to challenge this dogma. It served in both World Wars as a convenient pretext for innumerable measures of government interference with business which in many countries step by step led to full "war socialism." When the hostilities ceased, a new slogan was launched. The period of transition from war to peace and of "reconversion," people contended, requires even more government control than the period of war. Besides, why should one ever turn to a social system which can work, if at all, only in the interval between two wars? The most appropriate thing would be to cling permanently to government control in order to be duly prepared for any possible emergency.

An examination of the problems which the United States had to face in the second World War will clearly show how fallacious this reasoning is.

What America needed in order to win the war was a radical conversion of all its production activities. All not absolutely indispensable civilian consumption was to be eliminated. The plants and farms were henceforth to turn out only a minimum of goods for nonmilitary use. For the rest, they were to devote themselves completely to the task of supplying the armed forces.

The realization of this program did not require the establishment of controls and priorities. If the government had raised all the funds needed for the conduct of war by taxing the citizens and by borrowing from them, everybody would have been forced to cut down his consumption drastically. The entrepreneurs and farmers would have turned toward production for the government because the sale of goods to private citizens would have dropped. The government, now by virtue of the inflow of taxes and borrowed money the biggest buyer on the market, would have been in a position to obtain all it wanted. Even the fact that the government chose to finance a considerable part of the war expenditure by increasing the quantity of money in circulation and by borrowing from the commercial banks would not have altered this state of affairs. The inflation must, of course, bring about a marked tendency toward a rise in the prices of all goods and services. The government would have had to pay higher nominal prices. But it would still have been the most solvent buyer on the market. It would have been possible for it to outbid the citizens who on the one hand had not the right of manufacturing the money they needed and on the other hand would have been squeezed by enormous taxes.

But the government deliberately adopted a policy which was bound to make it impossible for it to rely upon the operation of the unhampered market. It resorted to price control and made it illegal to raise commodity prices. Furthermore it was very slow in taxing the incomes swollen by the inflation. It surrendered to the claim of the unions that the workers' real take-home wages should be kept at a height which would enable them to preserve in the war their prewar standard of living. In fact, the most numerous class of the nation, the class which in peacetime consumed the greatest part of the total amount of goods consumed, had so much more money in their pockets that their power to buy and to consume was greater than in peacetime. The wage earners—and to some extent also the farmers and the owners of plants producing for the government—would have frustrated the government's endeavors to direct industries toward the production of war materials. They would have induced business to produce more, not less, of those goods which in wartime are considered superfluous luxuries. It was this circumstance that forced the Administration to resort to the systems of priorities and of rationing. The shortcomings of the methods adopted for financing war expenditure made government control of business necessary. If no inflation had been made and if taxation had cut down the income (after taxes) of all citizens, not only of those enjoying higher incomes, to a fraction of their peacetime revenues, these controls would have been supererogatory. The endorsement of the doctrine that the wage earners' real income must in wartime be even higher than in peacetime made them unavoidable.[11]

As this most remarkable passage clearly shows, even the exceptional exigencies of total war, that is, of war in which all private interests are necessarily subordinated to, and even engulfed in the interests of the belligerent state, were not sufficient to divorce von Mises from his all-beloved economic liberalism. What is more significant, however, is his defense of *laissez-faire* in times and under conditions of peace. In spite of the present state of international relations, septuagenarians such as he and I may be excused from looking upon such times and such conditions as more normal and more durable than those referred to in my last quotation.

There is not, in *Human Action,* any precise delimitation of the state's legitimate activities. Von Mises expressly rejects the possibility of regulating this matter in accordance with any norms of right or wrong, just or unjust. Two points, however, stand out very clearly in his exposition.[12] On the one hand, besides the recognized necessity of national defense, the state must protect the individual against the consequences of social disorder and violence. "The only purpose of the laws and the social apparatus of coercion and compulsion is to safeguard the smooth functioning of social cooperation." [13]

However, even this admitted duty of the state is looked upon with more suspicion than favor, as is obvious from the following statement:

. . . government interference always means either violent action or the threat of such action. Government is in the last resort the employment of armed men, of policemen, gendarmes, soldiers, prison guards, and hangmen. The essential feature of government is the enforcement of its decrees by beat-

11 *Ibid.,* pp. 821-822.
12 *Ibid.,* pp. 715 *et seq.*
13 *Ibid.,* p. 718.

ing, killing, and imprisoning. Those who are asking for more government interference are asking ultimately for more compulsion and less freedom.[14]

On the other hand, all government interference, even when it is imposed by circumstances, is restrictive and not productive. Thus we read:

On the unhampered market there prevails an irresistible tendency to employ every factor of production for the best possible satisfaction of the most urgent needs of the consumers. If the government interferes with this process, it can only impair satisfaction; it can never improve it.
. . . While government has no power to make people more prosperous by interference with business, it certainly does have the power to make them less satisfied by restriction of production.[15]

This general view, expounded throughout *Human Action,* of course makes its author a determined opponent of tariff protection, labor legislation, high taxation, socialization of the means of production, and of all other forms of state intervention in the market economy such as are universally practiced by contemporary states.

I must resist the temptation of reproducing here many pungent statements on these various matters which I have noted in the preparation of these pages. Just one exception to characterize the severity of his judgment:

The outcome of the municipalization and nationalization policies of the last decades was almost without exception financial failure, poor service, and political corruption. Blinded by their anticapitalistic prejudices people condone poor service and corruption and for a long time did not bother about the financial failure. However, this failure is one of the factors which contributed to the emergence of the present-day crisis of interventionism.[16]

Some points of his attack on labor legislation may also be quoted. This would seem justified both because these statements display their author in one of his most isolated intellectual attitudes, and by reason of their bearing on one of the most widely discussed issues of the day, that of so-called underdeveloped countries. In his remarks on the industrial revolution of the eighteenth century in Great Britain he writes:

The history of capitalism in Great Britain as well as in all other capitalist countries is a record of an unceasing tendency toward the improvement in the wage earners' standard of living. This evolution coincided with the development of prolabor legislation and the spread of labor unionism on the one hand and with the increase in the marginal productivity of labor on the other hand.

14 *Ibid.,* p. 715.
15 *Ibid.,* pp. 736-737.
16 *Ibid.,* p. 373.

The economists assert that the improvement in the workers' material conditions is due to the increase in the per capita quota of capital invested and the technological achievements which the employment of this additional capital brought about. As far as labor legislation and union pressure did not exceed the limits of what the workers would have got without them as a necessary consequence of the acceleration of capital accumulation as compared with population, they were superfluous. As far as they exceeded these limits, they were harmful to the interests of the masses. They delayed the accumulation of capital thus slowing down the tendency toward a rise in the marginal productivity of labor and in wage rates.[17]

This conception of the futility of labor legislation in the country of its birth leads him to the following remarks on the subject of economically backward countries:

Vast areas—Eastern Asia, the East Indies, Southern and Southeastern Europe, Latin America—are only superficially affected by modern capitalism. Conditions in these countries by and large do not differ from those of England on the eve of the "Industrial Revolution." There are millions and millions of people for whom there is no secure place left in the traditional economic setting. The fate of these wretched masses can be improved only by industrialization. What they need most is entrepreneurs and capitalists. As their own foolish policies have deprived these nations of the further enjoyment of the assistance imported foreign capital hitherto gave them, they must embark upon domestic capital accumulation. They must go through all the stages through which the evolution of Western industrialism had to pass. They must start with comparatively low wage rates and long hours of work. But, deluded by the doctrines prevailing in present-day Western Europe and North America, their statesmen think that they can proceed in a different way. They encourage labor-union pressure and alleged prolabor legislation. Their interventionist radicalism nips in the bud all attempts to create domestic industries. These men do not comprehend that industrialization cannot begin with the adoption of the precepts of the International Labor Office and the principles of the American Congress of Industrial Organizations. Their stubborn dogmatism spells the doom of the Indian and Chinese coolies, the Mexican peons, and millions of other peoples, desperately struggling on the verge of starvation.[18]

Another phase of von Mises' advocacy of *laissez-faire* in economic affairs is displayed in his views on banking and money. I quote some of his relevant statements to show to what extremes of severity he is led by his abhorrence of state intervention in this field. Thus he writes:

The attitudes of the European governments and their satellites with regard to banking were from the beginning insincere and mendacious. The pretended solicitude for the nation's welfare, for the public in general, and for the poor ignorant masses in particular was a mere blind. The governments wanted inflation and credit expansion, they wanted booms and easy money.

[17] *Ibid.,* p. 617.
[18] *Ibid.,* pp. 618-619.

. . . . It is a fable that governments interfered with banking in order to restrict the issue of fiduciary media and to prevent credit expansion. The idea that guided governments was, on the contrary, the lust for inflation and credit expansion.

. . . . Many governments never looked upon the issuance of fiduciary media from a point of view other than that of fiscal concerns. In their eyes the foremost task of the banks was to lend money to the treasury. The money-substitutes were pacemakers for government-issued paper money. The convertible banknote was merely a first step on the way to the nonredeemable banknote. With the progress of statolatry and the policy of interventionism these ideas have become general and are no longer questioned by anybody. No government is willing today to give any thought to the program of free banking because no government wants to renounce what it considers a handy source of revenue. What is called today financial war preparedness is merely the ability to procure by means of privileged and government-controlled banks all the money a warring nation may need. Radical inflationism, although not admitted explicitly, is an essential feature of the economic ideology of our age.

But even at the time liberalism enjoyed its highest prestige and governments were more eager to preserve peace and well-being than to foment war, death, destruction, and misery, people were biased in dealing with the problems of banking.[19]

Much as I would like to pursue this recital of the anti-state views of L. von Mises, notably in the field of public instruction,[20] where his radical individualism leads him into a position of almost complete isolation amongst our contemporaries, it is time to conclude.

*   *   *

In the first part of this study we have shown him as an uncompromising foe of all pseudo-scientific judgments of value in economic affairs. In the second, we have just caught some glimpses of him on the warpath, denouncing often with extreme vigor of thought and language the aberration of all contemporary governments and the folly of almost all contemporary economists who practice and preach interventionist policies.

How are these intellectual attitudes to be reconciled? My purpose in undertaking this study was to discover the solution of this problem, which, I admit, had often perplexed me in the score of years I had the privilege of knowing our friend von Mises. My satisfaction in bringing it to a close is that this problem perplexes me no longer. Any careful and fair-minded reader of *Human Action* must recognize that it contains a clear and unequivocal answer to the question posed. Not that the reader will necessarily follow

[19] *Ibid.*, pp. 438 and 439.
[20] *Ibid.*, pp. 872 *et seq.*

our author in his denunciations of all the economic policies he attacks. But the accusation, or at least the suspicion, of logical inconsistency will have been invalidated.

Why and how?

Throughout his work von Mises maintains that there is and can be no justification for the scientific assertion of ends as the only desirable aims of policy. But he claims that most, if not absolutely all, governments, parties, and economists today have chosen and pretend to be pursuing the same aims. Under this assumption, what separates men is much less a variety of ends, about which science is impotent and must therefore remain mute, than means, which it is the right and duty of all economists to examine as to their adequacy.

That the ultimate aims pursued by all in matters economic are substantially the same, is a claim clearly made and constantly repeated in *Human Action*. The following quotations may suffice to show it:

It is true that the appetite for food and warmth is common to men and other mammals and that as a rule a man who lacks food and shelter concentrates his efforts upon the satisfaction of these urgent needs and does not care much for other things. The impulse to live, to preserve one's own life, and to take advantage of every opportunity of strengthening one's vital forces is a primal feature of life, present in every living being.[21]

Notwithstanding all declarations to the contrary, the immense majority of men aim first of all at an improvement of the material conditions of well-being. They want more and better food, better homes and clothes, and a thousand other amenities. They strive after abundance and health.[22]

While praxeology, and therefore economics too, uses the terms happiness and removal of uneasiness in a purely formal sense, liberalism attaches to them a concrete meaning. It presupposes that people prefer life to death, health to sickness, nourishment to starvation, abundance to poverty. It teaches man how to act in accordance with these valuations.[23]

It is a fact that civilization, when judged from this point of view, is to be considered a benefit and not an evil. It has enabled man to hold his own in the struggle against all other living beings, both the big beasts of prey and the even more pernicious microbes; it has multiplied man's means of sustenance; it has made the average man taller, more agile, and more versatile and it has stretched his average length of life; it has given man the uncontested mastery of the earth; it has multiplied population figures and raised the standard of living to a level never dreamed of by the crude cave dwellers of prehistoric ages.[24]

Asceticism teaches that the only means open to man for removing pain and

21 *Ibid.*, p. 19.
22 *Ibid.*, p. 96.
23 *Ibid.*, p. 154.
24 *Ibid.*, p. 170.

for attaining complete quietude, contentment, and happiness is to turn away from earthly concerns and to live without bothering about worldly things. There is no salvation other than to renounce striving after material well-being, to endure submissively the adversities of the earthly pilgrimage and to dedicate oneself exclusively to the preparation for eternal bliss. However, the number of those who consistently and unswervingly comply with the principles of asceticism is so small that it is not easy to instance more than a few names. It seems that the complete passivity advocated by asceticism is contrary to nature. The enticement of life triumphs.[25]

All present-day political parties strive after the earthly well-being and prosperity of their supporters. They promise that they will render economic conditions more satisfactory to their followers. With regard to this issue there is no difference between the Roman Catholic Church and the various Protestant denominations as far as they intervene in political and social questions, between Christianity and the non-Christian religions, between the advocates of economic freedom and the various brands of Marxian materialism, between nationalists and internationalists, between racists and the friends of interracial peace. . . .

The pompous statements which people make about things unknowable and beyond the power of the human mind, their cosmologies, world views, religions, mysticisms, metaphysics, and conceptual phantasies differ widely from one another. But the practical essence of their ideologies, i.e., their teachings dealing with the ends to be aimed at in earthly life and with the means for the attainment of these ends, show much uniformity.[26]

In the field of society's economic organization there are the liberals advocating private ownership of the means of production, the socialists advocating public ownership of the means of production, and the interventionists advocating a third system which, they contend, is as far from socialism as it is from capitalism. In the clash of these parties there is again much talk about basic philosophical issues. People speak of true liberty, equality, social justice, the rights of the individual, community, solidarity, and humanitarianism. But each party is intent upon proving by ratiocination and by referring to historical experience that only the system it recommends will make the citizens prosperous and satisfied. They tell the people that realization of their program will raise the standard of living to a higher level than realization of any other party's program. They insist upon the expediency of their plans and upon their utility. It is obvious that they do not differ from one another with regard to ends but only as to means. They all pretend to aim at the highest material welfare for the majority of citizens.[27]

No religion in its exoteric activities ever ventured to tell people frankly: The realization of our plans for social organization will make you poor and impair your earthly well-being. Those consistently committed to a life of poverty withdrew from the political scene and fled into anchoritic seclusion. But churches and religious communities which have aimed at making converts and at influencing political and social activities of their followers have espoused the principles of secular conduct. In dealing with questions of man's earthly pilgrimage they hardly differ from any other political party. In canvassing,

[25] *Ibid.*, pp. 178-179.
[26] *Ibid.*, pp. 180-181.
[27] *Ibid.*, p. 183.

they emphasize the material advantages which they have in store for their brothers in faith more than bliss in the beyond.[28]

The immense majority strives after a greater and better supply of food, clothes, homes, and other material amenities. In calling a rise in the masses' standard of living progress and improvement, economists do not espouse a mean materialism. They simply establish the fact that people are motivated by the urge to improve the material conditions of their existence. They judge policies from the point of view of the aims men want to attain. He who disdains the fall in infant mortality and the gradual disappearance of famines and plagues may cast the first stone upon the materialism of the economists.[29]

We call a progressing economy an economy in which the per capita quota of capital invested is increasing. In using this term we do not imply value judgments. We adopt neither the "materialistic" view that such a progression is good nor the "idealistic" view that it is bad or at least irrelevant from a "higher point of view." Of course, it is a well-known fact that the immense majority of people consider the consequences of progress in this sense as the most desirable state of affairs and yearn for conditions which can be realized only in a progressing economy.[30]

All varieties of the producers' policy are advocated on the ground of their alleged ability to raise the party members' standard of living. Protectionism and economic self-sufficiency, labor union pressure and compulsion, labor legislation, minimum wage rates, public spending, credit expansion, subsidies, and other makeshifts are always recommended by their advocates as the most suitable or the only means to increase the real income of the people for whose votes they canvass. Every contemporary statesman or politician invariably tells his voters: My program will make you as affluent as conditions may permit, while my adversaries' program will bring you want and misery.

It is true that some secluded intellectuals in their esoteric circles talk differently. They proclaim the priority of what they call eternal absolute values and feign in their declamations—not in their personal conduct—a disdain of things secular and transitory. But the public ignores such utterances. The main goal of present-day political action is to secure for the respective pressure group memberships the highest material well-being. The only way for a leader to succeed is to instill in people the conviction that his program best serves the attainment of this goal.

What is wrong with the producers' policies is their faulty economics.[31]

These many quotations all go to show that in the mind of von Mises the statement is justified that, in economic matters, men differ much less in the ultimate aims they pursue than in the means they recommend or adopt as best calculated to attain these ends. This view, he holds, is valid not as an abstract truth but as an assumption based on general observation. It is the contrary opinion which, in his estimation, is responsible for the "semantic

28 *Ibid.*, p. 184.
29 *Ibid.*, pp. 193-194.
30 *Ibid.*, p. 292.
31 *Ibid.*, p. 315.

confusion" above referred to. His final statement on this matter may be taken as a satisfactory conclusion. He writes:

The semantic confusion in the discussion of the problems concerned is due to an inaccurate use of terms on the part of many economists. An economist investigates whether a measure *a* can bring about the result *p* for the attainment of which it is recommended, and finds that *a* does not result in *p* but in *g*, an effect which even the supporters of the measure *a* consider undesirable. If this economist states the outcome of his investigation by saying that *a* is a bad measure, he does not pronounce a judgment of value. He merely says that from the point of view of those aiming at the goal *p*, the measure *a* is inappropriate. In this sense the free trade economists attacked protection. They demonstrated that protection does not, as its champions believe, increase but, on the contrary, decreases the total amount of products, and is therefore bad from the point of view of those who prefer an ampler supply of products to a smaller. It is in this sense that economists criticize policies from the point of view of the ends aimed at. If an economist calls minimum wage rates a bad policy, what he means is that its effects are contrary to the purpose of those who recommend their application.[32]

This paper has fulfilled its purpose if it has shown the reader, as it has convinced the author, that there is no logical inconsistency between Ludwig von Mises the rational agnostic and Ludwig von Mises the persistent and intolerant advocate of liberalism as a policy based on economic science.

*   *   *

It does not follow, of course, that all economists who share his rational agnosticism must of necessity also favor his *laissez-faire* policies in their absolute intransigence. The escape from the dilemma is not far afield. It is to be found much less in disagreement with his remarkable scientific dialectics than in doubts as to the universal validity of his fundamental assumption. As he declares himself, in the final pages of *Human Action*:

Economics does not assume or postulate that men aim only or first of all at what is called material well-being. . . . It is neither more nor less rational to aim at riches like Croesus than to aim at poverty like a Buddhist monk. . . .
It is a question of fact whether or not . . . men in general and our contemporaries especially are driven more by the wish to realize myths and dreams than by the wish to improve their material well-being.[33]

This question of fact strikes me as being susceptible of various answers, according to one's conception of myths and dreams. Does the British voter, for instance, favor confiscatory taxation of large

[32] *Ibid.,* p. 879.
[33] *Ibid.,* p. 880.

incomes primarily in the hope that it will redound to his material advantage, or in the certainty that it tends to reduce unwelcome and irritating social inequalities? In general, is the urge towards equality in our modern democracies not often stronger than the desire to improve one's material lot?

Let me conclude with a statement for which I truly believe I can vouch and which flatly contradicts that made by the author of *Human Action* when he declares:

> . . . in the predominantly industrial countries of Europe the protectionists were first eager to declare that the tariff on agricultural products hurts exclusively the interests of the farmers of the predominantly agricultural countries and of the grain dealers.[34]

Now, Switzerland is undoubtedly one of those countries. It is furthermore a completely democratic state in which the voter not only chooses his legislators but in which issues such as that of agrarian portectionism are often settled directly at the polls by means of the popular referendum after prolonged and very outspoken political campaigns. My country, in which farmers represent less than 20 per cent of the population, has in the course of the last generations repeatedly favored this small and dwindling minority by protectionist measures on corn, dairy products, and wine. The urban industrial and commercial majority have done so, neither in what would obviously be an absurd belief that they were thereby increasing their real income, nor out of what would be a no less absurd desire to hurt foreign producers. Quite deliberately and expressly, political parties have sacrificed the immediate material welfare of their members in order to prevent, or at least somewhat to retard, the complete industrialization of the country. A more agricultural Switzerland, though poorer, such is the dominant wish of the Swiss people today. It may be dismissed as a myth or a dream. In fact it is a somewhat costly, but a sincerely professed national ideal of a real democracy.

Such cases are not as exceptional as they may seem in the world of today. What, for instance, of the anti-colonialism professed in Bandoeng today? Does it not show that many, if not most, people in the world today prefer national freedom to individual wealth? To recall all these cases is not to deny the overwhelming validity of the doctrines expounded in *Human Action,* nor to belittle the truly magnificent intellectual achievement of its highly esteemed and dearly beloved author.

[34] *Ibid.,* p. 313.

III

Two of Ludwig von Mises' Most Important Works

by HENRY HAZLITT

In symposiums written "in honor of" some dintinguished writer, the individual contributors too often go off on tangents of their own, and develop points of view that may be irrelevant or even alien to the writer they are supposed to honor. In order to pay homage to the great contribution of Ludwig von Mises in a more direct way than in my following essay, therefore, I herewith take the liberty of reprinting reviews that I wrote of two of his most important books.

The first is my review of his *Socialism,* which appeared in *The New York Times* of January 9, 1938:

LUDWIG VON MISES is professor of Economics in the University of Vienna. His volume *Die Gemein-wirtschaft,* published in 1922, was a thorough analysis of socialism and socialistic ideas. A new edition appeared in 1932. This, with some additions contributed by the author, has now been translated under the title of *Socialism,* and becomes available for the first time to English readers.

In the years since its original publication the volume has attracted increasing attention as the course of events has made its contentions increasingly pertinent. Though considerably more than 200,000 words long, it is never prolix. On the contrary, it is written with remarkable concision. Its length is due solely to its thorough and comprehensive character. It examines socialism from almost every possible aspect—its doctrine of violence as well as that of the collective ownership of the means of production; its ideal of equality; its relation to problems of sex and the family; its proposed solution for the problem of production as well as of distribution; its probable operation under both static and dynamic conditions; its national and international consequences. It considers particular forms of socialism and of pseudo-socialism; the doctrine of the class war and the materialist conception of history; various Socialist criticisms of capitalistic tendencies or alleged tendencies; socialistic ethics; and finally various forms of "gradual socialism" and "destructionism."

No open-minded reader can fail to be impressed by the closeness of the author's reasoning, the rigor of his logic, the power and unity of his thought. This is by far the ablest and most damaging answer to the Socialist philosophy since Boehm-Bawerk, another Austrian economist, also from the University of Vienna, published his memorable *Karl Marx and the Close of His System* in 1898. It is more than that. Boehm-Bawerk confined himself mainly to an examination of Marx's technical economics. Mises, apparently on the assumption that Boehm-Bawerk disposed so thoroughly of Marx's strictly economic analysis of capitalism that the work does not have to be done again, does not go over this ground, except by incidental reference. But he recognizes that socialism does not stand or fall with Marx's economic analysis; and therefore he devotes himself to the much wider task of examining all the arguments against capitalism or in favor of socialism from whatever source.

He does this with such power, brilliance and completeness that this book must rank as the most devastating analysis of socialism yet penned. Doubtless even some anti-Socialist readers will feel that he occasionally overstates his case. On the other hand, even confirmed Socialists will not be able to withhold admiration from the masterly fashion in which he conducts his argument. He has written an economic classic in our time.

Mises analyzes his problem from so many sides that it is difficult even to outline his argument in a brief review. The contention most closely associated with his name is that socialism is certain to fail because it is incapable by its very nature of solving the problem of economic calculation. Unable to solve this, a Socialist society would not know how to distribute its labor, capital, land and other factors of production to the best advantage. It would not know which commodities it was producing at a social profit and which at a social loss. It would not know what any worker, or what any other factor, was actually contributing to the production of economic values. Unable to determine any worker's productive contribution, the Socialist society would be unable to fix his reward proportionately or know how to maximize his incentives.

The greatest difficulty to the realization of socialism in Mises' view, in short, is intellectual. It is not a mere matter of goodwill, or of willingness to cooperate energetically without personal reward. "Even angels, if they were endowed only with human reason, could not form a socialistic community." Capitalism solves this problem of economic calculation through money prices of both consumers' and producers' goods which are fixed in the competition of the open market. State and municipal and even Soviet socialism, in other words, are parasitic on their capitalist environment in a double sense. State or municipal socialism pays its open or hidden deficits by taxing private business. Both it and Russian socialism, in addition, are able to make calculations only with the aid of prices established by private enterprise. Pure or complete socialism, as Mises shows, could not make these calculations. Unfortunately, it is impossible here to outline the argument by which he reaches this conclusion, or even to indicate the nature of his other arguments.

Mises is a traditional liberal. He defends the private ownership of the means of production purely on utilitarian grounds: such ownership is most desirable from the standpoint of social happiness, peace, freedom and productivity. "Liberalism upholds private property not in the interests of the owners but in the general interest." It is Marxian ideology and not an opposition of real interests, he holds, which has made the modern world "class conscious."

He is not hopeful regarding the future:

Several generations of economic policy which was nearly liberal [he writes] have enormously increased the wealth of the world. Capitalism has raised the standard of life among the masses to a level which our ancestors could not have imagined. Interventionism and efforts to introduce socialism have been working now for some decades to shatter the foundations of the world economic system. We stand on the brink of a precipice which threatens to engulf our civilization.

Opposition in principle to socialism there is none. Today no influential party would dare openly to advocate private property in the means of production. The word "capitalism" expresses, for our age, the sum of all evil. Even the opponents of socialism are dominated by Socialist ideas.

And yet he maintains that these ideas are wholly false. But he does not despair altogether: "It is true that the masses do not think.

But just for this reason they follow those who do think." So he still holds forth a faint hope that sober, dispassionate reasoning may turn the world Socialist tide in time.

* * *

The following review of *Human Action* appeared in my column in *Newsweek* magazine of September 19, 1949:

There has just been published by the Yale University Press a book that is destined to become a landmark in the progress of economics. Its title is *Human Action,* and its author is Ludwig von Mises. It is the consumation of half a century of experience, study, and rigorous thought.

No living writer has a more thorough knowledge of the history and literature of economics than Mises, and yet no living writer has been to more pains to take no solution of any problem on faith, but to think out each solution, step by verified step, for himself. The result is a work of great originality written in a great tradition. Although it builds on what was sound in the classical economists and on the revolutionary revision of Menger, Böhm-Bawerk, Jevons, Clark, and Wicksteed, it extends beyond any previous work the logical unity and precision of modern economic analysis.

I know of no other work, in fact, which conveys to the reader so clear an insight into the intimate interconnectedness of all economic phenomena. It makes us recognize why it is impossible to study or understand "collective bargaining" or "labor problems" in isolation; or to understand wages apart from prices or from interest rates or from profits and losses, or to understand any of these apart from all the rest, or the price of any one thing apart from the prices of other things.

It makes us see why those who specialize merely in "monetary economics" or "agricultural economics" or "labor economics" or "business forecasting" so often go astray.

So far is Mises' approach from that of the specialist that he treats economics itself as merely part (though the hitherto best-elaborated part) of a more universal science, "praxeology," or "the science of every kind of human action." This is the key to his title and to his 889 comprehensive pages.

Mises is so concerned to lay the foundations of his work with unassailable solidity that he devotes the first 142 pages to a discussion of "epistemological" problems alone. This is apt to discourage all but the most serious students of the subject. Yet there is nothing pretentious or pedantic in Mises' writing. His sentences and vocabulary are as simple and clear as his profundity and closely woven logic will permit. Once his more abstract theoretical foundations have been laid his chapters are models of lucidity and vigor.

Outstanding among his many original contributions are his "circulation credit" theory of business cycles, which emphasizes the harm of cheap-money policies, and his demonstration that partial socialism is parasitic on capitalism and that a complete socialism would not even know how to solve the problem of economic calculation.

This book is in fact, as the publishers declare, the counterweight of Marx's *Das Kapital,* of Lord Keynes's *General Theory,* and of countless other books recommending socialization, collectivist planning, credit expansion, and similar panaceas. Mises recognizes inflationism under its most sophisticated disguises. He demonstrates repeatedly how statist interventions in the market economy bring about consequences which, even from the standpoint of those who originally advocated the interventions, are worse than the state of affairs they were designed to improve.

Human Action is, in short, at once the most uncompromising and the most rigorously reasoned statement of the case for capitalism that has yet appeared. If any single book can turn the ideological tide that has been running in recent years so heavily toward statism, socialism, and totalitarianism, *Human Action* is that book. It should become the leading text of everyone who believes in freedom, in individualism, and in the ability of a free-market economy not only to outdistance any government-planned system in the production of goods and services for the masses, but to promote and safeguard, as no collectivist tyranny can ever do, those intellectual, cultural, and moral values upon which all civilization ultimately rests.

PART TWO

On the Nature of Man
and Government

IV

Order vs. Organization

by Bertrand de Jouvenel

THIS paper deals with man's taste in configurations and consequences arising therefrom. "The Problem of the Orchard" may introduce the subject better than any abstract statement.

The Problem of the Orchard

Let there be an apple orchard and two distinct groups of school children. The first group is assembled in class and is asked the following question: "In a given orchard, 100,000 apples are to be picked and collected in heaps. How should the heaps be formed?" No child will regard the problem as indeterminate; most will answer that the apples should be collected in a hundred heaps of a thousand apples each. Possibly some few may give different answers, but always in round numbers of heaps with equal numbers of apples to the heap. In the meantime let us send out the second group of children actually to heap up the 100,000 apples. When their task is completed we will find a varied collection of uneven mounds.

Thus the same problem has been given contrasting solutions: A in the classroom, B in the field; A by a process of thought, B by a process of action. This affords us our first general statement: given a set of factors, there is no necessary coincidence between their arrangement by a process of thought (type A) and their arrangement by a process of action (type B).

After the apples are gathered an observer strolls into the orchard. He beholds the B arrangement, and its irregularity faintly displeases him, while his eye would be gladdened by a more regular distribution of the A type. Indeed the unseemliness of the B arrangement may affect him sufficiently to evoke action—he may apply his own labor or that of others to a rearrangement. This affords us our second and third general statements loosely worded: Man delights in perceived order; he is willing to expend labor on its achievement.

The Feeling of Orderliness

We are enamored of order; this passion runs through all of mankind, from the housewife to Einstein. True enough, but what is "Order"? So Platonic an approach is to be shunned. It is a more sensible and modest course to note that some arrangements evoke an immediate pleasure and approval, while others do not. We shall call the first "seemly" and the second "unseemly," hoping that we thereby emphasize that we start from subjective appreciations. We do not then have to answer the question, "what is Order?" Our concern is merely to detect when the feeling of seemliness is experienced.

Tests of seemliness can easily be devised. On your desk, next to the visitor's chair, place twelve pencils, six blue and six red ones, arranged in two heaps, six red and one blue in one heap and then five blue ones in the other. A visitor will itch to transfer the "mislaid" blue pencil to the blue lot, while he will remain quiescent if two heaps of six each contain three blue and three red pencils. Or again, if the pencils are arranged by size with one discrepancy, the visitor will experience something like relief if you restore the continuity of the series. As one goes on to less naive experiments, it becomes apparent that the feeling of seemliness is experienced when we grasp the law of structure according to which the factors are arrayed. If five beads are presented, three large ones in succession and then two small ones, the individual will want to place each small one between two large beads, but if the pattern of three large ones and then two small ones is frequently repeated, its periodicity will make it acceptable.

An office has a stock of envelopes of various sizes. Their arrangement pleases if they are stacked by sizes in a progression. Let there be two collections on two different shelves, each containing the whole range of sizes. A new secretary undoubtedly will set out to assemble all same-sized envelopes, substituting one series for two. She will, however, refrain from this rearrangement when she finds that the envelopes on the first shelf carry an engraved address on their back while those on the second shelf do not. The principle of classification has become clear to her and she now regards as orderly an arrangement which did not seem so at the outset.

We want factors to "obey" some understandable principle by reference to which each has and falls into "its place." The understanding can be either artistic or intellectual. Every eye enjoys the shapes of shells, but few minds could formulate that the shapes are generated from an equi-angular spiral. The eye may thus jump to a conclusion while the mind may recognize an organizing principle which does not jump to the eye as in the foregoing example of the envelopes. Thus there are two modes of understanding, appreciation of seemliness involves one or the other form of recognition of an organizing principle.

Our desire to find things "obedient" to some principle is the mainspring of intellectual inquiry. We seek "hidden" principles of organization whose discovery reveals the orderliness of phenomena that seem disorderly to us.

Our achievements in so marshalling phenomena have been connected with and are dependent upon the progress of mathematics. Mathematics mainly consist in the thinking out of more complex configurations. When an additonal "function" or "series" is studied, one more "shape" is thereby added to our intellectual store of "orderly configurations." Let us take a grossly simplified example. Let us assume that we have been unable to form any idea of a closed curve other than the circle. We are then told that the earth "circles" around the sun. But by some means we find that the earth does not in fact describe a circle around the sun.[1] Its movement therefore does not conform to any model of orderliness held in our mind, *ergo* we adjudge it disorderly. This is meant to stress that the probability of our experiencing orderliness is a function of the store of configurations worked out in our minds. A lognormal distribution[2] may seem orderly to a mathematician but to no one else.[3]

---

[1] Though in fact we would presumably have no means of establishing this if our geometric knowledge were so restricted.

[2] See the notable paper on lognormal distributions by Prof. J. H. Gaddum (*Nature*, Oct. 20, 1954) to which our attention was drawn by Prof. Allais.

[3] A collection of phenomena becomes orderly for me if and when I can tersely formulate the law of structure whereby each item is assigned the position which it holds.

Fitting and Tidying-up

A scientist may be thought of as having access to a great store of patterns into which he delves to find one that will fit the facts he seeks to integrate into a theory. Such a pattern may not be available to him, in which case he must acknowledge failure. For to him the facts are supreme; the theory must fit them. Success may come later in this field because some mathematician, possibly quite ignorant of his concern, has worked out a pattern [4] which will now suit the phenomena.

The inverse relation holds true in the case of those many diverse human activities which we may blanket under the term "tidying-up." Take the simple example of the housewife who holds in her mind a given pattern of arrangement to which the objects of "tidying-up" are made to conform.

In terms of our orchard example, the progress of science depends upon the ability of the mind to move away from the simplest type A arrangements to the conception of more intricate shapes. One of these shapes will bear a great likeness to the B arrangement which actually occurs. This is an achievement of science. On the other hand, tidying-up activities consist in moving objects from B configurations, which just occur, towards type A arrangements which are recognized as orderly and therefore desirable.

We can there reformulate our second and third general statements: Men have a tidiness-preference for arrangements of which they grasp the structural law, and they have a tidiness-propensity to recast arrangements in accordance with models held in their minds.

Contrasted Meanings of Rationality

The root of the word "rationality" is ratio, i.e., proportion. Considering a given arrangement of factors, we may call it "rational," because the proportions obtaining between parts are such as to spring immediately to the eye, or to be immediately (or readily) understood by the mind.[5] Our pleasure is then bound up with the

[4] Consider the number of processes which come to be recognized as orderly when related either to the Verhulst-Pearl logistic curve, or even better to Gaston Backman's more elastic model. For an inspired eulogy of these patterns cf. D'Arcy Thompson: *On Growth and Form*, new ed. Cambridge, 1942.

[5] Let us recall that the eye of an ignorant man may appreciate the harmony of proportions of an arrangement the structural law of which he could not formulate; conversely, a mathematician may formulate a law of arrangement which cannot be transcribed in a visible form.

assent we grant to existing proportions. But an arrangement may be "rational" in quite another sense: if the proportions between factors are suitable to produce the result at which the arrangement is aimed. We thus find two distinct meanings of "rationality": subjective enjoyment of proportions, and objective adequacy of proportions to the purpose of the arrangement. To be more precise, in the first case the arrangement is judged as "a sight"; in the second case, as "an organization for results." [6]

In everyday language, people tend to call arrangements "rational," "reasonable" and "orderly" if their principle is simple enough to be immediately grasped; conversely, they tend to call them "irrational," "unreasonable" and "disorderly," if the principle is not clear to them. Thus order and reason tend to be identified to seemliness rather than to operativeness.

The Case of the Library

In the course of his life an author has collected a private library attuned to his needs. The volumes he uses least have been relegated to the highest and least accessible tiers, while the works of reference are ready at hand. Regardless of authorship and formal subject-matter, those works that hold for him some affinity of significance and that are apt to be used simultaneously are placed together. The owner could not easily account for the distribution of his tools (which indeed shifts over time), but it serves his purpose.[7] While he is on a holiday, a well-meaning daughter decides to tidy up and aligns the volumes according to format and alphabetical order. Having wrought, she feels that "it looks better now"; and so it does, but a working arrangement has been destroyed in the name of seemliness. No doubt, the previous arrangement was imperfect and could have been reformed to serve the author's purpose even better. But such an improvement would have been based on a considered judgment of the operator thinking out his process, or by someone else capable of seeing the problem from the operative angle—an "operator-judgment." The reform effected by the daughter was not "operator-based," if I may so express it.

[6] A third meaning of rationality need not concern us here; any configuration whatever is, of course, the outcome of its causes and therefore may be called "rational." In this sense, everything that is real is rational, but then the term becomes so all-embracing as to be useless.

[7] For a striking treatment of the general problem of arrangement of tools around an artisan, see Gerald K. Zipf, *Human Behavior and the Principle of Least Effort*, Addison-Wesley Press, Cambridge, Mass., 1949.

Thinking in general terms, let us consider an arrangement of factors that serves some purpose and is instrumental to some process. Let us call it an operational arrangement. A mind concerned with this purpose, well aware of the process, dwells upon the operational arrangement and finds that it might be made more effective by certain alterations. We shall call a judgment passed from this angle an O-judgment to denote that the arrangement is appreciated from the operational standpoint. O-judgments are the principle of all technical progress made by mankind. Quite different in kind is the judgment passed upon the same arrangement of factors by a mind that regards it without any intensive interest in or awareness of the process. Such a judgment is then passed as it were from an external, extra-processive standpoint. We shall call it an S-judgment (S for sightseer).

The Genesis of Absurdity

Whenever I recognize that an arrangement of factors is instrumental to an operation, I cannot call this arrangement irrational (this would be saying in the same breath that it is related and unrelated to the same operation). But being concerned *ex hypothesi* with this operation I may well call the arrangement more or less rational. In this case I am really comparing a current method or path which I have explored with another method or path which I have discovered. This is an O-judgment.

Addressing myself to the same arrangement, I may fail to identify it as processive and instrumental to an operation, or I may fail to interest myself in this operation, or again I may fail to sufficiently scrutinize the process and arrangement to recognize their complex connection. If I nonetheless pass a judgment upon what I perceive of the configuration, this must be an S-judgment whose principle is a spontaneous and undeliberate comparison of the shape perceived to simple models of seemliness. If this is my attitude, the more complex the process is to which I have denied my attention, and the more complex the attending configuration, the more unseemly I shall find the latter, and the more unfavorable must be my S-judgment. I shall then call the arrangement disorderly and irrational.

An O-judgment is costly in terms of attention and time. It cannot be formed immediately or without effort; therefore, the number of such judgments which I may form is limited. But while I must focus my attention intensively on the process and arrangement in question, a great number of other shapes float into the field of my attention, and my glimpses at them immediately call forth uncostly S-judgments. The more extensive the field over which I may thus roam effortlessly, the greater the number of my S-judgments. Therefore, my store of judgments will tend to be made up of a small minority of O-judgments and a great majority of S-judgments. But while my O-judgments tend to improve arrangements whose processiveness I have grasped and which I endeavor to make more rational (i.e., effective), my S-judgments tend to impeach arrangements of which I considered only the seemliness and which I therefore pronounce irrational. Therefore the larger the number of arrangements upon which I venture to pass judgments, the higher the proportion of the arrangements examined which I shall pronounce unseemly, and the more the world will seem to me to be made up of "bad" and "wrong" arrangements.

But O-judgments are also in a small minority within every other mind. Moreover, diverse minds do not form O-judgments on the same subject matters. It follows that a summation of individual judgments arrived at independently within a society would show that there is of necessity a huge majority of S-judgments over O-judgments. And second, there must be a majority of S-judgments over O-judgments on every arrangement. S-judgments generally entail a verdict of unseemliness, disorder, and irrationality; therefore, a summation of all judgments must result in a general verdict of unseemliness, disorder, and irrationality. It must result in a condemnation of "the absurdity of the universe," and more specifically of all social arrrangements.

We actually find that such a philosophy has arisen in our times possibly because we have overextended the field of individual judgment.

The Case of the Judge

Of course, it runs contrary to the principle of division of labor that I should pass judgment on a great number of arrangements. Take a simple simile. As a judge I have to rule on a number of cases per year. It has never been suggested that every litigation in the country should be submitted to every judge. If this would be the case a great number of minds would be conscripted for each case, but no attention at all could be paid to each. Such a procedure would seem inane, and yet consider how many "cases" the daily paper brings to our private court and tempts us to adjudge.

It takes no great psychological acumen to observe that we enjoy

passing judgments on matters of which we know very little. This
is bound up with our taste in configurations. Problems to which we
have devoted scrupulous scrutiny and arrangements which we have
delved into deeply offer no scope for application of the simple
models that we inherently prefer. It is a relief to turn to problems
of which we are ignorant and to which we therefore may apply
our models. Be it noted that the greatest scientists who have mastered prodigious complexities are apt to come out with the most
naive views on social problems, for example. Their minds are taking
a holiday, reverting to the effortless and invalid judgment of seemliness. We could assume that those who are best aware of the
difficulties of grasping a process in their own fields, should be most
chary of passing S-judgments on other matters; but this is contrary to reality. Our affection for simple patterns is so basic to our
nature that the more we must bow to the actual complexities of
organizations we understand, the more we want to find simplicity
in other organizations.

The Attraction of Simple Figures

All that is known of man's past is testimony to the fact that he
has ever associated the idea of perfection with simple figures, which
he therefore used to denote Divinity. Basic to every ritual is the
circle in which the eye finds no lack and which thus represents (or
indeed suggests) the concept of Wholeness. The circular crown
seems to have been invented independently by all human societies;
the operations of magic have involved everywhere the tracing of
figures within a circle.[8] We are told that primitive places of worship
and assemblies of worshippers were circular.[9] Movement forming
simple geometric patterns was a form of homage to Divinity. Military parades have also been derived from this, as well as our word
"theory," which in barrack language still meant quite recently
"training in geometric marching."

The setting of effective values upon the simplest geometric figures is strikingly exemplified in the history of warfare. The Mace-
donians were so enamored with the squareness of their phalanx that
they thoughtlessly adhered to their order of battle even when circumstances made it most inadvisable. Frederick the Great and
Napoleon's victories owed much to the aesthetic sense of their oppo-

[8] Cf. for instance Robert Ambelin, La Kabbale Pratique, Paris, 1951.
[9] Cf. among many other sources Louis Hautecoeur, Mystique et Architecture;
Symbolisme du Cercle et de la Coupole, Paris, 1954.

nents who arrayed their troops with an eye for symmetry. Frederick and Napoleon gave themselves the advantage of an operative arrangement over a seemly one.

Complex Structures are Characteristic of Life

"Proteins may well be considered the most important of all the substances present in plants and animals."[10] This induces me to ask for a description of proteins. In answer the chemist must first remind me that he regards as elementary factors the atoms of pure substance, though they themselves display a complex inner architecture. Starting from them as simple, the chemist must draw my attention to amino-acids, a family of different compounds constructed by different arrangements of a different kind of atoms. Taking pity upon my ignorance, he may invite me to regard these amino-acids as a varied collection of queerly designed jewels, built by different arrangements of different kinds of precious stones. Then he must tell me about polypeptide chains, the stringing together in and from a line of many such "jewels," with a twisting of the chain and in many cases an inter-twisting of several chains. "Considering their structure, we see that the existence of a great number of different proteins (perhaps 50,000 different proteins in the human body) is not surprising. Protein molecules may differ from one another not only in the number of residues of different amino-acids, but also in the order of the residues in the polypeptide chains, and the way in which the chains are folded."[11]

In order to account for the operative properties of proteins, scientists have found themselves compelled to successively work out this extremely complicated picture, which stands in sharp contrast to the simple configurations that haunt our mind.

It is a trite remark that our dead body, regarded as a mine of inorganic chemicals, would not yield more than ten dollars worth of chemicals. And while this makes a pretty poor joke, it can be used to emphasize the value of intricate operative organization. Is it not therefore disquieting that our minds should spontaneously favor the tidiness of crystals over the intricacy of active arrangements?

Nothing is more orderly than a crystal of pure copper; therein we find regularity and symmetry at their best. Nothing is more opera-

[10] Taken from that admirable introduction to chemistry, *General Chemistry* by Linus Pauling, 2nd ed., San Francisco, 1953, pp. 592-600.
[11] *Ibid.*

tive than a gene, of which the intricacy baffles our science. A child can grasp and reproduce the structure of the copper crystal, but no human agency can forge this fantastically complicated signature which the gene repeats all over the body of one specific person. Surely so glaring an opposition should teach us not to confuse order with organization!

The Threat of Orderliness

This train of thought leads us to regard the simplicity-preference and tidiness-propensity of the human mind as potentially destructive. Such tendencies run counter to the diversity and intricacy of operative structures. If I could recast the molecule proteins of my body to give them a simpler and identical structure, I would be committing suicide. Practically all men enjoy the orderliness of a military parade, but they are dangerously prone to mistake this enjoyment for the recognition of a supreme form of organization. In fact, the men assembled on the field achieve no operation whatever beyond offering a sight. The idea of over-all organization is frequently aligned to an image of perceivable regularity in human movements as can be found in a parade. But this is the very opposite of organization.

A parade is costly; equally costly is the parade spirit with which we approach the operations of men in general. We tend to believe that society is at its best when its functioning offers to our minds a clear, distinct, and simple pattern. But the only thing then maximized is our intellectual enjoyment. We are prone to mistake our endeavors to maximize our intellectual enjoyment for the spirit of reform. But we have no warrant for the belief that a simplification of pattern that would please our minds would constitute an improvement of society, unless we define improvement as increasing coincidence of arrangements with the figures held in our mind—an extreme of intellectual pride.

Let us now picture a group of operators, each engaged in a process and therefore prone to arrange factors at hand in a manner suitable to his process. Imagine that they meet at regular intervals to devise a general structure. Now if they all individually and responsibly perform the same operations, we can assume that their general decisions as to the over-all structure will take into account operational needs that are experienced by all participants. This cannot be so, however, if the participants are engaged in very different processes and if only a minority of them are in fact responsible for the performing of operations. Then the common ground for the participants will be provided by those general shapes and figures that inhabit our minds and of which the simplest are the most common to all of us. Agreement shall then most easily be reached on orderly arrangements adverse to operational arrangements in proportion to the intricacy of the latter. The rule of order and the operational urge shall thenceforth be in conflict. This is, of course, in itself a pattern of deceitful simplicity. But it may serve to explain some tensions of contemporary society.[12]

[12] Much more could be said on the subject. It might, for instance, be useful to dwell upon our natural tendency, when sight-judging a mechanism or process, to reform or improve it by breaking down whatever feedback it is provided with. But what use, if any, can be made of the views advanced here must be left to better judgments.

V

On Democracy

by Hans F. Sennholz

<hr>

THE major conflict of our time is the struggle between the "People's Democracies" and the "Western Democracies." Both sides claim to represent the "true" democracy and the truly democratic way of life. Each side claims to represent a system of society that is diametrically opposed to that of the other, based on contradicting beliefs and values and on distinct systems of economic organization.

The subject of this study is the nature of both "democracies," and the nature and limit of the power which both kinds of society exercise over the individual. For it is the organization of society and the individual's position in his society that constitute the nucleus of the controversies. Stated in its broadest terms, the problem of the forms of social organization has occupied thinkers since the beginning of civilization. The problem of true or false democracy, however, is the specific problem of our age. "Democracy" is the ambiguous catchword with a multiplicity of connotations harboring conflicting political and economic ideas and practices.

On the Nature of People's Democracies

A thorough analysis of the nature of the communist social order and political constitution would have to include a discussion of the nature of society, the division of labor, private and collective property, the doctrines of class interests, the economics of a communist community, and many other important problems. Indeed voluminous volumes are and still could be written on the nature of the communist social order. In this essay we merely would like to

examine the communist form of government in relation to democracy, i.e., the system of political organization in which the supreme
power is retained by the people and exercised directly or indirectly
through a system of representation.

The most eminent architects of present-day communism, Marx,
Engels, Lenin, and Stalin, have repeatedly and distinctly stated
their views on the nature of "capitalist" and "communist" democracies. *Karl Marx* dealt with this subject on the occasion of the Paris
uprising by the communist proletariat which took possession of the
city from March 18 to May 28, 1871. According to Marx, the insur-
rectionary government called Commune was the "positive form" of
a republic. Not only legislation and administration were laid into
the hands of the Commune but also the judicatory. Thus the three
branches of government power were united by the Commune Delegation whose members were to be at any time "revocable and bound
by the *mandat impératif*" of their constituents.[1]

To Marx the capitalist state is the organ of class domination, the
organ of subjugation of one class by another. The function of Western democracy is "to perpetuate the rule of capital, the slavery of
labor."[2] Its objective is the creation of a political and economic
order that "legalizes and perpetuates the oppression of the workers." In connection with a discussion of his doctrine of the inevitable collapse of the capitalist democracies and the inevitability of
socialism and communism, Marx foresaw a stage of political transition in which the suppressed and impoverished proletariat would
seize dictatorial power through revolution. In his own words, "Between capitalist and communist society, there lies a period of
revolutionary transition from the former to the latter. A stage of
political transition corresponds to this period, and the State during
the period can be no other than the revolutionary dictatorship of
the proletariat."[3]

Similar ideas on state and society were expressed by Marx's friend
and collaborator, *Friedrich Engels*. In a letter to the German socialist party leader, Bebel, F. Engels vividly described the communist state as a "transitional institution which we are obliged to use
in the revolutionary struggle in order forcibly to crush our opponents. . . . During the period when the proletariat still *needs* the

[1] Karl Marx, *The Paris Commune*, 1871, edition New York Labor News Co., 1920,
p. 74 et seq.
[2] Karl Marx, *Class Struggles in France*, Lawrence & Wishart, London, 1942, p. 60.
[3] Letter of Marx to Bracke, May 15, 1875; see also Marx, *Zur Kritik des sozial-
demokratischen Parteiprogramms von Gotha*, Berlin, 1912, p. 23 et seq.

State, it does not require it in the interests of freedom, but in the interest of crushing its antagonists."[4] Once it has taken control of the state and has crushed its opponents, the proletariat, according to Engels, "converts the means of production into State property. But by this very act it destroys itself, as a proletariat, destroying at the same time all class differences and class antagonisms, and with this, also, the State. Past and present Society, which moved amidst class antagonisms, had to have the State, this is, an organization of the exploiting class for the support of its external conditions of production. . . . When, ultimately, the State really becomes the representative of the whole of Society, it will make itself superfluous. From the time when, together with class domination and the struggle for individual existence, resulting from the personal anarchy in production, those conflicts and excesses which arise from this struggle will all disappear—from that time there will be nobody to be oppressed; there will, therefore, be no need for any special force of oppression—no need for the State. The first act of the State, in which it really acts as the representative of the whole of Society, namely, the assumption of control over the means of production on behalf of Society, is also its last independent act as a State."[5] Under those conditions, Engels continues, "the State will not be 'abolished'; it will wither away." Of course, this does not mean that the *capitalist* state will wither away; it must be destroyed by the proletariat through revolution and war. Only the proletarian state withers away after the revolution.[6]

During his exile from czarist Russia, *W. I. Lenin* made similar remarks on the nature of capitalist and proletarian democracies. In his *The State and Revolution*,[7] which he wrote in 1917 while in Zurich, Switzerland, he reiterated the teachings of Marx and Engels and expounded his theory of proletarian revolution. To him the Western democracies were organizations with the express purpose of proletarian exploitation. "In capitalist society," said Lenin, "under the conditions most favourable to its development, we have a more or less complete democracy in the form of a democratic republic. But this democracy is always bound by the narrow framework of capitalistic exploitation, and, consequently, always remains, in reality, a democracy only for the minority, only for the possessing

[4] Letter of 18th-28th March, 1875, published in August Bebel, *Aus meinem Leben*, Stuttgart 1911, Vol. II, p. 322.
[5] *Ibid.* See also F. Engels, *Herrn Eugen Dührings Umwälzung der Wissenschaft*, 7th ed., Stuttgart, 1910, pp. 302, 303.
[6] *Ibid.*
[7] George Allen & Unwin, Ltd., London, 1920.

classes, only for the rich."[8] Or at another place, "To decide once every few years which member of the ruling class is to repress and oppress the people through parliament—this is the real essence of middle class parliamentarianism, not only in parliamentary and constitutional Monarchies, but also in the most democratic Republics."[9] Regarding the American, Swiss, French, and English democracies he remarked that "Parliament itself is giving up to talk for the special purpose of fooling the 'common people.'"[10] To sum up, "we have a democracy that is curtailed, wretched, false; a democracy only for the rich, for the minority."[11]

In his discussion of the alleged evolution of capitalism to imperialism Lenin applied his theory of proletarian revolution and temporary dictatorship also in the field of international relations. "It must be added," says Lenin, "that imperialism leads to an increase of national oppression and subsequently to the growing of resistance not only in new territories just opened up, but also to territorial annexations among the old countries."[12] Modern capitalism means "striving for power instead of freedom, exploitation of an increasing number of small and weak nations by very few and wealthy nations." To avoid subjugation by capitalist nations and to repulse any capitalist attempt at exploitation of the proletariat, that is, truly democratic societies, the proletarian state is still needed. Only when the resistance of the capitalists in all countries has finally been broken, when all capitalists have disappeared, only then will all states wither away.

In a speech before the Supreme Soviet in a special session in November 1936, *Joseph Stalin* compared capitalist constitutions with the new Russian constitution about to be adopted by the Supreme Soviet. "The characteristics of the new Constitution," according to Stalin, "is its consequent and fully realized democratization. From the point of view of democracy two groups of bourgeois constitutions can be distinguished: one group directly denies the equality of citizens and democratic freedoms or renders their realization unfeasible. The other group indeed accepts the democratic principles and even emphasizes them, but then embarks upon conditions and limitations that completely mutilate the democratic rights and freedoms. They speak of equal rights to vote for all

[8] *Ibid.*, p. 89.
[9] *Ibid.*, p. 48.
[10] *Ibid.*, pp. 48, 49.
[11] *Ibid.*, p. 92.
[12] W. I. Lenin, *Der Imperialismus als höchstes Stadium des Kapitalismus*, Moscow, 1946, p. 151.

citizens, but then make them contingent on domiciliation, on education and even wealth. They speak of equal rights, but immediately provide for limitations completely or partially voiding the rights of women, etc., etc." [13]

According to J. Stalin, the Soviet Constitution "does not merely announce the democratic freedoms, but also assures them through certain material means. It is evident that the democratization of the new Constitution is no 'ordinary,' but a *socialist* democratization." [14] Comparing the Capitalist Democracies with the People's Democracies Stalin arrived at the following conclusions: "Democracy in the capitalist countries divided into antagonistic classes, in final analysis, is a democracy for the strong, a democracy for the possessing minorities. The democracy in the Soviet Union, on the contrary, is a democracy of workers, of everybody. . . . I therefore believe that the Constitution of the U.S.S.R. is the only one in the world that is democratic throughout." [15] All power in the U.S.S.R. lies with the workers acting through the Soviets of deputies who are the political foundation of the U.S.S.R. and of the dictatorship of the proletariat. [16] Capitalism is abolished; unearned riches and exploitation profits are socialized and labor has become "the duty and honour of every able-bodied citizen according to the principle: Who does not labor, shall not eat." [17]

These, in short, are the opinions of the most eminent founders of the "People's Democracies." Their understanding and conception of the nature of capitalist democracies is based on the belief in the existence of antagonistic class interests under capitalism and in exploitation of the workers by the owners of the means of production. Their contentions obviously would lack any foundation if they failed to prove the existence of class conflicts and capitalist exploitation. We shall endeavor to show in the following that Marx, Engels, Lenin, and Stalin never succeeded in offering cogent proof of class conflict and exploitation under capitalism, nor could they ever succeed because both phenomena are incompatible with the nature of capitalism. Where there is capitalism there can be no class conflict, no exploitation. And where there are class conflicts and exploitation, there can be no capitalism.

In an unhampered market economy the determination of wages is

---

[13] J. Stalin, *Über den Entwurf der Verfassung der USSR*, Moscow, 1945, pp. 23, 24.
[14] *Ibid.*, p. 26.
[15] *Ibid.*, p. 37.
[16] Article 2 of the Soviet Constitution, *Ibid.*, p. 61.
[17] Article 12 of the Soviet Constitution, *Ibid.*, p. 63.

the outcome of the valuations and decisions of consumers. Through buying or abstaining from buying they determine what is produced, at what price, in what quantity, quality, etc. With the valuation of the ultimate consumption goods the consumers also determine the value of labor services and achievements necessary for the production of the final product. Labor services are valued like the services of any other factor of production. Their prices, i.e., wage rates, tend to coincide with the marginal productivity of labor. That is to say, the supply of labor and of other factors of production and the anticipated future prices of the ultimate product determine the height of wage rates. It is obvious that businessmen cannot pay more for services than they obtain for the ultimate product in the market. To pay more would mean to suffer losses and to risk bankruptcy. On the other hand, a businessman cannot pay less than the market value of each service because he would lose his workers to competing entrepreneurs. Under free enterprise I cannot hold a worker by paying him less than he can obtain from my competitors. To assume that employers could keep wages down is absurd, for new entrepreneurs would immediately enter the labor market and bid up the labor price. Already operating entrepreneurs would expand their employment and thus bid up wages until the market height had been reached. As long as an opportunity to earn a profit from low wages existed, employers would continue to bid for additional labor and thus cause wage rates to rise until this source of profit were eliminated.

Of course, in an interventionist society actual wage rates may differ from the potential rate which would exist in an unhampered market. If we erect institutional barriers that impede competition and hinder entrance into certain industries and occupations, we falsify the actual demand and supply situation and bring about disparities of labor prices. But in every instance our interference with competition has inevitable effects. That is to say, we create unemployment, or shortages, depending on the nature of the discrepancy between the interventionist price from that of the unhampered market. Thus it is conceivable that *under absence* of capitalism wage rates may be lower than the height determined by labor's marginal productivity. Exploitation is a common phenomenon in all non-capitalist countries, i.e., in interventionist, socialist, and above all, in communist societies where wage rates are determined by central decrees.

Equally indefensible is the contention of the antagonistic class interests under capitalism. The notion of the irreconcilable conflict between the interests of "capital" and "labor" is Marxian, though it enjoys popularity also among non-Marxian socialists and interventionists. In a free market society it is in the vital interests of all its members that the social division of labor be fully developed and each member be most productive. The higher productivity of the division of labor removes all conceivable sources of conflict. It is true, in a society without division of labor additional wealth cannot be produced and each man's share curtails the shares of all others. But in a market economy the preservation and further development of the division of labor and its greater productivity become the uniting common interest. The greater the productivity of my fellow men, the more will I obtain in exchange for my labor. Thus everybody benefits from the smooth operation of the market economy.

Consumers also determine everybody's share in the process of production. Their choices and preferences determine who shall be in possession of capital. Whoever serves them best in the satisfaction of their wants is allotted control. Whoever fails to satisfy their most urgent wants suffers losses of capital through the operation of the market. Under capitalism ownership in the means of production has a social function: it serves the satisfaction of the consumer's wants.

Under communism labor and the material means of production are directed by government. Central planners and officials determine what shall be produced and who shall produce it. It is no longer the consumer whose choices and preferences direct the economy, but government officials who determine the production process and allocate the material factors. Property is divested of its social function and becomes a privilege for officials whose power of management is absolute. To encroach upon their rights and decisions becomes a crime subject to severe punishment. According to Article 131 of the Soviet Constitution, "Persons who transgress against public socialist property are enemies of the people." That is to say, whoever transgresses against the means of production in the hands of the planners is an enemy of the state.

To maintain that capitalist democracies are democracies "only for the minority, only for the possessing classes, only for the rich," or that the capitalist state is a state of "class domination" in which "elections decide once every few years which member of the ruling class is to repress and oppress the people through parliament," either reflects an extraordinary insensibility toward reality or is outrightly malicious. In the United States more than seven million people own the stock of American corporations and more than five million own farms; that is to say, more than twelve million Americans are capitalists in the Marxian sense. But about a hundred million Americans are eligible to vote in all elections. If the Marxian contention were correct, only the twelve million capitalists could vote, make laws, and determine who should "repress and oppress the people through parliament." The emptiness of the Marxian contention is apparent.

Let us look at this case from another viewpoint. If it were the American capitalists who make and execute the laws, the taxes paid by the capitalists indeed would be insignificant. Also state controls would not be laid on the business transactions of the capitalists, but rather on all matters concerning the workers. American reality looks different. It is a matter of fact that the highest taxes are paid by the capitalists and especially by the bankers and brokers in Wall Street. As owners of corporations they often pay up to 82% of corporate income and up to 88% of the remaining income in the form of federal income taxes. In addition, state and city governments help themselves to revenues by taxing Wall Street transactions. Numerous government controls are imposed upon the credit and money market. Can anybody honestly maintain that these taxes and controls are imposed upon the capitalists by themselves? Or is it the vast majority of American voters who, ignorant of the fact that their very livelihood and existence depends on capital accumulation and investments, elect representatives who are bent on dissipating and enjoying past capital accumulations for the benefit of the moment? The answer is obvious.

According to Marx, Engels, Lenin, and Stalin, the capitalist democracies must be destroyed by the workers in violent revolutions and be replaced by the "dictatorship of the proletariat." For "communism alone is capable of giving a really complete democracy, and the fuller it is the more quickly will it become unnecessary and wither away."

Capitalism and exploitation are two incompatible concepts excluding each other. But let us disregard this conclusion for a moment in order to discuss the alleged necessity of proletarian revolutions in the Western democracies. If it were correct that the workers under capitalism are subjugated and exploited, why do they not vote the few ruling capitalists out of office? As we have seen, the workers are in the vast majority in all elections. Why should they favor violent revolutions if they can most easily form a proletarian dictatorship through their votes at the polls? In 1933, for example, the majority of Germans did not rise in revolution in order to make Hitler the dictator of Germany. They simply voted him into office, observing all provisions of the law. In a democracy where the workers comprise the majority of the constituency, there is no logical justification for the majority to overthrow the government. The majority of a nation only rises in revolution if and when it cannot remove an undesired government through free elections. A dictatorship that is not backed by the majority of the people faces the constant danger of revolution and overthrow.

The predilection of Marx and his followers for violent revolutions merely reveals their palliate intent to seize governmental power with the fanatical support of small minorities. Such an uprising may be successful provided the majority sympathizes with the minority and sooner or later approves the *fait accompli*. In Russia the majority of the people finally acquiesced in the communist seizure of power after a long and bloody civil war. But as soon as Russian public opinion should begin to disapprove of the dictatorship of the few in power, their overthrow through revolution is imminent. This is the most serious danger to the communist regime in Moscow.

The phrase of the "withering dictatorship of the proletariat" is a catchword coined to lure the bewildered masses. Devoid of any intelligent meaning it even presupposes realization of a series of conditions. First, all means of production must be in the possession of the state and the resistance of the capital owners must be broken. Second, the formula "from each according to his ability, to each according to his needs" must be fully realized. Third, and this is Lenin's contribution, capitalism must be destroyed in all countries and communism must prevail all over the world. Provided all these conditions are given, the communist states are said to wither away.

The first condition raises the problem of whether a society, in which all means of production are in the hands of an economic planner, can afford to be without a social apparatus of compulsion and coercion. Is central planning and directing of millions of production processes conceivable without coercion? Is the directing of a labor force of many millions of individuals possible without a disciplinary power? We deny this vehemently. Even if we assume that all material means of production are in the hands of a single planner whose position and decisions are uncontested by all his fellow men, we deny that they, without coercion, would work where he wants them to work and in accordance with his instructions. Of course, he may attempt to direct the labor force through education and persuasion. But if his attempt should fail only in exceptional cases, the central director would have to impose control over the engagement of labor. That is to say, he would resort to coercion through the apparatus of coercion: the state. All socialist governments, in order to control and direct the production process, sooner or later applied to a certain extent the use of powers of labor direction. Central planning always means central management of the factors of production, including labor. This holds true in all human societies.

The second condition, that the formula "from each according to his ability, to each according to his needs" must first be realized before the withering process can commence, is an empty political slogan which is to hypnotize the people. Every student of economics knows that the concept of "need," for example, permits a number of interpretations. And Marx and his followers are said to have been economists. They must have known that human need may pertain to anything requisite, desired, or useful for individual well-being, that it may be physical, intellectual, spiritual, that it refers to individual ends or to imperative demands for the realization of ultimate ends, that it implies indeterminable degrees of urgency. What do they mean? To fail to discuss these concepts of a future society they are striving to attain either reflects an astonishing shallowness of political and economic thought or bad faith. Could they have referred to the need of subsistence, to the provisions for the maintenance of human life? This, indeed, would be surprisingly modest as it implies a considerable reduction in the standards of living of the American and European nations. Or could they have promised the satisfaction of every conceivable want of every individual on this earth? Could they have meant a paradise on earth? This is most likely and equally fantastic. It seems quite unnecessary to expound on the limitations of our material resources and human energies. There are limits to what man can produce, limits of time and strength, of nature's cooperation, and above all, of the instruments of production. It is true the latter can be increased and improved through irksome saving and investing, but always in time-consuming narrow limits.

Or let us take the Marxian concept "from each according to his ability." It immediately reveals a similar ambiguity. Let us assume that ability refers to the physical, intellectual, and moral capacity to perform valuable labor services. But who is to determine a man's ability to add value to the social product? Is each individual himself to determine his position in the division of labor? Millions of people undoubtedly are convinced of their skill and competence to conduct central planning, to direct the production process, to supervise the labor of others. And who would openly admit that his faculties and talents merely suffice for the performance of primitive labor services? In such a society each individual indeed would endeavor to shift the disutility of hard and base labor to others, and the division of labor would disintegrate. Or should each man's ability be judged by his fellow men through the operation of the market? In a market society it is the consumers who determine the value of a man's contribution and, above all, his position in the production process. No, this is not what the communist fathers could have meant, for this is capitalism. Or is a central director to determine a man's ability and position in the production process? Is the economic dictator to determine everybody's ability and contribution to the total product? This indeed is conceivable; but this is enslavement and no proletarian paradise.

Finally, the third condition for the promised realization of the withering process is the destruction of capitalism all over the world. The communist state is said to wither away, provided the means of production are nationalized, the formula "from each according to his ability, to each according to his needs" is fully realized, and communism reigns all over the world. These are the communist conditions. In reality communism cannot be realized on a national basis, not to mention on a world-wide basis. It is a system of thought without a trace of logical coherence. Its realization is inaccessible to the human mind. But the unrealizability of the conditions serves the rulers in Russia as a welcome justification for their dictatorial position.

But let us assume for a moment that this nebulous system of social organization is actually realized. Let us assume that all the world is communistic. A glance at the hazy contour of such a world immediately reveals numerous sources of antagonistic conflict which would turn the world into an arena of war and chaos. At first, the problem of economic leadership could not be solved. We would continue to have as many planning agencies and economic directors as we now have states. Diverging policies of national economic planning would be conducted causing confusion, conflict, and chaos. If a world planning board is to direct the production of the whole world's population, who is to be the supreme economic leader? Even if he should be found, his central planning in the "interest of the world" would create more problems because the absence of the market economy would render the calculation of capital and costs of production impossible. A communist world planner would be deprived of a method of ascertaining whether or not a certain production or method of production were economically worth while. Furthermore, certain parts of the world would be favored to the detriment of others. The richer nations would probably take the view that the capital invested in their areas is their property which they would be reluctant to share with the poorer nations. It is true the American worker is eager to share in the profits of American capitalists and businessmen. But he would be very reluctant to share his wealth and income with the Chinese coolie. He undoubtedly would oppose a reduction of his annual income from, let us say $3,000 to the world average of $200-$300. On the other hand, the poorer nations would insist upon sharing the benefits from the capital and favorable production conditions enjoyed by the richer nations. They would undoubtedly insist upon the right to migrate in vast numbers to the areas with more favorable production conditions. How would a world board for economic planning solve all these problems? They are insoluble under communism.

The communist democracy before its actual realization through the withering process is said to be a "dictatorship of the proletariat." This phrase is as ambiguous and misleading as all other Marxian concepts. Taken literally it means that all workers are to be dictators. Such a state of society obviously would be identical with anarchism in which millions of workers would wield terroristic power over all others. Or could Marx have meant that the proletariat is to invest their leader with dictatorial power through a system of representation? Let us deliberate on this idea of leadership for a moment.

By far the larger part of the world's population clings to the pernicious belief that political and economic power concentrated in the hands of virtuous and capable leaders ensures a just and beneficial administration of political and economic matters. They believe that good laws are enacted and bad ones are repealed, that justice is fairly administered and that all branches of administration industriously and intelligently conduct their affairs in the best interest of the public. The virtuous, capable, and trustworthy leaders are said to operate the nation's facilities of economic production unselfishly and more efficiently than millions of businessmen under capitalist competition. Justice, order, and prosperity are said to prevail where nations have found great leaders in whom they have laid their trust.

This notion fully adopted by the communist world and embraced in large parts of the rest of the world permeates contemporary political thinking. The assumption of the virtuous and capable leader who establishes and enforces the law and plans economic life is without reason or force, for it contradicts the very nature of collectivism. In a collectivist society in which the individual serves the ends established by its illustrious leaders and where the "selfish" interests of the individual are forcibly superseded by collective duties imposed, only the unscrupulous and uninhibited get to the top. It cannot be otherwise. If there is only one end, that of society, and one leader under whose direction the individuals serve toward that end, the problem of dissent arises. How is the leader to deal with the dissenter who disputes the established end or merely the method by which it is to be attained? Is the citizen to be free to pursue diverging ends and unauthorized methods? Is the leader to exert tolerance and indulgence? If he does, the collective ends may not be realized or their realization may be impeded. The question inevitably arises whether the collectivist society should forego the desired ends or whether dissent should be suppressed. There is no other alternative. If superiority and priority are ascribed to the collective end, dissent *must* be eliminated lest its realization be a failure. Once we have arrived at this conclusion, we clearly perceive the problem of suppressing dissent. The leader who exerts the greatest degree of tolerance towards dissenters is least efficient in their suppression. A leader who is most ruthless and unscrupulous is most successful. As society tends to entrust the realization of its collective ends to those who are most likely to be successful, the most ruthless become its rulers. The notion that the leader of a collectivist society can be virtuous is not borne out by logic or reason. It is senseless and dangerous.

If the leader should abstain from exercising his power and be tolerant and indulgent in the pursuit of the collective end, he must be prepared to face a public opinion that no longer echoes his own. If he should grant his subjects freedom of discussion and the press, a public opinion will form and dissenters will express their doubts and objections. The dissenters now having regular organs will express opinions adverse to the policies of the leader. It is true that the leader may endeavor to "educate" the people in order to counteract adverse opinion and unmask it as a manifestation of selfish private interests. But what is he to do when the unfavorable opinions are embraced by the majority of his subjects? Is he to abdicate or to counteract with power and suppression? This would be the ultimate alternative of the indulgent dictator.[18]

But even if we were to concede that the dictator can be virtuous, capable, and indulgent, we must deny that it is humanly possible for him to give attention and superintendence to all parts of his legislature, administration, and judiciary. He must select a great number of collaborators of integrity and talent whom he can entrust with the power of supervision and control. And finally, he must depend on millions of honest and able men to inform him correctly at all times, so that he may guide them towards the execution of the collective program. He must direct them, for their passivity is implied in the very idea of his leadership.

It is inevitable that a nation that has transferred its political and economic matters to its illustrious leaders will suffer severely in intellectual and moral capacities. The development of human faculties depends among other things upon their practical application or the prospect of such application. Passivity does not call forth the development of intellectual or active faculties. Who puts himself to the trouble of thought and training if he lacks the prospect of some practical use of his efforts? Moral capacities must suffer where the ultimate decision of human welfare is released from the responsibility of the individual and transferred to government. Morality depends on voluntary good deeds and offices. If the field of personal morality is reduced and that of government responsibility enlarged, it follows that the domain of personal virtue is narrowed by the increasing area of collective coercion.

The very principle that the collective end is the sole end includes the principle that the collective end justifies all means. For the "good of the whole" the individual must be prepared to sacrifice his own ends and apply every means necessary for the attainment of the common end. There is literally nothing that he must not be prepared to do. The collective end as understood by the leader is the sole criterion of what ought to be done. It is obvious that this system of collectivist morals violently contrasts with the morals of our civilization. According to Judeo-Christian moral doctrines the influence of every single action on human good will and gratifica-

---

[18] See also John Stuart Mill, "Representative Government" in *Utilitarianism, Liberty, and Representative Government*, E. P. Dutton and Co., N.Y., 1951, p. 271 et seq.; Ludwig von Mises, *Human Action*, Yale University Press, 1949, pp. 42, 43, 145-153, 772; Clarence Manion, "Legalized Immorality" in *Essays on Liberty*, The Foundation for Economic Education, Inc., Irvington-on-Hudson, N.Y., 1952, p. 23 et seq.: Hans Kelsen, *Vom Wesen und Wert der Demokratie*, Tübingen, 1929, p. 53 et seq.

tion is the predominant consideration. The tendencies and effects of all our actions upon every individual and, indeed, upon the whole sentient creation form the yardstick of our morality. To exclude the consequences of our actions and means applied from our moral consideration and to limit our conscience to the consequences of the collective end is in fact to deny all morals.

We readily admit that an authoritarian society will not be wholly destitute of intellectual power. A select class of scholars may embark upon speculations that do not approach politics, the collective ends, and their realization. There may be skill in the common business of life or training in the proper execution of central orders and directives. Finally there may be an attempt on the part of the leader to direct the best mental power in the country in a direction where it will enhance his position and grandeur. This may be the political party, police, or armed forces. The vast majority of the people, however, will tend to lack knowledge of and interest in the more important matters of political and economic life.

It is true there is a bureaucratic variety of competition. The collectivist state in which the market and its competition is eliminated is necessarily organized according to bureaucratic principles. As the sphere of government is expanded to almost all spheres of human activity, the system of bureaucratic management is all-embracing. It cannot be otherwise. If the central leader would abstain from issuing directives and instructions to his subordinates, it would be tantamount to renouncing his own power. Therefore he issues codes, decrees, and statutes that limit and restrict the power of his subordinates. Only through numerous rules and regulations does the leader inform his subjects of the collective will and the methods of its realization. And only through scrupulously abiding by these detailed directives can it be realized. The individual in a collectivist society merely carries out orders; he is not free to act according to his own judgment and conviction.

Competition in an all-embracing bureaucracy pertains to the zeal with which the central directives are executed. To be docile, submissive, and obedient to the superior is to be most virtuous and most likely to gain his favor. There is no room for initiative, for there are regulations which a subordinate cannot change. He is not free to make decisions or to manage his own life and rely on his own strength. There is no hope but in obeying. To follow regulations and directives even if they are harmful or conflict with his conscience is the only way toward promotion. Under these conditions intelligence, initiative, and other personal talents are of little avail.

A young man who enters one of the innumerable bureaus has his life predetermined by established rules and practices. He is buried for life. It is true he enjoys security, similar to that enjoyed by the inmates of penitentiaries. But he will never be free to run his own life and be master of his own fate. He belongs to what Ludwig von Mises calls a "lost generation." [19]

The bureaucratic regimentation in a collectivist society breeds a passive type of character, which learns to endure and bend to all circumstances. No longer does the individual struggle against evil or strive for achievement through his own exertion, but he becomes acquiescent and submissive to his superiors and the conditions of his surroundings. Active and energetic characters are eyed with suspicion. Passivity and contentment are held in high esteem. But the advancement of society is solely the work of the uncontented and struggling. Without them civilization must fall into stagnation or even decline.

The moral consequences of all-round bureaucratic regimentation are far-reaching. Where people have desires which they cannot hope to realize through application of their own efforts and energies, they are apt to look with envy and hatred on those enjoying the opportunity of their realization. Only those who believe in the opportunity of success through exertion of individual efforts and energies tend to be free of malice towards those who in the past have succeeded. People who desire what others possess but are too inert to expend the necessary effort, and people whose system of social organization hinders them from ever realizing their hopes, are apt to be grumbling characters with envy and ill will towards all others. It is no coincidence that the nations of the Orient and of the Communist hemisphere embrace a great degree of envy and malice towards the Western nations because they would like to enjoy the advantages of the citizens of the West. They are envious of the standard of living which they cannot attain and are hindered from attaining through application of their own energies. It is a matter of fact that the hostility of numerous nations in the underdeveloped parts of the world flows from this very envy and malice which is the moral consequence of their own system of individual limitation. Russian soldiers in the occupation forces in Europe have learned to envy Europeans for their better living conditions and are thereby stirred to the desire for further conquest and occupation. These

---

[19] For an excellent comparison between the bureaucratic system of management and management under the system of free enterprise, see L. von Mises, *Bureaucracy*, New Haven, Yale University Press, 1946.

moral faults are the inevitable consequence of a system of social organization that rejects individual freedom and initiative. It is no coincidence that Americans in the past felt little ill will towards wealthier fellow men because it was the country of opportunity and reward for individual efforts and exertion. Of course, this too has begun to change with the growth of government regimentation and its attendant decline of individual opportunity, accompanied by the ideology of class struggle, collective bargaining, and strikes as the only remedy for individual enhancement.

Summing up, we may state that the "People's Democracies" are tyrannies of the states over the individual. They are organizations of destruction of human society, the division of labor, and the values that created human civilization. "People's Democracy" merely is a catchword with a multiplicity of connotations harboring conflicting political and economic ideas and brutal practices. The Marxian illusion of the stateless society cannot be realized. But any attempt of its realization necessarily must lead to suppression, conflict, and chaos.

On the Nature of Western Democracies

If we compare the political systems of the "People's Democracies" with those of the West we cannot fail to recognize instantly that the political power in the Western democracies ultimately lies with the people and is exercised indirectly through a system of representation. Government power flows from the consent of the people and is divided among many. Government is an organization set up by individuals for their protection from violent actions of domestic and foreign peace-breakers and has the monopoly of the use of coercion in order effectively to meet transgressions and preserve peaceful interhuman relations. By means of elections the majority of the constituency is free to replace an unpopular government with other representatives who promise to conduct more agreeable policies. It is a social organization that aims to prevent conflict, revolutions, and civil wars.

An historical sketch of Western democracies in theory and practice would have to include the political teachings of Aristotle and his followers, of Jean Jacques Rousseau, John Stuart Mill, and other modern theorists of democracy. It would have to include comparative studies of the legislatures, executives, and judiciaries in the most important Western countries, and finally a discussion of the historical significance of political events in Great Britain, France, the United States, and Germany. In this study, however, we may refrain from entering into a detailed discussion of all these problems and restrict our deliberation to the differences and similarities between the "People's Democracies" and those of the West.

Our political institutions are the work of men. They are the outcome of past and present political thought and application of human will. In every stage of development the political apparatus was devised and operated by men. Like all things made by man it is either well or ill made and is either capable of attaining desired objectives or not. Our criticism of present-day Western democracies will hinge upon this criterion.

One of the fundamental differences between the "People's Democracies" and those of the West lies in the political apparatus that guarantees accord between the will of the government and the will of the majority of the people. It is fundamental to the Western democracies and foreign to the "communist democracies." The significance of the democratic form of government lies in this dependence of legislation and administration on the will of the popular majority. They are dependent on the people's will through the institution of free elections which can peaceably change the government according to the people's liking. Under such a legal system conflicts between the rulers and the people are avoided and the smooth operation of the division of labor is safeguarded. Democracy thus performs a function that is of grave social importance and that civilized nations cannot do without.

It is obvious that the Marxian concept of democracy, the dictatorship of the proletariat through violent overthrow of nonproletarian governments, is diametrically opposed to the democratic concept of the West. In the communist states persons and systems in the government can be changed by violence only; in the West they are constantly changed through the institution of free election. Therefore, the will of the Western public continuously redetermines the will of the organs of government, whereas the popular will in the communist states may or may not concur with that of the state. If it actually does, the communist system does not suffer from the absence of the institution of free elections and the legal apparatus of government readjustment. However, if the popular will in the communist states should begin to diverge from the will of the state, the lack of the democratic form of government becomes fatal, and violence and revolution are unavoidable. All revolutions in human history resulted from this absence of the democratic institution of readjustment of government to the will of the public. And sooner or later the communist empires will be plunged into internal strife and civil war because of this shortcoming. For change is intrinsic to human nature.

Human coexistence and cooperation are safeguarded through a form of government that prevents conflict and strife. A democratic government whose single responsibility is this protection of society can discharge its function in an ideal manner. It does not matter whether every stratum of society is represented in accordance with its numerical importance in the making and administration of laws. As long as government is dependent on the will of the politically conscious and active members of society, peace and order are safeguarded. But democratic government suffers in its operation and becomes the source of insoluble conflicts as soon as the scope of its functions is enhanced. The proof of this point shall be attempted in the following.

In an *interventionist* system of society, government is given the additional task of directing the operation of the market economy into channels of "greater general welfare" as it is conceived by the welfare planners. The government apparatus of coercion is employed not only for the protection of social cooperation, but also to influence the utilization of the means of production. The sphere of government coercion is enlarged and that of individual freedom reduced. The individual's right to choose and to act is suppressed and government power is substituted for the discretion of the citizen. It is inevitable that the interests of the citizen who is forced to yield to an official's decision are impeded. His loss of freedom gives rise to conflict between him and the state. But government interventionism not only means bereavement of someone's freedom but also deterioration of someone's well-being. Government is an apparatus of coercion, and not an economic organization of production. Whatever benefits it may apportion to some of its citizens are taken from others whose material well-being is thus diminished. This deterioration of someone's well-being gives rise to conflict between individuals or groups of individuals and the state.

It is true this conflict created by the intervention of a democratic government for the sake of "greater general welfare" does not immediately endanger the peace and bring about domestic disorder. But human coexistence and cooperation suffer from every government act that creates and injects social conflict. It is obvious that such a policy constitutes a rejection of capitalism and is incompatible with the elementary function of democracy.

To restrain effectively governmental action that is likely to hinder the pacifying operation of government, the liberal philosophers and lawyers of the seventeenth, eighteenth and nineteenth centuries insisted upon and finally succeeded in making their governments constitutional, i.e., they established and maintained effective restraint upon governmental action. In its functional sense, a liberal constitution merely is an effective, regularized restraint of government to prevent it from becoming the source of insoluble conflicts. And man's "natural rights" as protected by the "bills of rights" merely constitute a pattern of such restraint upon governmental action. For limitation of the power of government over individuals does not lose its importance simply because government officials are freely removable by the majority of electors. Self-government does not mean government of each by himself, but of each individual by the majority of the rest. The will of the people does not mean the aggregate will of all individuals, but the will of the majority of the voters. This conception of government consequently demands precautions against any abuse of power and oppression by the government of the majority over the rest. It leads us to include the tyranny of the majority through acts of its governing authorities among the evils against which a democratic society must be on guard.[20]

Where democratic government is diverted from its true purpose—the protection of the smooth operation of the system of social organization—everyone will want to participate or at least be represented in the governing bodies. Participation in political matters becomes of greatest importance, for the interventionist coercion of government may be turned either against oneself or against others. We may observe furious bickering among the victims and beneficiaries of "progressive" policies in all parliaments rejecting unhampered capitalism. Various groups of beneficiaries struggle for the spoils of government intervention. And with every new act for the sake of "greater general welfare," new conflict and discord are created—until democracy itself is destroyed. The presence of capitalism does not call for destruction of the state, as Marx contends, but its very absence destroys democracy.

Take the example of the American income and inheritance taxation. It is the main instrument of progressive democracy. In order to raise the funds for popular spending programs or to equalize the material position of all members of society, the interventionists advocate systems of discriminatory taxation that confiscates "exces-

[20] See also John Stuart Mill, "On Liberty," in *Utilitarianism, Liberty, and Representative Government*, E. P. Dutton and Co., N.Y., 1951, pp. 88, 89.

sive" income and wealth. Our government employees and politicians enjoy spending billions of dollars of tax funds which are their very source of livelihood. To improve their own living conditions they must succeed in reducing the income of others. Numerous recipients of public revenues are eager to increase taxes in order to increase their income. Thus conflict of interest is created between two distinct classes of citizens: the bureaucrats and other beneficiaries of public revenues on the one hand, and those citizens from whom the funds are taken. Since taxes on "excess" income and inheritance are paid by the successful capitalist and entrepreneur, the conflict mainly arises between the bureaucrats and the most able and beneficent members of society—those who serve the wishes of the consumers in the cheapest and most efficient way. But this is not the only conflict created. Under capitalism millions of consumers ultimately determine, through their buying or abstention from buying, each individual's income and wealth. Confiscatory taxation, in fact, means removal of the consumers from this position. They no longer can determine who shall be in possession of the means of production, nor can they issue the ultimate instructions regarding the production process. Their material well-being, finally, is diminished by the consumption of the tax funds taken out of the sphere of production. Again, conflict is created between progressive government and certain groups of the people.

We readily admit that this policy of confiscation and redistribution by fiscal means is lauded and authorized by the majority of modern progressive governments. But it cannot be denied that it impedes human coexistence and cooperation. Conflict arises wherever nations abandon the system of unhampered capitalism for that of interventionism, socialism, and communism. The Western nations in fact have abandoned this road of true democracy that led them to the unprecedented achievements. Under the influence of the enemies of capitalism they have embarked upon the road of interventionism and socialism that leads to the ultimate destruction of Western democracies. Karl Marx and his followers, German holistic philosophers, Western reformers and planners, and other destructionists are leading the way—a way on which the legislator feels free of all limitations, a way of limitless rule of the majority which proclaims itself above the natural conditions of social and economic life.

But this is not all. There is the possibility and actual existence of conflicts between the interests of the parliamentary majority and those of the vast majority of the people. That is to say, the interests of the majority of legislators as expressed in parliamentary acts and resolutions no longer coincide with the interests of the majority of the people. Although it is the uncontested feature of constitutional government that coincidence of interests and will of constituents and representatives is most essential in all the various forms of representation, in modern "progressive democracy," however, the interests of representatives often differ from and prevail over those of their constituents. It is true, a member of the representative body is not a delegate but a representative; and his duty is to use his own judgment on any question that comes before him. But he ought not to sacrifice the interests of his constituents to diverging interests of his own.

The way in which modern progressive government necessarily is managed too often results in the public being unaware of the true nature of progressive legislation. Hundreds of bills and resolutions have to be dealt with in each parliamentary session. The great number of laws which socialist and interventionist governments ask the representative to pass makes adequate consideration by the public, and often even by the very members of the legislative body, impossible. Furthermore, "time-tables" for the various stages of bills before parliament often are introduced to shorten the time for public discussion of complicated government measures which are unintelligible to most constituents. Under these conditions the formation of a public opinion on each single bill is prevented, providing the leeway for representatives to further their own special interests or those of special favor groups.

In an increasing number of cases the representative is either a "professional politician" entirely dependent on his parliamentary salary with no expectation of earning a comparable livelihood outside his public employ, or he is the representative of economic interest groups, a lawyer for trade associations, or an official of a labor union. In these cases the representative tends to speak and vote in accordance with the recommendations of the local and national organizations of his party, a labor union or any organization whose endorsement and support he deems important for his re-election. Since organized pressure groups or lobbies can offer powerful support, such as monetary contributions to campaign funds, or can threaten organized opposition to his re-election, the representative tends to act in harmony with the wishes of the lobbyist. Thus the ignorance of the vast majority of the public on the one hand, and the opportunity to promote his own interests on the other hand, tend to make the representative sacrifice the interests of his constituency.

Under socialism, and progressively so under interventionism, where the means of production are either owned or controlled by the state, the material well-being of each citizen, including that of representatives, depends on the decisions of the rulers of the state. The representative cannot afford to flout their instructions, for the socialist state is his sole employer whose wrath may spell economic ruin after his expulsion from party and legislature at the next election. A man who may be threatened with a "return to the mine" tends automatically to record approval of decisions by the men in power. Under capitalism the material independence of a representative is mostly secured by independent means or by income not derived from public employment. He can always be sure of earning his livelihood in private enterprise. But under socialism and interventionism, where personal incomes derived from rent, interest, and profit are abolished or severely curtailed through progressive taxation, the representative lacks the material independence which is the basis for independent judgment. Thus through his cooperation with the leaders in power the representative may further his own interests even if he must sacrifice the interests of his constituency. But democracy perishes where the representative has no independence of decision and where the state is constituted merely according to the will of the men in power.[21]

It lies in the nature of interventionism and socialism that the intellectual and moral qualifications of men in parliamentary life deplorably decline. Dexterity, energy, and independence of judgment no longer are the criteria of election. The special-interest groups, such as agriculture and labor, prefer and promote the passive and subservient character, the one who faithfully represents their special interests. To struggle for spoils and privileges is repugnant to the generous spirit anxious for the advancement of mankind. He does not choose to run for a political office or stands no chance of being elected where success in such a struggle is the only criterion.

Let us look at an example offered by present-day American politics where the lawmakers no longer act to represent the interests of the vast majority of the people. Because there is a tiny pres-

[21] For an excellent discussion of parliamentary democracy in socialist Great Britain see Ivor Thomas, *The Socialist Tragedy*, The MacMillan Company, New York, 1951, p. 139 et seq. See also Carl J. Friedrich, *Constitutional Government and Democracy*, Ginn and Company, New York, 1946, pp. 255-267, and 414-442.

sure group well organized and financed—the lobby of the American peanut growers—Congress repeatedly passed legislation requesting the Administration to raise the price for peanuts through government purchases with tax money. There cannot be any doubt that the majority of the American population favors lower peanut prices which mean lower costs of living. And yet the majority of lawmakers enacts legislation that increases peanut prices at the expense of the vast majority of the constituency. Protected by the indifference of the people, the legislator readily yields to the pressure by special-interest groups and sacrifices the interests of his constituents.

In an increasing number of cases the American Congress passes legislation that favors tiny minorities who can command support and offer benefits to legislators. Indeed most representatives have become the spokesmen and delegates of minorities in their struggle for spoils and privileges at the expense of the public. There are delegates of peanut growers, producers of cotton, sugar, potatoes, butter and cheese—each group comprising a tiny minority of the people. The fundamental function of government is flagrantly disregarded at the risk of creating discontent and strife among numerous groups of society. This serious defect of progressive democracy tends to lead to its functional inactivation and to political catastrophe.

In defense of minority legislation the advocates for the special favor and privilege groups advance the following argument: the group we represent is an essential part of the whole economic body. If we suffer from economic distress and unemployment of capital and labor, all other members of the body inevitably will be contaminated by the plight that has overcome us. But if we should prosper, the whole economic body will prosper with us. Therefore, it is in the interest of the whole to assist its parts in distress.

In the first place, the concept of "economic distress" is very ambiguous. Who is to determine the plight in which an industry claims to have fallen? Are we to take each industry's own contentions? All other industries may claim and actually may prove similar states of distress which merely is another term for productive maladjustment. Unprofitable enterprises exist in every industry. Furthermore, the term implies a factor of temporariness and the possibility of recuperation and recovery. But if we look at the industries that, in the past, have received economic aid and privilege, we find that the beneficiaries have been enjoying their position for many decades. The American sugar industry, for example, which is constantly clamoring for public aid and protection, has been receiving public favors for more than a hundred years. The American silver industry, another special favor industry, tried to get its hands into the public treasury for almost a hundred years and repeatedly succeeded. Certain farm groups have been drawing funds from the treasury for more than three decades; and the present Administration is still spending two to three billion dollars anually to raise the prices of their products. Are these industries still suffering from temporary distress and unemployment? Or are they rather permanent guests loitering at the doors of our public treasuries?

Let us also inquire into the economic reasons for an industry's maladjustment and plight. Why does an industry suffer from low income? In a market economy it is the consumer who ultimately determines prices and thereby the income of every producer. If the price of certain commodities and services are lower than the producers would like them to be, it is because the consumers established lower prices. To accept the contentions of producers means to reject the sovereignty of consumers and to abolish the free market economy. Government intervention hampers economic readjustment to the wishes and decisions of consumers.

The contention that the whole economic body must prosper if a certain industry prospers is not only misleading but downright incorrect. How can the public prosper if some industries continuously extract heavy doles and contributions? The means of production and subsistence are scarce. If the government gives to someone, it must first take from someone else. If, some fifty or sixty years ago, the American government had heeded the same contention advanced by the once prosperous industries of horse breeding and buggy manufacturing, it would have encouraged them not to readjust to new economic conditions and would thus have prolonged their adjustment plight. It would have retarded the growth of the automobile industry or made it impossible altogether. If government were to guarantee everybody's income, changes and progress would be rendered impossible. Economic conditions would be arrested forever. Indeed, an enemy of the United States could have no greater wish than that such policies would have been conducted since the beginning of this nation's history, at a time when 95% of the American population was earning its livelihood in agriculture. If a New Deal government in 1800 had arrested this ratio of 95% to agriculture and 5% to trade and industry, the consequences would indeed be indescribable.

A conceivable remedy against special privilege legislation would be the development and extended application of the legislative *referendum,* i.e., the process of submitting a bill to a direct vote of the citizens for approval or rejection. The advantages of this legislative procedure are twofold. First, being faced with definite political problems and issues, a larger part of the constituency would endeavor to form an opinion on the proposed government measure and its effects. The sovereignty of the people would no longer be limited to the exercise of election, but would be extended to the direct act of legislation. That is to say, the will of the people would be formed and made known in each case subject to the referendum. Second, the referendum would eliminate the opportunity for representatives to rush through hundreds of acts that further their own interests or those of special favor groups through individual action and assistance of another. The power of lobbies and pressure groups would be instantly reduced to its proper size, i.e., that of tiny minorities. Thus the danger of discontent and strife through minority legislation would be eliminated in each case of referendum.

In the case of the American peanut legislation a referendum would ascertain whether the American public wants the government to raise prices through purchases of peanuts with tax funds or whether it favors market prices as determined by the actions of consumers. There cannot be any doubt that the vast majority of Americans would prefer market prices which mean lower prices and a higher standard of living. The American public undoubtedly would rebuke the majority of its representatives for its special favor legislation.

It is significant that the American government frequently uses a limited referendum when this serves its own political purpose or defends minority legislation. Government officials, for instance, arbitrarily select certain members of a pressure group and ask them to endorse the government policy of price supports, subsidies, acreage controls, etc. If the majority of this lobby group approves of the handouts to itself, government embarks upon legislation that benefits this minority at the expense of the vast majority of the public. The fact that 87 per cent of the voting wheat farmers comprising less than 30 per cent of all American wheat farmers and less than 1 per cent of the public endorsed government support of prices through acreage controls and enforced restraint of production, served to justify the policy of favoring a small minority of wheat farmers at the expense of the taxpayers. It is obvious that such a referendum fails to express the will of the majority of the people; it rather ascertains the will of the majority of a tiny pressure group.

Thus the referendum as employed by present-day government is apt further to separate the will of the public from that of its officials, and to create conflict rather than to alleviate it.

The ever-increasing scope of functions of progressive democracy not only creates classes of beneficiaries and victims of special-interest legislation, but also separates nations joined in division of labor. Most welfare measures by national governments produce inescapable effects on foreign relations and the international exchange of goods. Most welfare measures are identical with economic nationalism and are the causes of international conflicts. International conflicts among the Western nations, however, endanger the existence of the Western democracies and the continuance of the democratic form of government. The principle of progressive planning, for instance, requires government to maintain wage rates by limiting the labor supply through rigid immigration laws and other institutional barriers. Welfare planning requires government to raise costs of production to assist and favor certain industries and especially labor groups. These measures depend for their effectiveness upon complementary trade barriers, on tariffs, foreign exchange control, import restrictions, etc. All these measures constitute causes of international conflict.[22]

The cooperation of the various departments in each national government even suffers from this international conflict. On the one hand, the agricultural department, which is the public agency for the special interests of the farmers, is eager to dump on the international market "surplus commodities" purchased with public funds for the purpose of raising domestic agricultural prices and farm income. The State Department, on the other hand, is under pressure from foreign countries who compete in world markets, for international dumping harms foreign producers and constitutes international conflict. It is eager to avoid international conflict and therefore opposes the policies of the Department of Agriculture. All these effects are the consequences of modern progressive policies. They are inevitable when capitalism is abandoned.

The examples of sinister interests gnawing at the foundations of modern democracy can be easily extended. The ideological background for the social conflicts between the two classes of citizens created by interventionism, the beneficiaries and the tributaries, is provided by the prevailing ideology of the welfare state. It is ex-

---

[22] For a discussion of the problems of international relations under socialism and interventionism see this author's *How Can Europe Survive?*, D. Van Nostrand, New York, 1955.

pounded by a score of contemporary writers on political science demanding the realization of "social objectives" of the democratic state. They speak of the "general welfare" as the ultimate end of democracy, or of "morality," "economic order" and "world order," or the realization of "equality," etc. Governments willingly adopt their recommendations and continuously enhance the scope of functions of democratic government. But any expansion inevitably makes government a desirable instrument for the advancement of sinister interests and consequently the source of numerous social conflicts. The common feeling of disappointment over the ill effects of interventionist policies, finally, turns the people to a demand for further intervention and greater coercive power of government. The people ultimately become an agglomeration of organizations struggling for the favors of the state as the source from which all earthly blessings flow.

The deepening interventionist conflict generates social tension and causes government to embark upon a rapid succession of remedial policies to solve the problems, only to have these policies actually lead to more dissatisfaction. With the increased scope of governmental functions the power of governmental agencies is enhanced. All share in the expansion of authority—the federal, state, and municipal authorities, and the executive, legislative, and judiciary branches. This growth of political and economic authority and its need of coordination finally create a tendency for power to concentrate and fuse in the hands of those who apply that power: the executive.

The founders of Western democracy provided for functional and territorial division of powers in order to protect the people from abuses by government and to restrain effectively governmental action. To them it was a measure of caution against tyranny in government through undue concentration of power. It was to save the people from autocracy, for division of power makes it difficult for any one man or group to seize all the power and exercise it for the subjugation of the rest. Under modern interventionism and socialism, however, the traditional separation of powers gradually vanishes and the ultimate right to make and enforce laws is vested with fewer but more powerful men.

Contemplating the course of Western democracy during the last four decades leads to a despair for its future. Critics have raised their voices and condemned democracy as the rule of the common man. "It is the rule of demagoguery and deceit," they say, "a rule of the low and mean clamoring for policies of follies. Democracy in a triumph of platitude will ultimately vest the power of decision with the most incapable. It lies in the nature of democracy to destroy itself." These critics fail to understand the true nature of democracy. They fail to see that it constitutes the only form of government that is capable of avoiding conflict between the governing minority and the politically conscious part of the people. Democracy makes the governing body dependent on the will of the people for the sake of peaceful social coexistence and cooperation. No other form of government can conceivably discharge this most essential social function. Lasting coexistence and cooperation require democracy. There is no other alternative.

It is true, democracy is in grave danger because the large majority of Western nations step by step are abandoning the only economic system in the soil of which democracy can grow. People are not infallible; they can be led astray. If they prefer unsound principles to sounder principles, the policies conducted will reflect their choice with all its consequences. To defend democracy, we must defend capitalism. For it is in the soil of capitalism that democracy has grown and without which it must vanish. To defend capitalism we must demonstrate the advantages of freedom and free enterprise to the people. We must oppose the demagogues and agitators and convince the people of the beneficial effects of capitalism. This is the task of our philosophers and economists. But if they themselves embrace ideologies that are destructive, democracy must perish. If they themselves embrace holistic concepts of social life, society must suffer from turmoil of mental confusion, social conflict, and political and economic chaos.

Democracy, this pride of Western man, is a political concomitant of capitalism. If capitalism should perish, democracy must also perish. And with every step towards the destruction of capitalism, democracy is hastening towards its own end.

VI

The Road to Totalitarianism

by HENRY HAZLITT

I<small>N</small> SPITE of the obvious ultimate objective of the masters of Russia to communize and conquer the world, and in spite of the frightful power which such weapons as guided missiles and atomic and hydrogen bombs may put in their hands, the greatest threat to American liberty today comes from within. It is the threat of a growing and spreading totalitarian idealogy.

Totalitarianism in its final form is the doctrine that the government, the State, must exercise total control over the individual. The *American College Dictionary,* closely following *Webster's Collegiate,* defines *totalitarianism* as "pertaining to a centralized form of government in which those in control grant neither recognition nor tolerance to parties of different opinion."

Now I should describe this failure to grant tolerance to other parties not as the essence of totalitarianism, but rather as one of its consequences or corollaries. The essence of totalitarianism is that the group in power must exercise total control. Its original purpose (as in communism) may be merely to exercise total control over "the economy." But "the State" (the imposing name for the clique in power) can exercise total control over the economy only if it exercises complete control over imports and exports, over prices and interest rates and wages, over production and consumption, over buying and selling, over the earning and spending of income, over jobs, over occupations, over workers—over what they do and what they get and where they go—and finally, over what they say and even what they think.

If total control over the economy must in the end mean total control over what people do, say, and think, then it is only spelling out details or pointing out corollaries to say that totalitarianism suppresses freedom of the press, freedom of religion, freedom of assembly, freedom of immigration and emigration, freedom to form or to keep any political party in opposition, and freedom to vote against the government. These suppressions are merely the end-products of totalitarianism.

All that the totalitarians want is total control. This does not necessarily mean that they want total suppression. They suppress merely the ideas which they don't agree with, or of which they are suspicious, or of which they have never heard before; and they suppress only the actions that they don't like, or of which they cannot see the necessity. They leave the individual prefectly free to agree with them, and perfectly free to act in any way that serves their purposes—or to which they may happen at the moment to be indifferent. Of course, they sometimes also compel actions, such as positive denunciations of people who are against the government (or who the government says are against the government), or groveling adulation of the leader of the moment. That no individual in Russia today gets the constant groveling adulation that Stalin demanded chiefly means that no successor has yet succeeded in securing Stalin's unchallenged power.

Once we understand "total" totalitarianism, we are in a better position to understand *degrees* of totalitarianism. Or rather—since totalitarianism is by definition total—it would probably be more accurate to say that we are in a better position to understand the steps on the road to totalitarianism.

We can either move, from where we are, toward totalitarianism on the one hand or toward freedom on the other. How do we ascertain just where we now are? How do we tell in what direction we have been moving? In this ideological sphere, what does our map look like? What is our compass? What are the landmarks or constellations to guide us?

It is a little difficult, as nebulous and conflicting usage shows, to agree on precisely what liberty means. But it isn't too difficult to agree on precisely what slavery means. And it isn't too difficult to recognize the totalitarian mind when we meet one. Its outstanding mark is a contempt for liberty. That is, its outstanding mark is a contempt for the liberty *of others*. As de Tocqueville remarked in the preface to his "France Before the Revolution of 1789":

"Despots themselves do not deny the excellence of freedom, but they wish to keep it all to themselves, and maintain that all other men are utterly unworthy of it. Thus it is not on the opinion which may be entertained of freedom that this difference subsists, but on the greater or the less esteem that we have for mankind; and it may be said with strict accuracy, that the taste a man may show for absolute government bears an exact ratio to the contempt he may profess for his countrymen." The denial of freedom rests, in other words, on the assumption that the individual is incapable of managing his own affairs.

Three main tendencies or tenets mark the drift toward totalitarianism. The first and most important, because the other two derive from it, is the pressure for a constant increase in governmental powers, for a constant widening of the governmental sphere of intervention. It is the tendency toward more and more regulation of every sphere of economic life, toward more and more restriction of the liberties of the individual. The tendency toward more and more governmental spending is a part of this trend. It means in effect that the individual is able to spend less and less of the income he earns on the things he himself wants, while the government takes more and more of his income from him to spend it in the ways that *it* thinks wise. One of the basic assumptions of totalitarianism, in brief (and of such steps toward it as socialism, state paternalism, and Keynesianism), is that the citizen cannot be trusted to spend his own money. As government control becomes wider and wider, individual discretion, the individual's control of his own affairs in all directions, necessarily becomes narrower and narrower. In sum, liberty is constantly diminished.

One of the great contributions of Ludwig von Mises has been to show through rigorous reasoning, and a hundred examples, how government intervention in the market economy always finally results in a worse situation than would otherwise have existed, even as judged by the original objectives of the advocates of the intervention.

I assume that other contributors to this symposium will explore this phase of interventionism and statism rather fully; and therefore I should like to devote particular attention here to the *political* consequences and accompaniments of government intervention in the economic sphere.

I have called these political accompaniments *consequences*, and to a large extent they are; but they are also, in turn, causes. Once the power of the State has been increased by some economic intervention, this increase in State power permits and encourages further interventions, which further increase State power, and so on.

The most powerful brief statement of this interaction with which I am acquainted occurs in a lecture delivered by the eminent Swedish economist, the late Gustav Cassel. This was published in a pamphlet with the descriptive but rather cumbersome title: *From Protectionism Through Planned Economy to Dictatorship.*[1] I take the liberty of quoting an extensive passage from it:

> The leadership of the State in economic affairs which advocates of Planned Economy want to establish is, as we have seen, necessarily connected with a bewildering mass of governmental interferences of a steadily cumulative nature. The arbitrariness, the mistakes and the inevitable contradictions of such policy will, as daily experience shows, only strengthen the demand for a more rational coordination of the different measures and, therefore, for unified leadership. For this reason Planned Economy will always tend to develop into Dictatorship. . . .
>
> The existence of some sort of parliament is no guarantee against planned economy being developed into dictatorship. On the contrary, experience has shown that representative bodies are unable to fulfill all the multitudinous functions connected with economic leadership without becoming more and more involved in the struggle between competing interests, with the consequence of a moral decay ending in party—if not individual—corruption. Examples of such a degrading development are indeed in many countries accumulating at such a speed as must fill every honorable citizen with the gravest apprehensions as to the future of the representative system. But apart from that, this system cannot possibly be preserved, if parliaments are constantly over-worked by having to consider an infinite mass of the most intricate questions relating to private economy. The parliamentary system can be saved only by wise and deliberate restriction of the functions of parliaments. . . .
>
> Economic dictatorship is much more dangerous than people believe. Once authoritative control has been established it will not always be possible to limit it to the economic domain. If we allow economic freedom and self-reliance to be destroyed, the powers standing for Liberty will have lost so much in strength that they will not be able to offer any effective resistance against a progressive extension of such destruction to constitutional and public life generally. And if this resistance is gradually given up—perhaps without people ever realizing what is actually going on—such fundamental values as personal liberty, freedom of thought and speech and independence of science are exposed to imminent danger. What stands to be lost is nothing less than the whole of that civilization that we have inherited from generations which once fought hard to lay its foundations and even gave their life for it.

Cassel has here pointed out very clearly some of the reasons why economic interventionism and government economic planning lead toward dictatorship. Let us now, however, looking at another aspect of the problem, see whether or not we can identify, in an

[1] Cobden-Sanderson, London, 1934.

unmistakable way, some of the main landmarks or guideposts that can tell us whether we are moving away from or nearer to totalitarianism.

I said a while back that three main tendencies mark the drift toward totalitarianism, and that the first and most important, because the other two derive from it, is the pressure for a constant increase in governmental intervention, in governmental spending, and in governmental power. Let us now consider the other two tendencies.

The second main tendency that marks the drift toward totalitarianism is that toward greater and greater concentration of power in the central government. This tendency is most easily recognizable here in the United States, because we have ostensibly a Federal form of government and can readily see the growth of power in Washington at the expense of the states.

The concentration of power and the centralization of power, I may point out here, are merely two names for the same thing. This second tendency is a necessary consequence of the first. If the central government is to control more and more of our economic life, it cannot permit this to be done by the individual states. The pressure for uniformity, and the pressure for centralization of power, are two aspects of the same pressure.

It is not difficult to see why this is so. Obviously, if government is to intervene in business, there cannot be forty-eight different kinds of conflicting interventions. Obviously, if government is to impose an over-all "economic plan," it cannot impose forty-eight different and conflicting plans. Planning from the center is possible only with centralization of governmental power. And so deep is the belief in the benevolence and necessity of uniform regulation and central planning that the Federal government assumes more and more of the powers previously exercised by the states, or powers never exercised by any state; and the Supreme Court keeps steadily stretching the interstate commerce clause of the Constitution to authorize powers and Federal interventions never dreamed of by the Founding Fathers. At the same time recent Supreme Court decisions treat the Tenth Amendment to the Constitution practically as if it did not exist.[2]

A notable example of this tendency exists with regard to labor legislation. Supreme Court decisions regarding the Wagner Act and

[2] The Tenth Amendment reads: "The powers not delegated to the United States by the Constitution, nor prohibited by it to the States, are reserved to the States respectively, or to the people."

its successor the Taft-Hartley Act (legally, and essentially, a mere amendment of the Wagner Act) have not only steadily widened the sphere of Federal regulation to cover activities and labor relations that are primarily, if not almost wholly, *intra*-state, but have ruled that the states themselves have no power over these primarily internal activities and relations if Congress has chosen to "pre-empt" the field.

The third tendency that marks the drift toward totalitarianism is the increasing centralization and concentration of power in the hands of the President at the expense of the two co-ordinate branches of the government, Congress and the courts. In the United States this tendency is very marked today. To listen to our pro-totalitarians, the main duty of Congress is to follow the President's "leadership" in all things; to be a set of yes-men; to act as a mere rubber-stamp.

The dangers of one-man rule have been so emphasized and dramatized in recent years—we have seen so many appalling examples, from Hitler and Stalin to their many pocket-sized editions, the Mossadeghs and Peróns—that any warning of this danger to Americans may seem needless. Yet most Americans, like the citizens of the countries already victimized by their native Mussolinis, may prove incapable of recognizing this evil until it has grown beyond the point of control. One invariable accompaniment of the growth of Caesarism is the growing contempt expressed for legislative bodies, and impatience with their "dilatoriness" in enacting the "Leader's" program, or their actual "obstructionist tactics" or "crippling amendments." Yet in recent years derision of Congress has become in America almost a national pastime. And a substantial part of the press never tires of reviling Congress for "doing nothing" —that is, for not piling more mountains of legislation on the existing mountains of legislation; or for failing to enact in full "the President's program." [3]

If we ask how it comes about that Congress and other legislative bodies throughout the contemporary world have tended to fall into public disrepute, we again find that the answer lies in the apparently unshakeable contemporary faith in the necessity and benevolence of a continually expanding government intervention.

[3] It is instructive to recall in this connection that the 80th Congress, which President Truman condemned as a "do-nothing" Congress, actually passed 457 private bills and 906 new public laws—a total of 1363. This record was typical of our modern legislative mills. The 79th Congress passed 892 private bills and 734 new public laws. And so on.

Congress and the planners can never agree among themselves on precisely what the government should do to remedy some supposed evil. They cannot agree on an unambiguous general law, whose application in specific cases could be safely left to the courts. All that they can agree upon is that "something should be done." In other words, all they can agree upon is that the government must intervene, that the special area of economic activity under discussion must be "controlled." So they frame a law setting forth a number of vague but high-sounding goals and create an agency or commission whose function it is to achieve these goals through its own omniscience and discretion. The National Labor Relations Law (the Wagner-Taft-Hartley Act) is a typical example. It sets up a National Labor Relations Board, which thereupon proceeds to become a prosecutor, court, and legislative body all rolled into one, and starts laying down a series of rulings and handing down a series of decisions, many of which surprise no one more than the Congressional members who created the agency in the first place.

From then on, Congress in that particular sphere is treated mainly as a nuisance. The administrative bodies that it has set up resent its "interference" and "meddling" with their activities. These administrative bodies devote themselves in large part to extolling "administrative discretion" at the expense of the Rule of Law—that is, of any body of clear rules to be applied by the courts. Any subsequent effort of Congress to reduce the range of administrative discretion, arbitrariness, and caprice is denounced as "crippling" to administrative bodies, and as interfering with that "flexibility" of action so dear to the administrative heart.

Along with this growth of administrative agencies and administrative power, less and less controlled either by Congress or the courts, there has been a constantly widening interpretation of the President's constitutional powers. This has occurred both in the foreign and in the domestic field.

It is especially marked in the sphere of foreign relations. The Constitution, contrary to the repeated assumptions of the champions of Presidential omnipotence, nowhere specifically gives the President power to conduct foreign relations. Specifically, he has merely the formal power to "receive ambassadors and other public ministers." Perhaps this implies power over the routine conduct of foreign affairs, which could hardly be carried on by Congress; but it certainly does *not* apply to any crucial decision. For the Founding Fathers gave Congress *alone* the power to declare war. And they specifically provided that no treaty could be made by the President without "the advice and consent of the Senate." In practice, ever since George Washington, presidents have generally ignored the instruction to seek the advice of the Senate in treaty-making. And in recent years they have repeatedly tried to evade the requirement even for Senatorial consent. They have done this by three extra-constitutional devices.

One of these is to frame and sign a complicated multilateral treaty and then argue that the Senate must ratify it without suggesting amendments because any attempt to introduce amendments would make the whole treaty impossible.

A second device, coming more and more into practice, has been to frame a treaty setting up an international agency which is authorized from then on to take its own actions or makes its own rulings by discretion. This applies to the United Nations, with its innumerable sub-agencies, to the International Monetary Fund, and to the International Bank for Reconstruction and Development. Once the Senate has approved such an arrangement it loses any real say regarding the decisions of the agency it has set up, though the President can still have some partial control through his executive appointments to such a body.

The third extra-constitutional device is, of course, that of resorting to an "executive agreement" instead of a "treaty," claiming that this is just as binding on Congress and the country as a treaty would have been, and thereby evading the Constitutional requirement for Senate ratification. When the Senate tried to pass a clarifying amendment (and missed only by a single vote the necessary two-thirds majority for doing so) to assure the supremacy of the Constitution over treaties, and to prevent back-door amendment of the Constitution through the treaty-making device, President Eisenhower and his advisers opposed it. In this debate, the pro-Presidential press, in its news columns, constantly referred to this proposed amendment as an attempt to curb "the President's treaty-making powers." They used this phrase repeatedly in face of the fact that there are no exclusively Presidential treaty-making powers in the Constitution. The President has no treaty-making powers whatever that do not require the advice and consent of the Senate, and the concurrence of two-thirds of the Senators present. The claim that there is a Presidential power of making "executive agreements" with foreign nations binding on this country, which the Senate has no right to control, is completely without foundation.

In the domestic sphere, the President's powers have grown chiefly through the steady multiplication of Federal agencies. Many of these, through their rule-making and rule-enforcing powers, and their wide discretionary latitude, have become combined legislative and policing agencies to a large extent outside the control of the Congress.

The major wars in which the United States has engaged in the last forty years have also led to an enormous growth in the President's so-called "war powers." Now there is no specific mention of "war powers," or any listing of them, in the Constitution. This growth of war powers derives mainly from the precedents created by the unchallenged assumption or usurpation of such powers by presidents in the past. Hence their steadily cumulative nature.

Finally, the mere habit of huge Presidential power has led to the assertion of still more power. An outstanding example of this was President Truman's action in seizing the nation's steel plants in 1952, in order to force the steel companies to accept the wage decision of the Wage Stabilization Board that he appointed. Attorneys for the Government blandly argued, and Mr. Truman himself contended, that the President could do this under his "reserve powers" or "inherent powers" in the Constitution. This was again an assertion of powers that the Constitution itself nowhere mentions. And though this claim was finally rejected by the Supreme Court, it was only by a vote of six to three. Minority members argued that the President could seize anything he wished under these so-called inherent or reserve powers. Had this become the majority decision, no private property anywhere in the country would be safe from seizure. Presidential power would be unchecked and practically unlimited.

It should hardly be necessary to point out that this constant expansion of the claims for Presidential powers has almost necessarily been accompanied by a constant reduction of the powers and prerogatives of Congress. Today we find increasing resentment even of the Congressional power of investigation of the executive branch. This is surely a minimal power, without which Congress could not intelligently exercise its other functions. But Congressional investigations have in late years been constantly denounced either on the ground that they prevent the executive agencies "from getting any work done," or under the pretense that they undermine the morale of Federal officials and are almost invariably unfair. It is ironic that Congress, whose ability to check Presidential power has been steadily shrinking in the last forty years, should today be more often than ever before accused in the press of "usurping" the functions, powers, or prerogatives of the President.

One of the remarkable developments of the last decade, in fact, has been the frequency with which the President, on one excuse or another, has "forbidden" members of the executive branch to testify on certain executive activities before Congressional committees. More and more of the activities of the Federal government tend to become "top secret," even in peacetime. Congress is said to be prying into something that is none of its business. People presuming to speak for the President have frequently come close to asserting what we may call the principle of executive irresponsibility or non-accountability—that is, the principle that the President does not have to account to the elected representatives of the people for his official actions.

One would think that the horrible examples of Mussolini, Hitler, Stalin, Mossadegh, Perón, etc., would give pause to our own advocates of more and more executive power in the United States. Why haven't they done so? Partly, no doubt, from the deep-rooted habit of putting one's own country in a category by itself, as if what went on abroad could have no relation to anything going on at home. It is the old illusion that "It can't happen here."

Another reason why these dictatorial trends abroad are not related to our own domestic trends is that we are in the habit of using different vocabularies to describe similar developments, depending on whether they occur abroad or at home. We may call a foreign tendency a trend toward dictatorship, but argue for the same tendency at home on the ground that we need a "strong" executive.

Now there is, true enough, a possible danger of having an executive so weak, so incapable of maintaining law, order, and firmness and dependability of policy, that the executive weakness itself breeds a threat of revolutionary uprising followed by dictatorship. But this happens only under rare and special conditions, not a sign of which exists in present-day America. At the moment of writing, the nearest prominent example we have of a "weak" executive in the Western world is in France. But when we examine even that case closely we find that the real defect in the French system is less that the Premier lacks sufficient *legal powers* as long as he remains in office, as that he lacks *security of tenure*. The French Assembly can irresponsibly vote him out of power at any time. He has no corresponding power of dissolution to force the French Parliament to exercise its removal powers responsibly. Having no security of tenure, he is too often paralyzed in action. Yet the French, instead of giving him the unequivocal power of dissolution possessed, for example, by the Prime Minister of Great Britain, have tried to solve the problem in the wrong way by often giving the Premier in office "decree law powers" that he ought not to have. In other words, the French, instead of forcing the Assembly to exercise its powers of approval or disapproval responsibly, periodically give the Premier powers that should be properly exercised only by a legislature.

Regardless of whether or not this analysis of the present French situation is accepted as correct, it is certainly clear that outside of France no major nation today suffers because of "too weak" an executive. Most of the so-called "free" nations, including ourselves, already suffer from dangerously excessive powers in the hands of the executive, and above all from a *government* that has acquired dangerously excessive powers.

In a Federal government restricted to its proper sphere, the President might properly be given more powers than he has at present in some directions, and fewer powers in others. But any *general* argument for a "stronger" executive can seem plausible only as long as it remains ambiguous and vague in its specifications. If we must speak in broad general terms, then we are entitled to say in such general terms that the powers and the responsibilities of the President have grown far beyond those that either can or should be exercised by any one man.

We have now outlined what I have called the three main tendencies that mark a drift toward totalitarianism. They are (1) the tendency of the government to attempt more and more to intervene, and to control economic life; (2) the tendency toward greater and greater concentration of power in the central government at the expense of local governments; and (3) the tendency toward more and more concentration of power in the hands of the executive at the expense of the legislative and judiciary.

To these I am tempted to add a fourth tendency—the pressure for a world state.

The addition of this will doubtless come as a shock to many self-styled liberals and well-intentioned idealists who would regard the establishment of a world state as the crowning achievement of liberalism and internationalism. A little examination, however, will show us that the present pressure for a world state represents a false internationalism and a retreat from freedom. It is, on the contrary, merely the equivalent on a world scale of the pressure for centralized government on a national scale. It aims to set up the coercive machinery of a world state before the world is remotely prepared in sentiments or in ideology to accept a world state. The zealots for such machinery are too impatient to study the necessary preliminaries to a world state (even assuming that a world state, which would concentrate all world political powers in a few hands, is even ultimately desirable). Such zealots for a centralized world government with coercive powers fail to recognize that if international good-will and intellectual clearsightedness existed on the part of national statesmen, practically all the reasonable objectives of a so-called world state could be achieved without setting up such a world state. And until this good-will and clearsightedness are achieved within individual nations, the creation of a compulsive world state would be either futile or catastrophic.

The pressure for a world state, in fact, represents not true internationalism, but inter-*governmentalism,* inter-*statism.* It would lead to the setting up of machinery for a universal and procrustean coercion. We seem to be moving, in the present era, toward more and more restriction of the liberties of individuals by governmental agencies. This is the tendency that has produced the pressure for international price-fixing; for the creation of "buffer stocks" of international commodities; the institution of international subsidies and handouts; the paternalistic governmental establishment of industries in "underdeveloped" nations without regard to their appropriateness, efficiency, or need; and finally the growth of an international inflationism, as represented by such institutions as the International Monetary Fund.

This whole tendency makes a travesty of international freedom for the individual, which is the essence of true internationalism. For true internationalism does not consist in *compelling* the taxpayers or citizens of one nation or the inhabitants of one part of the globe to subsidize, or give alms to, or even to do "business" with, the citizens of any other nation or the inhabitants of any other part of the globe. True internationalism, on the contrary, consists in *permitting* the individual citizen or firm in any nation to buy from, or sell to, or trade with, the individual citizen or firm of any other nation. It consists, in brief, in the freedom of trade advocated so eloquently by Adam Smith in the eighteenth century and practically achieved in the nineteenth—a freedom of trade that (notwithstanding scores of international agencies and multilateral treaties) has now been destroyed.

We are losing our freedoms today, in brief, through a false ideology—or, to use an older expression, because of intellectual confusion. Nothing is more typical of this contemporary intellectual confusion than the enunciation by the late President Roosevelt of the so-called

Four Freedoms. As George Santayana points out in a footnote in his *Dominations and Powers:*

Of the "Four Freedoms" demanded by President Roosevelt in the name of mankind, two are negative, being freedoms *from,* not freedoms *to.* Had he chosen the word "liberty," he would have stumbled on reaching these desired exemptions, because the phrase "freedom from" is idiomatic, but the phrase "liberty from" would have been impossible. "Liberty" thus seems to imply vital liberty, the exercise of powers and virtues native to oneself and to one's country. But freedom from want or from fear is only a condition for the steady exercise of true liberty. On the other hand it is more than a demand for liberty; for it demands insurance and protection by provident institutions, which imply the dominance of a paternal government, with artificial privileges secured by law. This would be freedom from the dangers of a free life. It shows us liberty contracting its field and bargaining for safety first.

The contemporary world has gone astray, in sum, because it has sought freedom from the dangers and risks of liberty.

VII

The Greatest Economic Charity

by F. A. HARPER

WHEN asked to contribute an essay to Professor Mises' *Festschrift,* I was at first inclined to dip my pen in the well of humility and then lay it aside unused. On what economic theme has Professor Mises himself failed to write with a superiority to anything I could offer? Yet honor is due him. So I trust that friends of this great and patient teacher will tolerate an essay's imperfections for the sake of the spirit of an offering.

Professor Mises' main renown is as an economist. Yet to me he is a charitable person even more than an economist. His charity is not of the fashionable kind that ladles out economic pleasantries from a caldron filled with socialist loot obtained by theft. His is not even primarily of the material sort at all but is, instead, in the form of his inspiring mind and spirit. In my opinion there can be no greater charity than this, for it endures beyond any material form of benevolence.

In this essay I shall be dealing, however, with one aspect of economic charity—a form inferior to charity of the mind and the spirit. People spend vast sums trying to do good with economic alms in forms which, to me, seem open to serious question. In their haste to do good and to bask in the glow of immediate glory as purveyors of alms, they are being exceedingly wasteful of the means of benevolence. The methods they use would come to appear unbenevolent, I believe, if they would view them by the test of alternatives in the longer perspective of economic science. That is the thought I should like to explore here, in honor of Professor Mises.

❀   ❀   ❀

A certain Talmudical philosopher once offered us this apothegm:

The noblest charity is to prevent a man from accepting charity, and the best alms are to show and enable a man to dispense with alms.[1]

A profound observation! It deserves to be kept in mind constantly as we fumble along in attempts to do good to others.

The greatest charity of all, in the light of this apothegm, would be to assist a person toward becoming wholly self-reliant within nature's limitations, and therefore totally free. The non-material, non-economic things of the mind and spirit are supreme to this end and therefore comprise the greatest charity. Bread and raiment and abode are trivial indeed as compared with these, in the furtherance of human progress.

The greatest aids to self-reliance are educational, broadly speaking—the tools for pursuing the eternal embryo of truth. The root of progress is a sincere love of truth *per se*. Devotion to truth in the abstract must surpass love for any specific belief one holds at the moment, if the pursuit is to continue rather than to bog down in stagnant dogma. Exploratory shoots can then sprout from these roots in the form of specific "truths"—more accurately, mere beliefs—however dimly and even erroneously they may be seen at any moment. Among these sprouting shoots will be some sound ones capable of bearing the economic fruits and other passing joys of our daily living.

With things of the mind and spirit duly recognized as the greatest charity of all, this essay will explore one aspect of *economic* charity. When the word "charity" is used hereinafter, I shall be referring to charity in its economic form according to one definition given in the Oxford Dictionary—material benevolence, sometimes called alms or munificence or philanthropy.[2]

The social fashion of our age is the attempt to do good to others in a confused profusion of economic transfusions. Other times have been less afflicted in this respect for the simple reason that they

---

[1] Paraphrased by Mary Baker Eddy from Moses Maimonides in his *Code of Jewish Law*, Chapter X, paragraph 7.

[2] Some will resist my use of the word "charity" in connection with the object of my acclaim. They will point to the earlier meaning of the word, which refers to a mental attitude of brotherly love and compassion. Yet standard works on the meanings of words reveal no substitute that seems lacking in the same sort of difficulty. All have multiple meanings, and are generally given as synonyms for one another. In fact, the word "charity" has come to refer increasingly to some form of alms-giving rather than to its earlier meaning. So I decided to hazard its use for want of anything better, in the hope that most of those who will be reading this essay will be charitable enough to try to glean my meaning and intent.

could not afford as much waste as we can. For them, sheer survival of self and family absorbed nearly all their effort.

The charitable endeavors characteristic of our time are, in my opinion, often futile for their intended purpose. In fact, they may even be harmful to the recipient by making him less self-reliant than before. According to the Talmudical definition of the noblest charity, whatever reduces self-reliance is negative charity.

I believe there is another use for this vast amount of time and energy that would support a positive charity, fruitful beyond the fondest dreams of most persons. The prevailing notion is that such a use is wholly selfish. But its charitable aspect can be seen by testing it step by step against certain requisites of true charity.

The Nature of Charity

True economic charity has three characteristics:

1. Charity requires the transfer of ownership from one person to another of something having economic worth. The receiver must get a clear title to it, or it cannot be charity. The giver must have had clear title to it, or the giving is like a gift of stolen property—which is not an act of charity. Private ownership at both ends of the transfer, never public ownership, is therefore required.
2. The transfer must be voluntary with both parties. If forced upon the receiver against his will, it is not charity. If taken from the source against the prior owner's will, it is theft rather than an act of charity.
3. True charity requires anonymity. This is difficult to attain, to be sure. But if the conditions of the transfer result in a personal obligation in any form or degree, it is a grant of credit and not an act of charity. Devices other than anonymity usually fail to prevent the creation of a personal obligation.

It is a temptation to list as a fourth requirement that the gift shall, in the long run, be beneficial to the recipient. This aspect is important, but it tests the wisdom of the giving and not its charity.

The third requirement of charity—anonymity—is in harmony with the Biblical admonition that one who gives alms should not sound his trumpet before him as do the hypocrites.[3] If the act is motivated by vainglory, it is not charity; it is then merely salve for the ego of the giver. If the giver expects repayment in any form or degree,

[3] Matthew 6:2.

other than in unselfish personal satisfaction, it is something other than charity.

These are strict requirements for true charity and most "charitable" activities would fail to qualify.

Enslavement Through "Charity"

Unfortunately a common purpose of acts of "charity" is to entice somebody to become obligated to the giver. The way it works is this: Under guise of a gift or personal favor, an unspecified *quid pro quo* is assumed. "Some day you can do something for me." Perhaps it is some business favor in that wide arena where an unfree market allows special privileges to be traded. Such acts obligate the receiver for an amount not agreed upon in advance. There is no specific *quid pro quo* as with a loan or an outright trade. So the act of "charity" really becomes a debt that can never be repaid with precision because the amount of repayment is not known by both parties by prior agreement.

An attempt to repay such an obligation almost never satisfies both parties. A residual obligation, one way or the other, becomes suspended in uncertainty forever. That is why anonymity is required if this pernicious feature is to be avoided. Credit should be correctly labeled as credit and trade should be called trade.

The process just described is really a means by which one person permanently obligates himself to another. It is really a moderated form of enslavement.

Plutarch must have had this in mind when he said: "The real destroyer of the Liberties of any people is he who spreads among them bounties, donations, and largesses." Plutarch's other comments make it amply clear that he was not opposed to real charity. But he was opposed to the sham of charity that feeds the vainglory of the giver and enslaves the recipient.

Aesop's Fables—presumably written by a wise slave who had astutely observed these processes—repeatedly pointed out the dangers of enslavement under guise of charity.

False charity destroys security. Having once allowed one's self to become permanently obligated to another by debts that can never be repaid, the recipient loses his self-reliance and becomes insecure. As St. Thomas Aquinas expressed it: "There is no security for us so long as we depend on the will of another man."[4]

[4] Acton, *Essays on Freedom and Power*, p. 64.

Just as one person can allow himself to become enslaved to another by a debt that cannot be repaid, so can persons within a group allow themselves to become enslaved to the group. National socialism is a common form, where the state becomes the dispenser of loot collected by force. The recipients lose their self-reliance in the process and come to feel indebted forever to the collective for their very lives. They have by then become enslaved.

There is not space here to trace in full the ideological ancestry of mass enslavement in this way, but the influence of Rousseau and Marx should be mentioned in passing.[5] Rousseau, though he pleaded for "back to nature" in the education of *Emile*, was untrusting of natural self-reliance in economic and social affairs. So in his *Social Contract* he revived Plato's cult of reliance upon the state and became, according to Janet, the uncontested founder of modern communism.[6] Then Marx later built further upon the same concept when he said that man is merely a complex of social relations, and that he is responsible to society for his real existence. For if one really owes his existence to society because his life depends upon society, he then owes servitude to the state or to some other collectivity of society. That is how men like Rousseau and Marx, with their mass programs of social dependency and socialized "charity," have helped socialize masses of humanity into dependency, insecurity, and slavery.

Enslavement on either a personal or mass basis could not happen if charity were to be kept in pure form, supplementing free exchange and voluntary credit arrangements between persons.

Common Forms of Charitable Activity

Of the various forms of economic charity in which we commonly indulge, the simplest would seem to be something such as buying a vagrant a cup of coffee or giving him a dime for the purpose.

Most of the colossal amount of activity which today goes by the name of charity is of this type, where the intent of the giver is to provide something for direct consumption or relief of a destitute recipient. But little giving is direct from the giver to the object of need—often the sufferer from some physical ailment or the victim of devastation from "acts of God." Most is given to some organization which acts as an intermediary.

[5] Thomas Davidson, *Rousseau and Education According to Nature* (1898); also, Leopold Schwarzschild, *The Red Prussian, the Life and Legend of Karl Marx* (1947).
[6] P. Janet, *Les Origines du Socialisme Contemporain*, (1883), p. 119.

If one will tabulate requests of all types during a year, it will become evident how numerous are the forms of request for charitable assistance. A few solicitors still stand on street corners with their tin cups. But most solicitation stems from intricately organized endeavors to wrest funds from would-be givers, frequently with the aid of the fund-raising profession. Often goodly neighbors are enlisted as unpaid solicitors to knock at one's door, and the giving in many instances is really little more than the cost of peacefully evicting a well-intentioned trespasser.

In doubting that much of this sort of thing is charity at all—at least not the wisest form of charity—I am not questioning the right of anybody to support anything voluntarily with his own means. I am merely questioning his wisdom and suggesting a better alternative. His glow of self-satisfaction over having given in the usual way is no more assurance of its wisdom than any other misguided but well-intentioned act. One can grow in wisdom only as he is willing to review acts he previously judged to be wise.

Tools As a Form of Charity

Both fact and logic seem to me to support the view that savings invested in privately owned economic tools of production amount to an act of charity. And further, I believe it to be—as a type—the greatest economic charity of all.

By economic tools of production I mean, of course, things with exchange value—trucks, factories, railroads, stores—which assist human effort in the production of other items of economic worth.

Does saving and investment in these tools qualify as charity? Does it meet the three tests of an act of charity?

The first test is whether there has been a transfer of privately owned things having economic worth. It is true that when one saves and invests in a tool which he uses in production, although he retains title to the tool, most of the extra production which the tool makes possible passes on to others, as we shall see. For that reason the first requisite of an act of charity seems to be met as a certain consequence of saving and investment in tools. It is this feature of the creation of privately owned capital which is its charitable aspect.

The second test of charity is that the transfer of economic benefits shall be voluntary. Did anybody steal anything? Was anybody coerced? So long as the tools are privately owned and their use functions in a free market, the process has to be voluntary for everybody involved. But state ownership or control of tools, as is common in Russia, violates this requirement.

The third test of charity is anonymity. The charitable feature of savings and tools arises from the extra production that flows from it as a consequence and which goes in large degree to others than the one who saved and invested in the tool—to others than the owner of the tool. It is anonymous because the beneficiaries do not know its source. Most of them do not even know how they are benefitting from it at all. They do not know this because they have been victimized by a thorough saturation with the surplus value theory. They even think of themselves as being victimized by these capitalists who own the tools they are using.

One can easily test from his own experience the anonymity of the charity that flows from savings and investment in tools. If one will list all the economic items he consumes or enjoys in a day, the test is to try in each instance to name specifically all the persons whose savings and investment made the item possible. Most of us, I dare say, could not name even one person responsible for an item we use and enjoy. This illustrates the anonymity of the millions of unknown persons responsible for the things we enjoy.

So savings and the tools of production meet all three tests of charity, and thus qualify as charity. How many of the things we commonly call "charities" can equally qualify by these three tests?

The Productive Power of Tools

A large part of the high level of economic living we now enjoy in the United States arises from the use of tools.

The average person in the United States has available for consumption upwards of ten times that of persons in the less prosperous half of the world. The reason for their poverty is a lack of savings invested in tools of production. In all their history over the ages they have accumulated little beyond the most primitive and simple tools, such as crude plows and hoes.

Harder work by us is not the reason why we can enjoy ten times as much economic welfare as they do. Persons in the United States work no harder, if as hard, as do the poorer half of the world's population. Even including mental work along with sheer muscular effort, both of which contribute to output, I doubt if we work any harder—over-all.

Nor does innate intelligence seem to explain the difference. We probably have no more geniuses per thousand population than they do.

Lacking any of our accumulation of tools, our output per worker probably would be even lower than that of the poorer half of the world at the present time; even their production is aided considerably by their simple tools. Comparison of their output with ours suggests that without any tools whatsoever our output would be reduced to perhaps one-twentieth of what it now is. To say it another way, perhaps 95 per cent of our present output in the United States is made possible by the presence of our tools. These tools are available because in the past some wise people saved and invested in tools.

Who Gets the Output Due to Tools?

The next question is: Who gets this great increase in production? Evidence shows that a large part of it goes to others than those who did the saving and who hold the titles of ownership to the tools. It goes mostly to those who use the tools.

It has been estimated that only about 15 per cent of the national income in the United States goes to the owners of capital as current income.[7] This is the amount of dividends, interest, rents, and royalties together with their equivalents in owner-operated businesses. The other 85 per cent of the national income is paid currently for work, as distinguished from pay to owners for savings they have invested in tools. This figure for current work includes both wages paid to employees and its equivalent to those self-employed.

The question at once arises as to why so small a proportion of the product goes for capital, when capital is so highly productive? If we were to assume that those who save and invest in tools are entitled to the full increase in output that comes from the use of these tools as an aid to manual labor, it would appear from the evidence already given that justice would decree a division about like this: 95 per cent for the owners and 5 per cent for the users.

And so we may summarize:

	To the Tool Owners	To the Tool Users	Total
If full production increase were to go to the owners	95	5	100
Actual division in the United States at present	15	85	100
Division according to Marx's surplus value theory	0	100	100

Presuming these figures to be accurate, one must conclude that the saver-investor is receiving less than one-sixth of the return

[7] F. A. Harper, *The Crisis of the Free Market*, 1945, p. 66.

which his saving and investing has made possible—15 received from the 95 produced. The other five-sixths of the increase goes to the users of the tools, enhancing their pay seventeen times—85 received and 5 produced.

A person is lucky if by chance he happens to have been born in the United States where he can share directly in the bounty tools create. By having been born here he is enabled to work with tools that are now available because others have saved in the past. His income from current effort will, by these figures, be enhanced seventeen times (85 versus 5) because of these tools. Had he been born where no tools had been accumulated whatsoever but would have to work as hard or even harder than in the United States, he would be getting only one-seventeenth as much for his labors.

This bounty to the users of tools is what I call the greatest economic charity.

Surplus Value Theory Reviewed

These facts are significant in appraising Marx's surplus value theory. Marx said, in effect, that the 15 per cent which goes to the owners of the tools is surplus value because the user of the tool—according to Marx—deserves the full 100 per cent.

It is from the productive power of tools as aids to the manual efforts of man that something which might be called a surplus value arises. This surplus, as has been indicated, has raised United States production from a level of 5 to a level of 100. So a counter claim to that of Marx would be that the full increase of 95 (100 minus 5)—the amount of surplus value created by the tools—should go to the one whose savings created the tools. But who really gets this surplus value of 95? The owner gets 15 and the user gets 80. Not a bad deal for the user!

Surplus value of a different sort arises in every instance of voluntary exchange in a free market. If one farmer trades a bushel of wheat to a merchant for a shirt, it is because the farmer prefers the shirt to the wheat and the merchant prefers the wheat to the shirt. The trade creates a surplus value for each of the participants, but the amounts of surplus value thus created are not subject to measurement by any device we now know or can contemplate. They are compensating in direction but not necessarily in amount, because the amount is entirely a matter of subjective appraisal. Being unknown in amount by both parties and probably not even thought of in these terms at all, no sense of residual obligation is created.

This makes the process closely akin to anonymity. The center of interest of this discussion, however, is surplus value of the type created by tools as an act of economic charity. Therefore the phenomenon of surplus value created by exchange will not be dealt with further here.

In a free economy the process of deciding the division of the surplus value created by the use of tools occurs in the free market. We must accept the decree of private ownership and free exchange as having fairly decided the division, whatever the answer. Yet the answer given in the free market reveals that private capitalists—the "selfish owners," as those who save and invest are so often called—are really the greatest charity-givers of all.

It is also interesting to note the magnitude of charity arising from private capital in relation to "religious and welfare activities" contributions. About two billion dollars are given to religious and welfare activities in the United States each year. This is less than 1 per cent of the amount of charity which the users of tools receive in their pay envelopes, according to this concept, in the same length of time.

Bread vs. Seed Grain

I would certainly not scorn the giving of bread to a starving person in need. Nor would I scorn any other endeavors of a charitable nature by agencies which conduct recurrent campaigns for funds and materials for needy persons, so long as the offering is voluntary with one's own means. But I would emphasize strongly that the urgency of the plight of the needy can blind one to the possibilities of this greatest charity of all.

Those who benefit from the charity that flows from the creation of tools are the persons engaged in productive labor. This makes an excellent claim to worthiness, for as Samuel Johnson once said: "You are much surer that you are doing good when you *pay* money to those who work, as the recompense of their labor, than when you *give* money merely in charity." [8]

If we will but pause long enough to view with wider perspective the consequences of some of our customary acts of presumed charity, we can see their short-sightedness. Perhaps we should view with some question even the giving of grain to a starving person, if the same grain could better serve as seed for a harvest that would

[8] James Boswell, *The Life of Samuel Johnson*, Charles E. Lauriat Company, Boston, 1925—Vol. II, p. 636.

keep twenty persons from starving later. Savings, when used wisely by private enterprise to produce capital tools of venture, serve as economic seed in a like manner. The use of it as seed becomes an act of charity with a high leverage. But its creation requires enough patience and restraint from demands for immediate consumption so that the tools will be created. One must have foresight and economic insight enough to see beyond the exceedingly conspicuous and tempting need for present consumption.

When a neighbor knocks at one's door for a contribution to some charity, it may seem selfish to wonder if perhaps greater good could not be done by buying a share of new investment stock instead. But such an alternative is worth pondering, even with the perspective of charity in mind.

Many foundations have been established to engage in charity with the accumulated profits from the use of tools created in an earlier day. It may be a novel idea to suggest that greater charity might have been the consequence if these funds had been reinvested in new tools rather than to be used for direct-consumption charity, wherever that has been the policy. Use of foundation funds for the purpose of research and discovery is, of course, another matter because it is the creation of a form of tool and therefore highly charitable in its effects.

The one point I wish to make above all others is that, whereas a crust of bread may save a man from starving for a short while, the creation and use of tools are the only effective means by which people can be pulled completely out of the mire of poverty and placed on the solid base of sustained plenty. One cannot heal all the sick, relieve all the poor, comfort all in distress, nor father all the fatherless. And so it is important that in one's efforts to do good he lend his limited support where it will bear the most fruit on a long-time basis—after he is gone and after his own direct efforts have ceased.

The Incentive Factor

There must be some incentive if there is to be saving and investment in tools. This is best done by private ownership. The nature of man being what it is, the prospect of some rewards under private ownership surpasses all other incentives. A carrot will entice the donkey better than a whip will drive him.

The label of charity on anything having as a motive any personal gain at all will probably be questioned by many. They will say that, unless 100 per cent of it is relinquished, none is truly charity. But I would pose some questions in reply. Does the fact that a person gives only 10 per cent of his yearly income, not 100 per cent, deny any of his gifts being charity? Does the fact that a charitable agency uses part of its income for organizational expenses deny any of it as being charity?

He who would serve his fellow men by charity can best do so by saving and investing in tools. Even though he may benefit himself a little, in the process, he unavoidably and anonymously benefits others by many times as much.

One who would be wholly self-sacrificing in the matter is free to refrain from any personal benefits in consumption at all, if he wishes. He can do this by reinvesting his profits in more tools. He can use that small part of the product of the tools which the free market allocates to him in the form of owner-reward to extend this greatest charity, foregoing all personal gain beyond the title to tools which are wholly benefiting others.

Beating Communism at its Own Purpose

Has socialism-communism anything to offer to compare with this? Can their proposals benefit mankind in any such way, even though the capitalist may get a little out of it for himself? Do they have any such benefits to offer the commonweal in a parade of progress, benefiting his children and his children's children on a continuing basis?

No. A socialist-communist regime, instead of being truly charitable, kills off this greatest charity of all. Taxes for "public welfare" kill the goose that lays this golden egg of charity. As taxes increase more and more and the chance for reward disappears, savings and venture are discouraged more and more. As rewards become thinner, the players turn away from the game. Original hopes of a charitable plenty turn into a poverty enforced by orders and police measures.

There is always the danger that when one has grasped the idea of the productive power of tools he will propose confiscating funds from private citizens in order to build more tools. But this denies the very process of charity. One person cannot be truly charitable with funds which he steals from another, any more than church collections can be increased by having the members of the congregation pick each other's pockets every Sunday. If tried, the source will dry up because those attending will learn to keep their pockets empty or else stay away from church.

True charity must remain purely private rather than public and socialized. It must be voluntary. That is the nature of the greatest economic charity of all—savings invested in privately owned tools of production.

Conclusion

The intent of this essay has been to bring into focus the conflict between two views toward economic charity, and to give a basis for choice between them.

An analogy may illustrate the difference. According to one view, sharing a crust of bread is advocated as the method of charity. The other advocates savings and tools for the production of additional loaves of bread, which is the greatest economic charity.

The two views are in conflict because the two methods are mutually exclusive in absorbing one's time and means in all the choices he makes day by day. These cannot be twice used.

The reason for the difference in view really stems from different concepts about the nature of the economic world. The former view stems from the belief that the total of economic goods is a constant. The latter view is built on the belief that expansion in production is possible without any necessary limit.

The difference between the two views is like the difference between a two- and three-dimensional perspective of production. The two-dimensional size is fixed at any instant of time, but the third dimension and therefore the size of the total is expandable without limit by savings and tools.

If the total of economic goods were fixed, it might seem humane to spend all one's time dividing it into pieces and carrying them here and there. If man is assumed to be selfish, voluntary methods would seem inadequate and centralized control of supplies and their distribution would seem to be necessary—if only there could be any assurance of finding unselfish men to rule.

All the history of mankind denies that there is a fixed total of economic goods. History further reveals that savings and expansion of tools constitute the only way to any appreciable increase. Christ seemed to be telling us this in the story of the talents, two thousand years ago.[9] Were we to grasp fully the meaning of this story, con-

---

[9] Matthew 25.

cepts about what is the best form of economic charity would undergo a revolutionary change.

The greatest economic charity is that which enables persons to become independent of alms and therefore most self-reliant and secure under freedom. Only when that happens—when persons advance from the brink of starvation—is time released for devotion to things of the mind and spirit, which comprise the supremely great charity.

PART THREE

On Scientific Method

VIII

The Place of Economics Among the Sciences

by Wilhelm Röpke

(from the German by George D. Huncke)

To announce an essay on the place of economics among the sciences may seem to be short of reckless temerity. For there is hardly any subject which offers a more seductive invitation to be verbose, pedantic, and boring. Such an invitation virtually amounts to an authorization to iterate observations which have been made often enough to need no further emphasis. To be sure, it would be very malicious of me to apply to economics the characterization once levelled at philosophy which defined it as "the continuous abuse of a terminology created for that express purpose." But it must be admitted that philosophy and economics exhibit certain common features which distinguish both from most other sciences. One of these is that it can be said of each that the history of its doctrines constitutes an essential part of the science itself. Another is the highly characteristic tendency of each toward excessive and incessant preoccupation with itself, its nature and its methods. Both sciences resemble the introvert whose gaze is ever turned inward, whose conscience, staggering under the load of its own sins, is forever engaging in a searching of its own soul. No science outdoes economics in this sort of "soul-searching," in puzzling at the crossroads about signposts and direction-pointers, in discussing the whence, the whither, the whereby, and the wherefor. No science is more persistent in its repetition of a query whose

111

general formula has been made famous by Schiller in his opening
lecture, "What is, and for what purpose do we study, economics?"

If, despite all that, we again broach that question today, there
must be some especially cogent reason to justify us. And in order
to recognize that reason clearly, we should do well to consider two
facts which are as conspicuous as they are important. One of them
is a source of pride to the economist; the other spells humiliation for
him and danger to the position accorded to his branch of knowledge
among the sciences in general, and in the estimation of society at
large.

For on the one hand we note that throughout the civilized world
there has been an increase in the last few decades in the technical
equipment of economic science such as we older economists would
not have dreamed possible when we started our career. Thirty
years ago a university might have twenty to thirty students regis-
tered in courses in economics, and their existence would be regarded
by a faculty of law or philosophy as a bizarre appendage to be
tolerated rather than respected.[1] Each year doctorates were conferred upon a dozen or so candidates who were thereby launched
on a practice that was nearly as difficult to define as their science
itself. Today the enormously augmented scope which organized
research, instruction, and dissemination have attained in the field of
economics is no less remarkable than the corresponding increase
in the student body. In numbers that are positively unwieldy they
swarm about our "chairs in economics," crowd into seminars, hud-
dle over our library tables, and despite the immeasurably increased
amount of scientific material to be mastered, including even algebra
and geometry, they make heroic efforts to plumb the meaning of all
of it.

That is one of the two facts that demand our consideration. In
contrast to it stands the other which is no less striking but for that
very reason highly disquieting. I refer to the fact that the extraordinary expansion of economics in research, organization, expert personnel, and practical effectiveness has taken place at a stage which
could not conceivably be more critical in the development of a
science which already has a history replete with crises and critical
turning points.

The fact that our science has attained such a high rank in public
esteem at the very moment when it is less sure of itself than ever
before must appear striking to anyone who concerns himself with

---

[1] The author is particularly referring to conditions as they existed in Germany.

economics—a science which may truly lay claim, by reason of its maturity, experience, and methods, to a place second to none among the sciences which seek to establish the essential laws that govern society itself. Are we not here faced with a very serious contradiction which might almost move us to disapproval and gloomy foreboding? Are we not accustomed to feeling extremely uneasy whenever outward appearance does not correspond to inner solidarity? The question itself is no more than natural, yet the contradiction is only apparent. Would it not be more accurate to say that both facts are attributable to a common cause, namely, the profound crisis which confronts society itself? And that they are so attributable for the very reason that economics revolves about society, and especially about those of its problems which are most amenable to rational analysis?

In the course of the last two decades significant changes in the political, economic and social structure of our society have taken place, and these still continue to exert marked influence. It is to these changes that we may ascribe the extraordinary increase in the importance which our times accord to economic science. But it is those same changes, too, and the profundity of the intellectual sources from which they arise and the conflicts to which they lead, that are reflected in the altered appearance of that science, in its tensions, its problems and—let us openly admit—its errors. What at first seems to be a contradiction between external appearance and inner content is in fact an inevitably indissoluble combination that lies in the very nature of the science itself. Recourse is eagerly taken to economics in the expectation that it will furnish orientation for problems arising in an era of confusion which looks upon the birth of much that is new and the death of much that is old. And there is an intensely practical justification of that expectation. It lies in the new economic structure of society with its ever-increasing organization, institutionalization, and collectivization; and it lies in the fact that those characteristics give rise to an exceptionally augmented need for trained personnel capable of handling the problems these changes bring, as well as capable of publicly representing the interests that thereby come into play.

But by the same token it need not be too astonishing that the science to which recourse is taken is itself caught in the maelstrom of this era of confusion, and that it, too, is subject to turbulation and fluctuation. Such would not necessarily have to be the case. And there is every reason for us to combat with all our power the forces that tend to sweep economic science from its moorings.

There is no justification for treating as mere cause and effect the relationship between the cultural and social upheaval of our times, on the one hand, and the dubious aberrations, on the other, of which economic science has been guilty. However, it can hardly be denied that some such relationship does exist and that we are thereby put upon notice as to our obligation to establish the higher truth which must reconcile the paradox. And such denial becomes all the more out of the question when we consider the possibility of the recipro- cal influence of the two members of the paradox. For attention must be called to the probability that certain tendencies exhibited by economic science, while much in accord with the spirit of our times, are themselves in no small measure responsible for some of the spasmodic manifestations exhibited by our society and our economy.

I now propose that we explore the two facts of our paradox, one after the other, in order to discover what problems they present. And I suggest that we begin with the second, the internal conditions of economic science as they affect its position in relation to its fel- low sciences. A few observations respecting the first member of our paradox may constitute our concluding paragraphs.

With respect to the present situation in economics and to its position among the sciences, we may state that it is pregnant with questions to the point of crisis; but we need not linger unduly long over a number of well-known matters of a general nature. It is easy to state in general terms what economics is concerned with, even though great difficulty may be encountered in the treatment of its specific problems. The commonest point of departure for the latter is the general scarcity of goods, which can in turn be attributed to the scarcity of forces of production except, of course, for the absolutely rare goods. Thence follow those inescapable rules of all economic activity which constitute the uttermost in generality—such as the necessity for evaluation, the exercise of choice among alterna- tives, optimum utilization of scarce forces of production, and the like. These are the imperatives which even a collectivist economy cannot disregard with impunity. In this sense it is, of course, a mis- take to think of economics as a science whose scope is limited to one definite *method* of responding to those general imperatives, that is to say, as the science of a market economy controlled by free prices and competition. Quite on the contrary, a purely collectivist eco- nomic system is better fitted than any other to place those supreme imperatives in the correct light and so progress to a better understanding of how a market economy functions. And it is so fitted, if for no other reason than that a collectivist economy is in itself a demonstration that it cannot satisfactorily control those imperatives and hence that it must necessarily result in disorder and poverty. There could hardly be anything better calculated to further contemporary science than this inordinately costly and painful "instruction by the case method" which makes whole nations the guinea pigs on which to demonstrate so utterly convincingly the *modus operandi* and the irreplaceable functions of free determination of price and of the presuppositions behind it.

However, the difference in practice between these two opposing economic systems finds its counterpart in theory. Only a market economy makes it possible for economic science to go beyond those general and platitudinous truths and to discover relationships that have the objective definitiveness and validity which a market economy actually establishes by means of the mechanism of price. Only a market economy makes of economic science an *analytical* social science rather than a science which is merely a descriptive-understanding one having a logical structure like that of historiography. In the collectivistic state the science of economics is condemned to limit the scope of its activity to two extreme positions. The first of these is the preliminary and introductory stages of instruction which do not go beyond the general truths and their imperatives; the other is the doctrine of an economy controlled for the attainment of certain political objectives, not unlike the cameralism of the old absolute and paternalistic state.

But in saying this much we have not yet told the whole truth. In fact, we shall see later that it is dangerous to exaggerate the truth of what we have found so far. But it is indisputable that economics is, in the main, a science which is rooted in our market economy. It is, to speak with Ludwig von Mises, pre-eminently catalactics. That is the field where its actual scientific discoveries have been made; and it is still true that we can forget only at our dire peril what really constitutes the content of economic theory, namely, the economic organization which functions through a system of determined and determining prices, wages, rates of interest, and other magnitudes of value. We are, of course, aware that reality differs to a greater or lesser degree from our theoretical pattern of a free price mechanism which complies in every respect with the laws of unhampered competition. Nevertheless that pattern is indispensable to us if we are to arrive at any reasoned judgment at all concerning the importance of the degree to which, in every case, reality does so differ from the pattern of free and competitive markets.

We have thus more or less determined the intellectual site of the field where actual economic thinking takes place, and which constantly serves as its point of reference for reorientation. Let us then proceed a step further in order to characterize that thinking as to its individuality, its difficulties, its pitfalls. As Keynes once observed, economics is not difficult in the same sense as, say, theoretical physics is difficult. But I believe I can hazard a judgment based on my experience at our own university, where students of international problems have the option of approaching them from the point of view of law, of economics, or of "Political Science." And within that group of the social sciences, at least, economics has the reputation of presenting heights that are particularly difficult to scale. If I charitably debar the supposition that the reason might lie in the professors, then we are confronted by a problem which deserves considerable reflection.

Indubitably economics demands a kind of thinking which, if not difficult, is certainly peculiar to itself and which must be the product of training as well as of intensive practice. Such must inevitably be the case since its subject, economic activity, is so prodigiously varied and complex that it eludes our best efforts to grasp it by the methods customary in scientific study generally. The same Keynes who made the remark about economics and theoretical physics told us on another occasion (*Economic Journal,* 1924) that a man like Professor Planck, the famous originator of the Quantum Theory, confessed to him that he thought of studying economics but found it too difficult. He could have mastered, says Keynes, the whole corpus of mathematical economics in a few days, but what he seems to have found so difficult was the "amalgam of logic and intuition and the wide knowledge of facts, most of which are not precise, which is required for economic interpretation in its highest form."

> "Thee, boundless Nature, how make thee my own?
> Where you, ye breasts? . . . ."

The descriptive method does not advance our cause. Experimentation is ruled out by the very nature of the subject. The weaving of a fabric spun from ingeniously devised lines of thought only too often proves an escape from what is relevant and factual. When confronted by that difficulty, the mind of the untutored and the unsuspecting is prone to take refuge in the dangerous world of analogy, of metaphor, of the unwarranted transfer of what is manifest and what is observed in individual experience to economic activity of the community as a whole. But the latter field is the very place where the determining influence is exerted, not by that which is obvious, but by something that must be logically deduced, and where that which is valid in particular is not necessarily valid in general. Under these circumstances we get that dreaded "home-grown economics" which bristles with all the obvious blunders that characterize the mercantilist thinking of which David Hume and Adam Smith disposed once and for all and against which the best antidote is still that collection of essays published a century ago by Bastiat under the eloquent title "Ce qu'on voit et ce qu'on ne voit pas." That kind of thinking is the source of one of the most disastrous of economic fallacies to be designated, perhaps, as anthropomorphism, or as "realism of conception" or by Whitehead's phrase "fallacy of misplaced concreteness." It is especially to be encountered where discussions treat questions of international economic relations, and unfortunately it rears its ugly head even within the ranks of the professional economists themselves.[2] Indeed, the latter have unfortunately and in no inconsiderable numbers succumbed to the blandishments of still another influence which I shall describe shortly; and they have betrayed a tendency to relapse anew into the mercantilistic thinking that antedated the attainment by economics of its scientific maturity.

The present occasion is not the one on which to describe what methods economics does employ in lieu of those erroneous ones, nor to describe how our science makes use of abstraction, idealization, typification and the creation of models, in order to make a gradual approach to reality. But it *is* in order, on this occasion, to emphasize that in this process economic science requires the constant application of supreme attentiveness and a large dose of that intuitive power which enables us to keep our eyes on all the complicated threads at once, and to emulate the juggler who never loses sight of a single one of the balls he is keeping aloft. If that power forsakes the economist, the result is that commonest of economic errors which consists in a failure to think an economic process through to its conclusion and hence to lose sight of an important part of it. Such an error arises, for instance, if we conclude that profit must have a deflationary effect because (and this is the everlasting fallacy of all underconsumption theories) demand is thereby barred from

[2] On this point cf. my *Internationale Ordnung*, new ed. 1954 (Erlenbach–Zurich), pp. 118, 133, 241.

reaching the market. The truth of the matter is that we are dealing with a demand which is expressing itself in a different direction—and a direction, incidentally, which as a rule means greater economic progress. The particular intellectual effort required of us economists consists in recognizing that economic science deals essentially, not with constants but with functions, with relations, with interdependent forces. The logic peculiar to economic science is the logic of relationships. As one scholar of my generation somewhat exaggeratedly puts it, "such thinking in terms of relationships . . . undoubtedly" is one of "the most difficult problems the human intellect can encounter."[3]

Small wonder, then, that it is at this very point that the economic reasoning of the untrained mind most frequently comes to grief, whereas the trained economist is most clearly to be recognized by the fact that thinking in terms of relationships has become second nature with him. He knows that imports and exports, or that wages and employment are most intimately and reciprocally related. And the diagrams setting forth the mutual interdependence of supply, demand, and price are as much a part of the economist's mental "stock-in-trade" as, let us say, is for the jurist the distinction between claims *ad personam* and those *ad rem*. The economist will not commit the fundamental error of considering the demand for a particular good in any other light than the relative demand with respect to a certain price and with respect to the conditions which determine the demand curve itself. He does not need to be told that one cannot speak of a "shortage," of a "scarcity of dollars" or of a "deficit in the balance of payments" as something absolute. He knows that those terms apply only with respect to a definite price which is fixed in such a way as to inhibit the normal function of price, which is to equalize supply and demand. And he knows that this is so even if, in view of certain social or political postulates, it seems preferable to deprive price of that function and to assign the latter to a governmental agency, if not to such agents as the black market, political corruption, "influence" or the mere physical prowess of those who, at that price, can force their way into the market. The economist who is trained to reason along such lines must indeed wince when he reads—as it was possible for him to do in 1943, for instance, in the London *Economist*—of a "scarcity of dollars" which is destined to be permanent because the United

[3] O. Morgenstern—*Die Grenzen der Wirtschaftspolitik*, Vienna, 1934, p. 69.

States "needs" so little from other countries, while the latter "need" so much from the United States. Just as if this "needing" had any sense at all, except with respect to certain prices and, in this case of international economic relations, with respect to a certain rate of exchange; and as if it were not the theory of comparative costs (that incontrovertible basic law of international trade) which alone can explain the necessity, even under these unusual circumstances, of establishing an equilibrium in international trade.

To be sure, that all sounds a lot simpler than it really is. For it is another difficulty of economic science that we are everlastingly confronted by a painful dilemma. As Alfred Marshall once observed, all simple statements in economics are erroneous. But when we modify them and make them conform to pertinent relationships, we soon arrive at a point where the process gets out of control and where it would be possible to reason out economic justification for any abuse that assumes the name of economic policy. To the field of economics we can perhaps apply more aptly than to any other the dictum which Leibnitz applied to the entire system of human knowledge. There is no truth, said Leibnitz, which does not have something erroneous commingled with it, and no error which does not contain a bit of truth. If we recognize that, we ought to be secure against all extremes and eccentricities. But it is just as important for us to shun a thoroughly debilitating relativity. And if we are to do that, it is imperative from each occasion to the next, that we distinguish clearly between that which is our fundamental thesis and our general truth, and that which is a modification of the fundamental thesis. It is equally imperative that we be aware that the particular circumstances decide in each case how much practical significance attaches to the qualifying modification.

But that demands of the economist a further special virtue. He must possess judgment, sound common sense, a feeling of proportion and perspective—in a word, qualities that are the exact opposite of those which so often characterize the average type of modern intellectual.[4] In the words of Solomon,[5] "To everything there is a season, and a time to every purpose under the heaven." That which

[4] Cf. my *Mass und Mitte*, Erlenbach-Zurich, 1950, p. 54 et seq. "Celui qui regarde naturellement les choses a le bon sens," says Vauvenargues (*Introduction à la connaissance de l'esprit humain*, 1746, VII). Then he adds, "Pour avoir beaucoup de bon sens il faut être fait de manière que la raison domine sur le sentiment, l'expérience sur le raisonnement."

[5] Ecclesiastes 3:1.

is ordinarily folly, may by exception be wisdom, and vice versa. In a desperate situation, such as the depression of 1930-1933, it may be correct to place every emphasis on a policy of "spending" and not on saving. But the economist must possess sufficient judgment not to make that into an article of faith, but must promptly recall the general truth, only temporarily modified, which teaches the exact opposite. Or let us choose a different example. It is, of course, quite correct, that a "passive balance of payments" can be brought about not only, as Ricardo taught, through the internal financial and money policy of a state, but also, as his opponent Malthus emphasized, by "real" factors which lie completely outside the sphere of things for which such a policy is responsible. But the more stubborn and more pronounced this passivity is, the more does the monetary policy operate causatively, and the more importance is to be attributed to the responsibility borne by the state and its central bank. In the long run, Ricardo's position is right and Malthus's wrong; and this is all the more true the more violent the departure from the norm. In the period of the German inflation which followed World War I, the most primitive conception of the quantity theory laying the entire blame for the soaring prices and the disruption of foreign exchange on the increase in the issue of currency, was a thousand times superior to the most ingeniously worked out theory that looked for the trouble elsewhere, e.g., in the "passive" balance of payments. And even today time is running out for those countries in Europe that want to excuse the stubbornly continuing "dollar scarcity" on the ground that it is an effect of the war or the result of other "real" factors.

These things, unfortunately, require emphasis, even among professional economists. For it cannot be denied that these very qualities—the ability to exercise judgment, of "bon sens" and of a sense of reality—have suffered diminution. They have tended to cede their position to a formalistic facility in the manipulation of methods which have been unwarrantably adopted from the natural sciences and used in economics. That brings me to the painful subject of a revolution in the field of economics which, on the whole, invites severe criticism, and which has led to an undeniable crisis in the status of economic science. I need not do more than mention the name of Lord Keynes to indicate the origin and character of that revolution. It is a broad subject, and as any adequate treatment of it would go far beyond the limits of my present observations, I shall therefore restrict myself to a few remarks which shall serve to bring out what is important for us in this connection.[6]

Keynes, more than any other one person, became responsible for a certain lamentable development in the economic science of our day. It is probable that he did so contrary to his own basic intention, but that is at this point irrelevant. That development takes on the high-sounding name of "the new economics" or "Macroëconomics" and consists of a tendency to regard the whole economic process as something purely objective and mechanical. Hence purely mathematical and statistical methods, it seems, can be applied and the whole economic process can therefore be quantitatively determined and even pre-determined. Under those circumstances an economic system readily takes on the appearance of a sort of huge waterworks, and the science which treats of that economic system quite logically assumes the appearance of a kind of engineering science, which teems with equations in ever-increasing profusion. And so oblivion threatens to engulf what, as I see it, is the actual fruit of a century and a half of intellectual effort in the field of economics, namely, the doctrine of the movement of individual prices.

That brings in its train a number of other tendencies well calculated to arouse anxiety. One of these is an ever-increasing specialization in research which promotes a sort of fragmentation process throughout the field of the social sciences. Another phenomenon, inevitably consequent to the first, is an occultism which at times positively glories in the esoteric incomprehensibility of its presentation and proudly points to its use of mathematics as something which raises the "new economics" almost to the dazzling heights of physics itself. We encounter, too, a species of intellectualism or scholasticism which is bereft of all sense of proportion, loses itself in a maze of hair-splitting, and sets up "models" or "patterns" which abandon any possible approach to reality. And that leads, finally, to a stiff-necked intolerance which can justly be termed a "rabies economica" since it is no whit less intransigently bigoted than the comparable "rabies theologica." It has come to the point where we must often ask ourselves, as we open the pages of one of the technical publications of our science, whether we have not inadvertantly gotten hold of a technical journal on chemistry or hydraulics.

There is pressing need, then, for calm reflection and critical

[6] For a fuller treatment I refer the reader to my essay "Alte und neue Oekonomie" which appeared as a contribution to a symposium entitled *Wirtschaft ohne Wunder*, Eugen Rentsch, Erlenbach–Zurich, 1953.

deliberation.[7] Their starting point must be the self-evident fact that economics belongs to the estimable family of the *Geisteswissenschaften* and that it is a "moral science" in the sense that it deals with man as an intellectual and moral being. But our reflection and deliberation must also not lose sight of the point previously established, that economics occupies a special position, in that it deals with that institution which we call a market economy. Now that is an institution which goes so far in translating subjective feelings into objective actions, that we economists are able to employ methods which are foreign to other moral sciences. And this special position makes economics truly a "border science" with all the attractive possibilities the term implies, but also subject to all the great dangers inherent therein. Economics does, in actual fact, permit of recourse to mathematics to illustrate and to formulate with precision causal relationships of a quantitative character. And there are indeed few modern economists who would reject all utilization of mathematics. But this very method is open to question because it will lure the unwary into pushing forward unduly the frontier that delimits the border territory, the zone between what is human and what is mechanical. They will thus advance too far into the region of the mechanical, the statistical, the mathematical, and they will be prone to neglect that which lies on the hither side of the boundary, that which is human and unmathematical, that which is intellectual and moral and hence not quantitatively measurable. There should be a readiness to forgo the technique and methods of the natural sciences except occasionally and for illustrative purposes, particularly in view of the fact that the possible gain from their employment involves disproportionate danger of gross error. *"Parturient montes—nascetur ridiculus mus"* is truly an apothegm that should be borne in mind by those who engage in studies of this kind.

And it is an error to attempt to defend mathematical economics by pointing out that our science does, after all, deal with quantities. That statement is true. But it is true in even greater measure of strategy, and yet battles are no mere mathematical problem of computation that can be consigned to the care of an electronic calculating machine. The determining factor in economic activity is furnished by things that are as downright unmathematical as a love letter or a Christmas festival, by forces that are moral and intellectual, by reactions and opinions that simply have no place in curves

[7] The reader hardly needs to be told how much the author is indebted to the writings of Ludwig von Mises for much of what follows.

and equations, but lie in the domain of the everlastingly incalculable and unpredictable. We must not, in our "border science," demand more from the mathematical method than it can accomplish. I know of no really effectual economic theory that could be discovered by that method alone, nor indeed any that has actually been so discovered. There are profound reasons for this, for any economic doctrine deserves the jaundiced eye of suspicion if it can be demonstrated only mathematically without being at the same time unmathematically comprehensible. Wherever any attempt is made to advance such a doctrine, it would be well to apply the wise principle laid down by a brilliant Viennese economist who used to say in such cases, "Before I marvel, I'd rather disbelieve."

I find equally sound that remark of Voltaire's which Goethe once quoted in the course of a letter to Zelter, "J'ai toujours remarqué que la géometrie laisse l'esprit où elle le trouve." As one of our contemporary economists, L. A. Hahn, wittily remarks, mathematical economics all too often resembles the game of egg-hiding that children play at Easter. How they shout for joy when they find the eggs in the very place where they hid them! But even that is one of the most innocent objections that can be raised against this method. Its worst feature is, that it deludes us into a dehumanization of economic science. To rediscover hidden Easter eggs is an innocent pleasure that we need not, after all, begrudge anyone. But it becomes a serious matter when the game exposes us to the danger of sticking our hands into a rattlesnake's nest.[8]

The French statesman Philippe Berthelot once said, after the First World War, "un homme qui meurt—ça m'émeut. Quinze-cent mille hommes—c'est de la statistique." It is an observation as bitter as it is true, and the economist is the last person who should be deaf to the warning it contains. Of course, we economists cannot avoid the use of a species of technical shorthand. We speak of supply and demand, of the purchasing power of money, of the amount of production, the volume of savings, the volume of investment, not to mention a pork sector, and we cannot forever be emphasizing that behind all these pseudo-mechanical concepts there stand individual human beings with their feelings, their deliberations, their appraisals of value, their collective suggestions and decisions. But neither should we ever forget those things ourselves, nor play heedlessly with these collective symbols as children do with building blocks. Certain economists today speak of "coefficients of elasticity,"

[8] On the limitations of the mathematical method cf. G. F. Stigler, *Five Lectures on Economic Problems*, London, 1950.

"marginal propensities," "multipliers," "accelerators," and other ingenious devices, just as if it were a question of physical constants, so to speak, with which they were going through mathematical procedures. Then the moment has come when we have to express our disapproval in no uncertain terms.

Those are aberrations which make it very clear why the word "crisis" is hardly too strong a term to describe the present situation in economic science. But we have now arrived at the point where we must revert to a remark I made earlier in these pages. This tendency toward a quantitative and mechanical conception of our branch of the moral sciences is, of course, merely a reflection of a general inclination in the same direction in all the thinking of our era. It expresses itself with especial clarity in all questions bearing on our social life and in this respect runs parallel to developments in the practical politics of our day. The tendencies I deplore in economics are merely one particular case exemplifying the general tendency toward impersonalization, toward collectivization, toward mechanization, toward dehumanization. The spirit of our times is in very fact predominantly collectivistic, predominantly hostile to the human being, the human soul, the human personality. Anyone who perceives in that spirit a threat to human destiny must needs watch vigilantly for every manifestation whereby that spirit expresses itself. And that applies to economic theory just as truly! I make bold to aver that basically Keynes and Picasso both demonstrate that they belong to the same era, and that even in their alternation between classicism and ultramodernism they are remarkably alike. Ortega y Gasset has written a famous essay on "The Banishment of the Human Being from Art." We economists can well supplement it by making some observations on "The Banishment of the Human Being from Economic Science." And unfortunately here, too, developments in the field of theory parallel those in the field of its practical application.

That brings us back to the original point of departure for these observations. After we have attempted to explain and appraise the place of economics as a science, it still remains for us to say a concluding word on its place in modern society. What is it accomplishing here? What are its specific functions, and how can it fulfill them?

Let us not linger over the trivial truth that it is the function of economics to provide governments, organized groups, and public opinion with orientation and guidance in all decisions concerning economic policy, and to supply a training ground for the forces that specialize in these pursuits. There still remain two important observations to record.

The first of these is the need for repeating emphatically an old complaint. It is to the effect that hardly any other science has to struggle as hard as does economics against the layman's stubborn proclivity to adhere to the "home-grown economics" I mentioned earlier. Despite a complete lack of training and in naïve reliance on the obvious evidence of his senses, he opposes his own economies to two centuries of not entirely fruitless reflection and research by the economist. For economics is the one field where every layman feels able to render a competent opinion because it is the field where his interests are involved and his sentiments are aroused. And, as Frank H. Knight, then president of the American Economics Association, somewhat bitterly remarked a few years ago, that is all the more remarkable because it is just the more essential economic truths which are of such a nature that people would be bound to understand them without any elucidation by the economist, if they only wanted to. But they *will* not see "that imports are either paid for by exports, as a method of producing the imported goods more efficiently, or else are received for nothing. Can there be any use in explaining, if it is needful to explain, that fixing a price below the free market level will create a shortage and one above it a surplus?" And Knight adds the further remark, "Let me observe that rent freezing, for example, occurs not at all merely because tenants have more votes than landlords. It reflects a state of mind, a mode of reasoning, even more discouraging then blindness through self-interest." [9]

The second point that I feel requires to be recorded is that the task which confronts economic science, difficult enough in itself, becomes virtually impossible of accomplishment if that science itself betrays in its answers the uncertainty that is evident in the critical situation that obtains today. That seems even more emphatically true if economics enrolls under the Keynesian banner and bestows the blessings of mathematical science on the pronouncements of unlettered laymen. It is to be expected that the overwhelming majority of laymen will look upon the "passive balance of payments" as an Act of God. We may further take for granted that in the eyes of those same laymen the only cure for this affliction is an economy that relies on forcible control of exchange rates plus American sub-

[9] Frank H. Knight, "The Role of Principles in Economics and Politics," *American Economic Review*, March 1951, p. 4.

sidies. But what are we to think of a science of economics that confirms an ingenious version of that lay theory—a theory already exploded back in the days of David Hume and David Ricardo? Much of what goes today under the name of "New economics" has virtually deprived humanity of every last bit of firm ground on which to stand and combat such things, and there should be no divided opinion as to the crying need for something to heal the rupture they have caused in the body structure of our science as a whole. Fortunately, indications are increasingly numerous that granulation of the wound is progressing apace.

In the meantime economic science has other social functions which far transcend the aforementioned orientation and guidance in matters of economic policy. Thus, it is unquestionable that economics has become indispensable to modern man as a component element of his "culture." By "culture" I mean here the system of concepts which comprise his universe. In that sense it is the function of economics to provide the individual with that orientation—so supremely important for the genuine inner life—which instructs him concerning the structure and functioning of society and the place which he himself occupies within it.[10] It is necessary to add that orientation of that kind is vitally necessary to the existence of society and to economic order itself. For as Lucien Romier justly observed some twenty years ago,[11] no cultural system can long survive if the great mass of people who are its bearers no longer understand its inner laws and its essential structure. And it is that very understanding of our economic system which has gradually become lost in the ever-increasing complexity of its own bustling activity.[12] One of the primary tasks confronting present-day economic science is to make that system transparently intelligible, to explain its functioning with elementary clarity to every man, and thus to indicate beyond question the place he occupies in his world. But such a task presupposes that the economic scientist is wholeheartedly convinced of the compelling necessity for so presenting economics that it should be clearly intelligible, well synthesized and universal in scope—in short, so that it shall be a living part of the

[10] This characterization of economics gives it its proper place in the total program developed by Ortega y Gasset in his book, *Schuld und Schuldigkeit der Universität*, Munich, 1952.

[11] Lucien Romier, *Si le capitalisme disparaissait*, Paris 1933, "Aucune société, aucune humanité n'a pu vivre longtemps sans savoir pourquoi elle vivait et comment elle devait vivre, sans philosophie et sans moral." (pp. 156-157.)

[12] Cf. Walter Eucken, *Grundsätze der Wirtschaftspolitik*, Bern-Tübingen, 1952, p. 194.

body of our era's cultural knowledge. And that task imposes on economic science (and here we echo another demand by Ortega y Gasset) the further requirement that it emerge from its esoteric seclusion and recognize the necessity for making such intimate contact with society's organs of public opinion as to become a vital factor in its intellectual life.

And as if that were not enough, economics has, besides, a very specific function to perform in the modern democracy. It has an humble but all the more useful mission. Amidst the passions and self-interest of politics, it must assert the logic of things, it must bring to light all the inconvenient facts and relationships, must put them in their proper place with dispassionate justice, must prick all the soap bubbles, must unmask illusion and confusion, and must defend before all the world the proposition that two and two make four. It should be the one science *par excellence* which disillusions, which is anti-visionary, anti-Utopian, and anti-ideological. Thus it can render society the priceless service of cooling off political passion, of combating mass superstition, of making life hard for all demagogues, financial wizards, and economic prestidigitators. At the same time it must avoid becoming the willing handmaiden of that social emotionalism of which Solomon says in the 13th canto of *Il Paradiso,* "E poi l'affetto l'intelletto lega."

That does not by any means imply that we economists may or can retreat to the ivory tower of an economic neutrality. We, beyond all others, are representatives of the social sciences and under the duty to make up our minds at the great cross-roads of our civilization. It is not enough for us merely to decipher the roadmarkers; we must know whether we are sending society along the road to freedom, to humane living, to unalterable truth, or in the opposite direction and toward slavery, the prostitution of man, and crassest falsehood. To evade that decision would just as assuredly be a "trahison des clercs" as if we were to betray the sanctity that lies in the truth of science to the political passions and the social emotionalism of our era. The performance of that duty means no less than the erection of the most important possible "guide-post" for determining the place of economics among the sciences of today.

IX

On Methodology in Economics

by FAUSTINO BALLVÉ

(from the Spanish by O. L. Ballvé)

W HEN, in 1783, Immanuel Kant published his *Prolegomena* in order to dispel the confusion caused in the philosophical world by his revolutionary *Critique of Pure Reason,* he headed the chapters with a number of questions that could be condensed as follows: "How Is Metaphysics Possible?" If we, in turn, had to condense Ludwig von Mises' methodological position, we would have to phrase the question as follows: "How Is Economics Possible?"

As Manuel Reventós points out in his prologue to the Catalan translation of Chapman's *Economy,* the science of economics, towards the end of the nineteenth century, found itself in the stage in which metaphysics had been at the end of the eighteen century: floating between dogmatism and empiricism. Dogmatism was born with the physiocrats, developed by the classicists, and left its mark on the mathematical economists. It postulated inescapable economic laws to which man had to conform under penalty of failure. Empiricism was born with mercantilism and, through List and the historical school, arrived at "state socialism," neo-mercantilism, and other forms of etatism. It considered economic events only as social data, the study of which could be profitably employed by politicians to give order to economic life, thus freeing it from anarchy.

Both these trends gradually declined and their failure stimulated inquiring minds to reflect. The discredit into which economic laws had fallen seemed to justify empiricism. But neither did the control of economic life by political means prove practical. For whenever the state applied an economic measure to attain certain results, the final results proved to be quite different. Something always intervened. If it was not the discredited economic laws, what then could it be? If the economic activities of man were not ruled by "natural laws," nor could be regulated at will, then they had to have a sense of their own. And this sense was to be searched for neither by observation nor by experimentation, but by *reflection*. The data on economic life were available; only its sense was missing. And this could only be searched for by methodical reflection. Economic life did exist. It disobeyed natural laws and also resisted social laws. How was this possible?

The economic problem is exposed in a critical manner. In our opinion, herein lies the great contribution of L. von Mises to the science of economics.

Economic life, unlike natural life, is not subject to the law of causality. In natural life the same causes always produce the same effects. In economic life the same causes may produce different effects. Why? Because man's volition interferes between causes and effects. And man's volition is not ruled by causes (past), but by aims (future). Events in human life are not ruled by the law of causality, but by that of finality. We can judge natural events starting from the two fundamental categories of Kant: time and place. In human events a third category intervenes: action. García Morente, who in our belief is the most lucid interpreter of Kant, stated that the nineteenth century further developed Kantism by discovering a third fundamental category explaining human evolution and progress. Action is the product of man's *elective faculty*. Confronted with facts, which in nature would be causes, man chooses and consequently acts. He acts whether he is confronted by an economic or any other human problem.

The study of human action is called praxeology. Economics is a part of praxeology. But what part? How do we categorize it within the praxeological group?

In economics the category of *exchange* which plays no role in other praxeological phenomena is added to the category of elective action. In economic life man acts to obtain what he wants. This is possible only in a bilateral way: *do ut des*. You give me something in exchange for what I give you; or I give you something in exchange for what you give me. Thus economics is catalactical praxeology. But the act of exchange must take place somewhere. This place (material or ideal) is the *market*. Everybody is always present and acting in the market, even if only in a negative way, i.e., not exchanging. Not to exchange is also to act in the market, just as the gambler at a gambling table may momentarily abstain from placing a bet.

We categorize a science on grounds of its essential, general, and permanent characteristics. Economics is human action employing the elective faculty in market exchange. Thus its fundamental categories are the elective faculty, the exchange of goods, and the market. Only in the recognition of these categories is economic thinking possible. Economics is *oikos nemo,* i.e., running of the home or caring for one's well-being. From the interplay of choosing between goods and services for the well-being of oneself and one's family, and choosing leisure, indifference, or sacrifice, economic life is born. Its driving force is the autonomous action of individuals. Its means is choice; its stage, the market.

Therefore, economics is neither pursuit of wealth, nor the production or distribution of commodities and services, nor their consumption. These are results, purely external manifestations which also appear outside the scope of economics. As L. von Mises has repeatedly stated, production, distribution, consumption, and the satisfaction of the urge to amass wealth are also feasible by means not freely elective, such as politics or, more concretely, totalitarianism in any of its forms. But this is not economics. These actions only concern economics when they originate from the autonomous action of man exercising his elective faculty in the market. Only under this condition could the following characteristic phenomena, which always were considered to comprise economics, be brought about: supply and demand, mechanism of prices, money and credit, etc.

What we have just set forth constitutes the fundamental basis of economic theory. As Rudolf Stammler very accurately asserted, a theory is a doctrine of general validity. It is the exposition of the pure form of a certain scientific matter by means of a special focus or method. In our case it is the praxeological-catalactical focus of human action. The concrete and changing matters of human activity lack unity, order, and individuality. They receive these characteristics only from the method. Thus human action resulting from reflection on goods to be desired and to be offered in exchange may be an economic case or one of a different nature, depending upon the method applied. If we inquire why a man acts in a certain way today, instead of yesterday or tomorrow, why he selects one commodity or service instead of others, and why he offers in exchange one good or medium of exchange instead of others, then we apply psychology and not economics. We are dealing with economics when we regard the individual act as an elective act in the market. We are not interested in motives or "causes" that may have brought about a definite action at a definite time and place. This is the field of the psychologist. For the economist the elective-catalactical action of man is the ultimate given. It is the point of departure for our science and provides unity for an organic theory, that is to say, an explanation of the phenomena and problems resulting from man's use of his elective faculty in the market. If we start from this point of view we can logically explain and relate all economic phenomena.

In short, no event in itself is economic. Only the methodical focus makes it so. Thus we cannot study an economic event until we know the meaning of an "economic event." Economics, like any other science, necessarily starts from an *a priori* synthetical assertion. For economics it is the following: economic activity is elective-catalactic action. This *a priori* synthetical assertion has its "raison d'être," for it allows us to understand and explain economic phenomena. It makes economics possible. Through its form it gives individuality and organic unity to material events which we used to consider intuitively as economic events. It also enables us to discard those concepts which, despite their economic appearance (monopolies, for example), are not economic events although they may influence economic life.

Starting from the synthetic assertion that defines economics, the science of economics proceeds in an analytical way, searching for fundamental elements, in order to construct the theory of economic life. First it searches for the primary categories of economic thought. According to L. von Mises, human action is the fundamental element; but not every action is economic—only catalactic action is. It necessarily concerns commodities and services, even in the case of elective rejection. Being directed to future uses it necessarily entails insecurity, risks, etc.

According to L. von Mises, the foregoing reasoning explains how the categories of economic thought flow from the primary category of action and from reflection on the circumstances in which action takes place. As he repeatedly points out, the science of economics does not study an imaginary economy but the real economic life which it endeavors to comprehend systematically through its general elements or essential forms. The primary categories then produce the secondary categories: value, price, cost, calculation, etc. Economics thus proceeds from fundamental to secondary and tertiary categories until the building of economic theory is completed.

However, there is one problem to which an answer has not yet been given by economists, not even by L. von Mises who in his *Human Action* did not give us a theory, but a treatise on economics. Even a theory is not the whole of a science, but merely the unitarian, organic, and exhaustive explanation of its object at which we arrive by the method implicit in the *a priori* synthetic assertion, establishing its definition. That is to say, theory furnishes us with the explanation of the object in question. Then the method of realization, which is a *technical* problem, must be searched for. This does not imply that man is to receive advice on the use of his elective faculty in catalactic action. L. von Mises stated correctly that economics is not an axiological science and does not solve problems of justice or morals. Our task is to search for the most adequate means to attain the end that man has chosen.

Economics encounters many *modus faciendi* problems in its path, especially in the fields of money, economic calculation, etc. In treatises on economics these problems usually are intermingled with purely theoretical problems, which is not only antimethodical but also dangerous. For sometimes this is the reason a technical solution is given too great an importance insofar as the fundamental theoretical problem is subordinated to it. We all remember the confusion created in economic theory by the feud between monometalists and bimetalists. In jurisprudence we are now witnessing a similar aberration. The state is a juridical person. Now, the juridical person is a fiction of the technique of law. But notwithstanding, the state has lately been invested with ontological reality. People talk of the interests of the state, of state sovereignty, etc. And so we arrive at the omnipotent government, so justly attacked by L. von Mises. We believe that in this area important work is to be done by the economist. Careful distinction must be made in economics between theoretical problems of principle and technical problems of application. Both must be presented distinctly separated in treatises on economics, especially those for students.

But economics is not only theory and technique, it is also practice, i.e., the solution of concrete cases. L. von Mises does not expressly mention it, but he does so implicitly when he speaks of "history."[1] According to him, the method of history is understanding, not comprehension which characterizes theory. He speaks of history as the understanding of past events. But man not only understands or

[1] Ludwig von Mises, *Human Action*, Yale University Press, New Haven, Conn., pp. 47-58.

endeavors to understand history, he makes it. He makes it by acting in concrete cases, by exercising his faculty of election—that is, he solves praxeological problems. As L. von Mises repeats so insistently, he solves them through reasoning, classifying the data, the pros and cons that cause him to elect and act in order to attain a panoramic view which enables him to choose the proper road. It is not enough for him theoretically to comprehend the kind of action to be taken (in this case an economic action), nor to master the technical instruments which were not invented for his specific case, but for a larger group of cases. He must also take into consideration the individual circumstances of the concrete case he is facing, estimating the relevancy of each circumstance in itself, its relation to others, its relation to the precedents of similar cases in the past, and to the desired end. In short, he must judge the case in perspective and in relief. To a certain degree he must consider it as if he were confronting a minor premise *(Untersatz)* searching for the major premise *(Obersatz)* to which he can submit the case and thus reach the conclusion which will determine his elective action. We repeat, neither a theoretical comprehension nor the mastery of the technical means is sufficient for this. He must go deeper and exercise what L. von Mises calls specific understanding, and which may also be called criterion, discretion, or *savoir faire.* In a word, he must interpret the case. His situation is like that of an historian who endeavors to understand an historical case, but he not only has to understand, he must also act. L. von Mises advances a number of rules of understanding for the interpretation of past events. We believe that economists should also endeavor to find interpreting rules that serve as guides for the solution of practical cases and the discovery of the major premise, even if such guides are not exact or infallible. Indeed, it is deplorable to err in the interpretation of past historical cases as, for example, in the interpretation of the last depression. But it is fatal to err in actions affecting the future, especially if they concern not only an individual, but also a collective body. The examples of the revaluation of the pound sterling after the first world war and its devaluation by the last labor government clearly demonstrate this. The fatal effects of both measures for British citizens and even for non-Britishers can only be attributed to a lack of understanding of the measures to be taken. We, therefore, believe that economists should not neglect the practical problems, that they should endeavor to find exact rules for the interpretation of economic phenomena. Books should be written and courses be organized to help all those who, in some way or other, endeavor to solve practical cases, to avoid the pitfalls that may divert them from the true path of realizing economics in practice.

Let us conclude by returning to the beginning. We believe that Professor von Mises has done in economics what Kant did in metaphysics. He has demonstrated how economics is possible. But it is one thing to know "what is possible," and another to know reality. Today nobody can philosophize ignoring Kant. In the future nobody will be able to deal with economics ignoring L. von Mises. But we are still only in the beginning. As he has put it so well, economics is a young science. It must be made to grow, and we have endeavored to make a few suggestions to stimulate this growth. Of course, we do not hope to achieve its perfection because "there is no such thing as perfection in human knowledge, nor for that matter in any other human achievement. Omniscience is denied to man. . . . Science does not give us absolute and final certainty. . . . A scientific system is but one station in an endlessly progressing search for knowledge. . . . But to acknowledge these facts does not mean that present day economics is backward. It merely means that economics is a living thing—and to live implies both imperfection and change." [2]

[2] *Ibid.*, p. 7.

X

Some Considerations on Economic Laws

by CARLO ANTONI

(from the Italian by Micheline Mitrani)

WRITING many years ago, Luigi Einaudi pointed out how it had become the fashion after World War I to proclaim that the war had demonstrated the spuriousness of all economic laws. In reality the war provided an almost experimental confirmation of their validity. The alleged spuriousness simply consisted in the fact that the war provided politicians with an opportunity to commit a multiplicity of blunders, the inevitable effects of which were then ascribed to the war.

During the period of dictators' miracles, the recurring phrase of the bankruptcy of economic theory became almost deafening. Those titans bragged of their power to bend to their will even economic laws, as if a politician needed strength of character to violate, rather than to respect those laws.

But this did not suffice. Even today we must listen to the fatuous talk by all kinds of administrators and economic planners on the "rejection" of economic theory for the sake of politics.

It seems strange that in these matters theorists are primarily accused of abstractness, as if it were possible for a science not to be abstract, for science proceeds by general, schematic concepts. The political "realists" probably do not believe that abstract intellect itself is an instrument of action, and that a concept, to prove useful, must be abstract. The laws of economics are practical only insofar as they are abstract. It goes without saying that action also requires the intervention of that faculty which the ancient logicians called "secunda Petri" and which Kant called "judgment." We may name it "intuition." It serves to apply the general scheme to the concrete case. Without this faculty, according to Kant, a judge can possess all of juridical knowledge and yet be a fool. But to assume that intuition can act alone would be to believe that the "clinical eye" can exempt the doctor from a knowledge of medicine.

It is possible that those who deny the validity of economic laws may assume the role of champions of human liberty against naturalistic determinism. Alluding to the physicists' discovery of the principle of indetermination in natural phenomena, they find it completely indefensible to believe in determination in the phenomena of the human world.

In reality the concept of law can be similarly applied to nature and human action alike. The difference does not lie in the object, but in the method and point of view. At the beginning of this century Dilthey, Windelband, and Rickert in Germany, and Croce in Italy opposed the positivists' application of the methods of natural science to history. They raised the objection that historical knowledge was not the science of classes and general laws, but of individual facts. Their objection was irrefutable even though certain philosophers of history are still pretending to arrive at the "laws" of history from events and then explaining the events themselves in the light of these "laws." But if historical knowledge actually deals with individual facts, the elaboration of experience for practical purposes deals with the general. Nothing prevents us from extending this method also to the world of human behavior, provided, however, we bear in mind that life is always more varied and unpredictable than our schematization. Economic history as an historical science must aim at the individuality of facts; but economics, with due respect for the memory of Schmoller and the historical school of economics, is not merely knowledge of the past. The economic theorist is the successor and heir of the economic adviser who, in the past, counseled the sovereign on matters of financial policy.

Indeed it is fallacious to assume that in formulating a law the economist subjects human will to necessity. On the contrary, he merely attributes to the individual the capacity to act freely according to his interest. Having established that man acts in a utilitarian manner, the economist proceeds from an established situation and then anticipates the action which man will freely choose in his own interest.

The champions of politics probably will be surprised to learn that they prove themselves to be pure idealists in contesting the validity of economic laws. They forget that man is and remains an economic creature in spite of his noble sentiments; that he must satisfy his own vital needs and that he does so with gratification. In final analysis, however, these idealists reveal themselves as believers in force and the efficacy of police measures which are to curb the egoism of individuals and, as Hegel proclaimed, are to raise them from the level of base nature to the "ethical" level of the state. The affirmation of the validity of economic laws thus is identical with the affirmation of an insuppressible economic "nature" in man, which indeed is not the whole man—for he is also art, thought, moral and religious life—but it is a factor or vital element of his nature.

It must be admitted, however, that a layman who turns to an economic treatise to search for economic laws will be disappointed. He usually finds a description of the structure and operation of modern economic society, its monetary system, markets, banks, stock exchanges, corporations, taxes, duties, etc. He will find an explanation of the disturbances and damages which may affect this organism together with suggested remedies. Such a treatise is apt to create the belief that the laws which it sets forth concern the proper functioning of a particular society, the capitalist society, under the assumption of a free market, free choice of consumers, and free initiative of private producers. Without these premises or in a different organization of society, the laws of economics are said to be different like the non-Euclidean geometries which proceed from different postulates. But the truth is that these laws operate in all human societies, even in associations of ascetic abnegation or monastic communities.

The active element in laws is the factor of utility which is always alike, for it is a form or category of activity of the human mind. From this point of view all laws are comprised in only one, namely, that man, besides being a "spiritual" being, is also utilitarian. He is so in a manner not only insuppressible but also legitimate because he lives on earth and not in the kingdom of heaven. An economic law classifies the situation, renders it typical, and thus abstracts. Economics determines a certain number of typical situations which may even be infinite, in order to calculate or rather to deduce the subsequent action of the economic factor, i.e., individual interest. Therefore, contrary to the natural sciences which are empirical and merely summarize the data of experience and group them in their classes and laws, the science of economics "calculates." It deduces from certain abstract premises. In the calculation it reduces the terms of the useful, such as damages, profits, losses, and gains, to quantity. For this reason it adopts the form of a mathematical calculation.

Max Weber, who sought to deprive the law of its character of naturalistic necessity, set forth the concept of "ideal type." According to him, given certain premises, it is probable that concrete action takes place in conformity to the "type" which is deduced from those premises. In reality, the "type" concerns the premises; in other words, the situation abstractly presumed, as for instance, free competition.

The typical situations from which laws are deduced are, we repeat, schemes which more or less adhere to reality. The economic factor, however, is not abstract, but a real force, even though science must reduce it to quantitative terms for the sake of calculation. There may be instances in which patriotic enthusiasm, charity, so-called social morality, etc., induce individuals to act outside of and perhaps against their immediate advantage. But in a society of men and not of saints and heroes, all these ideal impulses cannot normally and permanently expel and suppress this economic factor which by nature and definition is individualistic.

It is a matter of fact that the science of economics came into being in the eighteenth century as a result of the "discovery of the useful," that is to say, of positive value and the fecundity of the economic interest in man's life. Comparing the origin of economics with that of aesthetics, Benedetto Croce called both sciences "worldly" and even "diabolic." According to him, both attribute positive and autonomous value to activities which in themselves, strictly speaking, are not moral. But it is a fact that the forerunners of economics praised those private vices and transformed them into public benefits. They approved as courage, initiative, and enterprise what the ancient morality had condemned as sins of avarice and cupidity. From Adam Smith on, some economists even attempted in vain to reduce moral life itself to utility. On the other hand, socialism, though proclaiming itself "materialistic," attempts to revive ascetic morality. It does so not only by condemning entrepreneurial profit as theft, but also by advocating a "social" morality according to which the individual is to labor not for himself, but for society. Socialism claims to repress the very economic factor in the economic world itself, rejecting or even censuring that formidable vital force. But moralistic edification and ideological propaganda cannot suffice to stimulate zeal. Socialism then returns to individual interest by means of a system of "incentives." Since even this seems insufficient it turns to forced labor. And yet, since not even the merciless dictator can deprive the human soul of that vital motive, economic laws reappear also in collectivist societies, alive and petulant, in the form of guilt and crime, sabotage and treason, or less vividly as black markets.

XI

Averages and Aggregates in Economics

by Louis M. Spadaro

IN AN interesting, though apparently neglected, aside, Professor Hayek has remarked that ". . . neither aggregates nor averages do act upon one another, and it will never be possible to establish necessary connections of cause and effect between them as we can between individual phenomena, individual prices, etc. I would even go so far as to assert that, from the very nature of economic theory, averages can never form a link in its reasoning. . . ."[1]

Now, any serious doubt concerning the validity of aggregates and averages is a dagger aimed straight at the heart of much current empirical research and statistical analysis in economics. Therefore it deserves close and systematic attention, even if this involves, in the opinion of some dedicated empiricists, an annoying interruption of the "front-line" activity of measurement for the mere purpose of "armchair" discussion of methodological issues.[2] Yet such is our contemporary spirited march on "objective data" that one who begins to suspect that a wrong turn may have been made sometime back almost naturally feels guilty for harboring this traitorous thought, and, if he expresses it at all, must expect to be regarded as a ruminant obstructionist in the company of men of action.

[1] F. A. Hayek, *Prices and Production*, London, 1935, 2nd ed. rev., pp. 4-5.
[2] Even Marshall comes close to this view in his advice to Schumpeter; (cf. P. A. Samuelson, "Economic Theory and Mathematics—An Appraisal," *Amer. Econ. Rev.*, vol. xlii, May 1953, no. 2, p. 65).

But methodology should need no apology. In the first place, anyone concerned with policy and the "planned economy" should be the least able to deny the need for a "planned economics." Second, as even a little reflection will show, so great a proportion of our data is presently accumulating in the form of aggregates and averages[3] that it would be, in prudence, *uneconomic* to ignore a possibility which, if true, would largely vitiate their usefulness.[4] Nor can economics avoid the difficulty by leaning, methodologically, on the physical sciences. On the one hand, it is by no means established that the physical sciences can make more than tentative, hypothetical use of statistical inference and probabilistic reasoning; and, on the other, even if they could, it would not necessarily follow that the kind of problem which is posed by economics is amenable to the same treatment.[5] That the implications of the concept of "law" in the natural sciences rule out applicability to the social sciences has been pointed out by too many[6] to need further discussion here. Our task here is not to discuss any of the broad methodological and even philosophical aspects of economic science, important and interesting as these doubtless are; it is, rather, the relatively narrow one of inquiring into some of the characteristics of averages and aggregates which may escape the attention of research workers in our field, and to attempt to clarify a few of the implications in their use, since this use is so integral a part of empirical research.

It might be well for us to note at the outset of our discussion something frequently pointed out about the statistical method: that

[3] Cf., e.g., R. A. Gordon, "Business Cycles in the Interwar Period: The Quantitative-Historical Approach," *Amer. Econ. Rev.*, vol. xxxix, May 1949, No. 3, pp. 51-3. Gordon points out that both the econometric "models" of Tinbergen and the Cowles Commission group and the cycle studies of the National Bureau as well as other forms of statistical approach find it difficult to cope with information which cannot be quantified and expressed in the form of averages.

[4] We cannot, I think, simply accept "aimless floundering" as inevitable for the social sciences because of their "youth" as Miss Wootton appears to do (cf. *Testament for Social Science*, New York, 1950, p. 71). Indeed the very fact, which this writer rightly deplores, that ". . . many blind alleys are long ones, and . . . we do not always recognize this till we have gone a very long way off the right track. . . ." is evidence of the ultimate economy (much like that of *all* indirect production) of pausing for methodological issues.

[5] Cf. F. S. C. Northrop, *The Logic of the Sciences and the Humanities* (New York, 1949), pp. 33, 240-3; P. A. Samuelson, *Foundations of Economic Analysis* (Cambridge, Mass., 1948), pp. 91, 93, 226, 351-2.

[6] Cf., e.g., M. Weber, *The Methodology of the Social Sciences* (Glencoe, Ill., 1949), pp. 73-5, 86; J. Marschak, "Probability in the Social Sciences," in P. F. Lazarsfeld, ed., *Mathematical Thinking in the Social Sciences* (Glencoe, Ill., 1954), pp. 190, 194; Northrop, *op. cit.*, pp. 212, 243-9, 261, 263; T. G. Connolly and W. Sluckin, *An Introduction to Statistics for the Social Sciences* (London, 1953), p. 101.

it divides into two easily distinguishable, though, as we shall see, not entirely unrelated parts—(1) the description of phenomena, and (2) the drawing of inferences as to meaningful relations among these phenomena.[7] Inasmuch as the second of these aspects necessarily depends upon, and makes detailed use of, the first as its data, it follows that any averages which are an important part of descriptive statistical inquiry must also, *eo ipso*, enter the second, or inferential, stage. Nor is this the full extent of their involvement in statistical inference. Averages also enter inferential statistical analysis independently of their descriptive value; analysis has come to depend upon them not merely because its data are usually in that form, but also, more significantly, because it appears to be able to draw tighter inferences concerning probability distributions of data when these data are in the form of averages than when they are in the "raw" form of individual observations. The possibility that this seeming initial advantage may ultimately result in error or distortion is precisely the point of our discussion.

Regard for space and for the reader's patience does not permit an exhaustive examination of the many problems posed by the use of aggregative materials in general in our field; this discussion will therefore restrict itself to some reflections on averages as a special type of aggregate. It seems best to proceed by listing several characteristics of averages and examining their implications.

1. *The Average Is a Special Type of Aggregate*

It has been noted [8] that an average is merely a certain value of the variable which it measures and is therefore necessarily of the same dimensions as that variable. Thus, if the variable is age, or income, or a percentage, an average of that variable is expressed, respectively, as an age, income, or percentage.[9] In this fact, other-

[7] For a discussion of the application of this double aim to physical science generally, cf. P. Duhem, "Representation vs. Explanation in Physical Theory," in P. P. Wiener, ed., *Readings in the Philosophy of Science* (New York, 1953), pp. 454 ff. Cf. also J. M. Keynes, *A Treatise on Probability* (London, 1921), pp. 3, 327.

[8] G. U. Yule and M. G. Kendall, *Introduction to the Elementary Theory of Statistics* (New York, 1950), 14 ed. rev. and enl., p. 112.

[9] It is interesting to note that even σ, the other determining parameter of a distribution besides the mean, is itself not free of the difficulties of averaging. We compute *each* deviation from the mean in arriving at the variance, but in computing the standard deviation we extract the square root of the *average* of the squared deviations, thus causing extreme cases to affect the variance and the standard deviation unequally. Cf., e.g., L. Cohen, *Statistical Methods for Social Scientists* (New York, 1954), p. 46; W. E. Deming and R. T. Birge, *On the Statistical Theory of Sampling* (Washington, D.C., 1937), p. 147; P. G. Hoel, *Introduction to Mathematical Statistics* (New York, 1954), 2nd ed., p. 52.

wise so convenient, may lurk some danger. If averages are really theoretical constructs at some remove from reality (as further discussion will attempt to show), then the fact that they are expressed in the same terms as the variable itself may give them an illusory realism and may lead the incautious to confuse shadow with substance.[10] Of course, this danger is very much smaller in those areas where realities are unmistakably in discrete units; no one would be likely to overlook the fact that an average family of, say, 2.73 members is merely a symbol and describes no real family. But where reality is less discrete or the units less shudderingly indivisible, the danger persists. And it is just as serious, where the explanation of causality is concerned, in the case of even a perfectly continuous variable as in that of a clearly discontinuous one—it is merely much less obvious.

In its own way, the average admits of the cumulative addition which is more usually associated with other aggregates. It is commonplace procedure, wherever the number of individual observations is large, to avoid the pedestrian task of adding individual items by calculating from frequency distributions; yet this procedure will be seen necessarily to involve averaging within each class interval on the basis, not of specific and exact information (which may even be no longer available), but by making some broad assumptions about the distribution of individual values within the class grouping. These assumptions tend to introduce into our calculations a systematic error which even ingenious mathematical manipulations (like "Sheppard's corrections" for example) cannot entirely eliminate.[11] In current economic research, many entities which inspection would show to be themselves averages are then combined into further aggregations or super-averages of which the price-indices are, perhaps, the arch-example. If the process of averaging in any way logically involves a retreat from causally effective specificity, this process of cumulative averaging presents us more and more with a Gordian knot which only the usual drastic surgery, and not mere statistical adjustment, can undo.

[10] Curiously, Yule and Kendall (op. cit., pp. 113-4), appear to base their claim of easy comprehensibility for the average precisely by ignoring this danger; their example of an average income in this connection admittedly assumes an equalizing redistribution (statistically, of course) of income. Cf. also F. A. Hayek, The Counter-Revolution in Science (Glencoe, Ill., 1952), pp. 36-43.

[11] Cf., e.g., R. G. D. Allen, Statistics for Economists (London, 1949), pp. 86-7; J. F. Kenney, Mathematics of Statistics, Part One (New York, 1947) 2nd. ed., p. 78.

2. Averages Are Mental "Constructs"

An average is not an immediate datum of experience but an indirectly apprehended "summary" of the data of perception. In this regard, it seems fair to say that an average is of the form of a proposition,[12] and one whose determinacy may depend, as Marschak points out,[13] on "*a priori* information" in our possession even before we collect the data on which we base it. The immediately apprehended data of experience are relatively independent of concepts and theory; averages are not, but are, rather, *described* fact.[14] An average cannot, therefore, be regarded as a simple aggregation of individual observations; it attempts to summarize and thus necessarily sacrifices a certain measure of realism for the sake of numerical accuracy.[15] The desire for this form of "accuracy" is, of course, part of the age-old conviction in economics that, if we can quantify economic phenomena, we can then formulate "laws" applicable to them; [16] but it has not always been recognized that the requirements of quantification and of the formulation of laws may tend to subordinate the basically individual nature of phenomena—that is, to regard them as merely representative illustrations of laws.[17] Perhaps because of the special significance of differences in the social sciences, the suppression of the individuality of things as scientifically unimportant which Max Weber termed "naturalistic monism in economics" appears to have especially important consequences, among which may be the veneration of averages which we are discussing.[18]

12 Cf. Northrop, *op. cit.*, pp. 35, 39, 247, 261.

13 Cf. Marschak, *op. cit.*, pp. 198-9.

14 Cf. L. Robbins, *An Essay on the Nature and Significance of Economic Science* (London, 1935), 2nd ed., p. 105; C. V. Langlois and C. Seignobos, *Introduction to the Study of History* (London, 1898), p. 218; Hayek, *The Counter-Revolution in Science*, pp. 38-9.

15 Cf. L. von Mises, *Human Action* (New Haven, 1949), pp. 347-54; M. J. Maroney, *Facts from Figures* (Harmondsworth, Middlesex, 1951), p. 43.

16 Cf., e.g., A. Standen, *Science is a Sacred Cow* (New York, 1950), p. 82: "If the idols of scientists were piled on top of one another in the manner of a totem pole, the topmost one would be a grinning fetish called Measurement." Cf. also Hayek, *The Counter-Revolution in Science*, pp. 50-1.

17 Cf. Northrop, *op. cit.*, pp. 241 ff., 268; Kenney, *op. cit.*, p. 81; G. J. Stigler, *Five Lectures on Economic Problems* (New York, 1950), p. 43; R. A. Fisher, *The Design of Experiments* (London, 1937), 2nd ed., pp. 4, 119; C. E. Weatherburn, *A First Course in Mathematical Statistics* (Cambridrge, 1946), p. 30; Maroney, *op. cit.*, p. 37. Hayek points out (*op. cit.*, p. 214, note 45) that the use of mathematics has no necessary connection to the attempts to measure social phenomena, but may be used merely to represent relationships to which numerical values cannot ever be assigned.

18 Cf. Weber, *op. cit.*, pp. 73, 75, esp. 86; Standen, *op. cit.*, pp. 204-6.

In this connection, it is perhaps very important to realize that the average is, in a sense, the denial of the significance of differences and changes.[19] The notion of an average necessarily suppresses, in the dimension averaged, whatever variations or "deviations" there may be among its components; and, even if the *fact* of the individual differences is not deliberately thrown away, those differences, so long as the average substitutes for the original data in further computations, are rendered entirely indeterminate and thus causally inoperative. When we say that the average income of a group of, say, ten families is $4,000, and go on to use this figure in our explanations of economic results, we are implicitly transferring the causative power of the individual incomes which went into that average to a group of ten fictitious families each of which is presumed to have an income of $4,000. Some, indeed, even appear ready to proceed to draw imporant inferences as to the "propensity to consume" of this group as contrasted with that of another group whose average income is, say, $5,000. But it is possibly inconsistent to insist on the consequences of a difference between two averages in this respect while leaving out of account the differences *within* each of them; the latter type may even be the more causally significant of the two. In any event, there may be at least as much economic "force" explained by the fact that, within each group, there may be a very wide range of difference of individual incomes than by the necessarily attenuated differences between averages. If, in the first group in our example, there were 9 families with incomes of $1,000 and one with $31,000, (average: $4,000), and, in the second group, 4 with $11,000 each and 6 with $1,000 each, (average: $5,000), there would conceivably be much more causative "potential" present than is shown in the comparison of the averages. The "average propensity to consume" is thus possibly one of our crasser abuses of the average.

To the extent that economic action is ultimately dependent for explanation on individual differences,[20] the employment of averages puts us out of reach of such explanation simply by understating these differences. For an average, by its nature, can only minimize if not entirely eliminate, differences; it can never magnify them. There is thus no possibility of drawing comfort from any compensating effect of large numbers; for the distortion brought into play by the use of averages cannot, ironically, itself be "averaged out." The

[19] Cf. Mises, *op. cit.*, pp. 223-4, 410-11.
[20] Cf. R. M. MacIver, *Social Causation* (Boston, 1942), pp. 27, 65, 377; Kenney, *op. cit.*, p. 84.

least distortive possibility for an average is neither to minimize nor
magnify—and this only in the case of identical components (in our
example, that of 10 families each with an actual income of $4,000 or
$5,000)—in the very case, in other words, in which the average loses
most, if not all, of its representative usefulness. For the "construct"
of average will be seen on reflection to owe its very existence to
differences; there would be no need or even usefulness in its calculation or use were it not for such differences. The student of statistics
who experiences any surprise whatever in reading that the sum of
deviations from the arithmetic mean always equals zero either
never before really understood the meaning of average or is momentarily dazzled by a new terminology; the statement is merely
tautological—it is true "by construction."

Why any averages, then? Precisely because the individuality of
cases (in the physical as well as the social sciences) has often
proved intractable for those intent on the discovery of exact laws to
describe and predict events.[21] There is a principle of "safety in
numbers" even in science, it appears, and when the unit is recalci-
trant to exact ordering, we retreat into consideration of great masses
of such units and appear to find regularities in their group behavior
to compensate for our frustration vis-a-vis the single unit.[22] And
this, to repeat, is not true of the social sciences alone; [23] the reaction
of modern physics, for instance, to the Heisenberg principle of uncertainty was the recasting of sub-atomic hypothesis along probabilistic lines [24]—and only time will tell whether this turns out to
be a form of mere temporizing, since the methodological, and even
philosophical, implications of this approach have yet to be fully
faced.[25] In our science, the individual economic reality has shown
itself to be even less docile than the single electron; for, while it is at
least possible to posit average behavior for particles which are by
hypothesis identical in structure and unchanging in composition

[21] Cf. Weber, *op. cit.*, p. 119.

[22] Cf. Fisher, *op. cit.*, pp. 45, 225-6; T. C. Koopmans, "The Econometric Approach
to Business Fluctuations," *Amer. Econ. Rev.*, vol. xxxix, May 1949, no. 3, p. 64;
J. A. Schumpeter, "Science and Ideology," *Amer. Econ. Rev.*, vol. xxxix, March 1949,
no. 2, p. 345. See especially Mises, *op. cit.*, pp. 106-17, 396; the distinction here
made between "class" and "case" probability appears to apply pertinently to this
problem.

[23] Cf. P. A. Samuelson, "Economic Theory and Mathematics—An Appraisal," *Amer.
Econ. Rev.*, vol. xlii, May 1952, no. 2, pp. 61-2.

[24] Cf. Northrop, *op. cit.*, pp. 201-12; M. R. Cohen, *Reason and Nature* (Glencoe,
Ill., 1953), 2nd ed., p. 224; K. Pearson, *The Grammar of Science* (London, 1937),
pp. 128-9; MacIver, *op. cit.*, pp. 54, 60 n.

[25] Northrop, *op. cit.*, pp. 343-7.

over time, human action remains undeniably individual and capriciously changeable.[26] Yet it is the same mass analysis to which we have resort; and it is curious that social scientists—with less reason to be—appear much more comfortable in their adoption of the aegis of "large numbers" than are the physicists.[27]

The average is thus part of our response to the elusiveness of economic reality. And what is the price we pay for the elimination of the troublesome differences? One is that these differences are not really eliminated but merely made indeterminate. By extending our use of averages into "distributions" we appear still to have a hold on the differences; we can express a whole "population" with only two parameters: the mean and the standard deviation. Many assure us that a distribution is entirely determinate if only these two parameters are known; yet it is not often pointed out as clearly as it deserves that, in the first place, these are almost never known with any exactitude, but only within degrees of probability or "confidence limits," and, secondly, that within any realistic range of empirical practice, these are much lower scales of probability than obtain in other disciplines. It is not of much use for the proponents of the aggregative statistical approach to remind us that, after all, we know nothing inductively with absolute certainty; we may readily admit this and still be unable to order our economic affairs on the basis of the probabilities *they* offer; we can admit that we can expect night to follow day only with a very high degree of probability and still wish we were just as "uncertain" about market behavior. The inadequacy of current economic statistical inquiry cannot be avoided by simply substituting probability for certainty—where it was true that we were not able to derive laws with any certainty, it is now equally true that we cannot derive them with a sufficiently high degree of probability to be of any practical use. While the difference may be less embarrassing, it is no less real.

Another cost of abandoning research to the frenzied accumulation of averages and other aggregates has been the resulting loss of specificity in our data.[28] An average is indeterminate. Once it is computed, if the component individual items are not retained, it tells no unique story; there are literally an infinite number of constellations of data which might have resulted in this same average

[26] Cf. *ibid.*, pp. 245, 248-9, 261-3; Connolly and Sluckin, *op. cit.*, p. 101; P. A. Samuelson, *Foundations of Economic Analysis*, pp. 21-7; Marschak, *op. cit.*, pp. 190-2.
[27] Cf. *ibid.*, p. 194; Standen, *op. cit.*, pp. 146, 155-6; MacIver, *op. cit.*, p. 263; Wootton, *op. cit.*, pp. 17, 21, 25, 30-1, 34-5.
[28] Cf. Allen, *op.cit.*, p. 17.

figure. It is, therefore, also irreversible. It is impossible to reason back from an average to the original items which formed it; it is freely admitted that there is a "loss of information" involved. But it should be borne constantly in mind that this loss is, on the one hand, irretrievable—we cannot have recourse to averages as we do to logarithms: for ease of computation at the end of which we re-convert to real terms; and, on the other, that the loss may be precisely in the area where we can least afford it—that of particular differentials where economic causality appears to originate.[29] The attractive stability which aggregates, including averages, exhibit in contrast to individual events may thus be purely illusory; this "stability" appears to increase directly with the inclusiveness of totals and may be nothing more than the result of the progressive elimination of significant causative differences. If we average over long enough periods of time, even the business cycle itself will disappear. Therefore, even apart from other shortcomings of averages, there is a point beyond which even their most enthusiastic supporters must beware of going, or risk leaving all meaningfulness behind, regardless of the degree of mathematical sophistication. It is possible that this same phenomenon of loss is significant, though, of course, in minor fashion, in the simplest average; it is undoubtedly so in procedures which compound, out of already complex averages, still larger ones.

3. The "Superiority" of the Mean as a Measure of Location

It is common for texts in statistical method to point out that the mean is, for most purposes, the best of the available measures of "central tendency." This claim of superiority for the mean appears to be based primarily on the often observed phenomenon that it exhibits more stability over a number of samplings than do other measures of location.[30] In practice this stability shows itself in the fact that the means computed from a number of samplings tend to be clustered more closely than is usually the case with either individual observations or with other measures of location, like the median or the mode. Now this proves to be a crucial claim which deserves to be examined closely and critically,[31] since it relates not only to

[29] Cf. Hayek, "The Use of Knowledge in Society," *Amer. Econ. Rev.*, vol. xxxv, September 1945, no. 4, pp. 521-4.

[30] Cf. *ibid.*; also, Hoel, *op. cit.*, pp. 50-1.

[31] In this section is discussed only the descriptive side of this claim; the inferential side will be examined later. Cf. Keynes, *op. cit.*, p. 336; Deming and Birge, *op. cit.*, p. 160.

the average as a tool of description, but, even more importantly, to its use in statistical inference.

One might begin by asking whether the stability or clustering involved here inheres in the subject matter described by the mean or is contributed, partly or wholly, by the measure itself. When we say that the mean is a better measure of central location, are we praising it as a more accurate description of the distribution of the actual variable, or as a construct which, by its very composition, tends to manufacture more central tendency than may possibly inhere in the observations of reality as actually made? The illuminating fact that the means of samples drawn from certain populations show more clustering than the single observations themselves appears to be more indicative of the second possibility than of the first. An interesting further aspect of this phenomenon will be discussed in a later section; here we content ourselves with inquiring into what assumptions, if any, would appear to underlie the presumed superiority of the mean in its *descriptive* aspect.

It is perhaps worthy of note, in this connection, that if we assume a population which is perfectly "normal" in the statistical sense, the purely descriptive superiority of the mean over, say, the mode and the median largely disappears. In such a case, the three measures coincide completely and the mean would offer no descriptive advantage; indeed, since it is somewhat more laborious to compute, quite the reverse would appear to be true. Its sampling (i.e., clustering) superiority would, of course, remain, but this, as we have said, may be extraneously introduced by the very concept of averaging. It is only as we begin to leave "normality" of distribution that the descriptive superiority of the mean asserts itself. Let us see what this implies.

The two salient characteristics of a normal distribution are its symmetry and unimodality. If we consider small departures from normality by introducing some asymmetry into our distribution (but retaining, for the moment, its unimodality), the three measures will cease to coincide. Under this condition, the mode will still describe the most typical value, but will no longer be located at the center of the distribution; the median will no longer fall at the most typical value, but will still indicate the center (though now only of the *number of cases* and not the center of *total value*); the mean will no longer lie at the typical class, nor at the numerical center, but will still indicate, so to speak, the "center of gravity" of the distribution (that is, the total value of the distribution divided by the number of cases). Now, it is clear that each of these measures has retained, according to its nature, a different kind of descriptive centrality; therefore, it is logical to assume that the claim of superiority for the mean must be based on the conviction that it retains the kind of centrality which is deemed most important to accurate description, in this case, namely, the centrality of total value. A little reflection will show that this conviction must, in its turn, be based on some notion of the *additive* nature of the phenomena measured; (and we thus return, by another route, to recognition of the mean as one type of aggregate). But, at least in economics, it is no light matter to assume the additive nature of things; there are many who would deny vigorously, and with impressive arguments, such a possibility in any body of material relating to human valuations. Here, certainly, is an issue which should have been definitively settled before we could proceed to settle upon the average as a favored tool of calculative analysis; yet it was not. Until it is, it is at least permissible for some economists to regard the modal value, since it occurs more frequently in actual experience than a theoretically adjusted, virtual value like the average, as more useful for their field. The argument that the mean is representative of the *whole* distribution (while the mode is not) and can thus enter further algebraic calculation should not deceive us. In the first place, ease of further mathematical treatment is not, by itself, sufficient to justify the average; in the second, the representativeness alluded to may ultimately depend on the unsupported assertion of the additivity of economic phenomena.

If we depart from unimodality as well as from symmetry in distribution, the descriptive value of the mean recedes even further from actual cases and becomes more clearly a purely theoretical symbol whose superior applicability to problems of both description and estimation admittedly diminishes.[32] It turns out, therefore, that the area of superiority of the mean is the relatively narrow one determined by distributions which differ only mildly from complete normality. The scope of this paper does not permit any detailed examination of the important corollary which suggests itself: the question as to the extent to which real economic phenomena naturally arrange themselves in the shape of quasi-normal distributions; this consideration alone would take us far afield into such intricate

[32] Cf. Connolly and Sluckin, *op. cit.*, p. 29; L. Cohen, *op. cit.*, pp. 40, 155; Hoel, *op. cit.*, pp. 50-7. One extreme example is the so-called Cauchy distribution whose theoretical moments are infinite and hence where the median becomes a far better measure of location than the mean.

matters as the theory of probability,[33] the nature of causality and even the nature of reality.[34] For our special purpose here it is perhaps sufficient to recognize that much current research appears to be based on the proposition that near-normal distributions accurately describe many important economic realities. We must therefore cope, in the next two sections, with the possibility that some aspects of this seeming regularity in the statistical material we use may perhaps have been inadvertently introduced by ourselves in the very act of adopting averages as a tool of analysis.

4. *Some Assumptions about Phenomena Implicit in the Use of Averages.*

We have seen that the justification of the use of averages may depend to a great extent on the validity of the assumption that the phenomena so treated are *de natura* usually distributed in a manner more or less approximate of the normal curve.[35] This assumption implies, in turn, a number of propositions about the nature of the average and its components; it is therefore perhaps useful to examine each of these briefly to determine whether or not they appear to be valid, especially in the case of economic data.

(a) *"Continuous" variables.* In any strict sense, a variable cannot actually be perfectly normally distributed if it is of the discontinuous type.[36] As an illustration of this which will again be useful later on, let us consider the well-known convergence of the binomial and normal distributions. The binomial expression often used in the elementary theory of probability as applied to two events is:

$$(p + q)^n$$

[33] Cf., e.g., A. Eddington, *The Philosophy of Physical Science* (New York, 1939), p. 61; Marschak, *op. cit.,* pp. 2-3; C. S. Peirce, "The Doctrine of Necessity Examined," in P. P. Wiener, *op. cit.,* pp. 485-96.

[34] It is virtually impossible to discuss statistical distributions without being led, as most writers are, into probability theory. The works cited here are, of course, no exceptions; cf., e.g., Hoel, *op. cit.,* p. 30; L. Cohen, *op. cit.,* pp. 89-100; Yule and Kendall, *op. cit.,* pp. 207-12, 312, 335-43; Connolly and Sluckin, *op. cit.,* pp. 79, 87-8, 102; Lazarsfeld, *op. cit.* pp. 9, 168, 188, 423; Deming and Birge, *op. cit.,* pp. 131, 137; Fisher, *op. cit.,* p. 19; Kenney, *op. cit.,* p. 131; Weatherburn, *op. cit.,* pp. 34-5; Northrop, *op. cit.,* pp. 210, 218; Samuelson, *Foundations of Economic Analysis,* p. 23. Also see especially H. Poincaré, *Science and Hypothesis* (New York, 1952), ch. XI, pp. 183-210 and *Science and Method* (New York, 1952), pp. 64-6, 74-90, 87-8, 284-8 (both in English transl. by F. Maitland).

[35] Cf. Connolly and Sluckin, *op. cit.,* pp. 70-1; Yule and Kendall, *op. cit.,* pp. 180, 185, 437; Kenney, *op. cit.,* pp. 114-119; Fisher, *op. cit.,* pp. 40-51; Poincaré, *Science and Hypothesis,* pp. 206-7.

[36] Cf., e.g., L. Cohen, *op. cit.,* p. 61; Yule and Kendall, *op. cit.,* p. 176; Keynes, *op. cit.,* pp. 48-9.

The expansion of this binomial, as the exponent n is increased, produces coefficients (of p and q and their intermediate terms) which arrange themselves in a symmetrical and unimodal fashion. The resulting histogram—if one were to draw it to aid visualization—while it approaches the normal distribution [37] as the exponent increases, can never actually become identical with the smooth curve of the statistically-perfect normal distribution because the intervals of the variable n do not, in this case, decrease infinitely; in order to arrive at the normal distribution in this instance it is necessary to imagine n as being able to take any value, no matter how small; in other words, to become a continuous variable. The eminent French mathematician, Henri Poincaré, has generalized the demonstration of this by showing that what leads to this distribution is a property possessed by *any* continuous variable, namely, that its derivatives are limited.[38]

Now, how characteristic of economic phenomena is continuous variability? Are actual prices, production, income, market demand, or any of the other important data continuously variable? Not conceivably; therefore, the normal distribution can only apply to them theoretically (i.e., by a species of conceptual interpolation), and this fact should be carefully borne in mind in assessing the validity of any of the instrumentalities of analysis based on the dimensions of the perfectly normal curve—and that considerable part of statistical inference which depends, through the employment of some types of test of significance, for its validity on the "theory of errors" and other probability distributions should perhaps head the list.

(b) *Independence.* It is an important qualification of the application of the binomial we have been considering to the theory of probability that the events to which it refers be statistically independent; that is, that the occurrence of one have no effect whatever on the possibility of occurrence of others.[39] This is clearly the case when we are dealing with the tossing of a perfect coin or the throwing of perfect dice; but one can reasonably wonder about the cogency of applying this sort of independence to economic, or any other social events. Of how many human actions can we predicate

[37] Cf. Yule and Kendall, *op. cit.*, pp. 171-6; Poincare, *Science and Method*, p. 79; L. Cohen, *op. cit.*, pp. 71-2; Northrop, *op. cit.*, p. 207; Connolly and Sluckin, *op. cit.*, p. 69; Maroney, *op. cit.*, pp. 91, 96, 129.

[38] Poincaré, *Science and Hypothesis*, pp. 193-200; *Science and Method*, pp. 78-84. Cf. also Weatherburn, *op. cit.*, pp. 34-5; R. von Mises, "Causality and Probability," in Wiener, *op. cit.*, pp. 501-4.

[39] Cf. L. Cohen, *op. cit.*, pp. 64-5. For a special feature of the Poisson distribution in this connection, see Maroney, *op. cit.*, pp. 97-100.

the needed statistical independence, even when sampled at random? [40] The study of the social behavior of the individual is ever bringing to light new interrelationships in the economic responses of the gregarious social animal; we thus appear to be going toward the recognition not of less, but actually of more interconnection among social phenomena.[41]

(c) *Mutual exclusiveness.* Another requirement for the binomial is that the events p and q must be mutually exclusive; that the occurrence of both p and q together must be impossible. Again, this quality applies much more clearly to coins and dice than to people and their actions. The statistician may imagine he can satisfy this requirement by merely seeing to the form of his proposition: e.g., A either buys or does not buy. But how often is the real case one of buying less, or buying a substitute, which, when reduced to the terms of this proposition, is equivalent to *both* buy and not-buy. We can easily construct mutually-exclusive semantic categories which satisfy every analytical requirement except the crucial one of corresponding to everyday actualities.

(d) *Exhaustiveness.* Not only is the probability of p in our binomial exclusive of that of q, it is also necessary that, between them, they be exhaustive of the total probability. In the usual mathematical formulation, the entire range of probability is contained from 0 to 1, and what is required of p and q here (or, in the case of a multinomial, of the whole set of terms) is that they must invariably add exactly to unity.[42] Now it is patently impossible for the social scientist even to conceive of all the possibilities in his subject, much less to compute the probability-weight of each of them. And this certainly not for lack of trying; current economic literature gives eloquent, if inconclusive, evidence of heroic attempts to approach all-inclusiveness by the use of "models," or systems of simultaneous equations—a method which appears to be able to explain nothing unless it explains everything. One cannot avoid the impression, in this regard, that economists may have been guilty of trying to arrive directly at the equivalent, in their field, of a Unified

[40] Statistical independence can also be described as "obedience to the multiplication theorem of probability," (cf. Weatherburn, *op. cit.*, pp. 26-7, 81); the distinction made by the latter between "statistical" and "functional" independence does not, I believe, necessarily eliminate the difficulty mentioned in this section. Cf. also Keynes, *op. cit.*, p. 54.

[41] Cf. Marschak, *op. cit.*, pp. 202-4; MacIver, *op. cit.*, pp. 93, 300, 309; Fisher, *op. cit.*, pp. 222-3.

[42] That this applies all the way to the limiting case of a perfectly continuous variable is illustrated by the similar equating to unity of the area under the normal curve; (cf., e.g., Maroney, *op. cit.*, p. 113).

Field Theory without yet having formulated the component laws of gravitation and of electro-magnetism. We can readily admit that there is, after all, no science like omniscience and yet question the practical value of this approach as an avenue of knowledge for mortal man.[43]

(e) *Homogeneity.* It is a consequence of the additive implications of the average that the items entering it be homogeneous, or "of the same genus."[44] This requirement assumes greater importance, indeed insistence, in measure as we are engaged—as is currently frequently the case—in *compounding* averages without always fully assessing their comparability; for most economic statistics are what R.G.D. Allen has called[45] "mixed bags" of heterogeneous items, whose claim to any homogeneity is either partial or contrived or both. In this regard, the statistical analyst must constantly guard against gross misinterpretation of the scope of his measurements; for a person of "average" income may be average in nothing else and, as we have seen, may be very far from typical even in that. Moreover, where data spanning an appreciable interval of time are concerned, certainty of homogeneity requires checking to exclude the possibility that any of those directly unobservable variations which have been termed "structural changes"[46] have entered to vitiate any real comparability of data. Consequently, the homogeneity requisite for valid quantification of economic data is, or should be, one of the most discouraging obstacles to mathematical analysis in economics.[47] One is never sure, for example, whether the prices (probably the most frequently used numerical quantities in our field) paid by different individuals, or by the same individual at different times, really differ by more or by less than their ratio seems to indicate, since the unit in which they are expressed is itself the object of varying individual appreciation. An average made up of prices with different valuation-meanings would have only a

[43] Cf. Hayek, "The Use of Knowledge in Society," *Amer. Econ. Rev.*, vol. xxxv, September 1945, no. 4, p. 521.

[44] Cf. Maroney, *op. cit.*, p. 35.

[45] *Op. cit.*, p. 19.

[46] Cf. T. C. Koopmans, ed., *Statistical Inference in Dynamic Economic Models* (New York, 1950), p. 266; A. G. Hart, "Model-building and Fiscal Policy," *Amer, Econ. Rev.*, vol. xxxv, September 1945, no. 4, p. 538; P. A. Samuelson, *Foundations of Economic Analysis*, pp. 354-5; L. Cohen, *op. cit.*, pp. 131-2; A. Marshall, *Principles of Economics* (New York, 1925) 8th ed., pp. 36-7.

[47] The instantaneous or timeless character of mathematics has no "passage" or duration and cannot represent, in its equations, the irreversibility of time; (cf. Mac-Iver, *op. cit.*, pp. 66-7). Cf. also Koopmans, *op. cit.*, p. 3; Samuelson, *op. cit.*, p. 4; and L. von Mises, *op. cit.*, p. 56.

superficial homogeneity and therefore dubious validity.[48] This may very possibly be one reason for the puzzling inability of even the most elaborately devised price-index to furnish us a coefficient which can then be exactly and meaningfully applied to the very same individual data out of which the index itself was computed.

5. The Average is a "Multiplier"

It is commonly thought that one of the clear advantages of the average is that it summarizes the information of many individual observations into the relatively brief compass of a single representative figure. In one sense this is undoubtedly true; where there were previously a number of items there appears now to be only one— and we have discussed some of the implications of the descriptive power of this "single" figure. Yet a curious fact emerges if we start with a finite number of actual observations and then consider the total number of possible averages which this finite number of items can produce. It is that, for any number of original observations in excess of two, the total number of averages possible: (a) exceeds the number of original items, and (b) rapidly outdistances the latter as these increase in number. Ordinarily, since we tend to regard the number of averageable events to be infinite, or at least indefinite,[49] this aspect of the matter is not apparent and we are likely to go on unquestioningly accepting the average as a distillation or summarization of information. (The concept of infinity, necessarily vague and elusive for us, is a poor frame of reference for our finite minds and experience; a larger finite number is, for instance, not perceptibly any nearer to infinity than a smaller, and the deduction that it is will be found to be based on a comparison of the finite numbers with each other and not with infinity.) Let us therefore, in the following discussion, consider only a finite and definite number of events or observations, say ten, and, in order to avoid any unintended numerical connotations, let us further designate these ten by $A, B, C, \ldots J$.

Now, how can we determine the number of averages which these

[48] Cf. Marschak, op. cit., p. 175; Northrop, op. cit., pp. 33, 239-43.

[49] Cf. Yule and Kendall, op. cit., p. 333. On the resort to probability analysis as a method of dealing with what we are ultimately ignorant of, cf. Poincaré, Science and Hypothesis, pp. 184-5, 189-90, 208-9; and Science and Method, pp. 64-5, 87-90, 284-8. Further, reasoning from probability—and tests of significance based upon it —may have only a permissive force; cf. Connolly and Sluckin, op. cit., pp. 87-8, 102, 153-5; L. Cohen, op. cit., pp. 89-99; Yule and Kendall, op. cit., pp. 207-12, 312, 335, 423, 437; Lazarsfeld, op. cit., pp. 9, 168, 188, 423; Deming and Birge, op. cit., pp. 131, 137 ff; Fisher, op. cit., p. 19; Maroney, op. cit., pp. 219-20.

ten make possible? Here the mathematical theory of combinations comes readily to our aid;[50] according to this principle, the total number of combinations, C_r^n, of n things taken r at a time is:

$$C_r^n = \frac{n!}{r!(n-r)!}$$

Now, n things can variously be taken 0, or 1, or 2 . . . or n at a time, so that by simply solving the above formula successively for $r = 0, 1, 2, \ldots n$ and adding the results will give us the total number of possible combinations. In our example, in which n was taken to be 10, the results can most graphically be shown by reference to the famous Pascal triangle:

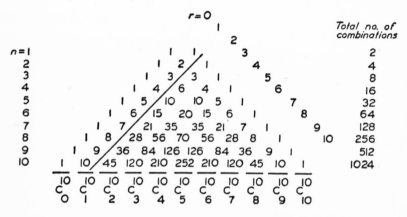

Entered below the last line (that corresponding to our example of ten items) are the symbols indicating, respectively, 10 things taken 0 at a time (C_0^{10}), 1 at a time (C_1^{10}), and so on to 10 at a time (C_{10}^{10}). The number directly above each of these symbols and along the line $n = 10$ indicates the number of different combinations possible in each case.

The first and second diagonal columns along the left side of the triangle will be seen to relate to the cases $r = 0$ and $r = 1$ respectively (that is, to things taken O and 1 at a time). Since neither of these types of combination can be considered an average, we have, for our purpose, excluded them by drawing a line between them

[50] This is on the supposition that the *order* of the events is not a factor; (cf., e.g., Hoel, *op. cit.*, p. 293). If the order of events entering the average were germane (as it very possibly could be in economics), we would have to deal not with "combinations," but with "permutations"—an even more numerous group.

and the rest of the triangle, the latter representing the whole gamut of combinations which can properly be considered as averages. Moreover, since the $r = 0$ column gives the value of unity throughout and the $r = 1$ column a value equal in each instance to the corresponding value of n, we can easily adapt the above formula for the total number of combinations so as to give us the total number of *averages*, (A_r^n):

$$A_r^n = \frac{n!}{r!(n-r)!} - (n+1).$$

Tabulating these results as n is increased from 1 to 10:

No. of events (n):	1	2	3	4	5	6	7	8	9	10
Total no. combinations (ΣC_r^n):	2	4	8	16	32	64	128	256	512	1024
Total no. averages (ΣA_r^n):	0	1	4	11	26	57	120	247	502	1013

Inspection of the progression of the total number of combinations shows that this figure is a function of n:

$$\Sigma C_r^n = 2^n;$$

as is, too, the total possible number of averages:

$$\Sigma A_r^n = 2^n - (n+1).$$

It is clear that the total number of averages it is possible to form out of a given number of items increases at a rate only slightly less than the number 2 raised to a power equal to the number of items. A glance at our tabulation shows that even for the relatively small number of components in our example (10) the number of possible averages has already exceeded 10^3. It is therefore not necessary to go beyond our very modest example to see the steeply multiplicative effect of averaging. Not only are averages, therefore, theoretical constructs and not data of experience, but they are also increasingly more numerous than the items of which they are usually presumed to be summaries. Here, perhaps, is loss of information of another sort; so that if, for example, we are given a set of five averages (still within the ten ultimate items of our example) we have, in one sense, much less of the total picture (5/1023) than we have if we are given five actual observations (5/10).

But it is a central part of much statistical inference that averages tend to cluster much more closely than do single observations themselves.[51] How can we account for this in the face of the multiplicative tendency just discussed? A brief examination of our Pascal triangle will show that the multiplicity of combinations, far from being evenly distributed, are heavily concentrated about the point $r = n/2$ as a center. This concentration is such that at $n = 10$ the three middle classes of combinations include well over half of all the possible combinations for that interval. It is, perhaps, especially worth noting that this triangle reports nothing other than the coefficients of expansion of our old friend the binomial

$$(p + q)^n$$

as n increases. The relation of the concentration of averages to the approximation of the normal curve appears, in consequence, to become a little clearer. Averaging does not simply multiply cases; it multiplies them according to a principle which progressively approximates the normal curve. It is therefore not a wondrous quality of *phenomena* that their averages cluster; it is something we may have extraneously introduced by the very act of applying the average to their measurement. For in admitting averages and their greater multiplicity we have also admitted a great deal of concentrated overlapping or repetition. If we take as a crude measure of this overlapping the number of times any same single item (say, A of our original $A, B, \ldots J$), plus the number of times each double (e.g., AB), plus the number of times each triple (e.g., ABC), and so on, are repeated within the total of combinations shown in our triangle, it can be shown by calculation with which we shall not further impose on the reader, that the greatest degree of overlap lies at the center of the average-size and decreases symmetrically on either side of it. Taking the last row of our triangle (i.e., at $n = 10$), and restricting ourselves to those combinations which can qualify as averages (i.e., from $r = 2$ to $r = 10$), and noting below each the total number of "repetitions" (singles, doubles, etc.) as described above, we have:

	$^{10}C_2$	$^{10}C_3$	$^{10}C_4$	$^{10}C_5$	$^{10}C_6$	$^{10}C_7$	$^{10}C_8$	$^{10}C_9$	$^{10}C_{10}$
No. of averages:	45	120	210	252	210	120	45	10	1
Total no. "repetitions":	10	45	120	210	252	210	120	45	10

Enough has perhaps been said to show that when it is pointed out by statistical workers that sample means approximate the normal

[51] Cf. Yule and Kendall, *op. cit.*, pp. 382-7; 434-7; L. Cohen, *op. cit.*, pp. 87-90; Connolly and Sluckin, *op. cit.*, pp. 28, 81-5, 92-3; Deming and Birge, *op. cit.*, p. 123; Weatherburn, *op. cit.*, pp. 119-25; Allen, *op. cit.*, p. 117; Keynes, *op. cit.*, pp. 337-66.

distribution even if the observations themselves are skewed, what they may be saying is, in effect, that the semblance of symmetry can be introduced into non-normal distributions[52] by applying to the latter a device which has a built-in tendency to multiply differentially so as to lend centrality and unimodality to the data.

6. Averages, Aggregates and Public Policy

We have seen that it is characteristic of averages and other aggregates (1) that they tend to suppress individual differences and actual typicalness[53] for the sake of quantification or "summarization," and (2) that they represent, in economics as elsewhere in science, an attempt to deal with phenomena in the mass. In part, this latter is a reaction to the inability to deal, with any degree of certainty, with individual events and represents a compromise with epistemological difficulties.[54] Being unable to paint in clearly the details of our picture, we appear to have been content to back away from it by adopting the use of mass analysis and, further, to squint at reality through the half-closed lids of probabilistic reasoning.[55] Methods like these will make even a poor painting look good—but only so long as we neither come closer nor open our eyes. Ultimately, however, all will have to be judged in clear light and at close range; whatever we may do to disguise it, economic reality remains distressingly individual and particular. Moreover, it is unfortunately not yet widely enough appreciated—even by some scientists—that to adopt a probabilistic explanation of phenomena is tantamount to the flat denial of causality.

But in part, too, the current resort to aggregates of all kinds is a facet of our hastening approach to central control as an ideal in economic affairs. Bureaucracy requires classification of economic fact into relatively few broad bands of manageable "homogeneity"; it abhors differences because it simply cannot operate in a field of bewildering individual complexity. In a sense, Socialism itself can be defined as the political form of central tendency;[56] it uses the

[52] Cf. Hoel, op. cit., pp. 103-5; Maroney, op. cit., pp. 94, 135-40.
[53] Cf., e.g., Weber, op. cit., pp. 100-1; Fisher, op. cit., pp. 45, 225-6.
[54] Cf. L. von Mises, op. cit., pp. 39, 47, 57, 64, 86, passim.
[55] Cf. Hoel, op. cit., pp. 15, 29-30; Northrop, op. cit., pp. 210 ff. One part of this has been the resort to randomness and the related assumption of the equiprobability of whatever is not known; cf. Fisher, op. cit., pp. 23 ff; Poincaré, Science and Method, pp. 9-10, 66, 74-5, 80-1; Koopmans, op. cit., pp. 2-6; Connolly and Sluckin, op. cit., p. 79; Samuelson, op. cit., p. 23; Keynes, op. cit., pp. 7-15, 21-4, 42-4, 61-4.
[56] Cf. Northrop, op. cit., p. 355.

concept of average not only as a means of computation but also as an end. In the fully developed ideal socialist state the "average" individual will no longer be a statistical device of the sort discussed here, but an accurate description of every actual individual.[57] This accuracy, however, will not have been attained by the refinement of descriptive method so as to fit actuality better, but actually the reverse. The aggregative approach in economics suits this program very well. The word "average" even etymologically betrays its redistributive reference—in this case specifically the redistribution of losses of cargo in transit.[58] And our contemporary treatment of whole aggregates like "income," "wages," "capital" and the like is implicitly in the same vein. Within each of these aggregates lie innumerable functioning differences which have been merely suppressed by classification.[59] It is one thing to use these aggregates as a rough summary measure of past social and economic outcomes; it is quite another to regard them as causally operative upon one another.[60] Yet this appears to be what we are doing, and in no small measure as a result of the confusion as to the limitations of statistical devices in wide use. Our concern in this section is specifically with the average and with the somewhat desperate claim made by some that it is indispensable for the operation of controls in effecting public policy.[61] But this is a tenuous argument: one should be free to question the desirability of central planning and control—and therefore to point out that we cannot submerge the moral falsity of the assertion that the ends justify the means by the simple expedient of making the latter geometric or harmonic.

[57] Cf. K. Marx, *Capital* (New York, n.d.), Modern Library edition, p. 22; Samuelson, *op. cit.*, p. 223; Hayek, *The Counter-Revolution in Science*, pp. 53-63; L. von Mises, *op. cit.*, pp. 257, 697-9, 706-11.

[58] Cf. Maroney, *op. cit.*, p. 34.

[59] Cf. A. N. Whitehead, *An Introduction to Mathematics* (New York, 1948), p. 32 ff; Keynes, *op. cit.*, pp. 328-9. For a very recent and rather extreme example of faith in classification as the road to knowledge in economics, see E. C. Harwood, *Reconstruction of Economics* (Great Barrington, Mass., 1955), pp. 8-9; Mr. Harwood finds great comfort in the identification of "knowing" with the "naming transaction" as made by John Dewey and A. F. Bentley (*Knowing and the Known*, Boston, 1949, p. 296), and while he admits that ". . . nothing just said enables economists or anyone else to use the word 'knowledge' for the purpose of specifying (scientifically naming) anything in particular.", he nevertheless asserts that, as a result of this approach, ". . . the economists can at least climb down their various trees of 'knowledge' and survey the relatively firm ground of knowing and the known." [One hastens to add that they had been in the trees for epistemological rather than atavistic reasons.]

[60] Cf., e.g., Samuelson, *op. cit.*, pp. 9, 99, 118, 223-7, 351-2; Connolly and Sluckin, *op. cit.*, pp. 118-35.

[61] For some very optimistic expectations expressed by writers on statistics in this regard, cf. Kenney, *op. cit.*, p. 2. Cf. also, Yule and Kendall, *op. cit.*, p. 206.

XII

The Inferiority Complex
of the Social Sciences

by FRITZ MACHLUP

I$_T$ IS said and repeated over and over again that the social sciences are so very young, relatively speaking. Why is it that social scientists insist on this as a statement of fact and why do they consider it worth-while repeating?

The habit of not-so-very-young women of understating their age and emphasizing their youthfulness probably rests on the observation that, as a rule, younger women are regarded as more eligible, desirable and attractive, partly because from some point on beauty is a decreasing function of age, partly because inexperience and innocence are associated with youth and are highly valued by many men. This, however, is not a helpful analogy for us. Innocence, inexperience, beauty—these are surely not the attributes which social scientists wish to claim for their subjects as means of attracting more followers and admirers.

Another analogy may come closer to an explanation. Very young children are forgiven when they misbehave and do silly things. Perhaps social scientists wish to claim this privilege of childhood in order to secure the indulgence of the adult world; as if they were saying: "Pardon us for being so dumb, but we are still so very young." By implication they seem to promise: "Wait till we grow up, wait just a few hundred years, then you will see how smart we shall be." In any case, apparently, while they are children they should be accorded the privilege of being silly; after all, children do not know what they are doing.

The closest analogy, in my opinion, is the well-known apology of many people in games and in sports, trying to account for their awkwardness and clumsiness. If they admit that they are old practitioners of the game or sport, their poor performance may be attributed to lack of intelligence or talent; but for "novices" they are not doing so badly. Thus, "Excuse me, I am just a beginner," is an often-heard apology from participants in sports and games who have a feeling of inferiority. This is what is probably behind the social scientists' pronouncements emphasizing how young the social sciences really are: "Please do not think we are stupid; we are merely beginners."

Only those who feel that their accomplishments are unsatisfactory and inferior to those of others have a reason to point to the fact that they are relatively new at their business and thus should not be expected to be any better than they are. Whether or not they actually are poor performers is not of the essence: an inferiority complex may or may not be justified by some "objective" standards. It is the *feeling* of inferiority which makes the sufferers over-apologetic, excessively aggressive, or looking for other sorts of compensations.

The trouble with the protestations by social scientists is that their story about their "young" science is not true. We have only to open our text-books on the history of social theory, political science, or economics to find that we have no right to engage in that baby talk about being mere children, or in those novices' excuses of being mere beginners. Our subjects are as old as any; the scholars and writers in classical Greece had as much interest in problems of society as in problems of the physical world, and their achievements in the former are not less than those in the latter.

But the social science "youngsters" or "beginners" will quickly protest against my reference to our ancient predecessors and will proclaim: "What they did must not be called 'science'! Only recently has social thought become social *science*." Such pronouncements force me to return to the analogy of the "beginner" in sports. When I once heard the familiar "I am just a beginner" from a ski bunny whom I had seen snow-plowing many years before, I was impolite enough to remind her of it. But undaunted she said: "Oh, that does not count! That was not the right technique; you cannot call it skiing!"

This is precisely the line these perennial beginners, the social scientists, are trying to sell: "Oh, what all these people, long ago, were doing was not the right scientific method, you cannot call it

Social Science!" I do not buy this line about the "right method" and want to warn against it. The old students of society used whatever method they believed was right and expedient, and they thought—2500 years ago, 2000, 1000, 200 years ago—that they had succeeded in acquiring more knowledge, and more accurate knowledge, about human action than the man-in-the-street had. That should make them social scientists in no less "good standing" than anybody who uses the most fashionable methods of our day.[1]

That the old scholars engaging in the study of society did not call themselves "social scientists" is surely irrelevant. Until recently their subjects were part of "moral philosophy," just as physics was part of "natural philosophy." The fact that Newton and his contemporaries considered his work as natural philosophy does not prevent us from calling him a physicist (although he also wrote much on philosophy and theology and believed that his contributions to these subjects were of major importance). It is not by what *name* it was called, nor by what *method* was used, nor by what *success* was had from the point of view of posterity that we should judge whether a certain body of knowledge at some time past was "science." Knowledge is "scientific" if it is impartial, systematic, and more complete or more accurate than "popular" knowledge at the time. The fact that in the course of the last hundred years several writers have proposed rather narrow definitions of "science"—restricted in terms of particular subject matters or particular methods—and were allowed to get away with these restrictive definitions, has caused anguish to many social scientists. If the restriction had always been in terms of *subject matter* and had excluded social phenomena once and for all, less serious harm would have followed [2] —because the study of society could do nothing to "qualify" for the title of "science." But many of the restrictions were in terms of particular *methods* and this created an ambition on the part of social scientists to earn the right to the honorific title by adopting as

---

1 "We cannot refuse the name *science* to logic or to the non-quantitative branches of mathematics . . . etc. Nor is there good reason for refusing the adjective *scientific* to such works as Aristotle's *Politics* or Spinoza's *Ethics* and applying it to statistical 'investigations' or 'researches' that do not advance the understanding of anything." Morris R. Cohen, *Reason and Nature: An Essay on the Meaning of Scientific Method* (Glencoe, Ill.: Free Press, 1953), p. 89.

2 Of course, there are so many connections between physical nature and social phenomena, that a division of disciplines as "sciences" as far as they relate to "nature" and "non-scientific studies" as far as they relate to "human action" would be rather silly. Just think of physical and cultural anthropology, of physical and human geography, of physiological and social psychology.

far as possible, and even farther, the methods that were elected as the definitional characteristics of "Science."

It is in terms of some of these restrictive definitions that the social sciences are deemed to be so very young. Those who insist that a science must be a system of deductions inferred from a small number of axioms or postulates will date the birth of economic science with the publication of Ricardo's *Principles* and will reject the scientific character of political science, sociology and most other social disciplines. Those who insist that a science must be exclusively based on a series of inductions from a large number of exact observations and precise measurements of objectively discerned phenomena, will date the science of sociology as a rather recent creation and will reject the scientific character of economics, political science and most other disciplines commonly counted among the social sciences. These are only two of a large number of definitional restrictions. When in a recent textbook on the methodology of social science the author states that "If we are honest we have to admit that the *first century* of social science has left us somewhere short of victory,"[3] we can infer that he proclaims Auguste Comte as the progenitor of social science and accepts his method of "positivism" as the essential criterion of "science."

Perhaps it ought to be said that there exists no method-oriented definition of science under which all parts and sections of physics, chemistry, biology, geology and other generally recognized natural sciences could qualify as "sciences." Definitions of science which stress the theoretical *system,* the network of logically interrelated hypotheses using mental constructions of ideal exactness, undoubtedly exclude large parts of chemistry and biology. Definitions stressing repeatable experiments and verified predictions clearly exclude the parts of biology, geology and cosmology which deal with the evolution of life, of the earth and of the universe. And even within physics—the discipline which is the science *par excellence* because most definitions of science were formulated with physics in mind as *the* model—the authorities are by no means agreed as to whether the deductive system or the inductive technique constitutes its scientific nature.[4]

It would be interesting to catalogue the definitions of science

[3] John Madge, *The Tools of Social Science* (New York: Longmans, Green & Co., 1953), p. 290. (*Italics supplied.*)

[4] For an exposition of the former view see Henry Margenau, *The Nature of Physical Reality: A Philosophy of Modern Physics* (New York: McGraw-Hill, 1950). For an expression of the latter view see P. W. Bridgman, *The Logic of Modern Physics* (New York: Macmillan, 1927).

proposed or adopted by writers in different fields or in specialized branches of larger disciplines. They all formulate the specific characteristics in such a way that their own kind of work would still qualify as "scientific," while they have little concern, if not undisguised scorn, for fellow workers in their own discipline, in cognate fields, or in fields with which they are entirely unfamiliar. Many a scholar thus excluded from the honorary fraternity of "true scientists" suffers from severe frustrations and develops an inferiority complex, or aggravates the one he had to begin with. In defense against the humiliating "rejection" he either tries to change the definition of science [5] by enlarging the extension of "scientific method" just enough to have his own particular working techniques covered or he adopts working techniques which, however unsuitable to the subject matter or problems under investigation, are safely approved, or can somehow be represented, as "scientific."

A mere enumeration of the subjects now customarily regarded as social sciences will suffice to make it clear that a demand that they follow the same methods (let alone, the same method) is entirely impractical, if not fantastic. The list includes Sociology, Cultural Anthropology, Social Psychology, Human Geography, Demography and Population Theory, Ethnography and Ethnology, Political Science, Economics, History, International Studies. This list is incomplete and overcomplete, depending on whether particular fields are granted "autonomy." [6] Moreover, it can easily be shown that many

[5] An analysis of the attitude of German social scientists may well show that their inferiority complexes are relatively smaller than those of their Anglo-American colleagues. For they do not suffer from frustrations resulting from restrictive definitions of science. The German *Wissenschaft* cannot meaningfully be restricted to exclude any kind of scholarly inquiry, be it in the social sciences, the humanities, philosophy, or jurisprudence. When a lawyer writes an article for a law review he writes a scientific paper (*Wissenschaftliche Arbeit*); and the historians of literature, the philologists, the philosophers, the mathematicians, the sociologists, they all are scientists (*Wissenschaftler*) no less and no more than the physicists and biologists. Feeling secure in their title and status as scientists, they do not have to "assert themselves" as scientists and do not have to show off with working techniques unsuited to their work but "acceptable" under some restictive definition of science. This is not to say that German scholars or German social scientists are free from inferiority complexes—yet one source at least is removed.

[6] Sociology, for example, may be given a larger scope so that it may comprise some of the other subjects enumerated; or its scope may be narrowed so that other subjects, such as criminology, become independent. International Studies, which merely emphasize the international aspects of political science, economics, geography, and history, have recently been granted autonomy in many university curricula. History, customarily listed among the social sciences, is sometimes regarded instead as a "method" of social science and sometimes as an "application" of social sciences; again, there are those who insist on excluding it entirely from the social sciences, grouping it with "humanistic studies" (or cultural sciences).

of the supposedly separate fields are largely interdependent. Finally, most of the subjects call for several approaches, descriptive, historical, statistical, and theoretical, which have to be skillfully integrated in the application to concrete problems. An insistence on the use of "the" scientific method for all would be nonsensical.

What is really meant by "the" scientific method? In its narrowest sense, scientific method is supposed to mean *experimental* method, or the demand that every proposition be "verified" by repeated laboratory experiments with strict controls of all conditions. In a wider sense, scientific method is supposed to mean *statistical* method, or the demand that every proposition be "verified" by numerous sets of statistical data relating to sufficiently comparable situations. If no wider extension of the definition is conceded and if no proposition is deemed "scientifically" acceptable unless it is confirmed by such scientific method—alas, only a *minute* fraction of all propositions about human action in society would be acceptable, and only the most *insignificant* propositions at that. Needless to say, all sorts of additional concessions are proposed in order to accommodate other kinds of scientific inquiry. But there is no epistemologically defensible borderline short of the widest meaning of scientific method, defined in the *Encyclopedia Brittanica* as "any mode of investigation by which impartial and systematic knowledge is acquired." Such largess would give away any pretensions by which one scholar may assert superiority over another on grounds of the purity and sanctity of his method; it would remove any need for feelings of guilt or inferiority on the part of scholars who ably and diligently add to our store of knowledge by inquiries which are neither experimental, nor statistical, nor quantitative, nor of predictive usefulness. But this largess in the meaning of scientific method is not widely accepted and we must continue to labor under the restrictive definitions and to bear the consequences of the inferiority complex of the social sciences.

These consequences or manifestations of the inferiority complex of the social sciences are chiefly in the form of scientistic [7] compensations. Some of them are old and may yield to treatment; for some more recently observed forms no cures have as yet been developed. Some, though satisfactorily described have not even been given

---

[7] This expression, introduced though not coined by F. A. Hayek, is almost self-explanatory: It expresses the desire of an investigator of social phenomena to apply in his studies methods found useful in the natural sciences however ill-adapted for his own purposes. See F. A. Hayek, *The Counter-Revolution of Science: Studies on the Abuse of Reason* (Glencoe, Ill.: Free Press, 1952), p. 15. The present paper owes much to Hayek's essay.

technical names, and I shall have to propose nomenclature. Although there are probably several more, we shall deal here only with the following: (1) Historicism, (2) Institutionalism, (3) Holism, (4) Behaviorism, (5) Operationism, (6) Metromania, (7) Predictionism, (8) Prescriptionism, (9) Mathematosis, and (10) Experimentomania. Needless to say, most of the afflicted will not recognize their attitudes as aberrations in any sense, but will insist that they, and they alone, have the right insights and all others are "unscientific."

Before I attempt to formulate the briefest possible statements of the symptoms and manifestations of these conditions, it may be well, in order to avoid even temporary misunderstandings, to anticipate here in the form of examples some explanations that will later be given in greater detail. A historian need not be a historicist—indeed, few historians are—and, moreover, even a fanatic historicist may be an excellent historian. Scholars engaged in social statistics, quantitative economics, econometrics, mathematical economics, or mathematical analysis in the other social sciences—however exclusively their interests may be in quantitative and numerical research and analysis—may be far removed from the attitudes characterized as metromania and mathematosis; and even some who are afflicted may produce useful results. Thus, their work is not in question here. What I find unhealthy in the ten listed attitudes or beliefs is, above all, the attempt to urge certain methods on others in the name of "science" and to disparage the research of others, not perhaps because their arguments or findings are fallacious, self-contradictory, or contradicted by evidence, but because they fail to employ the method claimed to be the only "scientific" one.

Historicism insists on the accumulation of historical facts as the only legitimate beginning and as the sole basis of social research; on the prohibition of the use of theory in the interpretation of past events, though sometimes admitting that theories might eventually be distilled from large masses of historical data; but the validity (not merely applicability) of any such theories will be strictly limited as to time and place. What laboratory experiments are to the natural sciences historical research is to the social sciences: just as the experimental method is required in the study of nature, the "historical method" is required in the study of society and makes it "scientific." Pure theory is useless speculation, sheer metaphysics; history is the scientific method of the social sciences.

Institutionalism, sharing with historicism the view that social theory cannot be general theory and is neither "perpetual" nor "cosmopolitan," holds that human attitudes, objectives, and organizations —all called "institutions"—are subject to human control and, hence, must not be taken as fundamental assumptions in the analysis of human action; instead, social sciences must concentrate on factual descriptions of the institutions and their evolution; thus they will be based on facts rather than on speculation and preconceptions.

Holism (derived from "the whole" rather than "the holy") takes several forms; one insisting on the notion that the whole is prior (logically and historically) to its parts and that, therefore, the study of society must start with the "social wholes" or collectives—the nation, the community, the market, etc.,—rather than with the individual and some of his motivations and actions; another insisting that different aspects of human action should not be separated in analysis, but that social conduct and organization should be studied realistically and "as a whole." To start with the individual and to isolate particular aspects of his actions is held to be unrealistic speculation, whereas the observation of the undissected whole will permit scientific social research.

Behaviorism insists on confining social sciences (as well as psychology *per se*) to the establishment of regularities in the physical behavior of man under strictly controlled conditions. All interpretation of human action on the basis of introspective insights or in terms of mental constructions, postulating the existence of motivations or preferences, is rejected as speculative; in order to be scientifically sound research must be restricted to objectively discernible facts, observable and describable in physical terms.

Operationism (or operationalism) insists on the exclusive use of so-called operational concepts in scientific discourse; that is, all concepts must be defined in terms of operations, chiefly physical operations of the scientific observers. Mental constructs without operational counterparts—idealized concepts—are either rejected outright or only temporarily admitted on the expectation that they will soon be replaced by operational concepts. "Conceivably operational" concepts are sometimes, in exceptional cases and only grudgingly, condoned for want of "practically operational" concepts. As a concession it was (somewhat inconsistently) proposed to admit "mental operations" besides physical operations, but this was not widely accepted since it would open the door to metaphysical speculation.[8]

---

[8] Operationalism has been urged upon both natural and social sciences. In the social sciences, behaviorists are perhaps the truest observers of operationalism.

Metromania, stemming from a fixation on the dogma that "science is measurement," [9] takes the form of attempts to measure everything however faintly connected with the subject under investigation and to imagine the resulting figures to be relevant, and of urgent claims that any proposition not amenable to quantitative verification be rejected as "unscientific." The questions of the stability of computed numerical relations and of their historical relativity are usually ignored and ever new statistical figures for different or longer time intervals are produced in order to devise "corrected" parameters or coefficients "explaining" the measured magnitudes of social reality.

Predictionism, impressed by the success of natural scientists in predicting the outcome of controlled laboratory experiments, sees the sole purpose and justification of scientific inquiry in the formulation of propositions instrumental in successful predictions of events in the real world, including the social world in which only few relevant factors can be controlled or even reliably ascertained, let alone measured. Generalizations of merely explanatory, not predictive, usefulness are rejected as speculative.

Prescriptionism insists, in emulation of the great practical achievements of the physical sciences, on practical usefulness of the findings of research in the social sciences; it demands their use in devising improved social institutions and, especially, in economic organization that satisfies the needs of mankind substantially better than the present one; embracing the dogma *"savoir pour prévoir pour pourvoir,"* [10] it denounces pure theory as apology of the *status quo* and, in the name of "science," calls for action to carry out the prescriptions. These are usually for social control of economic life either on the basis of "scientific socialism" or by governmental planning and interventions.[11]

Mathematosis is the urge, incited by admiration of the paramount use of mathematics in the physical sciences, to employ higher mathematics in expressing propositions that could equally well be expressed in ordinary language. Purely "literary" arguments are

---

Another expression of operationalism in the social sciences is the demand that social scientists employ only statistically measurable concepts.

[9] Lord Kelvin.

[10] Auguste Comte. The teachings of certain brands of pragmatism are also invoked by prescriptionists.

[11] What distinguishes prescriptionism from controlism, interventionism, socialism and other programs of economic policy is its appeal to "science." It urges these practical applications of scientific findings as the *raison d'être* of science, as a requirement of the true scientific spirit.

scorned, and ideas or problems not reducible to mathematical formulation are suspected of being "metaphysical" or "pseudo-problems."

Experimentomania combines the firm conviction that practical experiments alone are "scientific" with the illusion that social research will eventually be "solidly" founded on practical experiments under strictest controls; all present research techniques are regarded as preparations for eventual experimental research, and research problems are invented that are immediately amenable to laboratory techniques even if they are of little relevance to any hypotheses significant in the systems thus far employed in the various social sciences.

All these attitudes, beliefs, and ambitions use the flag of "true science" as a means for gaining support and allegiance and for combatting the non-believers. Their own method is the best—not perhaps because it has proved particularly fruitful and has yielded results not obtained by other methods—but because it is the only "truly scientific" one. All other methods ought to be rejected—not perhaps because they have not been instrumental in producing or confirming knowledge or insights—but because they are "not scientific."

There is at least one other notion that the described attitudes, beliefs, ambitions have in common. The social scientists who display them are apparently ashamed of the one thing that really distinguishes social sciences from natural sciences, namely, the fact that *the student of human action is himself an acting human being* and therefore has at his command a source of knowledge unavailable to the student of the phenomena of nature. The student of atoms, electrons, magnetic fields, enzymes, genes, etc., is himself none of these things and has no immediate experience of them, whereas the student of human thinking and acting is a thinking and acting human being and knows a good deal about the subject of his inquiries before he starts inquiring. The close and unbreakable link between pre-scientific everyday knowledge and scientific knowledge about the subject matter of social sciences is both an aid and a burden. It is an aid in that it furnishes the social scientist with an initial stock of experiences, working hypotheses, and interpretations of fundamental importance. It is a burden in that it saddles him with the obligation to work with constructs that are understandable to him and his fellow men in terms of their everyday experiences; that is to say, he is under the obligation to make his scientific constructs correspond in all relevant respects to the constructs that are used in everyday life in the common-sense interpretation of our fellow men's actions.[12]

Social scientists laboring under the inferiority complex they have developed under the frustrating notion that the methods of the natural sciences are the only truly scientific ones refuse both to recognize the "obligation" and to take advantage of the "aid" just mentioned. They mistake the prescription of scientific "objectivity" for a proscription of "subjectivism"—confusing "subjective" in the sense of impartial with "subjective" in the sense of cognizant of inner experiences.

But we must also guard against a possible misunderstanding: that we do not respect the positive and constructive values in the described attitudes, convictions, and ambitions; such values should be recognized. Thus we must be sure not to confuse historians with *historicists,* nor to discount the value of good historical work merely because its author happened to cling to historicist views aggressively critical of all theoretical analysis. We must not underestimate the importance of descriptive work on the institutional features of our social organization, even if its author is a firm believer in *institutionalist* methodology and should be deadly opposed to all general theory. We should admit that the *holists'* fervor for integrated studies, though often destructive in their rejection of isolating abstraction, may at times result in the discovery of data and the development of promising hypotheses. We must acknowledge that *behaviorists* have done good work and have come out with significant findings, even if their campaign against introspection and speculative reasoning about intervening variables probably has obstructed progress in the social sciences more than a little. Although it is true that the attempts of the *operationalists* to ban pure constructs has had obscurantist effects, we must grant that they have been successful in developing a number of statistically operational concepts as useful counterparts for pure constructs and thus have contributed much to our stock of factual information. We must not take all specialists in social statistics, quantitative economics, or econometrics for *metromaniacs;* moreover, while some metromaniac may have wasted money on piling up mountains of stultifying statistics, and may have misdirected some of our best talents, his enthusiasm for empirical work has probably been productive also of useful quantitative studies, for which he deserves credit regardless of the damage done by his preaching about his exclusive scientific method.

[12] See Alfred Schuetz, "Common-Sense and Scientific Interpretation of Human Action," *Philosophy and Phenomenological Research,* vol. XIV, September 1953, p. 34.

The *predictionists* are of course perfectly right in encouraging the formulation of generalizations useful for prediction and testable by the success of predictions based on them, and we must thank them for such encouragement, despite the gratuitous and harmful disparagement of purely explanatory hypotheses. The *prescriptionists* have frequently turned the attention of the social analyst to practical problems of immediate urgency when the latter was preoccupied with spinning hypotheses of remote applicability; for this they must be given credit even if most of the time their zeal has badly messed up theoretical analysis as well as practical policy-making. We should be careful not to regard every mathematical analyst as a *mathematotic;* and even the latter should be thanked for having contributed to substantial improvements in the mathematical training of social scientists, useful for a better selection of talents and also for greater elegance of exposition. Perhaps there is also something good to say about the achievements of the social science *experimentomaniacs,* though I have not yet been able to find anything.

In brief, good historical and institutional studies, interesting holistic hypotheses and behavioristic research, the development of operational concepts, improved quantitative-empirical research, encouragement of attempts to predict and to test, attention to the practical problems of the day, and better training in mathematics —all these are highly desirable things in the social sciences. What is harmful is the attitude of snubbing, disparaging, excommunicating, or prohibiting the working habits of others and of preaching a methodology that implies that they are inferior in scientific workmanship.[13]

Good "scientific method" must not proscribe any technique of inquiry deemed useful by an honest and experienced scholar. The aggressiveness and restrictiveness of the various methodological beliefs which social scientists have developed—in subconscious attempts to compensate for their feelings of inferiority vis-a-vis the alleged "true scientist"—are deplorable. Attempts to establish a monopoly for one method, to use moral suasion and public defamation to exclude others, produce harmful restraints of research and analysis, seriously retarding their progress.

[13] Lest someone think that I myself have engaged in such activities, he had better re-read the last sentence with greater care. For I have not said anything against the *working* habits of others and have not questioned anybody's scientific workmanship. I have dealt with their claims of exclusive possession of the one and only scientific method.

PART FOUR

The Economics of Free Enterprise

XIII

The Market Economy and the Distribution of Wealth

by L. M. LACHMANN

EVERYWHERE today in the free world we find the opponents of the market economy at a loss for plausible arguments. Of late the "case for central planning" has shed much of its erstwhile luster. We have had too much experience of it. The facts of the last forty years are too eloquent.

Who can now doubt that, as Professor Mises pointed out thirty years ago, every intervention by a political authority entails a further intervention to prevent the inevitable economic repercussions of the first step from taking place? Who will deny that a command economy requires an atmosphere of inflation to operate at all, and who today does not know the baneful effects of "controlled inflation?" Even though some economists have now invented the eulogistic term "secular inflation" in order to describe the permanent inflation we all know so well, it is unlikely that anyone is deceived. It did not really require the recent German example to demonstrate to us that a market economy will create order out of "administratively controlled" chaos even in the most unfavorable circumstances. A form of economic organization based on voluntary cooperation and the universal exchange of knowledge is necessarily superior to any hierarchical structure, even if in the latter a rational test for the qualifications of those who give the word of command could exist. Those who are able to learn from reason and experience knew it before, and those who are not are unlikely to learn it even now.

Confronted with this situation the opponents of the market economy have shifted their ground; they now oppose it on "social" rather than economic grounds. They accuse it of being unjust rather than inefficient. They now dwell on the "distorting effects" of the ownership of wealth and contend that "the plebiscite of the market is swayed by plural voting." They show that the distribution of wealth affects production and income distribution since the owners of wealth not merely receive an "unfair share" of the social income, but will also influence the composition of the social product: Luxuries are too many and necessities too few. Moreover, since these owners do most of the saving they also determine the rate of capital accumulation and thus of economic progress.

Some of these opponents would not altogether deny that there is a sense in which the distribution of wealth is the cumulative result of the play of economic forces, but would hold that this cumulation operates in such a fashion as to make the present a slave of the past, a bygone an arbitrary factor in the present. Today's income distribution is shaped by today's distribution of wealth, and even though today's wealth was partly accumulated yesterday, it was accumulated by processes reflecting the influence of the distribution of wealth on the day before yesterday. In the main this argument of the opponents of the market economy is based on the institution of Inheritance to which, even in a progressive society, we are told, a majority of the owners owe their wealth.

This argument appears to be widely accepted today, even by many who are genuinely in favor of economic freedom. Such people have come to believe that a "redistribution of wealth," for instance through death duties, would have socially desirable, but no unfavorable economic results. On the contrary, since such measures would help to free the present from the "dead hand" of the past they would also help to adjust present incomes to present needs. The distribution of wealth is a datum of the market, and by changing data we can change results without interfering with the market mechanism! It follows that only when accompanied by a policy designed continually to redistribute existing wealth, would the market process have "socially tolerable" results.

This view, as we said, is today held by many, even by some economists who understand the superiority of the market economy over the command economy and the frustrations of interventionism, but dislike what they regard as the social consequences of the market economy. They are prepared to accept the market economy only where its operation is accompanied by such a policy of redistribution.

The present paper is devoted to a criticism of the basis of this view.

In the first place, the whole argument rests logically on verbal confusion arising from the ambiguous meaning of the term "datum." In common usage as well as in most sciences, for instance in statistics, the word "datum" means something that is, at a moment of time, "given" to us as observers of the scene. In this sense it is, of course, a truism that the mode of the distribution of wealth is a datum at any given moment of time, simply in the trivial sense that it happens to exist and no other mode does. But in the equilibrium theories which, for better or worse, have come to mean so much for present-day economic thought and have so largely shaped its content, the word "datum" has acquired a second and very different meaning: Here a datum means a necessary condition of equilibrium, an independent variable, and "the data" collectively mean the total sum of necessary and sufficient conditions from which, once we know them all, we without further ado can deduce equilibrium price and quantity. In this second sense the distribution of wealth would thus, together with the other data, be a DETERMINANT, though not the only determinant, of the prices and quantities of the various services and products bought and sold.

It will, however, be our main task in the paper to show that the distribution of wealth is not a "datum" in this second sense. Far from being an "independent variable" of the market process, it is, on the contrary, continuously subject to modification by the market forces. Needless to say, this is not to deny that at any moment it is among the forces which shape the path of the market process in the immediate future, but *it is* to deny that the mode of distribution as such can have any permanent influence. Though wealth is always distributed in some definite way, the mode of this distribution is ever-changing.

Only if the mode of distribution remained the same in period after period, while individual pieces of wealth were being transferred by inheritance, could such a constant mode be said to be a permanent economic force. In reality this is not so. The distribution of wealth is being shaped by the forces of the market as an object, not an agent, and whatever its mode may be today will soon have become an irrelevant bygone.

The distribution of wealth, therefore, has no place among the data of equilibrium. What is, however, of great economic and social interest is not the mode of distribution of wealth at a moment of time, but its mode of change over time. Such change, we shall see, finds its true place among the events that happen on that problematical "path" which may, but rarely in reality does, lead to equilibrium. It is a typically "dynamic" phenomenon. It is a curious fact that at a time when so much is heard of the need for the pursuit and promotion of dynamic studies it should arouse so little interest.

Ownership is a legal concept which refers to concrete material objects. Wealth is an economic concept which refers to scarce resources. All valuable resources are, or reflect, or embody, material objects, but not all material objects are resources: Derelict houses and heaps of scrap are obvious examples, as are any objects which their owners would gladly give away if they could find somebody willing to remove them. Moreover, what is a resource today may cease to be one tomorrow, while what is a valueless object today may become valuable tomorrow. The resource status of material objects is therefore always problematical and depends to some extent on foresight. An object constitutes wealth only if it is a source of an income stream. The value of the object to the owner, actual or potential, reflects at any moment its expected income-yielding capacity. This, in its turn, will depend on the uses to which the object can be turned. The mere ownership of objects, therefore, does not necessarily confer wealth; it is their successful use which confers it. Not ownership but use of resources is the source of income and wealth. An ice-cream factory in New York may mean wealth to its owner; the same ice-cream factory in Greenland would scarcely be a resource.

In a world of unexpected change the maintenance of wealth is always problematical; and in the long run it may be said to be impossible. In order to be able to maintain a given amount of wealth which could be transferred by inheritance from one generation to the next, a family would have to own such resources as will yield a permanent net income stream, i.e., a stream of surplus of output value over the cost of factor services complementary to the resources owned. It seems that this would be possible only *either* in a stationary world, a world in which today is as yesterday and tomorrow like today, and in which thus, day after day, and year after year, the same income will accrue to the same owners or their heirs; *or* if all resource owners had perfect foresight. Since both cases are remote from reality we can safely ignore them. What, then, in reality happens to wealth in a world of unexpected change?

All wealth consists of capital assets which, in one way or another, embody or at least ultimately reflect the material resources of production, the sources of valuable output. All output is produced by human labor with the help of combinations of such resources. For this purpose resources have to be used in certain combinations; complementarity is of the essence of resource use. The modes of this complementarity are in no way "given" to the entrepreneurs who make, initiate, and carry out production plans. There is in reality no such thing as A production function. On the contrary, the task of the entrepreneur consists precisely in finding, in a world of perpetual change, which combination of resources will yield, in the conditions of today, a maximum surplus of output over input value, and in guessing which will do so in the probable conditions of tomorrow, when output values, cost of complementary input, and technology all will have changed.

If all capital resources were infinitely versatile the entrepreneurial problem would consist in no more than following the changes of external conditions by turning combinations of resources to a succession of uses made profitable by these changes. As it is, resources have, as a rule, a limited range of versatility, each is specific to a number of uses.[1] Hence, the need for adjustment to change will often entail the need for a change in the composition of the resource group, for "capital regrouping." But each change in the mode of complementarity will affect the value of the component resources by giving rise to capital gains and losses. Entrepreneurs will make higher bids for the services of those resources for which they have found more profitable uses, and lower bids for those which have to be turned to less profitable uses. In the limiting case where no (present or potential future) use can be found for a resource which has so far formed part of a profitable combination, this resource will lose its resource character altogether. But even in less drastic cases capital gains and losses made on durable assets are an inevitable concomitant of a world of unexpected change.

The market process is thus seen to be a leveling process. In a market economy a process of redistribution of wealth is taking place all the time before which those outwardly similar processes which modern politicians are in the habit of instituting, pale into comparative insignificance, if for no other reason than that the market gives wealth to those who can hold it, while politicians give it to their constituents who, as a rule, cannot.

[1] The argument presented in what follows owes a good deal to ideas first set forth by Professor Mises in *Das festangelegte Kapital*. See "Grundprobleme der Nationaloekonomie," pp. 201-14.

This process of redistribution of wealth is not prompted by a concatenation of hazards. Those who participate in it are not playing a game of chance, but a game of skill. This process, like all real dynamic processes, reflects the transmission of knowledge from mind to mind. It is possible only because some people have knowledge that others have not yet acquired, because knowledge of change and its implications spread gradually and unevenly throughout society.

In this process he is successful who understands earlier than anyone else that a certain resource which today can be produced, when it is new, or bought, when it is an existing resource, at a certain price A, will tomorrow form part of a productive combination as a result of which it will be worth A'. Such capital gains or losses, prompted by the chance of, or need for, turning resources from one use to another, superior or inferior to the first, form the economic substance of what wealth means in a changing world, and are the chief vehicle of the process of redistribution.

In this process it is most unlikely that the same man will continue to be right in his guesses about possible new uses for existing or potential resources time after time, unless he is really superior. And in the latter case his heirs are unlikely to show similar success— unless they are superior, too. In a world of unexpected change capital losses are ultimately as inevitable as are capital gains. Competition between capital owners and the specific nature of durable resources, even though it be "multiple specificity," entail that gains are followed by losses as losses are followed by gains.

These economic facts have certain social consequences. As the critics of the market economy nowadays prefer to take their stand on "social" grounds, it may be not inappropriate here to elucidate the true social results of the market process. We have already spoken of it as a leveling process. More aptly, we may now describe these results as an instance of what Pareto called "the circulation of elites." Wealth is unlikely to stay for long in the same hands. It passes from hand to hand as unforeseen change confers value now on this, now on that specific resource, engendering capital gains and losses. The owners of wealth, we might say with Schumpeter, are like the guests at a hotel or the passengers in a train: They are always there but are never for long the same people.

It may be objected that our argument applies in any case only to a small segment of society and that the circulation of elites does not eliminate social injustice. There may be such circulation among wealth owners, but what about the rest of society? What chance have those without wealth of even participating, let alone winning, in the game? This objection, however, would ignore the part played by managers and entrepreneurs in the market process, a part to which we shall soon have to return.

In a market economy, we have seen, all wealth is of a problematical nature. The more durable assets are and the more specific, the more restricted the range of uses to which they may be turned, the more clearly the problem becomes visible. But in a society with little fixed capital in which most accumulated wealth took the form of stocks of commodities, mainly agricultural and perishable, carried for periods of various lengths, a society in which durable consumer goods, except perhaps for houses and furniture, hardly existed, the problem was not so clearly visible. Such was, by and large, the society in which the classical economists were living and from which they naturally borrowed many traits. In the conditions of their time, therefore, the classical economists were justified, up to a point, in regarding all capital as virtually homogeneous and perfectly versatile, contrasting it with land, the only specific and irreproducible resource. But in our time there is little or no justification for such dichotomy. The more fixed capital there is, and the more durable it is, the greater the probability that such capital resources will, before they wear out, have to be used for purposes other than those for which they were originally designed. This means practically that in a modern market economy there can be no such thing as a source of permanent income. Durability and limited versatility make it impossible.

It may be asked whether in presenting our argument we have not confused the capital owner with the entrepreneur, ascribing to the former functions which properly belong to the latter. Is not the decision about the use of existing resources as well as the decision which specifies the concrete form of new capital resources, viz. the investment decision, a typical entrepreneurial task? Is it not for the entrepreneur to regroup and redeploy combinations of capital goods? Are we not claiming for capital owners the economic functions of the entrepreneur?

We are not primarily concerned with claiming functions for anybody. We are concerned with the effects of unexpected change on asset values and on the distribution of wealth. The effects of such change will fall upon the owners of wealth irrespective of where the change originates. If the distinction between capitalist and entrepreneur could always easily be made, it might be claimed that the continuous redistribution of wealth is the result of entrepreneurial action, a process in which capital owners play a merely passive part. But that the process really occurs, that wealth is being redistributed by the market, cannot be doubted, nor that the process is prompted by the transmission of knowledge from one center of entrepreneurial action to another. Where capital owners and entrepreneurs can be clearly distinguished, it is true that the owners of wealth take no active part in the process themselves, but passively have to accept its results.

Yet there are many cases in which such a clear-cut distinction cannot be made. In the modern world wealth typically takes the form of securities. The owner of wealth is typically a shareholder. Is the shareholder an entrepreneur? Professor Knight asserts that he is, but a succession of authors from Walter Rathenau [2] to Mr. Burnham have denied him that status. The answer depends, of course, on our definition of the entrepreneur. If we define him as an uncertainty-bearer, it is clear that the shareholder is an entrepreneur. But in recent years there seems to be a growing tendency to define the entrepreneur as the planner and decision-maker. If so, directors and managers are entrepreneurs, but shareholders, it seems, are not.

Yet we have to be careful in drawing our conclusions. One of the most important tasks of the entrepreneur is to specify the concrete form of capital resources, to say what buildings are to be erected, what stocks are to be kept, etc. If we are clearly to distinguish between capitalist and entrepreneur we must assume that a "pure" entrepreneur, with no wealth of his own, borrows capital in money form, i.e., in a non-specific form, from "pure" capital owners.[3]

But do the directors and managers at the top of the organizational ladder really make all the specifying decisions? Are not many such decisions made "lower down" by works managers, supervisors, etc.? Is it really at all possible to indicate "the entrepreneur" in a world in which managerial functions are so widely spread?

On the other hand, the decision of a capital owner to buy new shares in company A rather than in company B is also a specifying decision. In fact this is the primary decision on which all the managerial decisions within the firm ultimately depend, since without capital there would be nothing for them to specify. We have to

---

[2] *Vom Aktienwesen*, 1917.

[3] This definition has, of course, certain social implications. Those who accept it can hardly continue to regard entrepreneurs as a class access to which is impossible for those with no wealth of their own. Whatever degree of the "imperfection of the capital market" we choose to assume will not give us this result.

realize, it seems, that the specifying decisions of shareholders, directors, managers, etc., are in the end all mutually dependent upon each other, are but links in a chain. All are specifying decisions distinguished only by the degree of concreteness which increases as we are moving down the organizational ladder. Buying shares in company A is a decision which gives capital a form less concrete than does the decision of the workshop manager as to which tools are to be made, but it is a specifying decision all the same, and one which provides the material basis for the workshop manager's action. In this sense we may say that the capital owner makes the "highest" specifying decision.

The distinction between capital owner and entrepreneur is thus not always easily made. To this extent, then, the contrast between the active entrepreneurs, forming and redeploying combinations of capital resources, and the passive asset owners, who have to accept the verdict of the market forces on the success of "their" entrepreneurs, is much overdrawn. Shareholders, after all, are not quite defenseless in these matters. If they cannot persuade their directors to refrain from a certain step, there is one thing they can do: They can sell!

But what about bondholders? Shareholders may make capital gains and losses; their wealth is visibly affected by market forces. But bondholders seem to be in an altogether different position. Are they not owners of wealth who can claim immunity from the market forces we have described, and thus from the process of redistribution?

In the first place, of course, the difference is merely a matter of degree. Cases are not unknown in which, owing to failure of plans, inefficiency of management, or to external circumstances which had not been foreseen, bondholders had to take over an enterprise and thus became involuntary shareholders. It is true, however, that most bondholders are wealth owners who stand, as it were, at one remove from the scene we have endeavored to describe, from the source of changes which are bound to affect most asset values, though it is not true of all of them. Most of the repercussions radiating from this source will have been, as it were, intercepted by others before they reach the bondholders. The higher the "gear" of a company's capital, the thinner the protective layer of the equity, the more repercussions will reach the bondholders, and the more strongly they will be affected. It is thus quite wrong to cite the case of the bondholder in order to show that there are wealth owners exempt from the operation of the market forces we have described. Wealth owners as a class can never be so exempt, though some may be relatively more affected than others.

Furthermore, there are two cases of economic forces engendering capital gains and losses from which, in the nature of these cases, the bondholder cannot protect himself, however thick the protective armor of the equity may happen to be: the rate of interest and inflation. A rise in long-term rates of interest will depress bond values where equity holders may still hope to recoup themselves by higher profits, while a fall will have the opposite effect. Inflation transfers wealth from creditors to debtors, whereas deflation has the opposite effect. In both cases we have, of course, instances of that redistribution of wealth with which we have become acquainted. We may say that with a constant long-term rate of interest and with no change in the value of money, the susceptibility of bond-holders' wealth to unexpected change will depend on their relative position as against equity holders, their "economic distance" from the center of disturbances; while interest changes and changes in the value of money will modify that relative position.

The holders of government bonds, of course, are exempt from many of the repercussions of unexpected change, but by no means from all of them. To be sure, they do not need the protective armor of the equity to shield them against the market forces which modify prices and costs. But interest changes and inflation are as much of a threat to them as to other bondholders. In the world of permanent inflation in which we are now living, to regard wealth in the form of government securities as not liable to erosion by the forces of change would be ludicrous. But in any case the existence of a government debt is not a result of the operation of market forces. It is the result of the operation of politicians eager to save their constituents from the task of having to pay taxes they would otherwise have had to pay.

The main fact we have stressed in this paper, the redistribution of wealth caused by the forces of the market in a world of unexpected change, is a fact of common observation. Why, then, is it constantly being ignored? We could understand why the politicians choose to ignore it: After all, the large majority of their constituents are unlikely to be directly affected by it, and, as is amply shown in the case of inflation, would scarcely be able to understand it if they were. But why should economists choose to ignore it? That the mode of the distribution of wealth is a result of the operation of economic forces is the kind of proposition which, one would think, appeal to them. Why, then, do so many economists continue to regard the distribution of wealth as a "datum" in the second sense mentioned above? We submit that the reason has to be sought in an excessive preoccupation with equilibrium problems.

We saw before that the successive modes of the distribution of wealth belong to the world of disequilibrium. Capital gains and losses arise in the main because durable resources have to be used in ways for which they were not planned, and because some men understand better and earlier than other men what the changing needs and resources of a world in motion imply. Equilibrium means consistency of plans, but the redistribution of wealth by the market is typically a result of inconsistent action. To those trained to think in equilibrium terms it is perhaps only natural that such processes as we have described should appear to be not quite "respectable." For them the "real" economic forces are those which tend to establish and maintain equilibrium. Forces only operating in disequilibrium are thus regarded as not really very interesting and are therefore all too often ignored. There may be two reasons for such neglect. No doubt a belief that a tendency towards equilibrium does exist in reality and that, in any conceivable situation, the forces tending towards equilibrium will always be stronger than the forces of resistance, plays a part in it.

But an equally strong reason, we may suspect, is the inability of economists preoccupied with equilibria to cope at all with the forces of disequilibrium. All theory has to make use of coherent models. If one has only one such model at one's disposal a good many phenomena that do not seem to fit into one's scheme are likely to remain unaccounted for. The neglect of the process of redistribution is thus not merely of far-reaching practical importance in political economy since it prevents us from understanding certain features of the world in which we are living. It is also of crucial methodological significance to the central area of economic thought.

We are not saying, of course, that the modern economist, so learned in the grammar of equilibrium, so ignorant of the facts of the market, is unable or unready to cope with economic change; that would be absurd. We are saying that he is well-equipped only to deal with types of change that happen to conform to a fairly rigid pattern. In most of the literature currently in fashion change is conceived as a transition from one equilibrium to another, i.e., in terms of comparative statics. There are even some economists who, having thoroughly misunderstood Cassel's idea of a "uniformly progressive economy," cannot conceive of economic progress in any other way![4] Such smooth transition from one equilibrium (long-run or short-run) to another virtually bars not only discussion of the process in which we are interested here, but of all true economic processes. For such smooth transition will only take place where the new equilibrium position is already generally known and anticipated before it is reached. Where this is not so, a process of trial and error (Walras' *"tâtonnements"*) will start which in the end may or may not lead to a new equilibrium position. But even where it does, the new equilibrium finally reached will not be that which would have been reached immediately had everybody anticipated it at the beginning, since it will be the cumulative result of the events which took place on the "path" leading to it. Among these events changes in the distribution of wealth occupy a prominent place.

Professor Lindahl[5] has recently shown to what extent Keynes' analytical model is vitiated by his apparent determination to squeeze a variety of economic forces into the Procrustean bed of short-period equilibrium analysis. Keynes, while he wished to describe the *modus operandi* of a number of dynamic forces, cast his model in the mold of a system of simultaneous equations, though the various forces studied by him clearly belonged to periods of different length. The lesson to be learned here is that once we allow ourselves to ignore fundamental facts about the market, such as differential knowledge, some people understanding the meaning of an event before others, and in general, the temporal pattern of events, we shall be tempted to express "immediate" effects in short-period equilibrium terms. And all too soon we shall also allow ourselves to forget that what is of real economic interest are not the equilibria, even if they exist, which is in any case doubtful, but what happens between them. "An auxiliary makeshift employed by the logical economists as a limiting notion"[6] can produce rather disastrous results when it is misemployed.

The preoccupation with equilibrium ultimately stems from a confusion between subject and object, between the mind of the observer and the minds of the actors observed. There can, of course, be no systematic science without a coherent frame of reference, but we can hardly expect to find such coherence as our frame of refer-

---

[4] For a most effective criticism of this kind of model-building see, Joan Robinson "The Model of an Expanding Economy," *Economic Journal*, March 1952.

[5] Erik Lindahl, "On Keynes' Economic System," *Economic Record*, May and November 1954.

[6] Ludwig von Mises, *Human Action*, Yale University Press, New Haven, Conn., p. 352.

ence requires ready-made for us in the situations we observe. It is, on the contrary, our task to produce it by analytical effort. There are, in the social sciences, many situations which are interesting to us precisely because the human actions in them are inconsistent with each other, and in which coherence, if at all, is ultimately produced by the interplay of mind on mind. The present paper is devoted to the study of one such situation. We have endeavored to show that a social phenomenon of some importance can be understood if presented in terms of a process reflecting the interplay of mind on mind, but not otherwise. The model-builders, econometric and otherwise, naturally have to avoid such themes.

It is very much to be hoped that economists in the future will show themselves less inclined than they have been in the past to look for ready-made, but spurious, coherence, and that they will take a greater interest in the variety of ways in which the human mind in action produces coherence out of an initially incoherent situation.

XIV

Unearned Riches

by LEONARD E. READ

O NE of the cornerstones of economic theory is the economic value we attach to commodities and services that possess a relation to our well-being. Economic value is the importance which a good possesses for us because it is useful and scarce.

It is to the everlasting credit and fame of Carl Menger and other scholars of the Austrian School to have found and expounded this elementary knowledge of subjective value. They then proceeded to apply the value analysis in the field of *complementary goods,* i.e., goods that are required to cooperate in the rendition of use services, and finally in the field of *capital goods,* which they called "goods of higher order." The theory of the value of complementary goods then became the key for the solution of one of the most important and difficult problems of economics: the problem of distribution.

The valuations of the consumers in a market economy, in final analysis, determine the way in which the ultimate product is distributed among the cooperating factors of production. How little this elementary knowledge of economic valuation is known can be seen at the widespread acceptance and circulation of wage theories that deny any relation to the valuation process. The American public embraces and most institutions of economic education teach theories of "bargaining-power," "purchasing-power," "standard-of-living," the "subsistence theory," or even the unadulterated "exploitation theory." Distribution through the valuation process seems to be known to a few remnants of "reactionary" and "outdated" scholars and writers only. It is to the enduring credit of Ludwig von Mises that he, for several decades, has been the foremost "reactionary" among scholars, a reactionary of reason and economic theory. For this he merits our admiration and gratitude.

Many people sincerely believe that the value of anything is determined by the labor used in producing it; that its price ought to reflect quite objectively the amount of labor put into it. The belief in this labor theory of value, however, is founded in myth, not fact. Day-to-day experiences reveal its error. For a far-fetched example, the same labor could be used to make mud pies as to make mince pies, yet the value in the market place would differ. A service or a product of little value at one time or in one place may be highly valued at another time and place. For instance, an artist may produce hundreds of paintings considered freakish by others and be rewarded with starvation for his labors. But, let his style become the fad, and for less labor than before, he can revel in luxury.

Lost and adrift on a raft for days, a man might offer his fortune in exchange for a hamburger. Yet, the same person, following a lusty meal, might not offer a penny in exchange, though the hamburger had changed not at all.

Individuals have varying value judgments. Value in the market sense, therefore, is a subjective rather than an objective determination. In a way, it is like beauty. What is beauty? It is what you or I or other individuals think is beautiful. It depends on subjective or personal value judgments, judgments characterized by constant variation. Value, as beauty, cannot be objectively determined. That all persons may think of a certain sunset as beautiful, a given monster as hideous, gold as desirable, or mud pies as useless does not alter the fact that these are subjective judgments. Such unanimity merely asserts that some subjective judgments are similar.

It is not at all surprising that many persons in the United States and throughout the world do not subscribe to the subjective nature of value. As far as can be determined, no one understood it well enough to try an explanation until the latter part of the nineteenth century. Prior to that, such a notable as John Stuart Mill and the very best of economists, including Adam Smith and Ricardo, were stymied in their development of economic theory because they accepted the cost-of-production or labor theory of value. They simply could not explain what they otherwise knew to be the great advantages of the free market process of voluntary exchange. They knew full well that both parties must gain when each traded what he wanted less for what he wanted more, yet they could not show that such gain had been "earned," for they were unable to explain it in terms of labor costs. In short, they were unable to see how the free market price might be competitively or subjectively determined by individuals who had no accurate knowledge of the labor or other costs involved in producing a particular item.

How Adam Smith, holding to this labor theory of value, could have seen the great advantages of trade—the untold blessings of others, or society, to the individual—and could have come out in favor of private enterprise instead of socialism, is a miracle more to be attributed to sound instinct than to economic reasoning.

Marx, as distinguished from Adam Smith, followed the labor theory of value to its logical conclusion: socialism. Marx looked upon all things useful as one great "wages fund" and believed that the entire fund ought to be distributed directly to laborers. To allow any part of this fund as a return on capital would amount to unearned increment and, he argued, would be exploitation. How any advocate of the cost-of-labor theory could believe in anything but socialism is difficult to understand. Smith, Ricardo, Mill, and many others instinctively, not logically, concluded otherwise.

Only if one understands the marginal utility or subjective theory of value based upon the judgments of countless individuals acting freely and voluntarily in the market may he proceed logically to a belief in private ownership and control of property. With this kind of an understanding, he can see why any person may have a perfect right to consume more than he could ever hope to produce by his own labor. He can, it is plain, properly own anything others will freely offer in exchange for what he has to offer them. This means gains for all participants in the exchange process, gains which must always appear to be unearned in terms of labor expended. Nonetheless, it reflects the approval of all who are properly concerned in any transaction. The marginal utility or subjective theory of value needs no other justification. Because it is based on willing exchange, it works without coercing anyone. The labor theory of value—the labor theory of price determination—on the other hand, founded on unwilling exchange, cannot function without coercion.

Now, let us proceed to the person whose father invested $500 in an early auto industry and who now wonders to whom he should give the resulting millions. He is no more the recipient of unearned increment than is the person who today works for a wage in the same company. Both exist on what they themselves do not and could not produce. And if the wage earner were to succeed in cutting off what he might think are the unearned riches of his "lucky" brothers, he would at the same time destroy his own source of livelihood.

Let us contemplate this wage earner. He lives in a house he could not build. Perhaps, given enough materials and tools properly fabricated and the plans some architect has drawn, he could put together something resembling a house. But he wouldn't know how to make a lowly nail: mine the ore, alloy the metals, construct the furnaces, build the extrusion and other machinery, and so on. Could he make a hammer? A saw? Bring the lumber to its finished state? Even make the string on which his plumb hangs? Grow and gin and spin and comb and weave the cotton from which it is made?

Could he build the machinery that mines the coal he uses to heat his house? He could not make the lamp the miners wear if every ingredient depended solely on his own resources.

What about the automobiles he helps to put together, one of which he owns? Neither he nor any other person on this earth could produce it alone. What about the food he eats? The clothes he wears? The books and magazines he reads? The telephone he uses? The counsel on health that is his? The opportunities that are constantly presented to him? All are done by a vast work and exchange process, millions of individuals with as many varied skills, laboring cooperatively and competitively, a world of complex and flowing energy, the organization of which is more complicated than any one person can understand, let alone control. Others—society past and present—place within his reach goods and services and knowledge in such an array and abundance that he could not himself produce in thousands of years that portion of it which he consumes in a single day. And he obtains all of this in exchange for his own meager efforts.

The astounding thing is that it is possible for him to gain without any change in his efforts, his skills, his knowledge. Let others become more inventive and more productive, and he may receive more in exchange for what he has to offer. Parenthetically, it is also possible for him to lose out entirely, as might happen if he persisted in offering nothing in exchange but buggy whips.

There is a fact still more astounding. Our wage earner may think of his plight as hapless when compared to the one who inherited his millions. True, the millionaire has gained much from the doings of others. *But the wage earner himself owes his life to the doings of others.* It is not that possessing millions and having life are alternative propositions. That is not the point. The point is that both flow from the same exchange process and that whatever each has—be it autos, houses, food, clothing, heat, millions, knowledge, or life itself —comes to him unearned in the sense that he alone did not produce all of it. We trade because we can all get more satisfaction from our labor by that means. Vast stores are available to those who have anything to trade that others value. In the free market, each earns all that he receives in willing exchange. This is fantastically more than one could produce by himself.

In order fully to grasp the process by which one can consume in a day that which he could not produce in thousands of years—the process by which he can earn in a day that which he could not earn by himself in thousands of years—it is only necessary for one to see that one's earning power is capable of unlimited expansion by the productivity and exchange and value judgments of others. This world of creative energy, this productivity exterior to self, then, becomes of singular importance to each one of us. Not only does our prosperity—material, intellectual, and spiritual—depend upon it, but life itself comes under its government. In short, each of us is the beneficiary of this productivity through division of labor and capital accumulation and investments by others.

Let us sample this world of productivity through division of labor from the standpoint of oneself as a potential beneficiary of its largess. The mathematics of nuclear fission is known to some scholars. I, however, do not know that much mathematics. Such knowledge conceivably can be mine. But I can possess it only by increasing my own perceptive powers. It may very well be that the required increase in perception is beyond my competency or that I may choose to increase my perception along other lines to the exclusion of perceptive powers along this line. But, assuming that I do gain this knowledge, do I earn it? Yes, as much as though I gained the knowledge by direct revelation. Direct, or indirect through study of the knowledge of others, does not alter the matter.

The same principle applies to a product as to an item of knowledge. Luxurious yachts are available. Their making is as foreign and as unrelated to me as presently is the mathematics of nuclear fission. I do not have one. Such a possession conceivably could be mine. I could become the beneficiary of its existence by increasing my own exchange powers or, should all others become sufficiently productive, I could have one in exchange for efforts no greater than I now exercise. But assume that I do obtain one in exchange for my present meager efforts, do I earn it? Yes, even though it is in the sense I earn a deer by choosing the path I will walk and by pulling the trigger on a gun. All else is supplied. The deer, a miracle about which man had nothing to do, crossed my path. The gun, the powder, the shot represented creative ingenuity flowing through space and time about which I have but the dimmest of notions. As with the deer, so with the yacht. I earn it as though I had done it all myself. Others in their productivity, knowledge, skills *willingly* exchanged what I offered them.

Someone may argue that I could have exchange power to obtain a yacht had I been born the son of a father who "hit it lucky." By the same token, I might have the perceptive powers to understand the mathematics of nuclear fission had my parentage been different.

Seeing oneself in true perspective as related to all others is utterly impossible. We but dimly comprehend ourselves; the comprehension of others is much dimmer. However, it is not necessary that this perspective be perfect. It is only necessary that we grasp the idea of being a beneficiary of this benefactor, this division of labor, and that we understand and appreciate our dependence on and our relationship to it.

No better example of the beneficent effects of the division of labor together with capital accumulation is to be found than in the area of our own 48 states. Here, less than 400 years ago, there were perhaps 200,000 Indians. Why was the population limited to this number? Certainly it was not for any lack of natural resources, friendly climates, or fertile soils. Nor was it because of the Indians' inability to breed. The population was limited and the standard of life was relatively impoverished because of a low form of cooperant society. They lived in a foraging economy, all of them in a near sameness. There was little in the way of division of labor, of variable skills, knowledge. Society was indeed so uncooperative that as a result only 200,000 could live in it, and they not very well.

Today, in this same area, 160,000,000 persons, 800 times as many, live in relative luxury, be luxury measured in terms of goods and services, leisure, opportunities, knowledge, or insights into the nature of things. It is fair to say that 159,800,000 of us have life, and a rather full one at that, due to a higher form of cooperant society, to the freeing of creative energy, to large capital investments per head of population, to an advanced state of division of labor. It is fair to say that nearly all of us exist and have the possessions we enjoy because of a greater division of labor in a market economy. These millions of people with their varied skills and specializations, taken together, constitute a benefactor without which most of us could have no life at all. Each one of us is a beneficiary of this phenomenon.

Looked at in this light—oneself as a beneficiary and division of labor as a benefactor—it becomes pertinent to re-examine one's own behaviors, attitudes, actions. If we would best serve our individual self-interest, we would do well to live in harmony with the facts of life, not in disharmony with them.

Looked at in this light, one should do everything possible to increase his own perceptive and exchange powers. It is only by self-improvement that one can best serve self. And, clearly, it is only by self-improvement that one can better serve others—that is, add to someone else's well-being.

Who composes this benefactor of ours, this storehouse of energy? It is composed of individuals who, like ourselves, are different from all others and who, like ourselves, depend on others. And what ought to be our attitude toward these millions of others if looked at from the standpoint of self-interest?

1. Self-reliance, a great virtue, should be emphasized. The way to be self-reliant is to keep off the backs of others and to engage in willing—never unwilling—exchange. This is the *free market*.

2. It is a primary fact of observation that these others, like oneself, will work at their best if permitted the ownership and control of the fruits of their own labor—and of their own participation in the exchange process. It is in one's interest to preserve his incentive. This is the institution of *private property*.

3. As with oneself, these others will act at their best creatively if left free to do so. One should, therefore, look with great disfavor on any interference with creative activity and on any inhibitions to free exchange and communication of creative action. One's own interest is impaired if there are marauders or robbers or authoritarians among these others; if there are men among them practicing violence, fraud, misrepresentation, or predation. One's own interest suffers if voters use the political apparatus to gain their own ends at the expense of the vast majority of the public. The form of government that protects the smooth operation of the free market economy and its voluntary division of labor is *limited government*.

For each individual to save his own skin and soul he must give at least as much concern to the rights of others as he does to his own. He would be as eager to protect the creative energies and the free exchange and communication of others as his own. For each of us can truly say, "I am the beneficiary of their existence."

If we as individuals would save our own skins and our own souls, we would use all the moral suasion at our command to see that all men are free:

... to pursue their ambition to the full extent of their abilities;

... to associate with whom they please for any reason they please;

... to worship God in their own way;

... to choose their own trade;

... to go into business for themselves, be their own bosses, and set their own hours of work;

... to use their honestly acquired property or savings in their own way;

... to offer their services or products for sale on their own terms;

... to buy or not to buy any service or product offered for sale;

... to agree or to disagree with any other person;

... to study and learn whatever strikes their fancy;

... to do as they please in general, as long as they do not infringe the equal right and opportunity of every other person to do as he pleases.

According to these observations, here is a way of life harmonious with the interests of others. The envy of others for accomplishments or rewards can be made naturally and easily to give way to appreciation and pleasure. Inequality, being but the team-mate of variation without which survival is impossible, would, therefore, be favored rather than disparaged.

Are the riches received in a free society unearned? Only in the sense that all producers reap fantastically more than they could earn in isolation. The benefits flowing from our division of labor are available to all of us in willing exchange if freedom prevails. Such are the thoughts of one who believes himself a beneficiary and who believes that all others who act creatively are his benefactors. I owe my life to them; hence if I would live and prosper, I shall work as diligently for their freedom as for my own.

XV

The Yield from Money Held

by W. H. HUTT

MY AIM in this essay is to attempt to carry the tenor of Mises' teaching a step further in the field of monetary theory. A feature of his great contribution, *Human Action,* is its insistence that all goods and services have the same *scarcity* significance, i.e., that they all stand in an identical relation to human choice and exchange. It seems to me that money and monetary services ought to be included under this principle, in a manner in which Mises himself has not argued. In this field all economists have shared, I feel, in a hindering tradition which, had the logic of his approach been extended, Mises would have thrown off. I refer to the notion that money is "barren," "sterile," "unproductive," "offering a yield of *nil.*" This view is held today by economists of all schools. Yet practically without exception they talk of the "services" rendered by money or the "utilties" derived from money. It is in this respect that we find the clearest justification for Wicksell's confession that in the field of monetary theory, "diametrically opposed and sometimes self-contradictory views are defended by the most famous writers." [1] To the best of my knowledge the doctrine of the sterility of money has so far been subject to *explicit* challenge only by T. Greidanus.[2] The latter has, however, not yet explained the full significance of his "yield theory." [3]

[1] Wicksell, *Lectures,* II, p. 190.

[2] T. Greidanus, *The Value of Money.*

[3] Mises has criticized Greidanus' work on the grounds that an analysis of the motives which lead people to keep money on hand cannot explain purchasing power without bringing in the notions of cash holding and the demand for and supply of money. But I have interpreted Greidanus as meaning that the "yield" he stresses *is* the return to the *holding* of money.

In three articles published since 1952,[4] I have discussed an ambiguity in the concept of the "volume of money." We have to distinguish, I have suggested, between the idea of *the aggregate amount of money measured in actual money units,* like pounds, dollars, francs, etc., and *the aggregate amount of money assets measured in "real terms,"* i.e., measured in units of constant value in terms of "things in general." [5] The former, I regard as "containers" of varying amounts of the latter.[6]

The notion that money has a "yield of *nil,*" i.e., that it differs from other assets in that it is "dead stock," persists, I think *in part* owing to the above-mentioned ambiguity. For one of the usual explanations of this supposed peculiarity of money relies on the fact that an increase in its "quantity" does not mean that there is any increase in "wealth" or "welfare" or "total utility." But this is true only of the number of money units or "containers" and not of what is contained in them. It is not true of the aggregate amount of money assets measured in real terms. Money so conceived is as productive as all other assets, and *productive in exactly the same sense.* And the fact that the number of "containers" (units) may be varied whilst *the aggregate amount* of what is contained in them may remain constant (or *vice versa*) in no way affects the truth that money assets offer prospective yields just as the rest of the assets possessed by individuals, firms, banks or governments. As objects of investment, they are chosen for the same reason that other objects are chosen. Thus, if their marginal prospective yield at any time is *below* that of other assets, it will pay to part with some of them, and if it is *above,* it will pay to acquire money assets up to the point at which the marginal prospective yield has fallen to the rate of interest. Now Mises himself, and several other economists, maintain explicitly that the amount of money which individuals and firms decide to hold is determined by the marginal utility

[4] In *The South African Journal of Economics* as follows: *The Nature of Money,* September, 1952; *The Notion of the Volume of Money,* March, 1953; *The Notion of Money of Constant Value,* September and December, 1953.

[5] The definitions which I have found useful differ from those which Mises employs, in that the term "money assets" as I use it covers all assets (tokens or commodities) the value of which is affected by reason of their being demanded for their "liquidity," i.e., for the *medium of exchange* services which they can perform. Commodities and securities which perform monetary services and other functions as well are included in the proportion to which they are money. On this point, see *The Nature of Money, op. cit.,* p. 61.

[6] Some of the difficulties arising from the concept of "real terms" are discussed in *The Notion of Money of Constant Value, op. cit.*

of its services.[7] Yet for some reason they have not made the next small step needed to recognize this prospective yield (of "utilities"), which invites the holding of money, as the normal return to investment.

The prospective yield from investment in money assets consists, I suggest, (a) of a prospective *pecuniary yield*, in which case the money assets are producers' goods;[8] or (b) of a prospective *non-pecuniary yield* in personal convenience, in which case the money assets are consumers' capital goods;[9] or (c) of a prospective "real," i.e., *non-pecuniary*, speculative yield, in which case the assets are producers' goods, whether held privately or in the course of business. In the case of (a) and (b), the yield is derived in the form of technical monetary services of various kinds, which permit the most economic acquisition of other factors of production or goods for consumption. In the case of (c), the yield is derived in the form of the greater command over non-money assets which a *unit* of money is expected to have at some later period. As we shall see, these statements are all *implied* by Mises' teaching, but never expressed by him in terms of prospective yield. In the following pages, I shall try to support my thesis that it is logically correct, and appropriate from the standpoint of exposition, to refer to the prospective yield or return from the holding of money assets, just as one does from the holding of non-money assets. I shall do so through an examination of the principal arguments which have been used by economists since the earliest times to explain why money has *no* yield, pecuniary or otherwise.

I am inclined to think that the tradition which I am questioning arose originally through the influence of Locke upon Adam Smith. The latter's description of "ready money . . . which a dealer is obliged to keep by him unemployed," as so much "dead stock, which . . . *produces nothing* either to him or to his country,"[10] gave influential emphasis to a bad precedent. Locke had three times used the very same words of money, "produces nothing." Unlike land, which produces something valuable to mankind, said Locke,

---

[7] E.g., Mises, *Human Action*, p. 445.

[8] E.g., cash in the till, which offers prospective *pecuniary* yields in exactly the same way that the site, or the buildings, or the materials, or the labor necessary in business offer pecuniary yields.

[9] E.g., the notes or cash in one's purse or the balance in one's personal current account, the yield from which is in terms of "gratifications," just as with one's furniture or house.

[10] Adam Smith, *The Wealth of Nations*, Cannan Edition, Vol. I, p. 303. (My italics.)

"money is a barren thing"; and yet it was, he argued, subject to the same laws of value as other commodities.[11]

But the idea is ancient. Several writers have attributed it to Aristotle,[12] for he condemned usury on the grounds that "the birth of money from money" was "the most unnatural" mode of making money.

Edwin Cannan insisted that it is by no means certain that Aristotle thought money *was* barren, but merely that he thought it *ought to be*.[13] Wicksteed pointed out that Dante, following Aristotle, emphasized the unnaturalness of money breeding money, by expressly associating usurers with sodomites! [14] Bacon (who argued for the toleration of usury) said, "They say that it is against nature for money to beget money," [15] but did not explain whether "they" meant that it was immoral or impossible. Shakespeare, in the same context of the controversy over usury, made Antonio, in *The Merchant of Venice*, refer to "a breed of barren metal." [16] We can hardly blame Shakespeare for what he made one of his characters say; yet through this passage, Bonar agreed, "a wrong twist" was probably given to Aristotle's meaning.[17] And Bentham, facetiously [18] ridiculing what Aristotle was supposed to have held, alleged that the "celebrated heathen" philosopher described money as barren because he "had never been able to discover, in any one piece of money, any organs for generating any other such piece." [19]

Now although this discussion of the legitimacy of usury continued to be clouded by the confusion of the concept of money with that of capital (all money is capital, but not all capital is money), it appears to have been responsible for the continuing and still current fallacy that "money does not mulitply itself," as do other forms

[11] Locke, *Some Considerations of the Consequences of the Lowering of Interest . . .*, 1691. In Locke, *Works*, Vol. V, 1801 Edn., pp. 36-7. Locke discussed payment for the use of money, but then became caught in the persistent confusion between capital and money which was so common before Mill's time.

[12] Aristotle, *Politics*, I, (10), Jowett Translation, 1258 b. Adam Smith was undoubtedly directly influenced also by Aristotle's remarkable insight into the nature of money. Senior pointed out that Adam Smith used a phrase which would serve as a translation of a phrase in Aristotle's *Ethics*.

[13] See the delightful symposium, *Who said "Barren Metal?"*, by Cannan, Ross, Bonar and Wicksteed, in *Economica*, 1922, No. 5. This paragraph is based on that symposium.

[14] Wicksteed, in *Ibid.*, p. 109.

[15] Bacon, *Essay on Usury*, quoted in *Ibid.*, p. 107.

[16] Quoted in *Ibid.*, p. 105.

[17] *Ibid.*, p. 107. Bonar pointed out also that Aristotle's ideas on the subject had come down *via* the canonists.

[18] Böhm-Bawerk described it as "witty," Cannan as "coarse."

[19] Bentham, *Defence of Usury*, quoted in *Ibid.*, p. 105.

of productive capital. And we must, I fear, blame either Locke, whose failure to throw off the ancient and barren notion of "barren metal" thereby perpetuated it, or else Adam Smith, who was too uncritically indebted to Locke (or Aristotle directly) and propagated the insidious fallacy.

Locke's influence was all the greater by reason of the impressive, rational treatment which he devoted to the role and functions of money. He had a remarkably modern grasp of the tasks which money has to perform.[20] Indeed, he perceived clearly what we call today the "institutional" factors determining the demand for money."[21] And most interesting of all, he saw that money had "the nature of land," the interest on land being but the rent.[22] In using these words, he seemed to come very near to stating the very truth for the recognition of which I am now pleading; for, he said, the "*income*" of land is called "rent" and that of money, "use." (See page 216) A little later on, however, he apparently remembered Aristotle (or Antonio!) and wrote: "Land produces something new and profitable, and of value to mankind; but money is a barren thing and produces nothing."[23] In part, the confusion here seems to be due to the narrow view of what constitutes productiveness; although, as I have said, the old confusion between the concepts of money and capital seems mainly to blame. He thought of money *lent* as productive to the lender, but presumably not productive to the borrower. Yet there is similarly no *direct* pecuniary return from land unless it is

[20] Thus, he recognised "the necessity of a certain proportion of money to trade" (Locke, *op. cit.*, p. 21); he saw that the necessary proportion "depends not barely on the quantity of money, but the quickness of its circulation" (*Ibid.*, p. 23); he explained that a coin could, "rest in the same hands one hundred days together," which would make it "impossible exactly to estimate the quantity of money needful in trade" (*Ibid.*, p. 23); and he gave a surprisingly complete treatment of the indispensability of money as an instrument in the hands of different classes of the community (laborers, farmers, tradesmen, landholders, brokers, consumers, etc.). (*Ibid.*, pp. 24 *et. seq.*).

[21] For example, he wrote: "It were better for trade, and consequently for everybody, (for money would be stirring, and *less would do the business*) if rents were paid by shorter intervals. . . . A great deal less money would serve for the trade of a country." *Ibid.*, p. 27 (my italics). If he had said, instead, that there would have been *less work for money to do,* he would have been much nearer to enunciating a really satisfactory theory.

[22] *Ibid.*, p. 33.

[23] Locke, *op. cit.*, p. 36. On other occasions he appeared to waver. Thus, at another place, he actually *implied* that money is productive, although *less frequently* than land. He referred to "the many and sometimes long *intervals of barrenness,* which happen to money more than land. Money at use, when returned to the hands of the owner, usually lies dead there, till he gets a new tenant for it" (*Ibid.*, p. 65, my italics). But as we shall see, money does not work by circulating.

hired out to someone else. Does that mean, then, that our land brings us no return, pecuniary or real, when it is not lent? Obviously not. Of course, if one finds that *the whole of* one's cash balance is unnecessary (i.e., if some part of the balance offers no speculative or convenience yield valued at above the rate of interest), and one then fails to make other use of the redundant sum, or to lend it to someone who can, the surplus *will* remain "barren," just like unutilized land. A trader's stocks of *anything* may be wastefully large. There is nothing unique about money in this respect. It was owing to Locke's failure to make the small further jump necessary, and to state that the productiveness of money does not differ in any material manner from that of land, that we may have the origin of the root fallacy which has confused monetary theory ever since. The subsequent tradition has been to regard money as having "resource value" or capital value, but no "service value."

Between Locke and Adam Smith, various writers perceived the *usefulness* of money, e.g., Cantillon and Hume, but they failed to see that "usefulness" is a mere synonym for "productiveness" or "yield." [24]

Adam Smith's contribution on the point, although obviously inspired by that of Locke, differed slightly from it. At times, he regarded money as "the instrument of commerce," [25] but at other times he *denied* that it was "a tool to work with." [26] "Gold and silver," he wrote elsewhere, "whether in the form of coin or of plate, are utensils . . . as much as the furniture of the kitchen." [27] But he would not have described furniture as "productive." This "dead stock," he said of money, "is a very valuable part of the capital of the country, which produces nothing to the country." [28] His acceptance of such a paradox can probably be explained, as with Locke, by the narrow conception of "productivity" of his day. "The gold and silver money which circulates in any country may," he said, "very properly be compared to a highway, which, while it circulates and carries to market all the grass and corn of the country, produces itself not a single pile of either." [29] To some extent he

[24] See Greidanus, *The Value of Money*, pp. 21-31.

[25] Adam Smith, *op. cit.*, Vol. I, p. 396. Hume also used the word "instrument" for money. (Quoted Greidanus, *op. cit.*, p. 31.)

[26] *Ibid.*, Vol. I, p. 279.

[27] *Ibid.*, Vol. I, pp. 406-7.

[28] *Ibid.*, Vol. I, p. 304. (He repeated these words—"dead stock," "produces nothing"—in the same paragraph.)

[29] *Ibid.*, Vol. I, p. 304.

was, I think, misled through his desire to refute the fallacies of the Mercantilists. He wanted to show the folly of accumulating money in the belief that it represented "wealth," and was accordingly led to the assertion that, whilst it "no doubt, makes always a part of the national capital, . . ." it is "always the most unprofitable part of it." [30]

It is surprising that, as the eighteenth century view of productivity was abandoned, the essential yield from money assets did not come to receive explicit recognition. But as Greidanus has pointed out, Ricardo failed to recognize that money is needed, not only for payments but to be kept on hand. [31] Senior recognized that money was "of the highest utility" [32] but contended that its use gave "no pleasure whatever." He added, "its abundance is a mere inconvenience" because we should have to carry more of it. [33] Obviously, he was here thinking of what I have called "money units."

J. S. Mill's insight was not very much deeper. He recognized that money assets had a task, he referred to "the quantity of work done" by them, he even spoke of their "efficiency," and he fully understood that the demand for such assets was a function of the amount of traffic which they facilitated. [34] But he confused the notion of "rapidity of circulation" with that of "efficiency." He did not realize that, *certis paribus*, if units of money circulated more slowly, that would be due to there being more work, not less work, for them to do. (See below, pp. 213, 214.)

Cairnes (like Adam Smith) was led astray through an attempt at easy refutation of mercantilist ideas. [35] He wanted to answer Tooke, who had discussed *metallic money* as though it were, in itself, a source of productive energy, and who had argued that "an addition to the quantity of money" was "the same thing as an addition to the Fixed Capital of a country"—as equivalent in its effects to "improved harbours, roads and manufactories." [36] But to deny that the acquisition of specie is necessarily a wise form of investment is not to deny that money is instrumental capital. Nor does the fact that it may take a wasteful form (e.g., gold coin, when convertible paper would

[30] *Ibid.*, Vol. I, p. 404.
[31] Greidanus, *op. cit.*, p. 39.
[32] Senior, *Industrial Efficiency and Social Economy*, Vol. II, p. 42.
[33] *Ibid.*, p. 41.
[34] J. S. Mill, *Principles*, Book III, Ch. viii, section 3.
[35] Cairnes, *Essays*, p. 45 *et. seq.*
[36] Tooke, *History of Prices*, Vol. VI, p. 216. He elaborated Adam Smith's comparison of money to a highway, and argued that more money was equivalent to broader, smoother and longer roads.

serve equally well) imply that money assets as such do not provide a flow of valuable services.[37]

Böhm-Bawerk was surprisingly contented with the naïvety of Aristotle, whose argument he summed up as follows: "Money is by nature incapable of bearing fruit."[38] And yet he recognized that interest "may be obtained from any capital, . . . from goods that are barren as well as from those that are naturally fruitful."[39] The explanation of the paradox again appears to lie in the dogged persistence of the crude notion of productiveness, a notion which was responsible for Böhm-Bawerk's rejection of the "use theories" of interest. He twice quoted the same trenchant passage from Hermann in which it was pointed out that "land, dwellings, tools, books, *money*, have a durable use value. Their use . . . can be conceived of *as a good in itself*, and may obtain for itself an exchange value which we call interest."[40] But this repeated quotation was merely for the purpose of refutation. To Böhm-Bawerk, "use" meant "physical" or "material" services only.[41] "For any 'use of goods' . . . other than their natural material services," he said, "there is no room,

[37] Cairnes argued (assuming a metallic currency) that if a merchant "can safely dispense with a portion of his ready cash, he is enabled, with the money thus liberated . . . to add to his productive capital. . . . On the other hand, if he finds it necessary to increase his reserve of cash, his productive capital must be proportionally encroached upon . . ." (Cairnes, *op. cit.*, p. 92.) And "precisely the same may be said of the currency of a nation"; for "the chief advantage of a good banking system consists . . . in enabling a nation to reduce within the narrowest limits this unproductive portion of its stock" (meaning metallic stock). (*Ibid.*, pp. 92-3.) Unfortunately, he was not led to face the paradox that, even under such a banking system, the metallic backing, reduced to these "narrowest limits," must have had some productive function or it could have been dispensed with entirely. Still less was he led to perceive that credit was performing a productive function of an identical nature at a much smaller social cost (i.e., at a much smaller sacrifice of other things). This was in spite of his recognition that credit will "affect prices in precisely the same way as if it were actually the coin which it represents." (*Ibid.*, p. 95.)

[38] Böhm-Bawerk, *Capital and Interest*, Smart Translation, p. 17.

[39] *Ibid.*, p. 1.

[40] Hermann, quoted in *Ibid.*, pp. 194 and 233. (My italics.)

[41] He admitted some fears about the "employment of this physical conception in regard to a certain limited class of material goods . . . e.g., a dwelling house, a volume of poems, or a picture. . . ." But, he argued, the fact that "a house shelters and warms, is nothing else than a result of the forces of gravity, cohesion, and resistance, of impenetrability, of the non-conducting quality of building materials"; and "the thoughts and feelings of the poet reproduce themselves . . . in a direct physical way, by light, colour, and form of written characters; and it is this physical part of the mediation which is the office of the book." (*Ibid.*, p. 222.) He would evidently have regarded the books in a library as wholly without use except when a reader's book was brought "into the necessary relation with his eye for the image, which is continually being formed by reflection, to fall on the retina." (*Ibid.*, p. 221.)

either in the world of fact, or in the world of logical ideas." [42] It is "theoretically inadmissible to recognise relations as real goods." [43]

Von Wieser mentioned various reasons why holdings of ready money were indispensable or speculatively profitable; [44] but he thought that the "advantage in value" is only *realized* by such holdings when the object is ultimately acquired for which the money was accumulated. [45] And although he used phrases which at first suggest that he had perceived that money units are useful or necessary for reasons of the same economic nature as other productive assets or durable consumption assets, [46] and although he clearly regarded money as part of circulating capital, [47] he used his chief concepts in a far from rigorous manner. One can hardly feel that he was visualizing, even dimly, the prospective yield which induces the acquisition of money assets. [48]

Wicksell accepted explicitly Aristotle's contention that money is "sterile." [49] It "does not itself enter into the processes of production," he said. [50] Yet, in discussing the various functions of money (e.g., as resources to meet unforeseen disbursements), he discussed also the factors determining its average period of "rest" or "idleness," notions which suggest that it must have periods of work or activity. He held that money was held "not to be consumed . . . *or to be employed in technical production,* but to be exchanged for something else. . . ." [51] He did not explain why the fact that money is not consumed, or intended to be exchanged for something else, should pre-

[42] *Ibid.*, p. 231. The argument which occurred to him, and should have shaken him, that "the possession of good machines might assist the maker to secure, say, a good credit, a good name, good custom," etc., he dismissed as "hairsplitting." (*Ibid.*, p. 230, footnote.)

[43] *Ibid.*, p. 261.

[44] Von Wieser, *Social Economics*, pp. 284-6.

[45] *Ibid.*, p. 169. (For a refutation of this view, see below, pp. 213-215.)

[46] E.g., ". . . in order to cover the same marginal use, more or less money has to be expended." (*Op. cit.*, p. 263.) "The theory of the value of money must start from the service of money, just as that of the value of wares starts from their serviceability." (*Ibid.*, p. 265.) ". . . The need of money is nearly akin to the need of commodities. In the monetary economy, everyone meets his personal need of goods by first covering the need of money. The latter, like the former, is also influenced in the final analysis by the magnitude of the needs and the law of satiety." (*Ibid.*, p. 285.)

[47] *Ibid.*, p. 294-9.

[48] The omission of references to important writers on money like Jevons, Menger and Irving Fisher is due to their having followed the tradition I am criticizing without having contributed any new slant on the point at issue.

[49] Wicksell, *Lectures*, Vol. II, p. 191.

[50] *Ibid.*, p. 190.

[51] *Ibid.*, p. 15. (My italics.)

vent it from providing continuous services in production.[52] But in criticizing Menger for his false distinction between "money on the wing" and "money in hand," he wrote, "Some money may often lie untouched for years in the till, though it has not, on that account, ceased to serve as a means of circulation."[53] Here, surely, is an admission that money in the till is *providing continuous services*, that it is *not economically idle*, or "resting," and that its usefulness is not concentrated into the moment at which it is spent.[54]

Marshall referred to the services (without using this word) rendered by holdings of currency, in making business "easy and smooth,"[55] and discussed the balancing of the "advantages" of holding resources in this form with the "disadvantages" of putting more of a person's resources into a form "in which they yield him no *direct* income or *other benefit*."[56] But somehow he did not see that he was comparing one "advantage" with another "advantage," i.e., one end or means with another end or means. It certainly seems that he also was in some measure misled by the realization that a mere increase in the number of *money units* (pounds, francs, dollars, etc.) does not, in itself, result in an increase in the flow of monetary services. He said, "currency differs from other things in that an increase in its quantity exerts no direct influence on the amount of services it renders."[57] That view, combined with the influence of the "barren money" tradition, appears to account for his insistence that the holding of resources in the form of currency "locks up *in a barren form* resources that might yield an income of gratifi-

[52] Wicksell seems to have had some misgivings on this point. He wrote: "Now this is also true of a merchant's goods." He says, however, that it is then "a question of *continued production* . . . or . . . an intermediate link in the process." (*Ibid.*. p. 15.) But are not a merchant's stocks of money just as much a link in the productive process?

[53] *Ibid.*, p. 21.

[54] Never quite happy on the subject, Wicksell argued also (a) that money assets are different from other assets because they always remain in the market, "though in different hands"; and (b) that "money itself has no marginal utility, since it is not intended for consumption." (*Ibid.*, pp. 19-20.) Yet are money assets any different in this respect from other durable assets? They do not come into the market unless we put them in. And no durable goods have marginal utility "in themselves," unless they are consumed or "used up" in production. Only the services which they render have marginal utility. He contended also that, whilst the supply of real capital is limited by physical conditions, "the supply of money is in theory unlimited." (*Interest and Prices*, p. xxvi.) Here he obviously meant "money units."

[55] Marshall, *Money, Credit and Commerce*, p. 45.

[56] *Ibid.*, p. 44. (My italics.) Why did Marshall use the word "direct"? I feel that he was almost on the point of recognizing explicitly the "indirect" yield (pecuniary or non-pecuniary) from money assets. He may have meant, "or other *direct* benefit."

[57] Marshall, *Money, Credit and Commerce*, p. 49.

cation if invested, say, in extra furniture; or a money income if invested in extra machinery or cattle."[58] *This contrast* of furniture and money (as opposed to Adam Smith's *identification* of furniture with money) curiously failed to suggest to him, or his critics and disciples, that he was making a false distinction. Money assets (held as consumers' capital goods) render non-pecuniary gratifications just like those rendered by furniture.

How much wiser was Edwin Cannan's insight, in his *Modern Currency:* "Our need for currency is analagous to our need for houses," he said.[59] And he was, I feel, ahead of his contemporaries in his recognition, from the beginning, that the demand for money is essentially *a demand to hold.*[60] Nevertheless, the passage quoted seems to be inconsistent with what he wrote elsewhere. Thus, in his *Money,* he wrote at one point in the traditional way, that "people only want money in order to buy other things with it. . . ."[61] In reality, people want money so as to be in a position to acquire other things *at the most profitable time, or at the most convenient time.* Had it been put this way to him Cannan, like anyone else, would have agreed at once.[62] As things are, after having recognized that the services of money are analogous to those of a house, he wrote that holdings of money "are not *directly* productive."[63] People would not diminish their holdings "without reason," he continued, "because it would, they believe, be inconvenient to have less in hand." But cash in hand and at the bank does not differ in this respect from any type of stock in trade. The main difference is that, in the case of money stocks, it is easier to rectify any mistaken judgment which has led to surplus stocks (but less easy to rectify any deficiency).

Wicksteed (agreeing with his interpretation of Aristotle) illustrated what he thought was "the exact nature of a circulating medium" as "something which X, when he has given Y something that Y wants, is willing to receive in exchange *though he has no use for*

---

[58] *Ibid.,* p. 45. (My italics.)

[59] Cannan, *Modern Currency and the Regulation of Its Value,* p. 11. It is interesting to notice that Keynes *contrasted* houses and money (*General Theory,* pp. 226-228).

[60] See T. E. Gregory, *Professor Cannan and Contemporary Monetary Theory,* p. 37, in *London Essays in Economics.*

[61] Cannan, *Money: Its Connexion with Rising and Falling Prices,* 4th Edn., p. 19.

[62] Had he consistently thought in this way, however, he would have made the point referred to in his passage quoted in my footnote 71 much more effectively.

[63] *Modern Currency,* p. 12. (My italics.) It is interesting to compare Marshall's phrase, "no direct income," with Cannan's "not directly productive." The word "direct" is not very helpful.

it himself, because he knows that he can, in his turn, get something that he does want in exchange for it." [64] No article, he contended, which is accepted as a medium of exchange, occupies "on its own merits . . . such a place on (people's) relative scale as would justify the exchange." [65] But if we had "no use for" money, would we not always part with it immediately we got it, so that the velocity of circulation would be infinite? The fact that we hold money assets for any period at all indicates that, although we do not want to use these assets *in any other way,* their services *do* occupy a place on our scale of preferences, just like the services of all the other capital resources which we refrain from exchanging.[66]

Cassel recognized that "an object in general demand" which develops "spontaneously into a general medium of exchange . . . naturally acquires a *new attraction,* in virtue of *its new property.*" [67] But he did not represent this "new attraction," or the "new property," as a new and additional *use* (personal or business); and on the next page he employed the words, "merely to be used later for exchange with another commodity." [68]

Robertson (Sir Denis H.), in spite of his highly independent and original approach to the question, has never torn himself away from the tradition which regards "idle money" as unproductive. The following passage from the 1947 edition of his delightful textbook is not one of the "little bits of specially dead wood" which he cut out of the 1928 version.

. . .The value of money is (within limits) a measure of the usefulness of any one unit of money to its possessor, but not to society as a whole: while the value of bread is also a measure (within limits) of the *social* usefulness of any one loaf of bread. And the reason for this peculiarity about money is the fact that nobody generally speaking wants it except for the sake of the control which it gives over other things.[69]

Again I ask, then why is the velocity of circulation not infinite?

Pigou, in *The Veil of Money,* refers to the damage which would be inflicted on us if we lost the services of money. It would be just

---

[64] Wicksteed, in *Who Said "Barren Metal?"* op. cit., p. 108. (My italics.)

[65] Wicksteed, *The Common Sense of Political Economy,* Vol. I, p. 136.

[66] Because I insist upon the continuity of services or yield from money assets, this does not mean that I deny the truism that such assets are demanded in order to be "exchanged for something else" *at the appropriate moment, i.e., when the services rendered have fully fulfilled their purpose.* But one eminent economist who read the typescript of this article assumed that I was denying this!

[67] Cassel, *Theory of Social Economy,* Vol. II, p. 350. (My italics.)

[68] *Ibid.,* p. 351.

[69] D. H. Robertson, *Money,* p. 31.

as if roads and railways were destroyed.[70] But he similarly insists that money is "only useful *because* it exchanges for other things," and he accepts the tradition that "a larger quantity does not, as with other things, carry more satisfaction on its back than a smaller quantity, but the same satisfaction." Nevertheless, he differs from previous writers (with the exception of Greidanus and the possible exception of Cannan)[71] because he makes it clear that by "quantity of money" he means "the *number of units of money* embodied" in the "instrument" or "institution" of money. (Pigou's italics.) The mere fact, however, that a particular economic good is capable of being diluted is no proof that it is not useful or productive. Milk does not cease to be useful because its adulteration does not increase its gross usefulness.[72]

Pigou has recourse also to a metaphor which previous writers have used, namely, that of comparing money to the oil in a machine. He refers to it as a "lubricant." [73] Now a lubricant is always *consumed*, whereas money assets are economically durable. If we use this metaphor, then, we must regard money assets as the resources which supply a continuous flow of lubrication. The comparison then succeeds in suggesting the continuous yield which money assets offer. But it may still leave the wrong impression that the services of money consist in "circulation." [74]

Keynes adopted the Marshallian view of money being resources, but barren resources (although Marshall seems to have been nearer

[70] Pigou, *The Veil of Money*. The pertinent passages are all on pp. 24-27.

[71] Greidanus (in his tract, *The Development of Keynes' Economic Theories*, p. 36), has distinguished between the "nominal amount of money" and "the quantity of money in terms of goods," for which I would use the terms "the number of money units" and, "the amount of money in real terms." In his earlier work, *The Value of Money*, p. 162, his exposition was less effective because he had not made this distinction clearly enough.

The germ of the distinction is present also in Cannan's article "The Application of the Theoretical Apparatus of Supply and Demand to Units of Currency," *Economic Journal*, 1921, in which he explained that the demand for money can only be said appropriately to have "increased" when more units *of the same value* would be demanded. At a lower value per unit there would have been, in my own terminology, a demand for the same amount of "money in real terms" (measurable only in abstract units of constant value but for more "actual money units," such units having been "diluted").

[72] I feel that if Pigou had conceived of the total value of assets demanded for and used for monetary purposes, being measured in "real terms," he would have stressed the term "instrument" rather than the term "institution" as a description of the aggregate collection of money assets. His comparison of this "institution" with the laws of property and contract does not seem to me to be appropriate or helpful.

[73] Pigou, *op. cit.*, p. 25. (Compare Marshall, *op. cit.*, p. 38; Robertson, *op. cit.*, p. 10.)

[74] See below, pp. 213-215.

than Keynes to a perception of the essential productiveness of money assets). Yet the terminology of *The General Theory* suggests, in itself, an awareness of the continuous services of money assets; for it appears at first to be conferring a definite name upon the yield which is expected to flow from an investment in such assets, namely, "liquidity." [75] Certainly, liquidity is regarded as (a) something valuable and (b) something continuously received or enjoyed. This is implicit in the contention that we *want* a "reward" for parting with it for any given length of time, and that we *shall be* "rewarded" for so doing. "The power of disposal" over money assets, said Keynes, although it offers "a potential convenience or security," and although people are "ready to pay something" (a "liquidity premium") for this advantage, brings forth, "so to speak, nothing . . . in the shape of output." [76] But if the capital value of my till is £ 100 and the average amount of cash in the till is also £ 100, may they not be expected to make an equal contribution to my output? However, Keynes contended that the liquidity which is provided continuously by *money held,* and for which people are prepared to pay a premium, represents a yield of *nil.* The holders of money are envisaged as refusing to part with this yield of *nil* unless they are paid the rate of interest. [77]

Keynes built a heavy structure on this thesis that money assets are absolutely sterile. So much is this so, that Greidanus actually contrasts him with Marshall. Greidanus contends that Keynes' view —first expressed in his *Tract*—that money has no utility apart from its exchange value, although supported by quotations from Marshall, [78] completely overlooked "the advantages of holding currency" which Marshall stressed. [79] "The place Marshall would have assigned to the 'advantages,' Keynes in his equation allots to the number of

---

[75] The term "liquidity" had not, I think, previously been used in the sense which Keynes gave it. It had been employed mainly in connection with the special case of the reserves of banks, insurance societies, etc. Discussing banks, Cassel defined "the *liquidity* of the assets as the ratio of the sum of the advances which falls due for repayment daily to the sum of the advances made." (*Op. cit.,* Vol. II, pp. 403-4.)

[76] Keynes, *General Theory,* p. 226.

[77] Keynes' equation (*General Theory,* top of p. 228) to illustrate the fact that, in equilibrium, "wealth owners" will have "nothing to choose in the way of advantage" between the holding or acquisition of houses, wheat and money, would, if it had stood alone, have given the impression that he was about to say: "The *liquidity premium* is, of course, simply another name for 'yield,' when we describe the services of money." But in fact, he stressed the opposite, in deliberately *contrasting* the yield from a house with the *absence* of a yield from money.

[78] Keynes quoted (in his *Tract on Monetary Reform,* pp. 78-9) some of the very passages from Marshall which I have quoted above.

[79] T. Greidanus, *The Development of Keynes' Economic Theories,* pp. 2-7.

consumption units we wish to buy in a certain period."[80] But the fact that Keynes did not realize that his views about the services of money diverged so fundamentally from those of his great teacher is surely due to Marshall's own exposition reflecting some conceptual confusion.[81]

Keynes' acknowledged followers have, as far as I am aware, failed to examine or test this crucial stone in his foundations. Apart from the false impressions created through his having excluded the acquisition of assets which provide liquidity from the concept of "investment," there remains this notion that money assets differ from other assets in that they do not multiply. For instance, L. Tarshis, in a 1948 exposition of Keynesianism, contends that, against the advantages of liquidity, "the holder of money must set the disadvantage that it does not multiply, that his wealth held in that form does not grow."[82] Of course, it does multiply in the sense that any agent of production provides valuable services which may be embodied into cumulable resources. The services of consumers' capital goods (including cash balances) *are* always consumed; but those of producers' goods (including cash balances) are incorporated into wanted things with exchange value. That is why they are acquired or retained.

Even Mises, who has so clearly perceived and emphasized the essential homogeneity of the scarcity concept, has not yet rejected the traditional view. Money, he says, is "an economic good,"[83] but neither a producer's nor a consumer's good.[84] It is not acquired by people "for employment in their own production activities,"[85] and it is "not a part of capital; it produces no fruit."[86] Although "indispensable in our economic order . . . [money] is not a physical component of the social distributive apparatus in the way that account books, prisons, or fire-arms are."[87] Adam Smith said that money was unproductive because it was like a highway.[88] But Mises would

---

[80] *Ibid.*, p. 6.

[81] Marshall certainly failed to realize clearly enough that money assets, in providing "advantages" or "benefits," were as productive as all other instrumental capital or all other durable consumers' goods. Like several writers before him and after him, he appears to have come very near to perceiving this truth, but for reasons which I find puzzling, he never managed to make the final jump.

[82] L. Tarshis, "A Consideration of the Economic and Monetary Theories of J. M. Keynes," *American Economic Review*, May 1948, pp. 261-271.

[83] Mises, *Theory of Money and Credit*, p. 85; *Human Action*, p. 415.

[84] Mises, *Theory of Money and Credit*, p. 79.

[85] Mises, *Human Action*, p. 398.

[86] Mises, *Theory of Money and Credit*, p. 90.

[87] *Ibid.*, p. 85.

[88] See above, p. 201.

insist that a highway *is* productive. Money, he says a little later, does not derive its value from that of its products, like other products, "for no increase in the welfare of the members of a society can result from the availability of an additional quantity of money." [89] Now it is true (as he puts it in his *Human Action*) that "*the services money renders* can be neither improved nor impaired by changing the supply of money," [90] for he is here referring to *the number of money units*. But it is not true that the aggregate stock of all commodities, securities or tokens which can serve the purposes of a medium of exchange and which are demanded for that purpose, does not contribute to "welfare" in proportion to its value. When society decides to use assets to a greater extent for the monetary services which they can perform, that *does* result in a preferred use of all scarce resources and an increase in "welfare" in that sense. Money assets held provide valuable services (utilities), and they do derive their value from their power to render these services. The fact that some assets held for medium of exchange purposes may have value because they can be used for other purposes also (e.g., a gold coin) does not affect this truth.

It may be objected that, when the assets held are mere tokens, as with currency notes and demand deposits, their value is derived, not from the value of their services, but (a) from their market convertibility into goods in general or (b) from their contractual or legal convertibility into a monetary metal or other currencies. But in the absence of *faith* in convertibility in some such sense, the assets would be incapable of rendering a medium of exchange services. They could not constitute money. It remains true, then, that we part with non-money goods and services in order to acquire money because we judge that money can render us services; and we hold so much of it as renders services which we value more highly than those rendered by non-money assets.

Far from denying the productiveness of money assets held, however, Mises constantly stresses their "services." And in a most lucid passage he describes the nature of their *productiveness* [91] (although without using this word). He insists that "what is called storing money is a way of *using* wealth." [92] One's holdings of money do not represent "an unintentional remainder," he says. Their amount "is

[89] *Ibid.*, p. 86.
[90] Mises, *Human Action*, p. 418. (My italics.)
[91] Mises, *Human Action*, p. 398.
[92] Mises, *Theory of Money and Credit*, p. 147. (My italics.)

determined by deliberate demand." [93] Money is "appraised on its own merits, i.e., the *services* which each man expects from holding cash." [94] And it does not perform its task by circulating, but by being held. Thus, he says: "Money is an element of change, not because it circulates but because it is kept in cash holdings." [95] Indeed "there is no fraction of time in between in which the money is not a part of an individual's or a firm's cash holding, but just in 'circulation'." [96] And although it is true that people are continuously acquiring money in order continuously to part with it, they accumulate it in the first place "in order to be ready for the moment in which a purchase may be accomplished." [97] For this reason, he *denies* that there is a difference between money and vendible goods.

I get the impression therefore that, in his *Human Action,* Mises is on the point of saying that it is merely the *pecuniary* yield which is missing from the *private* holding of money assets.

H. S. Ellis, in an early work on *German Monetary Theory* (1934), also comes remarkably near to stating the correct principle—so near, indeed, that it looks almost as though, having prepared for combat, he is unwilling actually to clash with the great weight of authority against him. He certainly appears to be trying to escape the conclusions of his own analysis. Thus, he recognizes the "flow of utilities" from money holdings and says that this flow "appears to the producer indirectly as a *plus* in quantity of product ascribable to his possessing a perfectly liquid asset and to the consumer as a *plus* in satisfactions in the form of convenience. . . ." [98] Moreover, he realizes that the circulation of money "*terminates* the flow of services. . . ." [99] On all these points, he is well ahead of most writers. Yet at the same time he wants to "preserve the undeniably separate character of monetary *services,*" [100] partly for reasons which I do not follow, but partly because he feels that money assets as such, although providing services or utilities, cannot be properly regarded as part of the aggregate assets of the community. This is so, he says, because it would be double counting, such as would result if

[93] Mises, *Human Action,* p. 399.
[94] *Ibid.,* pp. 414-5. (My italics.)
[95] *Ibid.,* p. 415. See also *ibid.,* p. 396, where Mises questions the assumption of the mathematical economists that services rendered by money "consist wholly or essentially in its turnover, in its circulation."
[96] Mises, *Human Action,* p. 399.
[97] *Ibid.,* p. 400.
[98] Ellis, *German Monetary Theory,* p. 109.
[99] *Ibid.,* p. 109 (footnote).
[100] *Ibid.,* p. 109.

one included mortgages or stocks and shares as well as the assets they represent, as part of society's aggregate capital.[101]

But to obtain the goods which money is said to "represent," one must *exchange* money assets for non-money assets, whereas, if a company is liquidated, the shareholders do not *exchange* assets, i.e., they do not *buy* the capital resources of the firm: they receive them without any exchange taking place (in practice after the assets are realized for money). Similarly, if a mortgage is foreclosed, there is no *exchange* of assets. Money assets do not, then, "represent" *in the same sense* the assets for which they can be exchanged. They are themselves assets which are just as productive (although in a different way) as those for which they are exchanged.[102] To appreciate this, one must try for a moment to forget about the number of units into which these assets are divided and to think of their aggregate amount in real terms.

As far as I know, only one economist has come at all close to *an actual enunciation* of what I regard as the true theory of the yield of money assets, namely, Greidanus, who has significantly described his theory, "the yield theory." [103] But his contributions on this subject appear to have had little influence upon other economists, whilst his treatment has not brought out explicitly what I conceive to be the full basic truth—the fact that money assets are not only subject to the same laws of value as other scarce things, but are equally productive in all intelligible senses.

Surely the reality is that, although money is always held (except perhaps by misers) with a view to its being ultimately passed on to others, the act of passing it on is merely the *culmination* of a service (technical or speculative) which it has been rendering to the possessor. Indeed, the transfer itself occupies a mere moment whilst the services which flow from the possession of money are continuous over time. The essence of all these services is *availability*. In the terminology which I suggested in my *Theory of Idle Resources*,[104] money assets are not unemployed or resting when they are in our pockets, or in our tills, or in our banking accounts, but in *pseudo-*

---

101 *Ibid.,* p. 110.

102 There is another argument used by Ellis to justify the separate classification of money assets. He argues that "individuals hold money *only because* it has exchange value, whereas they would desire shoes even if shoes were free goods." (*Ibid.,* p. 113). But the point at issue is the similarity of money *assets* and non-money *assets.* Free goods would not be assets; and only assets can be used as media of exchange.

103 Greidanus, *The Value of Money.*

104 See my *Theory of Idle Resources,* pp. 57-70, for the definition *pseudo*-idleness, and pp. 146-173 for the definition *of withheld capacity.*

idleness, like a piano when it is not being played, or a fireman or a fire engine when there are no fires. If it could be shown that there exist various forms of wasteful idleness in money which could be classed as *withheld capacity,* or which correspond, say, to a trader's redundant stocks (which, through mismanagement, he fails to realize), we could rightly talk of "idle money," but not otherwise. And the fact that money units may be held speculatively does not mean that they are not being *used.* Stocks of goods retained because their sale now would, it is anticipated, realize less than their sale later on, including all such goods in warehouses and shops, are normally [105] *being used,* in the course of the production of "time utilities." The same applies to money units. When speculatively held, they represent money *in use.*[106]

Hence money does not do its work by circulating. The common analogies of "the circulation of the blood," or "the oil of a machine," are both bad analogies. Because money units are exchange media, they just happen to change ownership more than other types of assets. If we imagine that the work of money is circulation, then we must conclude that money is always idle; for the transfer of money must be regarded as instantaneous![107] It has been suggested that, if people generally were paid quarterly instead of weekly, the demand for money would increase because more money would "be kept idling about at any one time."[108] That is quite the wrong way of putting it. There would be more work for money units to do,[109] more *monetary services* would be required, and more *money* would therefore be required. Changes in the average interval between purchases (i.e., changes in the velocity of circulation of money units) do not mean changes in the average period of *idleness* of those units, but changes in their average period of *service* to each holder, which is a very different thing.

[105] I use the word "normally" here because these stocks may represent not *pseudo-idleness* but *withheld capacity,* i.e., goods which are being withheld, not speculatively, but with a view to maintaining or forcing up prices.

[106] This passage must not be taken to imply that I regard the speculative holding of money as part of a state of affairs which society can passively accept. My point is simply that such money cannot be described as "wastefully idle."

[107] Cannan made this point in a reference to the "disastrous confusions" which can arise through the "common mistake" of dividing currency into that which is "actually circulating" and that which is "idle." (*Modern Currency,* p. 8.) The demand for houses, he said, does not depend upon the number of transactions in them, but comes from "those who want to *hold* houses: even the speculator wants to hold for a time." (*Money,* 4th Edn., p. 72.)

[108] D. H. Robertson, *op. cit.,* p. 37.

[109] No diseconomy would necessarily be involved. There might be less work for other productive factors.

During an inflation there might *appear* to be an enormous demand for money assets in the sense that people want them *for periods of time which they intend to keep as short as possible.* In such circumstances, in spite of a multiplication of transactions, and in spite of increased circulation, the amount of work actually needed from money assets falls off. Each money unit becomes less productive because the real yield in convenience etc., is *diminished* by a real loss. Certainly, people still want money units "for what they will buy," but they value them less than ever.[110]

It may be objected that the nature of money is such that it *does* do all its work in instantaneous skips from buyer to seller, or from debtor to creditor, or from giver to receiver. The objection may be answered by means of a comparison with a climber's rope. Can it be said that the rope on which the climber is belayed is of service to him only when he actually loses his grip and dangles on it? Obviously not, for without the security it provides, he would almost certainly not have been attempting that particular climb.[111]

Some may feel that I am stressing a point which is of verbal rather than of substantial importance. But as Greidanus has pointed out, in the minds of the Keynesians, the failure to recognize the real but non-pecuniary yield enjoyed has led to material fallacies. Once the productiveness of money assets is recognized, the notion that the rate of interest is determined by the demand for and supply of *money assets,* or the demand for and supply of the *services of money assets* ("liquidity"), ceases to have meaning. And the modifications of that theory, like the various compromise revisions of Keynes' theory of interest by his disciples, become equally untenable. For if money assets are demanded, like all other assets, up to the point

---

110 Cannan made this point in his *Money*, (4th Edn., p. 23). He said that "what every one wants the money for . . . is to buy commodities and services in the hopes of making a profit because 'things are going up.'"

111 An eminent "Keynesian" economist who read the typescript of this article wrote: "You contrast the view that money has utility on its own account by performing a definite service with the view that money is valued only by reference to what it will buy. You take these views to be contradictory to one another and criticize some authors for holding both views simultaneously. You seem to feel that an author who recognizes the inherent serviceability of money ought to shake off this other view that money is wanted for what it would get. I suggest, on the contrary, there is nothing mutually contradictory about these two views . . . Thus, the two theories are not mutually exclusive but support each other." I ought to make it clear that I do not regard the truism (it is hardly a "theory") that "money is wanted for what it would get" as conflicting in any way with the theory that money assets are productive. Hence I do not criticize any authors for holding "both views simultaneously," but for denying the productiveness of money assets, which they usually do in simple, unambiguous language.

at which their marginal prospective yield has fallen to the rate of interest, it becomes obvious that the demand for and supply of merely one category of capital assets cannot be held to be the determinants of the ratio between the value of the pure services of assets in general and their capital value, which is the best way of conceiving of the rate of interest. If interest is envisaged (as Keynes regarded it) as the "reward" for not hoarding, it has to be accepted equally as the "reward" for not investing in each and every other productive field. Or, more generally, the "reward" for not investing in any productive field (including that of money assets) is the "average" or "general" return which can be expected from all other fields of investment—allowance made for entrepreneurial remuneration.[112]

It might be argued that there *is* one respect in which money assets are different, namely, that their *real* volume or stock is not determined by their being produced and consumed. That is, whereas services may be embodied into non-money assets for replacement or net accumulation purposes, this is impossible with money (although the number of *money units* could be affected by the production of any commodity into which such units are contractually or legally convertible—e.g., gold, under the gold standard). The truth is, however, that money is in exactly the same position as certain other non-money assets in this respect. Thus, consider the case of land, in the sense of site. With the growth of population and the expansion of the productive purposes to which land can be put, its aggregate value in real terms will increase. Similarly (and *ceteris paribus*) the real value of money assets will increase to the same extent under such circumstances.[113] But the *services* of money assets *are* produced and, like all other services, they are either consumed or embodied into products.

In conclusion, I suggest that if we understand that the demand for money assets is a demand for *productive resources*, we are in a better position to grasp the nature of the difficult problems which arise owing to (a) *uncertainties about* the future value of the money *unit* (in practice, uncertainties about what governments or monetary authorities will do) or (b) (less important and rather less difficult) realized changes in the value of the money unit.

[112] It is unnecessary to discuss here the qualifications which this assertion requires when the value of the money unit is rising or falling.

[113] On the determinants of this real value, see my article, *The Notion of the Volume of Money, op. cit.*

XVI

The Accelerator and Say's Law [1]

by WILLIAM H. PETERSON

ECONOMISTS, like women, are not immune to the dictates of fashion. One such dictate in vogue among post-Keynesians is the accelerator, which enjoyed similar popularity in the early Twenties. At least a partial reason for the renewed popularity of the accelerator is that it forms an integral part of the *General Theory*.[2]

The acceleration doctrine holds that a temporary increase in consumer demand sets in motion an accelerated "derived demand" for capital goods. This action, according to adherents of the doctrine, explains at least part of the causation of the business cycle. As evidence supporting this theory, accelerationists point to boom-and-bust, feast-and-famine conditions prevalent in capital goods industries.

A typical illustration of the acceleration principle follows. Assume a "normal" annual demand for a certain consumer good at 500,000 units. Production is accomplished through 1000 durable units of capital goods; capacity of each capital unit: 500 consumer units per year; life of each unit: 10 years. Then assume a 10 per cent increase in consumer demand. Thus:

Annual Consumer Demand		Capital Goods	Annual Captl. Gds. Demand ("derived")
"normal year"	500,000	1000	100 (replacements)
next yr. + 10%	550,000	1100	200 (replacements plus new)
3rd yr.—new "nor."	550,000	1100	100 (replacements)

[1] This article is done at the inspiration of a series of lectures by Prof. W. H. Hutt of the University of Capetown, at Buck Hill Falls, Pa., June 13-25, 1955.

[2] See, e.g., J. M. Clark, "Business Acceleration and the Law of Demand," *JPE*, March 1917, pp. 217-235; T. N. Carver, *Principles of National Economy*, 1921, pp. 436-440; J. M. Keynes, *General Theory*, 1935; and R. F. Harrod, *Trade Cycle*, 1936.

Conclusion: *10% increase in consumer demand led to 100% increase in capital demand in same year but to 50% decrease in capital demand in following year.*

The argument against the acceleration doctrine simply shows so many unreal assumptions and a vital *non sequitur* as to nullify any validity in the doctrine whatsoever. An analysis of these objections follows:

1. *Rigid specialization in capital goods industries.* Accelerationists pose their doctrine on the basis of a given capital goods industry supplying equipment for a given consumer goods industry *and no other*. Thus a decrease in consumer demand or even a falling-off in its rate of growth immediately cuts off part of the capital goods market, and the "famine" phase of the capital goods industry begins.

Yet where is the capital goods industry so rigidly specialized as to preclude its serving other markets, with or without some conversion of its facilities? Are we to presume that businessmen under the pressure of overhead and profit maximization will twiddle their thumbs waiting for their consumer demand to "reaccelerate"? It is clear that accelerationists deny or ignore convertibility of facilities and substitutability of markets.

Within many capital goods industries, trends of diversification and complementarity are evident. Examples: A machine tool manufacturer which has undertaken lines of construction and textile equipment; a basic chemical producer which has engaged in the manufacture of home clotheswasher and dishwasher detergents. These trends break down the "industry" classifications, upon which the accelerator is based.

2. *No unutilized capacity in the consumer goods industry.* Holders of the acceleration doctrine assume the consumer goods industry is operating at the extensive margin of production and no intensive possibilities for greater production exist.

But very few consumer goods industries, typically, operate at constant peak capacity. To do so is generally to operate beyond the point of optimum efficiency as well as beyond the point of maximum profit. The usual case then, other than during wartime, is that an industry operates with some unutilized capacity, some "slack." Normally this unutilized capacity is to be found among the marginal and sub-marginal producers, and it is these producers which could and probably would absorb any increase in consumer demand—without, of course, the purchase of new equipment.

Yet even the successful and efficient producer would likely consider other means of absorbing higher consumer demand before committing himself to more equipment and greater overhead. For example, he could expand the existing labor force, resort to over-time, add one or two additional shifts, sub-contract work in over-loaded departments, and so on. That such alternatives are feasible without more equipment is evidenced by the experience of even the most efficient firms in the utilization of their capital equipment. Examples: A West Coast airplane manufacturer found his gear-cutting equipment in use only 16 per cent of the time; a New York newspaper plant utilized its presses only 11 per cent of the time. The concept of 100 per cent utilization of all capital equipment is not tenable.

3. *Automaton role for entrepreneurs.* Accelerationists share the danger common to all *holistic* and *macro* approaches to economic problems—namely, the submergence of individual and entrepreneurial decision (human action) to a constant factor within a pat formula. Such treatment implies on the part of entrepreneurs irrationality or sheer impulsiveness. Boulding described this situation thusly: [3]

The picture of the firm on which much of our analysis is built is crude in the extreme, and in spite of recent refinements there remains a vast gap between the elegant curves of the economist and the daily problems of a flesh-and-blood executive.

Accelerationists argue that a temporary rise in consumer demand automatically calls into being additional capital goods. If this were true, it follows that entrepreneurs in capital goods industries wit-lessly expand their capacity and thereby commit themselves to greater overhead without regard to future capital goods demand.

True, entrepreneurs can and do err in gauging future demand. But the concept of automatic response to any rise in demand, on the order of the conditioned reflex salivation of Pavlov's dogs, is not warranted. Increased capacity is less of a calculated risk in response to increased current demand than it is to *anticipated* future demand. This anticipation, in turn, is likely to be based upon market research, price comparison, population studies, cost analysis, political stability, etc., rather than upon impulse.

4. *Static technology.* It is not surprising that the accelerator perhaps reached the zenith of its popularity when professional journals were replete with terms like "secular stagnation" and "technological frontier." (Nowadays the term is "automation." Apparently we

[3] K. E. Boulding, "The Theory of the Firm in the Last Ten Years," *AER*, December 1942, p. 801.

have moved from the one extreme of too little technology to the opposite extreme of too much.) Such heavy-handed treatment of technology does not coincide with experience. Science and invention do not hibernate during depressions. Du Pont introduced both Nylon and Cellophane during the Thirties.

Adherents of the acceleration principle must either minimize or ignore the impact of technology on rising productivity, for, after all, a strict ratio of capital goods to consumer goods output must be maintained to substantiate the action of the accelerator. Technology, however, can and does obviate such ratios. Technological advances not only serve to increase the unit-volume of given capital goods through superior technical design but also through the improvement of fuel, the refinement of raw materials, the use of time-and-motion studies, the rearrangement of layout and production flow, and so on.

While the growth of technology is somewhat irregular, there can be no question of its progression. Progression tends to "accelerate" the obsolescence component of depreciation and thereby crimps the acceleration model, which, *ceteris paribus,* ignores the unpredictable dynamics of technology.[4]

5. *Arbitrary time periods.* Accelerationists must use time as a frame of reference for their doctrine. The most frequent time period used is a year. Such a time period, however, implies an even spread of the increase (or the decrease) of consumer demand in the time period. Thus a spasmodic strengthening and weakening of demand within the time period could distort the artificial taxonomics of the accelerator.

For example, a January-December period may carry one peak demand, whereas a July-June period may yield two peak demands. An accelerationist may read the first period as having an 8 per cent increase and the second as having a 10 per cent increase, which, in the long run, may average out to 9 per cent or some other figure.

Moreover, within a time period, the accelerationist assumes a fixed relationship between consumer goods and capital goods. Let alone the problem of technological advances, were such a fixed relationship to exist it would necessarily mean that the cycles of production for both sets of goods were perfectly synchronized. This, however, is rarely the case. Consumer goods generally have a short cycle; capital goods, a long cycle. Thus, current capital goods pro-

[4] Cf. J. R. Hicks, *The Theory of Wages,* 1932, pp. 112-135. Even though it is incidental to his distribution theory, Hicks formulates a theory of invention which could profit the accelerationists.

duction may be based on orders originating in an earlier "period." Two consecutive increases in consumer demand could conceivably be followed by a decrease, which may well mean that the latest order for capital goods would be cancelled. The flow of goods from the capital pipeline is not irrevocable.

6. *Implicit denial of Say's Law.* Previous objections to the acceleration doctrine were of the "other-things-are-*not*-equal" variety. In short, with so many independent variables *ceteris paribus* would not hold.

This objection—the implicit denial of Say's Law of Markets—is more fundamental. If it is valid, it would strike at the heart of the acceleration principle and reduce it to a *non sequitur*.

According to Say's Law, the source of purchasing power lies within production—i.e., supply creates its own demand—and therefore *generalized* overproduction or underconsumption is not possible. Barring external distortions to the economy, such as war or drought, Say's Law is operative under two conditions—the flexibility of prices and the neutrality of money. Thus it is not astonishing that a major accelerationist like Keynes who shunned price flexibility and upheld inflation should attempt a refutation of Say's Law and resurrect the dead body of underconsumption, rebaptized as the "consumption function" or "the propensity to consume."

If it is true, as accelerationists claim, that a rise in consumer demand will thereby create a demand for capital goods, then it must be explained what causes the rise in consumer demand in the first place. Should accelerationists concede that the rise is due to capital —or as Böhm-Bawerk put it, "the technical superiority of roundabout production"—they would then be forced to admit, logically, that they have put the cart before the horse, that the growth of capital preceded the growth of demand.

Indeed, if demand could arise without prior production to give it effectiveness, then we should witness the overnight industrialization of India, where such astronomical "consumer demand" exists as to induce the full flowering of the accelerator.

Say's Law not only points to the fallacy of the accelerator but to its corollary, "derived demand." There is a germ of truth in "derived demand"—"primary" consumer demand does affect "secondary" capital demand. But the consecutive sequence should be reversed. The effect of consumer demand upon capital is not demand for capital *per se.* Capital is always in demand as long as time-preference exists—as long as capital yields the reward of interest. Rather, the effect of "derived demand" will be, if strong enough, merely to change the *form* of capital goods, no more. If not otherwise impeded, capital will always flow to the most urgent of the least satisfied demands. The point is that capital accumulation—saving and investment—must come *before* "derived demand." So-called derived demand merely shifts already existing productive resources from present applications to alternative but more rewarding applications.

Insofar, as the acceleration explanation of the business cycle is concerned, accelerationists view deceleration with equal alarm to acceleration. The dilemma was stated by Samuelson: [5]

It is easy to see that in the acceleration principle we have a powerful factor for economic instability. We have all heard of situations where people have to keep running in order to stand still. In the economic world, matters may be worse still: the system may have to be kept running at an ever faster pace just in order to stand still.

To maintain such an argument, Samuelson and other accelerationists must discount the fact that a cut in consumer demand in one line releases consumer demand for other lines. Thus, the change in the composition of consumer demand releases factors engaged in certain suspended lines of capital goods production for new lines of endeavor. That this would cause frictional unemployment of factors is not denied, but frictional unemployment is far less of a problem than generalized unemployment. The notion of ever-accelerating consumer demand to achieve stability within its related capital goods industry thus loses sight of the interchangeability of factors. The essence of capitalism, as in life, is change. While some industries may be in decline, others will be in ascendancy. Capital is not eternally fixed; it can be liquidated and "recirculated." Nor does capital idly wait for consumer demand to "reaccelerate." Disinvestment and reinvestment, business mortality and business birth, industry expansion and industry contraction, constantly adjust the supply and form of capital to the demand for consumer goods. Samuelson overlooks the dynamics of capital in his essentially static, timeless acceleration thesis.

Say's Law places production as the controlling factor over consumption. The accelerator reverses this order. Thus accelerationist Keynes sought to accelerate consumer demand by having the unemployed uselessly dig holes or build pyramids, the important thing being to put "purchasing power" in the hands of spenders. Productionless "purchasing power," according to Say's Law, is a contradic-

[5] P. A. Samuelson, *Economics*, 2nd ed., 1951, p. 391.

tion in terms; it is nothing but inflation. In short, the false premise of "derived demand" in the acceleration principle has led to other false premises.

Conclusions. Four findings spring from this article. One, the accelerator is groundless as a tool of economic analysis. Two, Say's Law has yet to meet an effective refutation. Three, acceptance of the acceleration doctrine leads to false conclusions in other areas of economics. And four, accelerationists must look elsewhere for an answer to the business cycle.

While there is evidence that capital goods industries do suffer wide extremes of business activity during the course of the business cycle, it is also true that consumer goods industries undergo much the same cycle, even if their amplitudes are smaller. That there is correlation between the two phenomena is not denied. But correlation is not causation. This is the heart of the error in the accelerator.

XVII

Toward a Reconstruction of Utility and Welfare Economics

by Murray N. Rothbard

I. *Introduction*

INDIVIDUAL valuation is the keystone of economic theory. For, fundamentally, economics does not deal with things or material objects. Economics analyzes the logical attributes and consequences of the existence of individual valuations. "Things" enter into the picture, of course, since there can be no valuation without things to be valued. But the essence and the driving force of human action, and therefore of the human market economy, are the valuations of individuals. Action is the result of choice among alternatives, and choice reflects values, i.e., individual preferences among these alternatives.

Individual valuations are the direct subject matter of the theories of utility and of welfare. Utility theory analyzes the laws of the values and choices of an individual; welfare theory discusses the relationship between the values of many individuals, and the consequent possibilities of a scientific conclusion on the "social" desirability of various alternatives.

Both theories have lately been foundering in stormy seas. Utility theory is galloping off in many different directions at once; welfare theory, after reaching the heights of popularity among economic theorists, threatens to sink, sterile and abandoned, into oblivion.

The thesis of this paper is that both related branches of economic theory can be salvaged and reconstructed, using as a guiding principle of both fields the concept of "demonstrated preference."

II. *Demonstrated Preference*

a. A Statement of the Concept. Human action is the use of means to arrive at preferred ends. Such action contrasts to the observed behavior of stones and planets, for it implies *purpose* on the part of the actor. Action implies choice among alternatives. Man has means, or resources, which he uses to arrive at various ends; these resources may be time, money, labor energy, land, capital goods, etc. He uses these resources to attain his most preferred ends. From his action, we can deduce that he has acted so as to satisfy his most highly valued desires or preferences.

The concept of *demonstrated preference* is simply this: that actual choice reveals, or demonstrates, a man's preferences; i.e., that his preferences are deducible from what he has chosen in action. Thus, if a man chooses to spend an hour at a concert rather than a movie, we deduce that the former was preferred, or ranked higher on his value scale. Similarly, if a man spends five dollars on a shirt we deduce that he preferred purchasing the shirt to any other uses he could have found for the money. This concept of preference, rooted in real choices, forms the keystone of the logical structure of economic analysis, and particularly of utility and welfare analysis.

While a similar concept played a role in the writings of the early utility economists, it had never received a name, and it therefore remained largely undeveloped and unrecognized as a distinct concept. It was generally discarded in the 1930's, before it had even achieved recognition. This view of preference as derived from choice was present in varying degree in the writings of the early Austrian economists, as well as in the works of Jevons, Fisher, and Fetter. Fetter was the only one who clearly employed the concept in his analysis. The clearest and most thorough formulation of the concept has been in the works of Professor Mises.[1]

b. Positivism and the Charge of Tautology. Before developing some of the applications of the demonstrated preference principle to utility and welfare theory, we must consider the methodological objections that have been levelled against it. Professor Alan Sweezy, for example, seizes on a sentence of Irving Fisher's which

[1] Cf. Alan R. Sweezy, "The Interpretation of Subjective Value Theory in the Writings of the Austrian Economists," *Review of Economic Studies*, June 1934, pp. 176-85, for an historical survey. Sweezy devotes a good part of the article to a criticism of Mises as the leading exponent of the demonstrated preference approach. For Mises' views, cf. *Human Action* (New Haven, 1949), pp. 94-96, 102-03; *Theory of Money and Credit* (3rd Ed. New Haven, 1951), pp. 46 ff. Also cf. Frank A. Fetter, *Economic Principles* (New York, 1915), pp. 14-21.

very succinctly expressed the concept of demonstrated preference: "Each individual acts as he desires." Sweezy is typical of the majority of present-day economists in not being able to understand how such a statement can be made with absolute validity. To Sweezy, insofar as it is not an empirically testable proposition in psychology, such a sentence must simply reduce to the meaningless tautology: "each individual acts as he acts."

This criticism is rooted in a fundamental epistemological error that pervades modern thought: the inability of modern methodologists to understand how economic science can yield substantive truths by means of logical deduction (i.e., the method of "praxeology"). For they have adopted the epistemology of positivism (now dubbed "logical empiricism" or "scientific empiricism" by its practitioners), which uncritically applies the procedures appropriate in physics to the sciences of human action.[2]

In physics, simple facts can be isolated in the laboratory. These isolated facts are known directly, but the laws to explain these facts are not. The laws may only be hypothecated. Their validity can only be determined by logically deducing consequents from them which can be verified by appeal to the laboratory facts. Even if the laws explain the facts, however, and their inferences are consistent with them, the laws of physics can never be *absolutely* established. For some other law may prove more elegant or capable of explaining a wider range of facts. In physics, therefore, postulated explanations have to be hypothecated in such a way that they or their consequents can be empirically tested. Even then, the laws are only tentatively rather than absolutely valid.

In human action, however, the situation is reversed. There is here no laboratory where "facts" can be isolated and broken down into their simple elements. Instead, there are only historical "facts" which are complex phenomena, resultants of many casual factors. These phenomena must be explained, but they cannot be isolated or used to verify or falsify any law. On the other hand, economics, or praxeology, has full and complete knowledge of its original and basic axioms. These are the axioms *implicit in the very existence of human action,* and they are absolutely valid so long as human beings exist. But if the axioms of praxeology are absolutely valid for human existence, then so are the consequents which can logically be deduced from them. Hence, economics, in contrast to physics, can derive absolutely valid substantive truths about the real world

[2] Cf. the methodological treatises of Kaufmann, Hutchison, Souter, Stonier, Myrdal, Morgenstern, etc.

by deductive logic. The axioms of physics are only hypothecated and hence subject to revision; the axioms of economics are already known and hence absolutely true.[3] The irritation and bewilderment of positivists over the "dogmatic" pronouncements of praxeology stem, therefore, from their universal application of methods proper only to the physical sciences.[4]

The suggestion has been made that praxeology is not really scientific, because its logical procedures are verbal ("literary") rather than mathematical and symbolic.[5] But mathematical logic is uniquely appropriate to physics, where the various logical steps along the way are not in themselves meaningful, for the axioms and therefore the deductions of physics are in themselves meaningless, and only take on meaning "operationally," insofar as they can explain and predict given facts. In praxeology, on the contrary, the axioms themselves are known as true and are therefore meaningful. As a result, each step-by-step deduction is meaningful and true. Meanings are far better expressed verbally than in meaningless formal symbols. Moreover, simply to translate economic analysis from words into symbols, and then to retranslate them so as to explain the conclusions, makes little sense, and violates the great scientific principle of Occam's Razor that there should be no unnecessary multiplication of entities.

The crucial concept of the positivists, and the one that forms the basis for their attack on demonstrated preference, is that of "operational meaning." Indeed, their favorite critical epithet is that such and such a formulation or law is "operationally meaningless." [6] The

[3] On the methodology of praxeology and physics, cf. Mises, *Human Action, op. cit.*, and F. A. Hayek, *The Counter Revolution of Science* (Glencoe, Ill., 1952), Part I.

[4] It is even dubious that positivists accurately interpret the proper methodology of physics itself. On the widespread positivist misuse of the Heisenberg Uncertainty Principle in physics as well as in other disciplines, cf. A. H. Hobbs, *Social Problems and Scientism* (Harrisburg, Pa., 1953), pp. 220-32.

[5] For a typical suggestion, cf. George J. Schuller, "Rejoinder," *American Economic Review*, March 1951, p. 188. For a realization that mathematical logic is essentially subsidiary to basic verbal logic, cf. the remarks of André Lalande and René Poirier, on "Logique" and "Logistique," in (A. Lalande, ed.), *Vocabulaire Technique et Critique de la Philosophie* (6th Ed., Paris, 1951), pp. 574, 579.

[6] Paul Samuelson has added the weight of his authority to Sweezy's criticism of Mises and demonstrated preference, and has couched his endorsement in terms of "operational meaning." Samuelson explicitly rejects the idea of a *true* utility theory in favor of one that is merely hypothetical. Cf. Paul A. Samuelson, "The Empirical Implications of Utility Analysis," *Econometrica*, 1938, pp. 344 ff; and *id., Foundations of Economic Analysis* (Cambridge, 1947), pp. 91-92.

The concept of operational meaning was originated by the physicist Percy W.

test of "operationally meaningful" is derived strictly from the procedures of physics as outlined above. An explanatory law must be framed so that it can be tested and found empirically false. Any law which claims to be absolutely true and not empirically capable of being falsified is therefore "dogmatic" and operationally meaningless—hence, the positivist's view that if a statement or law is not capable of being falsified empirically, it must simply be a tautologous definition. And consequently, Sweezy's attempted reduction of Fisher's sentence to a meaningless identity.[7]

Sweezy objects that Fisher's "each man acts as he desires" is circular reasoning, because action implies desire, and yet desires are not arrived at independently, but are only discoverable through the action itself. Yet this is not circular. For desires exist by virtue of the concept of human action, and of the existence of action. It is precisely the characteristic of human action that it is motivated by desires and ends, in contrast to the unmotivated bodies studied by physics. Hence, we can say validly that action is motivated by desires, and yet confine ourselves to deducing the *specific* desires from the real actions.

c. Professor Samuelson and "Revealed Preference." "Revealed preference"—preference revealed through choice—would have been an apt term for our concept. It has, however been pre-empted by Samuelson for a seemingly similar but actually quite different concept of his own. The critical difference is this: Samuelson assumes the existence of an underlying preference scale that forms the basis of a man's actions, and that remains *constant* in the course of his actions over time. Samuelson then uses complex mathematical procedures in an attempt to "map" the individual's preference scale on the basis of his numerous actions.

The prime error here is the assumption that the preference scale remains constant over time. There is no reason whatever for making any such assumption. All we can say is that an action, at a specific point of time, reveals part of a man's preference scale *at that time.*

Bridgman *explicitly* to explain the methodology of physics. Cf. Bridgman, *The Logic of Modern Physics* (New York, 1927). Many founders of modern positivism, such as Mach and Boltzmann, were also physicists.

[7] The heroes of positivism, Rudolf Carnap and Ludwig Wittgenstein, disparaged deductive inference as merely drawing out "tautologies" from the axioms. Yet all reasoning is deductive, and this process is peculiarly vital to arriving at truth. For a critique of Carnap and Wittgenstein, and a demonstration that inference is not merely identity or "tautology," cf. A. Lalande, "Tautologie," in *Vocabulaire, op. cit.*, pp. 1103-04.

There is no warrant for assuming that it remains constant from one point of time to another.[8]

The "revealed preference" theorists do not recognize that they are assuming constancy; they believe that their assumption is simply that of *consistent* behavior, which they identify with "rationality." They will admit that people are not always "rational," but uphold their theory as being a good first approximation or even as having normative value. However, as Mises has pointed out, *constancy* and *consistency* are two entirely different things. Consistency means that a person maintains a transitive order of rank on his preference-scale (if A is preferred to B and B is preferred to C, then A is preferred to C). But the revealed preference procedure does not rest on this assumption so much as on an assumption of *constancy*—that an individual maintains the same value-scale over time. While the former might be called irrational, there is certainly nothing irrational about someone's value scales changing through time. Hence, no valid theory can be built on a constancy assumption.[9]

One of the most absurd procedures based on a constancy assumption has been the attempt to arrive at a consumer's preference scale not through observed real action, but through quizzing him by questionnaries. *In vacuo*, a few consumers are questioned at length on which abstract bundle of commodities they would prefer to another abstract bundle, etc. Not only does this suffer from the constancy error; no assurance can be attached to the mere questioning of people when they are not confronted with the choices in actual practice. Not only will a person's valuation differ when talking about them than when he is actually choosing, but there is also no guarantee that he is telling the truth.[10]

[8] Samuelson's analysis suffers from other errors as well, such as the use of invalid "index number" procedures. On the theoretical fallacies of index numbers, cf. Mises, *Theory of Money and Credit, op. cit.,* pp. 187-94.

[9] Cf. Mises, *Human Action, op. cit.,* pp. 102-03. Mises demonstrates that Wicksteed and Robbins committed a similar error.

[10] It is to Samuelson's credit that he rejects the questionnaire approach. Professors Kennedy and Keckskemeti, for different reasons, defend the questionnaire method. Kennedy simply says, rather illogically, that *in vacuo* procedures are being used anyway, when the theorist states that *more* of a good is preferred to *less*. But this is not *in vacuo;* it is a conclusion based on the praxeological knowledge that since a *good* is any object of action, more must be preferred to less while it remains a good. Kennedy is wrong, therefore, when he asserts that this is a circular argument, for the fact that action exists is not "circular."

Keckskemeti actually asserts that the questionnaire method is preferable to observing behavior in discovering preferences. The basis of his argument is a spurious dichotomy between utility and ethical valuations. Ethical valuations may be con-

The bankruptcy of the revealed-preference approach has never been better portrayed than by a prominent follower, Professor Charles Kennedy. Says Kennedy: "In what respectable science would the assumption of consistency (i.e., constancy) be accepted for one moment?"[11] But he asserts it must be retained anyway, else utility theory could not serve any useful purpose. The abandonment of truth for the sake of a spurious usefulness is a hallmark of the positivist-pragmatist tradition. Except for certain auxiliary constructions, it should be clear that the false cannot be useful in constructing a true theory. This is particularly the case in economics, which is explicitly built on *true* axioms.[12]

d. *Psychologizing and Behaviorism: Twin Pitfalls.* The revealed-preference doctrine is one example of what we may call the fallacy of "psychologizing," the treatment of preference-scales as if they existed as separate entities apart from real action. Psychologizing is a common error in utility analysis. It is based on the common assumption that utility analysis is a kind of "psychology," and that, therefore, economics must enter into psychological analysis in laying the foundations of its theoretical structure.

Praxeology, the basis of economic theory, differs from psychology, however. Psychology analyzes the *how* and the *why* of people forming values. It treats the concrete *content* of ends and values. Economics, on the other hand, rests simply on the assumption of the *existence* of ends and then deduces its valid theory from such a general assumption.[13] It therefore has nothing to do with the con-

---

sidered either as identical with, or a subset of, utility judgments, but they cannot be separated.

Cf. Charles Kennedy, "The Common Sense of Indifference Curves," *Oxford Economic Papers,* January 1950, pp. 123-31; Kenneth J. Arrow, "Review of Paul Keckskemeti's *Meaning, Communication, and Value,*" *Econometrica,* January 1955, p. 103.

[11] Kennedy, *loc. cit.* Kennedy's article furnishes the best brief explanation of the revealed-preference approach.

[12] This error again stems from physics, where such assumptions as absence of friction are useful as first approximations—to *known* facts from *unknown* explanatory laws! For a refreshing skepticism on the value of false axioms, cf. Martin Bronfenbrenner, "Contemporary Economics Resurveyed," *Journal of Political Economy,* April 1953.

[13] The axiom of the existence of ends may be considered a proposition in philosophical psychology. In that sense, praxeology is grounded in psychology, but its development then completely diverges from psychology proper. On the question of purpose, praxeology takes its stand squarely with the Leibnizian tradition of philosophical psychology as opposed to the Lockean tradition upheld by positivists, behaviorists, and associationists. For an illuminating discussion of this issue, cf. Gordon W. Allport, *Becoming* (New Haven, 1955), pp. 6-17.

tent of ends or with the internal operations of the mind of the acting man.[14]

If psychologizing is to be avoided, so is the opposite error of *behaviorism.* The behaviorist wishes to expunge "subjectivism," i.e., motivated action, completely from economics, since he believes that any trace of subjectivisim is unscientific. His ideal is the method of physics in treating observed movements of unmotivated, inorganic matter. In adopting this method, he throws away the subjective knowledge of *action* upon which economic science is founded; indeed, he is making any scientific investigation of human beings impossible. The behaviorist approach in economics began with Cassel, and its most prominent modern practitioner is Professor Little. Little rejects the demonstrated preference theory because it assumes the existence of preference. He glories in the fact that, in his analysis, the maximizing individual "at last disappears" which means, of course, that economics disappears as well.[15]

The errors of psychologizing and of behaviorism have in common a desire by their practitioners to endow their concepts and procedures with "operational meaning," either in the areas of observed behavior or in mental operations. Vilfredo Pareto, perhaps the founder of an explicitly positivist approach in economics, championed both errors. Discarding a demonstrated preference approach as "tautologous," Pareto, on the one hand, sought to eliminate subjective preferences from economics, and on the other, to investigate and measure preference-scales apart from real action. Pareto was, in more ways than one, the spiritual ancestor of most current utility theorists.[16, 17]

[14] Thus, the law of diminishing marginal utility does *not* at all rest on some postulated psychological law of satiety of wants, but on the *praxeological* truth that the first units of a good will be allocated to the most valuable uses, the next units to the next-most valuable uses, etc.

[15] I. M. D. Little, "A Reformation of the Theory of Consumers' Behavior," *Oxford Economic Papers,* January 1949, pp. 90-99.

[16] Vilfredo Pareto, "On the Economic Phenomenon," *International Economic Papers,* No. 3, (London, 1953), pp. 188-94. For an excellent rebuttal, cf. Benedetto Croce, "On the Economic Principle, Parts I and II," *ibid.,* pp. 175-76, 201. The famous Croce-Pareto debate is an illuminating example of early debate between praxeologic and positivist views in economics.

[17] V. C. Walsh is an interesting current example of the combinations of both types of error. On the one hand, he is an extreme behaviorist, who refuses to recognize that any preferences are relevant to, or can be demonstrated by, action. On the other hand, he also takes the extreme psychologizing view that psychological states *per se* can be directly observed. For this, he falls back on "common sense." But this position fails because Walsh's psychological "observations" are *ideal types* and not analytic categories. Thus, Walsh says that: "saying that someone is a smoker is different from saying that he is smoking now," upholding the former type of

e. A Note on Professor Armstrong's Criticism. Professor Armstrong has delivered a criticism of the revealed-preference approach which he would undoubtedly apply to demonstrated preference as well. He asserts that when more than one commodity is being ranked, individual preference-scales cannot be unitary, and we cannot postulate the ranking of the commodities on one scale.[18] On the contrary, it is precisely the characteristic of a deduced preference-scale that it is unitary. Only if a man ranks two alternatives as *more* and *less* valuable on one scale can he choose between them. Any of his means will be allocated to his more preferred use. Real choice therefore always demonstrates relevant preferences ranked on a unitary scale.

III. *Utility Theory*

Utility theory, over the last generation, has been split into two warring camps: (1) those who cling to the old concept of cardinal, measurable utility, and (2) those who have thrown over the cardinal concept, but have dispensed with the utility concept as well and have substituted an analysis based on indifference-curves.

In its pristine form, the cardinalist approach has been abandoned by all but a rearguard. On demonstrated preference grounds, cardinality must be eliminated. Psychological magnitudes cannot be measured since there is no objectively extensive unit—a necessary requisite of measurement. Further, actual choice obviously cannot demonstrate any form of *measurable* utility; it can only demonstrate one alternative being preferred to another.[19]

a. Ordinal Marginal Utility and "Total Utility." The ordinalist rebels, led by Hicks and Allen in the early 1930's, felt it necessary to overthrow the very concept of marginal utility along with measurability. In doing so, they threw out the Utility baby together with the Cardinal bathwater. They reasoned that marginal utility

---

statement for economics. But such statements are historical ideal types, relevant to history and psychology, but not to economic analysis. Cf. V. C. Walsh, "On Descriptions of Consumers' Behavior," *Economica*, August 1954, pp. 244-52. On ideal types and relation to praxeology, cf. Mises, *Human Action, op. cit.,* pp. 59-64.

[18] W. E. Armstrong, "A Note on the Theory of Consumers' Behavior," *Oxford Economic Papers*, January 1950, pp. 119 ff. On this point, cf. Little's rebuttal, in I. M. D. Little, "The Theory of Consumers' Behavior—A Comment" *ibid.,* pp. 132-35.

[19] Mises' priority in establishing this conclusion is acknowledged by Professor Robbins; cf. Lionel Robbins, "Robertson on Utility and Scope," *Economica*, May 1953, pp. 99-111; Mises, *Theory of Money and Credit, op. cit.,* pp. 38-47 and *passim.* Mises' role in forging an ordinal marginal utility theory has suffered almost total neglect.

itself implies measurability. Why? Their notion rested on the implicit neo-classical assumption that the "marginal" in marginal utility is equivalent to the "marginal" of the differential calculus. Since, in mathematics, a total "something" is the integral of marginal "somethings," economists early assumed that "total utility" was the mathematical integral of a series of "marginal utilities." [20] Perhaps, too, they realized that this assumption was essential to a mathematical representation of utility. As a result, they assumed, for example, that the marginal utility of a good with a supply of six units is equal to the "total utility" of six units minus the "total utility" of five units. If utilities can be subjected to the arithmetical operation of subtraction, and can be differentiated and integrated, then obviously the concept of marginal utility must imply cardinally measurable utilities.[21]

The mathematical representation of the calculus rests on the assumption of *continuity*, i.e., infinitely small steps. In human action, however, there can be no infinitely small steps. Human action and the facts on which it is based must be in observable and discrete steps and not infinitely small ones. Representation of utility in the manner of the calculus is therefore illegitimate.[22]

There is, however, no reason why marginal utility must be conceived in calculus terms. In human action, "marginal" refers not to an infinitely small unit, but to the *relevant* unit. Any unit relevant to a particular action is marginal. For example, if we are dealing in a specific situation with single eggs, then each egg is the unit; if we are dealing in terms of six-egg cartons, then each six-egg carton is the unit. In either case, we can speak of a marginal utility. In the former case, we deal with the "marginal utility of an egg" with various supplies of eggs; in the latter, with the "marginal utility of the cartons" whatever the supply of cartons of eggs.

[20] The error began perhaps with Jevons. Cf. W. Stanley Jevons, *Theory of Political Economy* (London, 1888), pp. 49 ff.

[21] That this reasoning lay at the base of the ordinalists' rejection of marginal utility may be seen in John R. Hicks, *Value and Capital* (2nd Ed., Oxford, 1946), p. 19. That many ordinalists regret the loss of marginal utility may be seen in the statement by Arrow that: "The older discussion of diminishing marginal utility as aiming for the satisfaction of more intense wants first makes more sense" than the current "indifference-curve" analysis, but that, unfortunately it is "bound up with the untenable notion of measurable utility." Quoted in D. H. Robertson, "Utility and All What?" *Economic Journal*, December 1954, p. 667.

[22] Hicks concedes the falsity of the continuity assumption but blindly pins his faith on the hope that all will be well when individual actions are aggregated. Hicks, *op. cit.*, p. 11.

Both utilities are marginal. In no sense is one utility a "total" of
the other.

To clarify the relationship between marginal utility and what has
been misnamed "total utility," but actually refers to a marginal
utility of a larger-sized unit, let us hypothetically construct a typical
value-scale for eggs:

Ranks in
Value
—— 5 eggs
—— 4 eggs
—— 3 eggs
—— 2 eggs
—— 1 egg
—— 2nd egg
—— 3rd egg
—— 4th egg
—— 5th egg.

This is a man's ordinal value, or preference, scale for eggs. The
higher the ranking, the higher the value. At the center is one egg,
the first egg in his possession. By the Law of Diminishing Marginal
Utility (ordinal), the second, third, fourth eggs, etc., rank below
the first egg on his value-scale, and in that order. Now, since eggs
are goods and therefore objects of desire, it follows that a man will
value two eggs more than he will one, three more than he will two,
etc. Instead of calling this "total utility," we will say that *the marginal utility of a unit of a good is always higher than the marginal
utility of a unit of smaller size.* A bundle of 5 eggs will be ranked
higher than a bundle of 4 eggs, etc. It should be clear that the only
arithmetic or mathematical relationship between these marginal
utilities is a simple ordinal one. On the one hand, given a certain
sized unit, the marginal utility of that unit declines as the supply
of units increases. This is the familiar Law of Diminishing Marginal
Utility. On the other hand, the marginal utility of a larger-sized
unit is greater than the marginal utility of a smaller-sized unit. This
is the law just underlined. And there is no mathematical relationship between, say, the marginal utility of 4 eggs and the marginal
utility of the 4th egg except that the former is greater than the
latter.

We must conclude then that *there is no such thing as total utility;*
all utilities are marginal. In those cases where the supply of a good
totals only one unit, then the "total utility" of that whole supply is

simply the marginal utility of a unit the size of which equals the whole supply. The key concept is the *variable size* of the marginal unit, depending on the situation.[23]

A typical error on the concept of marginal utility is a recent statement by Professor Kennedy that "the word 'marginal' presupposes increments of utility" and hence measurability. But the word "marginal" presupposes *not* increments of utility, *but the utility of increments of goods*, and this need have nothing to do with measurability.[24]

b. Professor Robbins' Problem. Professor Lionel Robbins, in the course of a recent defense of ordinalism, raised a problem which he left unanswered. Accepted doctrine, he declared, states that if *differences* between utility rankings can be judged by the individual, as well as the rankings themselves, then the utility scale can in some way be *measured*. Yet, Robbins says, he *can* judge differences. For example, among three paintings, he can say that he prefers a Rembrandt to a Holbein far less than he prefers a Holbein to a Munnings. How, then, can ordinalism be saved?[25] Is he not conceding measurability? Yet Robbins's dilemma had already been answered twenty years earlier in a famous article by Oskar Lange.[26] Lange pointed out that in terms of what we would call demonstrated preference, only pure rankings are revealed by acts of choice. "Differences" in rank are not so revealed, and are therefore mere psychologizing, which, however interesting, are irrelevant to economics. To this, we need only add that differences of rank *can* be

[23] This analysis of total utility was first put forward by Mises, in *Theory of Money and Credit, op. cit.*, pp. 38-47. It was continued by Harro F. Bernardelli, especially in his "The End of the Marginal Utility Theory?", *Economica*, May 1938, p. 206. Bernardelli's treatment, however, is marred by laborious attempts to find some form of legitimate mathematical representation. On the failure of mathematical economists to understand this treatment of marginal and total, cf. the criticism of Bernardelli by Paul A. Samuelson, "The End of Marginal Utility: A Note on Dr. Bernardelli's Article," *Economica*, February 1939, pp. 86-87; and Kelvin Lancaster, "A Refutation of Mr. Bernardelli," *ibid.*, August 1953, pp. 259-62. For rebuttals cf. Bernardelli, "A Reply to Mr. Samuelson's Note," *ibid.*, February 1939, pp. 88-89; and *id.*, "Comment on Mr. Lancaster's Refutation," *ibid.*, August 1954, pp. 240-42.

[24] Cf. Charles Kennedy, "Concerning Utility," *Economica*, February 1954, p. 13. Kennedy's article, incidentally, is an attempt to rehabilitate a type of cardinalism by making distinctions between "quantity" and "Magnitude," and using the Bertrand Russell concept of "relational addition." Surely, this sort of approach falls with one slash of Occam's Razor—the great scientific principle that entities not be multiplied unnecessarily. For a criticism, cf. D. H. Robertson, *loc. cit.* pp. 668-69.

[25] Robbins, *loc. cit.*, p. 104.

[26] Oskar Lange, "The Determinateness of the Utility Function," *Review of Economic Studies*, June 1934, pp. 224 ff. Unfortunately, Lange balked at the implications of his own analysis and adopted an assumption of cardinality, solely because of his anxious desire to reach certain cherished "welfare" conclusions.

revealed through real choice, whenever the goods can be obtained by money. We need only realize that *money* units (which are characteristically highly divisible) can be lumped in the same value-scale as commodities. For example, suppose someone is willing to pay $10,000 for a Rembrandt, $8000 for a Holbein and only $20 for a Munnings. Then, his value-scale will have the following descending order: Rembrandt, $10,000; Holbein, $9000, $8000, $7000, $6000 . . .; Munnings, $20. We may observe these ranks, and no question of the measurability of utilities need arise.

That money and units of various goods can be ranked on one value-scale is the consequence of Mises' money-regression theorem, which makes possible the application of marginal utility analysis to money.[27] It is characteristic of Professor Samuelson's approach that he scoffs at the whole problem of circularity which money-regression had solved. He falls back on Leon Walras, who developed the idea of "general equilibrium in which all magnitudes are simultaneously determined by efficacious interdependent relations," which he contrasts to the "fears of literary writers" about circular reasoning.[28] This is one example of the pernicious influence of the mathematical method in economics. The idea of mutual determination is appropriate in physics, which tries to explain the unmotivated motions of physical matter. But in praxeology, the *cause* is known: individual purpose. In economics, therefore, the proper method is to proceed from the causing action to its consequent effects.

c. The Fallacy of Indifference. The Hicksian Revolutionaries replaced the cardinal utility concept with the concept of indifference-classes, and for the last twenty years, the economic journals have

[27] Cf. Mises, *Theory of Money and Credit, op. cit.*, pp. 97-123. Mises replied to critics in *Human Action, op. cit.*, pp. 405 ff. The only further criticism has been that of Gilbert, who asserts that the theorem does not explain how a paper money can be introduced after the monetary system has broken down. Presumably he refers to such cases as the German *Rentenmark*. The answer, of course, is that such paper was *not* introduced *de novo*; gold and foreign exchange existed previously, and the *Rentenmark* could exchange in terms of these previously existing moneys. Cf. J. C. Gilbert, "The Demand for Money: the Development of an Economic Concept," *Journal of Political Economy*, April 1953, p. 149.

[28] Samuelson, *Foundations, op. cit.*, pp. 117-18. For similar attacks on earlier Austrian economists, cf. Frank H. Knight, "Introduction" in Carl Menger, *Principles of Economics* (Glencoe, Ill., 1950), p. 23; George J. Stigler, *Production and Distribution Theories* (New York, 1946), p. 181. Stigler criticizes Böhm-Bawerk for spurning "mutual determination" for "the older concept of cause and effect" and explains this by saying that Bohm was untrained in mathematics. For Menger's attack on the mutual determination concept, cf. T. W. Hutchison, *A Review of Economic Doctrines, 1870-1929* (Oxford, 1953), p. 147.

been rife with a maze of two- and three-dimensional indifference curves, tangencies, "budget lines," etc. The consequence of an adoption of the demonstrated preference approach is that the entire indifference-class concept, along with the complicated superstructure erected upon it, must fall to the ground.

Indifference can never be demonstrated by action. Quite the contrary. Every action necessarily signifies a *choice,* and every choice signifies a definite preference. Action specifically implies the *contrary* of indifference. The indifference-concept is a particularly unfortunate example of the psychologizing error. Indifference-classes are assumed to exist somewhere underlying and apart from action. This assumption is particularly exhibited in those discussions that try to "map" indifference curves empirically by the use of elaborate questionnaires.

If a person is really indifferent between two alternatives, then he cannot and will not choose between them.[29] Indifference is therefore never relevant for action and cannot be demonstrated in action. If a man, for example, is indifferent between the use of 5.1 ounces and 5.2 ounces of butter because of the minuteness of the unit, then there will be no occasion for him to act on these alternatives. He will use butter in larger-sized units, where varying amounts are *not* indifferent to him.

The concept of "indifference" may be important for psychology, but not for economics. In psychology, we are interested in finding out intensities of value, possible indifference, etc. In economics, however, we are only interested in values revealed through choices. It is immaterial to economics whether a man chooses alternative A to alternative B because he strongly prefers A, or because he tossed a coin. The *fact of ranking* is what matters for economics, not the reasons for the individual's arriving at that rank.

In recent years, the indifference concept has been subjected to severe criticism. Professor Armstrong pointed out that under Hicks' curious formulation of "indifference," it is possible for an individual to be "indifferent" between two alternatives and yet choose one over the other.[30] Little has some good criticisms of the indifference concept, but his analysis is vitiated by his eagerness to use faulty theorems in order to arrive at welfare conclusions, and by his radi-

---

[29] The "indifference theorists" also err in assuming infinitely small steps, essential for their geometric representation, but erroneous for an analysis of human action.

[30] W. E. Armstrong, "The Determinateness of the Utility Function," *Economic Journal,* 1939, pp. 453-67. Armstrong's point that indifference is not a transitive relation, (as Hicks assumed), only applies to different-sized units of *one* commodity. Also cf. Armstrong, "A Note on the Theory of Consumers' Behavior," *loc. cit.*

cally behaviorist methodology.[31] A very interesting attack on the indifference concept from the point of view of psychology has been levelled by Professor Macfie.[32]

The indifference theorists have two basic defenses of the role of indifference in real action. One is to cite the famous fable of Buriden's Ass. This is the "perfectly rational" ass who demonstrates indifference by standing, hungry, equidistant from two equally attractive bales of hay.[33] Since the two bales are equally attractive in every way, the ass can choose neither one, and starves therefore. This example is supposed to indicate how indifference can be revealed in action. It is, of course, difficult to conceive of an ass, or a person, who could be *less* rational. Actually, he is not confronted with *two* choices but with *three*, the third being to starve where he is. Even on the indifference theorists' own grounds, this third choice will be ranked lower than the other two on the individual's value-scale. He will *not* choose starvation.

If both bundles of hay are equally attractive, then the ass or man, who must choose one or the other, will allow pure chance, such as the flip of a coin, to decide on either one. But then indifference is still not revealed by his choice, for the flip of a coin has enabled him to establish a preference! [34]

The other attempt to demonstrate indifference classes rests on the consistency-constancy fallacy, which we have analyzed above. Thus, Kennedy and Walsh claim that a man can reveal indifference if, when asked to repeat his choices between A and B *over time*, he chooses each alternative 50 per cent of the time.[35]

If the concept of the individual indifference-curve is completely fallacious, it is quite obvious that Baumol's concept of the "community indifference curve," which he purports to build up from individual curves, deserves the shortest possible shrift.[36]

d. *The Neo-Cardinalists: the von Neumann-Morgenstern Approach.* In recent years, the world of economics has been taken by

[31] Little, "Reformulation" and "Theory," *locs. cit.* It is another defect of Samuelson's revealed-preference approach that he attempts to "reveal" indifference-curves as well.

[32] Alec L. Macfie, "Choice in Psychology and as Economic Assumption," *Economic Journal*, June 1953, pp. 352-67.

[33] Thus, cf. Joseph A. Schumpeter, *History of Economic Analysis* (New York, 1954), pp. 94 *n.*, 1064.

[34] Also cf. Croce's warning about using animal illustrations in analyses of human action. Croce, "Economic Principle I," *loc. cit.*, p. 175.

[35] Kennedy, "Common Sense," and Walsh, *locs. cit.*

[36] Cf. William J. Baumol, *Welfare Economics and the Theory of the State* (Cambridge, 1952), pp. 47 ff.

storm by a neo-cardinalist, quasi-measurement theory of utility. This approach, which has the psychological advantage of being garbed in a mathematical form more advanced than economics had yet known, was founded by von Neumann and Morgenstern in their celebrated work.[37] Their theory had the further advantage of being grounded on the most recent and fashionable (though incorrect) developments in the philosophy of measurement and the philosophy of probability. The Neumann-Morgenstern thesis was adopted by the leading mathematical economists and has gone almost unchallenged to this day. The chief consolation of the ordinalists has been the assurance by the neo-cardinalists that their doctrine applies only to utility under conditions of uncertainty, and therefore does not shake the ordinalist doctrine too drastically.[38] But this consolation is really quite limited, considering that some uncertainty enters into every action.

The Neumann-Morgenstern theory is briefly as follows: an individual can compare not only certain events, but also combinations of events with definite numerical probabilities for each event. Then, according to the authors, if an individual prefers alternative A to B, and B to C, he is able to decide whether he prefers B or a 50-50 probability combination of C and A. If he prefers B, then his preference of B over C is deduced as being greater than his preference of A over B. In a similar fashion, various combinations of probabilities are selected. A quasi-measurable numerical utility is assigned to his utility scale in accordance with the indifference of utilities of B as compared with various probability combinations of A or C. The result is a numerical scale given when arbitrary numbers are assigned to the utilities of two of the events.

The errors of this theory are numerous and grave:

(1) None of the axioms can be validated on demonstrated preference grounds, since admittedly all of the axioms can be violated by the individual actors.

[37] John von Neumann and Oskar Morgenstern, *Theory of Games and Economic Behavior* (2nd ed., 1947), pp. 8, 15-32, 617-32.

[38] Thus cf. the excellent expository article by Armen A. Alchian, "The Meaning of Utility Measurement," *American Economic Review*, March 1953, pp. 26-50. Also cf. Robert Strotz, "Cardinal Utility," *ibid.*, May 1953, pp. 384-97. The leading adherents of the Neumann-Morgenstern approach are Marschak, Friedman, Savage, and Samuelson.

Claims of the theory, even at its best, to measure utility in any way have been nicely exploded by Ellsberg, who also demolishes Marschak's attempt to make the theory normative. Ellsberg's critique suffers considerably, however, from being based on the "operational meaning" concept. Cf. D. Ellsberg, "Classic and Current Notions of Measurable Utility," *Economic Journal*, September 1954, pp. 528-56.

(2) The theory leans heavily on a constancy assumption so that utilities can be revealed by action over time.

(3) The theory relies heavily on the invalid concept of *indifference* of utilities in establishing the numerical scale.

(4) The theory rests fundamentally on the fallacious application of a theory of numerical probability to an area where it cannot apply. Richard von Mises has shown conclusively that numerical probability can be assigned only to situations where there is a class of entities, such that nothing is known about the members except they are members of this class, and where successive trials reveal an asymptotic tendency toward a stable proportion, or frequency of occurrence, of a certain event in that class. There can be no numerical probability applied to specific individual events.[39]

Yet, in human action, precisely the opposite is true. Here, there are no classes of homogeneous members. Each event is a unique event and is different from other unique events. These unique events are not repeatable. Therefore, there is no sense in applying numerical probability theory to such events.[40] It is no coincidence that, invariably, the application of the neo-cardinalists has always been to lotteries and gambling. It is precisely and *only* in lotteries that probability theory can be applied. The theorists beg the entire question of its applicability to general human action by confining their discussion to lottery cases. For the purchaser of a lottery ticket knows only that the individual lottery ticket is a member of a certain-sized class of tickets. The entrepreneur, in making his decisions, is on the contrary confronted with unique cases about which he has some knowledge and which have only limited parallelism to other cases.

[39] Richard von Mises, *Probability, Statistics, and Truth* (London, 1939). Also cf. Ludwig von Mises, *Human Action, op. cit.,* pp. 106-17. The currently fashionable probability theories of Rudolf Carnap and Hans Reichenbach have failed to shake the validity of R. von Mises' approach. Mises refutes them in the third German edition of his work, unfortunately unavailable in English. Cf. Richard von Mises, *Wahrscheinlichkeit, Statistik, und Wahrheit* (3rd ed. Vienna, 1951). The only plausible critique of R. Mises has been that of W. Kneale, who pointed out that the numerical assignment of probability depends on an *infinite* sequence, whereas in no human action can there be an infinite sequence. This, however, *weakens* the application of numerical probability even to cases such as lotteries, rather than enabling it to expand into other areas. Cf. Little, "Theory," *loc. cit.*

[40] Cf. Frank Knight's basic distinction between the narrow cases of actuarial "risk" and the more widespread, non-actuarial "uncertainty." Frank H. Knight, *Risk, Uncertainty, and Profit* (2nd ed. London, 1940). G. L. S. Shackle has also levelled excellent criticism at the probability approach to economics, especially that of Marschak. His own "surprise" theory, however, is open to similar objections; cf. C. F. Carter, "Expectations in Economics," *Economic Journal,* March 1950, pp. 92-105; G. L. S. Shackle, *Expectations in Economics* (Cambridge, 1949), pp. 109-23.

(5) The neo-cardinalists admit that their theory is not even applicable to gambling if the individual has either a like or a dislike for gambling itself. Since the fact that a man gambles demonstrates that he likes to gamble, it is clear that the Neumann-Morgenstern utility doctrine fails even in this tailor-made case.[41]

(6) A curious new conception of measurement. The new philosophy of measurement discards concepts of "cardinal" and "ordinal" in favor of such labored constructions as "measurable up to a multiplicative constant" (cardinal); "measurable up to a monotonic transform" (ordinal); "measurable up to a linear transform" (the new quasi-measurement, of which the Neumann-Morgenstern proposed utility index is an example). This terminology, apart from its undue complexity (under the influence of mathematics), implies that everything, including ordinality, is somehow "measurable." The man who proposes a new definition for an important word must prove his case; the new definition of measurement has hardly done so. Measurement, on any sensible definition, implies the possibility of a unique assignment of numbers which can be meaningfully subjected to all the operations of arithmetic. To accomplish this, it is necessary to define a fixed unit. In order to define such a unit, the property to be measured must be *extensive* in space, so that the unit can be objectively agreed upon by all. Therefore, subjective states, being *intensive* rather than objectively extensive, cannot be measured and subjected to arithmetical operations. And utility refers to intensive states. Measurement becomes even more implausible when we realize that utility is a praxeologic, rather than a directly psychologic, concept.

A favorite rebuttal is that subjective states *have* been measured; thus, the old, unscientific subjective feeling of heat has given way to the objective science of thermometry.[42] But this rebuttal is erroneous; thermometry does *not* measure the intensive subjective feelings themselves. It assumes an approximate correlation between the intensive property and an objective extensive event—such as the physical expansion of gas or mercury. And thermometry can certainly lay no claim to precise measurement of subjective states: we all know that some people, for various reasons, feel warmer or colder at different times even if the external temperature

---

[41] It is curious how economists have been tempted to discuss gambling by first assuming that the participant doesn't like to gamble. It is on this assumption that Alfred Marshall based his famous "proof" that gambling (because of each individual's diminishing utility of money) is "irrational."

[42] Thus, cf. von Neumann and Morgenstern, *op. cit.*, pp. 16-17.

remains the same.[43] Certainly no correlation whatever can be found for demonstrated preference scales in relation to physical lengths. For preferences have no *direct* physical basis, as do feelings of heat.

No arithmetical operations whatever can be performed on ordinal numbers; therefore, to use the term "measurable" in any way for ordinal numbers is hopelessly to confuse the meaning of the term. Perhaps the best remedy for possible confusion is to avoid using *any* numbers for ordinal rank; the rank concept can just as well be expressed in letters (A,B,C . . .), using a convention that A, for example, expresses higher rank.

As to the new type of quasi-measurability, no one has yet proved it capable of existence. The burden of proof rests on the proponents. If an object is extensive, then it is at least theoretically capable of being measured, for an objective fixed unit can, in principle, be defined. If it is intensive, then no such fixed unit can apply, and any assignment of number would have to be ordinal. There is no room for an intermediate case. The favorite example of quasi-measurability that is always offered is, again, temperature. In thermometry, centigrade and Fahrenheit scales are supposed to be convertible into each other *not* at a multiplicative constant (cardinality) but by multiplying and then adding a constant (a "linear transform"). More careful analysis, however, reveals that both scales are simply derivations from one scale based on an absolute zero point. All we need to demonstrate the cardinality of temperature is to transform both centigrade and Fahrenheit scales into scales where "absolute zero" *is* zero, and then each will be convertible into the other by a multiplicative constant. Furthermore, the actual measurement in temperature is a measurement of *length* (say, of the mercury column) so that temperature is really a derived measure based on the cardinally measurable magnitude of length.[44]

Jacob Marschak, one of the leading members of the Neumann-Morgenstern school, has conceded that the temperature case is

[43] Cf. Morris R. Cohen, *A Preface to Logic* (New York, 1944), p. 151.

[44] On measurement, cf. Norman Campbell, *What Is Science?* (New York, 1952), pp. 109-34; *id., An Account of the Principles of Measurement and Calculation* (London, 1928). Although the above view of measurement is not currently fashionable, it is backed by the weighty authority of Mr. Campbell. A description of the controversy between Campbell and S. S. Stevens on the issue of measurement of intensive magnitudes was included in the unpublished draft of Carl G. Hempel's *Concept Formation,* but was unfortunately omitted from Hempel's published *Fundamentals of Concept Formation in Empirical Science* (Chicago, 1952). Campbell's critique can be found in A. Ferguson, *et. al. Interim Report* (British Association for the Advancement of Science, 1938), pp. 277-334; and in *id.* (Final Report, 1940), pp. 331-349.

inappropriate for the establishment of quasi-measurability, because it is derived from the fundamental, cardinal, measurement of distance. Yet, astonishingly, he offers *altitude* in its place. But if "temperature readings are nothing but distance," what else is altitude, which is solely and purely distance and length? [45]

IV. *Welfare Economics: A Critique*

a. Economics and Ethics. It is now generally accepted among economists, at least *pro forma,* that economics *per se* cannot establish ethical judgments. It is not sufficiently recognized that to accept this need not imply acceptance of the Max Weber position that ethics can never be scientifically or rationally established. Whether we accept the Max Weber position, or we adhere to the older view of Plato and Aristotle that a rational ethics is possible, it should be clear that *economics* by itself cannot establish an ethical position. If an ethical science is possible, it must be built up out of data supplied by truths established by all of the other sciences.

Medicine can establish the fact that a certain drug can cure a certain disease, while leaving to other disciplines the problem whether the disease *should* be cured. Similarly, economics can establish that Policy A leads to the advancement of life, prosperity, and peace; while Policy B leads to death, poverty, and war. Both medicine and economics can establish these consequences scientifically, and without introducing ethical judgments into the analysis. It might be protested that doctors would not inquire into possible cures for a disease if they did not want a cure, or economists would not investigate causes of prosperity if they did not want the result. There are two answers to this point: (1) that this is undoubtedly true in almost all cases, but not *necessarily* so—some doctors or economists may care only about the discovery of truth, and (2) this only establishes the psychologic motivation of the scientists; it does not establish that the discipline itself arrives at values. On the contrary, it bolsters the thesis that ethics is arrived at apart from the specific sciences of medicine or economics.

Thus, whether we hold the view that ethics is a matter of non-rational emotions or taste, or whether we believe in a rational ethic, we must agree that economic science *per se* cannot establish ethical statements. As a political policy judgment is a branch of ethics, the same conclusion applies to politics. If prosperity vs. poverty, for

[45] Cf. Jacob Marschak, "Rational Behavior, Uncertain Prospects, and Measurability," *Econometrica,* April 1950, p. 131.

example, are political alternatives, economic science cannot decide between them; it simply presents the truth about the consequences of each alternative political decision. As citizens, we take these truths into account when we make our politico-ethical decisions.

b. The Problem of the New Welfare Economics: The Unanimity Rule. The problem of "welfare economics" has always been to find some way to circumvent this restriction on economics, and to make ethical, and particularly *political,* statements directly. Since economics discusses individuals' aiming to maximize their utility or happiness or welfare, the problem may be translated into the following terms: When can economics say that "society is better off" as a result of a certain change? Or alternatively, when can we say that "social utility" has been increased or "maximized"?

Neo-classical economists, led by Professor Pigou, found a simple answer. Economics can establish that a man's marginal utility of money diminishes as his money-income increases. Therefore, they concluded, the marginal utility of a dollar is less to a rich man than to a poor man. *Other things being equal,* social utility is maximized by a progressive income tax which takes from the rich and gives to the poor. This was the favorite demonstration of the "old welfare economics," grounded on Benthamite utilitarian ethics, and brought to fruition by Edgeworth and Pigou.

Economists continued blithely along this path until they were brought up short by Professor Robbins. Robbins showed that this demonstration rested on interpersonal comparisons of utility, and since utility is not a cardinal magnitude, such comparisons involve ethical judgments.[46] What Robbins actually accomplished was to reintroduce Pareto's Unanimity Rule into economics, and establish it as the iron gate where welfare economics must test its credentials.[47] This Rule runs as follows: We can only say that "social welfare" (or better, "social utility") has *increased* due to a change, if no individual is worse off because of the change (and at least one is better off). If one individual is worse off, the fact that interpersonal utilities cannot be added or subtracted prevents economics from saying anything about social utility. Any statement about social utility would, in the absence of unanimity, imply an ethical interpersonal comparison between the gainers and the losers from

[46] Cf. Lionel Robbins, "Interpersonal Comparisons of Utility," *Economic Journal,* December 1938, pp. 635-41; and *id., An Essay on the Nature and Significance of Economic Science* (2nd ed., London, 1935), pp. 138-41.

[47] Cf. Vilfredo Pareto, *Manuel d'Économie Politique* (2nd Ed., Paris, 1927), p. 617.

a change. If X number of individuals gain, and Y number lose, from a change, any weighting to sum up in a "social" conclusion would necessarily imply an ethical judgment on the relative importance of the two groups.[48]

The Pareto-Robbins Unanimity Rule conquered economics and liquidated the old Pigovian welfare economics almost completely. Since then, an enormous literature known as the "new welfare economics" has flourished, devoting itself to a series of attempts to square the circle: to assert certain political judgments as scientific economics, while still retaining the unanimity rule.

c. Professor Robbins' Escape Route. Robbins' own formulation of the Unanimity Rule far undervalues the scope of its restrictive power over the assertions of economists. Robbins stated that only *one* ethical assertion would be necessary for economists to make interpersonal comparisons: namely, that every man has an "equal capacity for satisfaction" in similar circumstances. To be sure, Robbins grants that this ethical assumption cannot be established by economics; but he implies that since all good democrats are bound to make this egalitarian assumption, we can all pretty well act *as if* interpersonal comparisons of utility can be made, and go on to make ethical judgments.

In the first place, it is difficult, upon analysis, to make sense of the phrase "equal capacity for satisfaction." Robbins, as we have seen, admits that we cannot scientifically compare utilities or satisfactions between individuals. But since there is no unit of satisfactions by which we can make comparisons, there is no meaning to any assumption that different men's satisfactions will be "equal" in any circumstances. "Equal" in what way, and in what units? We are not at liberty to make any ethical assumption we please, because even an ethical assumption must be framed meaningfully, and its terms must be definable in a meaningful manner. Since there is no meaning to the term "equality" without some sort of definable unit, and since there is no unit of satisfaction or utility, it follows that there can be no ethical assumption of "equal capacity for satisfaction," and that this cannot provide a shortcut to permit the economist to make conclusions about public policy.

The Robbins' position, moreover, embodies a highly oversimplified

---

[48] Kempt tries to alter the Unanimity Rule to read that social utility is only increased if *everyone* is better off, none being worse off *or* indifferent. But, as we have seen, indifference cannot be demonstrated in action, and therefore this alteration is invalid. Cf. Murray C. Kemp, "Welfare Economics: A Stocktaking," *Economic Record,* November 1954, p. 245.

view of ethics and its relation to politico-economic affairs. The problem of interpersonal comparisons of utility *is only one* of the very many ethical problems which must at least be discussed before any policy conclusions can rationally be framed. Suppose, for example, that two social changes take place, each of which causes 99% of the people to gain in utility and 1% to lose. Surely no assumption about the interpersonal comparison of utility can suffice to establish an ethical judgment, divorced from the *content* of the change itself. If, for example, one change was the enslavement of the 1% by the 99%, and the other was the removal of a governmental subsidy to the 1%, there is apt to be a great deal of difference in our ethical pronouncements on the two cases, even if the assumed "social utility" in the two cases is approximately the same.

d. The Compensation Principle. A particularly notable attempt to make policy conclusions within the framework of the Unanimity Rule was the Kaldor-Hicks "compensation principle," which stated that "social utility" may scientifically be said to increase, if the winners *may* be able to compensate the losers and still remain winners.[49] There are many fatal errors in this approach. In the first place, since the compensation principle is supposed to help economists form policy judgments, it is evident that we must be able to compare, at least in principle, *actual* social states. We are therefore always concerned with *actual*, and not *potential*, winners and losers from any change. Whether or not the winners *may* compensate the losers is therefore irrelevant; the important question is whether the compensation *does*, in fact, take place. Only if the compensation is actually carried out so that not a single person remains a loser, can we still assert a gain in social utility. But *can* this compensation ever be carried out? In order to do so, everybody's utility scale would have to be investigated by the compensators. But from the very nature of utility scales this is an impossibility. Who knows what has happened to anyone's utility scale? The compensation principle is necessarily divorced from demonstrated preference, and once this occurs, it is impossible to find out what has happened to

---

[49] On the compensation principle, cf. Nicholas Kaldor, "Welfare Propositions in Economics," *Economic Journal*, September 1939, p. 549; John R. Hicks, "The Foundations of Welfare Economics," *ibid.*, December 1939, p. 706. For a criticism, cf. William J. Baumol, "Community Indifference," *Review of Economic Studies*, 1946-47, pp. 44-48; Baumol, *Welfare Economics and the Theory of the State, op. cit.*, pp. 12 ff; Kemp, *loc. cit.*, pp. 246-50. For a summary of the discussion, cf. D. H. Robertson, *Utility and All That* (London, 1952), pp. 29-35. The weakness in Robbins' accession to the Unanimity Rule is demonstrated by his endorsement of the compensation principle. Cf. Robbins, "Robertson on Utility and Scope," *loc. cit.*

anyone's utility. The reason for the divorce is that the act of compensation is, necessarily, a unilateral gift *to* a person rather than an act *of* that person, and therefore it is impossible to estimate how much his utility has increased as compared to its decrease in some other situation. Only if a person is actually confronted with a *choice* between two alternatives can we say that he prefers one to the other.

Certainly, the compensators could not rely on questionnaires in a situation where everyone need only *say* that he has lost utility in order to receive compensation. And suppose someone proclaims that his sensibilities are so hurt by a certain change that no monetary reward could ever compensate him? The existence of one such person would null any compensation attempt. But these problems necessarily occur when we leave the realm of demonstrated preference.

e. The Social Welfare Function. Under the impact of criticisms far less thoroughgoing than the above, the compensation principle has been abandoned by most economists. There have been recent attempts to substitute another device—the "Social Welfare Function." But after a flurry of activity, this concept, originated by Professors Bergson and Samuelson, quickly struck rocky waters, and virtually sank under the impact of various criticisms. It came to be regarded as an empty and therefore meaningless concept. Even its founders have given up the struggle and concede that economists must import ethical judgments from outside economics in order to make policy conclusions.[50] Professor Rothenberg has made a desperate attempt to salvage the social welfare function by radically changing its nature, i.e., by identifying it with an existing "social decision-making precess." To uphold this shift, Rothenberg must make the false assumption that "society" exists apart from individuals and makes "its" own valuation. Furthermore, as Bergson has pointed out, this procedure abolishes welfare economics, since the function of the economist would be to observe empirically the social decision-making process at work, and to pronounce its decisions as gains in "social utility."

---

[50] Cf. Abram Bergson, "On the Concept of Social Welfare," *Quarterly Journal of Economics,* May 1954, p. 249; Paul A. Samuelson, "Welfare Economics; Comment," in (B. F. Haley, ed.), *A Survey of Contemporary Economics, Vol. II* (Homewood, Ill., 1952), p. 37. Also cf. Jerome Rothenberg, "Conditions for a Social Welfare Function," *Journal of Political Economy,* October 1953, p. 397; Sidney Schoeffler, "Note on Modern Welfare Economics," *American Economic Review,* December 1952, p. 881; I. M. D. Little, "Social Choice and Individual Values," *Journal of Political Economy,* October 1952, pp. 422-32.

f. The Economist As Adviser. Failing the establishment of policy conclusions through the compensation principle or the social welfare function, there is another very popular route to enable the economist to participate in policy formation while still remaining an ethically neutral scientist. This view holds that someone else may set the ends, while the economist is justified in telling that person (and to be hired by that person) the correct means for attaining these desired ends. Since the economist takes *someone else's* hierarchy of ends as given, and only points out the means to attain them, he is alleged to remain ethically neutral and strictly scientific. This viewpoint, however, is a misleading and fallacious one. Let us take an example suggested by a passage in Professor Philbrook's seminal article; a monetary economist advising the Federal Reserve System.[51] Can this economist simply take the ends set by the heads of this System, and advise on the most efficient means to attain them? *Not unless the economist affirms these ends as being positively good,* i.e., not unless he makes an ethical judgment. For suppose that the economist is convinced that the entire Federal Reserve System is pernicious. In that case, his best course may well be to advise that policy which would make the System highly *inefficient* in the pursuit of its ends. The economist employed by the System cannot, therefore, give any advice whatever without abandoning ethical neutrality. If he advises the System on the best way to achieve its ends, it must be logically inferred that he supports these ends. His advice involves no less an ethical judgment on his part if he chooses to "tacitly accept the decisions of the community *(sic)* as expressed through the political machinery."[52]

g. The End of Welfare Economics? After twenty years of florid growth, welfare economics is once more confined to an even tighter Unanimity Rule. Its attempts to say anything about political affairs within the confines of this rule have been in vain.

The death of the New Welfare Economics has begun to be reluctantly recognized by all of its supporters, and each has taken turns in pronouncing its demise.[53] If the strictures advanced in this

[51] Clarence Philbrook, " 'Realism' in Policy Espousal," *American Economic Review,* December 1953, pp. 846-59. The entire article is of fundamental importance in the study of economics and its relation to public policy.

[52] E. J. Mishan, "The Principle of Compensation Reconsidered," *Journal of Political Economy,* August 1952, p. 312. Cf. especially the excellent note of I. M. D. Little, "The Scientist and the State," *Review of Economic Studies,* 1949-50, pp. 75-76.

[53] Thus, see the rather mournful discussion in the American Economic Association's second volume of the *Survey of Contemporary Economics, op. cit.:* Kenneth E. Boulding, "Welfare Economics," pp. 1-34; Melvin W. Reder, "Comment," pp. 34-36; and

paper are conceded, the burial rites will be accelerated, and the corpse decently interred. Many New Welfare Economists understandably continue to grope for some way of salvaging something out of the wreckage. Thus, Reder suggests that economics make specific, piecemeal policy recommendations anyway. But surely this is only a despairing refusal to take the fundamental problems into account. Rothenberg tries to inaugurate a constancy assumption based on psychologizing about underlying basic personalities.[54] Aside from the fact that "basic" changes can take place at any time, economics deals with *marginal* changes, and a change is no less a change for being marginal. In fact, whether changes are marginal or basic is a problem for psychology, not praxeology. Bergson tries the mystical route of denying demonstrated preference, and claiming it to be possible that people's values "really differed" from what they chose in action. He does this by adopting the "consistency"—constancy fallacy.

Does the Unanimity Rule then spell the end of *all* possible welfare economics, as well as the "old" and the "new" versions? Superficially, it would seem so. For if all changes must injure nobody, i.e., if no people must feel worse off as a result of a change, what changes could pass muster as socially useful within the Unanimity Rule? As Reder laments: "Consideration of the welfare implications of envy, for example, make it impossible even to say that welfare will be increased by everyone having more of every commodity."[55]

V. *Welfare Economics: A Reconstruction*

a. Demonstrated Preference and the Free Market. It is the contention of this paper that the wake for all welfare economics is premature, and that welfare economics can be reconstructed with the aid of the concept of demonstrated preference. This reconstruction, however, will have no resemblance to either of the "old" or "new" edifices that preceded it. In fact, if Reder's thesis is correct, our proposed resurrection of the patient may be considered by many as more unfortunate than his demise.[56]

Samuelson, *loc. cit.* Also cf. the articles by Schoeffler, Bergson, and Kemp cited above.

[54] Jerome Rothenberg, "Welfare Comparisons and Changes in Tastes," *American Economic Review*, December 1953, pp. 885-90.

[55] Reder, *loc. cit.*, p. 35.

[56] "To a considerable extent, welfare (and related) theorizing of the 1930's and '40's was an attempt to show the variety and importance of the circumstances under which *laissez-faire* was inappropriate." *Ibid.*

Demonstrated preference, as we remember, eliminates hypothetical imaginings about individual value-scales. Welfare economics has until now always considered values as hypothetical valuations of hypothetical "social states." But demonstrated preference only treats values as revealed through chosen action.

Let us now consider exchanges on the free market. Such an exchange is voluntarily undertaken by both parties. Therefore, the very fact that an exchange takes place demonstrates that both parties benefit (or more strictly, *expect* to benefit) from the exchange. The fact that both parties chose the exchange demonstrates that they both benefit. The free market is the name for the array of all the voluntary exchanges that take place in the world. Since every exchange demonstrates a unanimity of benefit for both parties concerned, we must conclude that *the free market benefits all its participants.* In other words, welfare economics can make the statement that the free market increases social utility, while still keeping to the framework of the Unanimity Rule.[57]

But what about Reder's bogey: the envious man who hates the benefits of others? To the extent that he himself has participated in the market, to that extent he reveals that he likes and benefits from the market. And we are not interested in his opinions about the exchanges made by *others*, since his preferences are not demonstrated through action and are therefore irrelevant. How do we *know* that this hypothetical envious one loses in utility because of the exchanges of others? Consulting his verbal opinions does not suffice, for his proclaimed envy might be a joke or a literary game or a deliberate lie.

We are led inexorably, then, to the conclusion that the processes of the free market always lead to a gain in social utility. And we can say this with absolute validity as economists, without engaging in ethical judgments.

b. The Free Market and the "Problem of Distribution." Economics, in general, and welfare economics, in particular, have been plagued with the "problem of distribution." It has been maintained, for example, that assertions of increased social utility on the free market are all very well, but only within the confines of assuming

---

[57] Haavelmo criticizes the thesis that the free market maximizes social utility on the grounds that this "assumes" that the individuals "somehow get together" to make an optimal decision. But the free market is precisely the method by which the "get together" takes place! Cf. Trygve Haavelmo, "The Notion of Involuntary Economic Decision," *Econometrica*, January 1950, p. 8.

a given distribution of income.[58] Since changes in the distribution of income seemingly injure one person and benefit another, no statements, it is alleged, can be made about social utility with respect to changes in distribution. And income distribution is always changing.

On the free market, however, there *is* no such thing as a separate "distribution." A man's monetary assets have been acquired precisely because his or his ancestors' services have been purchased by others on the free market. There is no distributional process apart from the production and exchange processes of the market; hence the very concept of "distribution" becomes meaningless on the free market. Since "distribution" is simply the result of the free exchange process, and since this process benefits all participants on the market and increases social utility, it follows directly that the "distributional" results of the free market also increase social utility.

The strictures of the critics do apply, however, to cases of State action. When the State takes from Peter and gives to Paul it is effecting a separate *distribution* process. Here, there does exist a process *separate* from production and exchange, and hence the concept becomes meaningful. Moreover, such State action obviously *and demonstrably* benefits one group and injures another, thus violating the Unanimity Rule.

c. The Role of the State. Until quite recently, welfare economics has never analyzed the role of the State. Indeed, economics in general has never devoted much attention to this fundamental problem. Specific problems, such as public finance, or price controls, have been investigated, but the State itself has been a shadowy figure in the economic literature. Usually, it has vaguely been considered as representing "society" or "the public" in some way. "Society," however, is not a real entity; it is only a convenient short-hand term for an array of all existing individuals.[59] The largely unexplored area of the State and State actions, however, can be analyzed with the powerful tools of Demonstrated Preference and the Unanimity Rule.

The State is distinguished from all other institutions in society in two ways: (1) it and it alone can interfere by the use of violence with actual or potential market exchanges of other people; and (2) it and it alone obtains its revenues by a compulsory levy, backed by violence. No other individual or group can legally act in these

---

[58] It would be more correct to say given distribution of money *assets.*

[59] On this fallacy of methodological collectivism, and the broader fallacy of conceptual realism, cf. the excellent discussion in Hayek, *Counter Revolution of Science, op. cit.,* pp. 53 ff.

ways.[60] Now what happens when the State, or a criminal, uses violence to interfere with exchanges on the market? Suppose that the government prohibits A and B from making an exchange they are willing to make. It is clear that the utilities of both A and B have been lowered, for they are prevented by threat of violence from making an exchange that they otherwise would have made. On the other hand, there has been a gain in utility (or at least an anticipated gain) for the government officials imposing this restriction, otherwise they would not have done so. As economists, we can therefore say nothing about social utility in this case, since some individuals have demonstrably gained, and some demonstrably lost in utility, from the governmental action.

The same conclusion follows in those cases where the government forces C and D to make an exchange which they otherwise would not have made. Once again, the utilities of the government officials gain. And *at least one* of the two participants (C or D) lose in utility, because at least one would not have wanted to make the exchange in the absence of governmental coercion. Again, economics can say nothing about social utility in this case.[61]

We conclude therefore that *no government interference with exchanges can ever increase social utility.* But we can say more than that. It is the essence of government that it alone obtains its revenue by the compulsory levy of taxation. All of its subsequent acts and expenditures, whatever their nature, rest on this taxing power. We have just seen that whenever government forces anyone to make an exchange which he would not have made, this person loses in utility as a result of the coercion. But taxation is just such a coerced exchange. If everyone would have paid just as much to the government under a system of voluntary payment, then there would be no need for the compulsion of taxes. The fact that coercion is used for taxes demonstrates that less would have been contributed under a completely voluntary arrangement. Since some lose by the existence of taxes, therefore, and since all government actions rest on its taxing power, we deduce that: *no act of government whatever can increase social utility.*

Economics, therefore, without engaging in any ethical judgment whatever, and following the scientific principles of the Unanimity Rule and Demonstrated Preference, concludes: (1) that the free

---

[60] *Criminals* also act in these ways, but they cannot do so legally. For the purpose of praxeologic rather than legal analysis, the same conclusions apply to both groups.

[61] We cannot discuss here the praxeological analysis of general economics which shows that, in the long run, for many acts of coercive interference, the coercer himself loses in utility.

market always increases social utility; and (2) that no act of government can ever increase social utility. These two propositions are the pillars of the reconstructed welfare economics.

Exchanges between persons can take place either voluntarily or under the coercion of violence. There is no third way. If, therefore, free market exchanges always increase social utility, while no coerced exchange or interference can increase social utility, we may conclude that the maintenance of *a free and voluntary market "maximizes" social utility* (provided we do not interpret "maximize" in a cardinal sense).

Generally, even the most rigorously *Wertfrei* economists have been willing to allow themselves one ethical judgment: they feel free to recommend any change or process that increases social utility under the Unanimity Rule. Any economist who pursues this method would have to (a) uphold the free market as always beneficial, and (b) refrain from advocating any governmental action. In other words, he would have to become an advocate of *"ultra" laissez-faire.*

d. Laissez-faire Reconsidered. It has been quite common to scoff at the French "optimist" *laissez-faire* school of the nineteenth century. Usually, their "welfare economic" analysis has been dismissed as naïve prejudice. Actually, however, their writings reveal that their *laissez-faire* conclusions were *post-judices*—were judgments *based* on their analysis, rather than preconceptions of their analysis.[62] It was the discovery of the general social benefit from free exchange that led to the rhapsodies over the free exchange process in the works of such men as Frederic Bastiat, Edmond About, Gustave de Molinari, and the American, Arthur Latham Perry. Their analyses of State action were far more rudimentary (except in the case of Molinari), but their analyses generally needed only the ethical presumption in favor of social utility to lead them to a pure *laissez-faire* position.[63] Their treatment of exchange may be seen in this passage from the completely neglected Edmond About:

[62] Lionel Robbins' *The Theory of Political Economy* (London, 1952) is devoted to the thesis that the English classical economists were really "scientific" because they did *not* uphold *laissez-faire*, while the French optimists were dogmatic and "metaphysical" because they did. To uphold this, Robbins abandons his praxeological approach of twenty years before, and adopts positivism: "The final test whether a statement is metaphysical (*sic*) or scientific is . . . whether it argues dogmatically *a priori* or by way of appeal to experience." Naturally, Robbins cites examples from the physical sciences to bolster this fallacious dichotomy. *Ibid.*, pp. 23-24.

[63] Bastiat's writings are well known, but his "welfare" analysis was generally inferior to that of About or Molinari. For a brilliant analysis of State action, cf. Gustave de Molinari, *The Society of Tomorrow* (New York, 1904), pp. 19 ff., 65-96.

Now what is admirable in exchange is that it benefits the two contracting parties. . . . Each of the two, by giving what he has for that which he has not, makes a good bargain. . . . This occurs at every free and straightforward exchange. . . . In fact, whether you sell, whether you buy, you perform an act of preference. No one constrains you to give over any of your things for the things of another.[64]

The analysis of free exchange underlying the *laissez-faire* position has suffered general neglect in economics. When it is considered, it is usually dismissed as "simple." Thus, Hutchison calls the idea of exchange as mutual benefit "simple"; Samuelson calls it "unsophisticated." Simple it perhaps is, but simplicity *per se* is hardly a liability in science. The important consideration is whether the doctrine is correct; if it is correct, then Occam's Razor tells us that the simpler it is, the better.[65]

The rejection of the simple seems to have its root in the positivist methodology. In physics (the model of positivism), the task of science is to go beyond common-sense observation, building a complex structure of explanation of the common-sense facts. Praxeology, however, begins with common-sense truths as its *axioms*. The laws of physics need complicated empirical testing; the axioms of praxiology are known as obvious to all upon reflection. As a result, positivists are uncomfortable in the presence of universal truth. Instead of rejoicing in the ability to ground knowledge on universally accepted truth, the positivist rejects it as simple, vague, or "naïve." [66]

Samuelson's only attempt to refute the *laissez-faire* position was to refer briefly to the allegedly classic refutation by Wicksell.[67] Wicksell, however, also dismissed the approach of the French "harmony economists" without argument, and went on to criticize at length the far weaker formulation of Leon Walras. Walras tried to prove "maximum utility" from free trade in the sense of an interpersonally cardinal utility, and thus left himself wide open to refutation.

Furthermore, it should be stressed that the theorem of maximum

[64] Edmond About, *Handbook of Social Economy* (London, 1872), p. 104. Also cf. *ibid.*, pp. 101-12; and Arthur Latham Perry, *Political Economy* (21st Ed., New York, 1892), p. 180.

[65] Cf. T. W. Hutchison, *op. cit.*, p. 282; Samuelson, *Foundations, op. cit.*, p. 204.

[66] For an example of this attitude, cf. the critique of Hayek's *Counter-Revolution of Science* by May Brodbeck, in "On the Philosophy of the Social Sciences," *Philosophy of Science*, April 1954. Brodbeck complains that the praxeologic axioms are not "surprising"; if she pursued the analysis, however, she might find the *conclusions* surprising enough.

[67] Cf. Knut Wicksell, *Lectures on Political Economy, Vol. I* (London, 1934) pp. 72 ff.

social utility applies not to any type of "perfect" or "pure" competition, or even to "competition" as against "monopoly." It applies simply to any voluntary exchange. It might be objected that a voluntary cartel's action in raising prices makes many consumers worse off, and therefore that assertion of the benefits of voluntary exchange would have to exclude cartels. It is not possible, however, for an observer scientifically to compare the social utilities of results on the free market from one period of time to the next. As we have seen above, we cannot determine a man's value-scales over a period of time. How much more impossible for all individuals! Since we cannot discover people's utilities over time, we must conclude that whatever the institutional conditions of exchange, however large or small the number of participants on the market, the free market at any time will maximize social utility. For all the exchanges are exchanges effected voluntarily by all parties. Thus, in Period 1 the free market will maximize social utility. Then, suppose some producers voluntarily form a cartel in an industry. This cartel makes its exchanges in Period 2. Social utility is again maximized, for again no one's exchanges are being altered by coercion. If, in Period 2, the government should intervene to prohibit the cartel, it could not increase social utility since the prohibition demonstrably injures the producers.[68]

e. The State As a Voluntary Institution; A Critique. In the development of economic thought, far more attention has been paid to analysis of free exchange than to State action. Generally as we have indicated, the State has simply been assumed to be a voluntary institution. The most common assumption is that the State is voluntary because all government must rest on majority consent. If we adhere to the Unanimity Rule, however, it is obvious that a majority is not unanimity, and that therefore economics cannot consider the State as voluntary on this ground. The same comment applies to the majority voting procedures of democracy. The man who votes for the losing candidate, and even more the man who abstains from voting, can hardly be said voluntarily to approve of the action of the government.[69]

[68] It is also possible to argue, on *general* economic, rather than welfare-economic, grounds, that a voluntary cartel action, *if profitable*, will benefit consumers. In that case, consumers as well as producers would be injured by governmental outlawry of the cartel. As we have indicated above, *welfare* economics demonstrates that no governmental action can increase social utility. *General* economics demonstrates that, in many instances of governmental action, even those who immediately benefit lose in the long run.

[69] Schumpeter is properly scornful when he says: "The theory which construes taxes on the analogy of club dues or of purchase of services of, say, a doctor only

In the last few years, a few economists have begun to realize that the nature of the State needs careful analysis. In particular, they have realized that welfare economics must prove the State to be in some sense voluntary before it can advocate any State action whatever. The most ambitious attempt to designate the State as a "voluntary" institution is the work of Professor Baumol.[70] Baumol's "external economy" thesis may be put succinctly as follows: certain wants are by their nature "collective" rather than "individual." In these cases, every individual will rank the following alternatives on his value scale: (A) he would most prefer that *everyone but himself* be coerced to pay for the satisfaction of the group want (e.g., military protection, public parks, dams, etc.). But since this is not practicable, he must choose between alternatives B and C. In (B) *no one* is forced to pay for the service, in which case the service will probably not be provided since each man will tend to shirk his share; in (C) *everyone*, including the particular individual himself, is forced to pay for the service. Baumol concludes that people will pick C; hence the State's activities in providing these services are "really voluntary." Everyone cheerfully chooses that he be coerced.

This subtle argument can be considered on many levels. In the first place, it is absurd to hold that "voluntary coercion" can be a demonstrated preference. If the decision were truly voluntary, no tax coercion would be necessary—people would voluntarily and publicly agree to pay their share of contributions to the common project. Since they are all supposed to prefer getting the project to not paying for it and not getting it, they are then really *willing* to pay the tax-price to obtain the project. Therefore, the tax coercion apparatus is not necessary, and all people would bravely, if a bit reluctantly, pay what they are "supposed to" without any coercive tax system.

Secondly, Baumol's thesis undoubtedly is true for the *majority*, since the majority, passively or eagerly, must support a government if it is to survive any length of time. But even if the majority are willing to coerce themselves in order to coerce others (and perhaps tip the balance of coercion *against* the others), this proves nothing for welfare economics, which must rest its conclusions on *unanimity*, not majority, rule. Will Baumol contend that *everyone* has this

proves how far removed this part of the social sciences is from scientific habits of mind." Joseph A. Schumpeter, *Capitalism, Socialism, and Democracy* (New York, 1942), p. 198. For a realistic analysis cf. Molinari, *op. cit.*, pp. 87-95.

[70] Cf. William J. Baumol, "Economic Theory and the Political Scientist," *World Politics*, January 1954, pp. 275-77; and Baumol, *Welfare Economics and the Theory of the State, op. cit.*

value ordering? Isn't there *one* person in the society who prefers freedom for all to coercion over all? If one such person exists, Baumol can no longer call the State a voluntary institution. On what grounds, *a priori* or empirical, can anyone contend that no such individual exists? [71]

But Baumol's thesis deserves more detailed consideration. For even though he cannot establish the existence of a voluntary coercion, if it is really true that certain services simply cannot be obtained on the free market, then this would reveal a serious weakness in the free-market "mechanism." Do cases exist where only coercion can yield desired services? At first glance, Baumol's "external economy" grounds for an affirmative answer seem plausible. Such services as military protection, dams, highways, etc., are important. People desire that they be supplied. Yet wouldn't each person tend to slacken his payment, hoping that the others would pay? But to employ this as a rationale for State provision of such services is a question-begging example of circular reasoning. For this peculiar condition holds only and precisely because the State, not the market, provides these services! The fact that the State provides a service means that, unlike the market, its *provision of the service is completely separated from its collection of payment.* Since the service is generally provided free and more or less indiscriminately to the citizens, it naturally follows that every individual—assured of the service—will try to shirk his taxes. For, unlike the market, his individual tax payment brings him nothing directly. And this condition cannot be a justification for the State action; for it is only the *consequence* of the existence of the State action itself.

But perhaps the State must satisfy some wants because these wants are "collective" rather than "individual"? This is Baumol's second line of attack. In the first place, Molinari has shown that the existence of collective wants does not necessarily imply State action. But, furthermore, the very concept of "collective" wants is a dubious one. For this concept must imply the existence of some existent collective entity who does the wanting! Baumol struggles against conceding this, but he struggles in vain. The necessity for assuming such an entity is made clear in Haavelmo's discussion of "collective action," cited favorably by Baumol. Thus, Haavelmo grants that deciding on collective action "requires a way of thinking

[71] Galbraith, in effect, does make such an assumption, but obviously without adequate basis. Cf. John K. Galbraith, *Economics and the Art of Controversy* (Cambridge, 1954), pp. 77-78.

and a power to act which are outside the functional sphere of any individual group as such."[72]

Baumol attempts to deny the necessity for assuming a collective entity by stating that some services can be financed only "jointly," and will serve many people jointly. Therefore, he argues that individuals on the market cannot provide these services. This is a curious position indeed. For all large-scale businesses are "jointly" financed with huge aggregations of capital, and they also serve many consumers, often jointly. No one maintains that private enterprise cannot supply steel or automobiles or insurance because they are "jointly" financed. As for joint consumption, in one sense no consumption can be joint, for only individuals exist and can satisfy their wants, and therefore everyone must consume separately. In another sense, almost all consumption is "joint." Baumol, for example, asserts that parks are an example of "collective wants" jointly consumed, since many individuals must consume them. Therefore, the government must supply this service. But going to a theater is even more joint, for all must go at the same time. Must all theaters therefore be nationalized and run by the government? Furthermore, in a broad view, all modern consumption depends on mass production methods for a wide market. There are no grounds by which Baumol can separate certain services and dub them "examples of interdependence" or "external economies." What individuals could buy steel or automobiles or frozen foods, or almost anything else, if enough other individuals did not exist to demand them and make their mass-production methods worth while? Baumollian interdependencies are all around us, and there is no rational way to isolate a few services and call them "collective."

A common argument related to, though more plausible than, Baumol's thesis is that certain services are so vital to the very existence of the market that they must be supplied collectively outside the market. These services (protection, transportation, etc.) are so basic, it is alleged, that they permeate market affairs and are a prior necessary condition for its existence. But this argument proves far too much. It was the fallacy of the classical economists that they considered goods in terms of large *classes*, rather than in terms of *marginal units*. All actions on the market are marginal, and this is precisely the reason that valuation, and imputation of value-pro-

[72] Haavelmo, *loc. cit.* Yves Simon, cited favorably by Rothenberg, is even more explicit, postulating a "public reason" and a "public will," as contrasted to individual reasonings and wills. Cf. Yves Simon, *Philosophy of Democratic Government* (Chicago, 1951); Rothenberg, "Conditions," *loc. cit.*, pp. 402-03.

ductivity to factors, can be effected. If we start dealing with whole classes rather than marginal units, we can discover all sorts of activities which are necessary prerequisites of, and vital to, all market activity; land room, food, clothing, shelter, power, etc.—and even paper! Must all of these be supplied by the State and the State only?

Stripped of its many fallacies, the whole "collective wants" thesis boils down to this: certain people on the market will receive benefits from the action of others without paying for them.[73] This is the long and short of the criticism of the market, and this is the only relevant "external economy" problem.[74] A and B decide to pay for the building of a dam for their uses; C benefits though he did not pay. A and B educate themselves at their expense and C benefits by being able to deal with educated people, etc. This is the problem of the Free Rider. Yet it is difficult to understand what the hullabaloo is all about. Am I to be specially taxed because I enjoy the sight of my neighbor's garden without paying for it? A's and B's purchase of a good reveals that *they* are willing to pay for it; if it indirectly benefits C as well, no one is the loser. If C feels that he would be deprived of the benefit if only A and B paid, then he is free to contribute too. In any case, all the individuals consult their own preferences in the matter.

In fact, we are *all* free riders on the investment, and the technological development, of our ancestors. Must we wear sackcloth and ashes, or submit ourselves to State dictation, because of this happy fact?

Baumol and others who agree with him are highly inconsistent. On the one hand, action cannot be left up to voluntary individual choice because the wicked free rider might shirk and obtain benefits without payment. On the other hand, individuals are often denounced because people will not *do enough* to benefit free riders. Thus, Baumol criticizes investors for not violating their own time-preferences and investing more generously. Surely, the sensible course is neither to penalize the free rider nor to grant him special

---

[73] Cf. the critique of a similar position of Spencer's by "S.R.", "Spencer As His Own Critic," *Liberty*, June 1904.

[74] The famous "external diseconomy" problems (noise, smoke nuisance, fishing, etc.) are really in an entirely different category, as Mises has shown. These "problems" are due to insufficient defense of private property against invasion. Rather than a defect of the free market, therefore, they are the results of invasions of property, invasions which are ruled out of the free market by definition. Cf. Mises, *Human Action, op. cit.*, pp. 650-56.

privilege. This would also be the only solution consistent with the unanimity rule and demonstrated preference.[75]

Insofar as the "collective want" thesis is not the problem of the Free Rider, it is simply an ethical attack on individual valuations, and a desire by the economist (stepping into the role of an ethicist) to substitute his valuations for those of other individuals in deciding the *latter's* actions. This becomes clear in the assertion by Suranyi-Unger; "he (an individual) may be led by a niggardly or thoughtless or frivolous evaluation of utility and disutility and by a correspondingly low degree or complete absence of group responsibility."[76]

Tibor Scitovsky, while engaging in an analysis similar to Baumol's, also advances another objection to the free market based on what he calls "pecuniary external economies."[77] Briefly, this conception suffers from the common error of confusing the general (and unattainable!) equilibrium of the evenly rotating economy with an ethical "ideal," and therefore belaboring such ever-present phenomena as the existence of profits as departures from such an ideal.

Finally, we must mention the very recent attempts of Professor Buchanan to designate the State as a voluntary institution.[78] Buchanan's thesis is based on the curious dialectic that majority rule in a democracy is really unanimity because majorities can and do always shift! The resulting pulling and hauling of the political process, because obviously not irreversible, are therefore supposed to yield a social unanimity. The doctrine that endless political conflict and stalemate really amount to a mysterious social unanimity must be set down as a lapse into a type of Hegelian mysticism.[79]

---

[75] In a good, though limited, criticism of Baumol, Reder points out that Baumol completely neglects voluntary social organizations formed by individuals, for he assumes the State to be the only social organization. This error may stem partly from Baumol's peculiar definition of "individualistic" as meaning a situation where no one considers the effects of his actions on anyone else. Cf. Melvin W. Reder, "Review of Baumol's *Welfare Economics and the Theory of the State*," *Journal of Political Economy*, December 1953, p. 539.

[76] Theo Suranyi-Unger, "Individual and Collective Wants," *Journal of Political Economy*, February 1948, pp. 1-22. Suranyi-Unger also employs such meaningless concepts as the "aggregate utility" of the "collectivized want satisfaction."

[77] Tibor Scitovsky, "Two Concepts of External Economies," *Journal of Political Economy*, April 1954, pp. 144-51.

[78] Cf. James M. Buchanan, "Social Choice, Democracy, and Free Markets," *Journal of Political Economy*, April 1954, pp. 114-23; and *id.*, "Individual Choice in Voting and the Market," *ibid.*, August 1954, pp. 334-43. In many other respects, Buchanan's articles are quite good.

[79] How flimsy this "unanimity" is, even for Buchanan, is illustrated by the following very sensible passage: "a dollar vote is never overruled; the individual is never placed in the position of being a member of dissenting minority"—as he is in the voting process. Buchanan, "Individual Choice," *loc. cit.*, p. 339. Buchanan's ap-

VI. *Conclusion*

In his brilliant survey of contemporary economics, Professor Bronfenbrenner described the present state of economic science in the gloomiest possible terms.[80] "Wilderness" and "hash" were typical epithets, and Bronfenbrenner ended his article in despair by quoting the famous poem *Ozymandias*. Applied to currently fashionable theory, his attitude is justified. The 1930's was a period of eager activity and seemingly pathbreaking advances in economic thought. Yet one by one, reaction and attenuation have set in, and in the mid-1950's the high hopes of twenty years ago are either dying or fighting desperate rearguard action. None of the formerly new approaches any longer inspire fresh theoretical contributions. Bronfenbrenner specifically mentions in this connection the imperfect competition and the Keynesian theories, and justly so. He could also have mentioned utility and welfare theory. For the mid-1930's saw the development of the Hicks-Allen indifference curve analysis, and the New Welfare Economics. Both of these theoretical revolutions have been enormously popular in the upper reaches of economic theory; and both are now crumbling.

The contention of this paper is that while the formerly revolutionary and later orthodox theories of utility and welfare deserve an even speedier burial then they have been receiving, they need not be followed by a theoretical vacuum. The tool of Demonstrated Preference, in which economics deals only with preference as demonstrated by real action, combined with a strict Unanimity Rule for assertions of social utility, can serve to effect a thoroughgoing reconstruction of utility and welfare economics. Utility theory can finally be established as a theory of ordinal marginal utility. And welfare economics can become a vital *corpus* again, even though its new personality might not attract its previous creators. It must not be thought that we have, in our discussion of welfare economics, been attempting to set forth any ethical or political program. On the contrary, the proposed welfare economics has been put forward without inserting ethical judgments. Economics by itself and standing alone cannot establish an ethical system, and we must grant this regardless of what philosophy of ethics we hold. The fact that the free market maximizes social utility, or that State action cannot be considered voluntary, or that the *laissez-faire*

---

proach leads him so far as to make a positive virtue out of inconsistency and indecision in political choices.

[80] Bronfenbrenner, *loc. cit.*

economists were better welfare analysts than they are given credit for, in itself implies no plea for *laissez-faire* or for any other social system. What welfare economics does is to present these conclusions to the framer of ethical judgments as part of the data for his ethical system. To the person who scorns social utility or admires coercion, our analysis might furnish powerful arguments for a policy of thoroughgoing Statism.

PART FIVE

The Hampered Market Economy

XVIII

Progressive Taxation
Reconsidered

by F. A. Hayek

AMONG the measures of economic
policy which are gradually transforming our society and producing
far-reaching results which few people yet clearly grasp, few are as
firmly established and as widely accepted as the redistribution of
income by progressive taxation. Though it is a comparatively recent
feature and one which only in the course of the last generation has
assumed the proportion of a major factor in social change, there has
been until quite recently very little re-examination of its effects. It
is accepted as right and desirable even by most people who are
anxious to preserve a free market economy, and to most of them
it indeed appears as the main hope of establishing within such a
system the greater degree of economic justice or equality for which
they yearn. So firmly has the opinion that progressive taxation is
both innocuous and desirable been established that even those who
were alarmed by some of its visible effects seem to feel that any
critical examination of the principle as such would be a futile waste
of effort and that anyone who undertook it would thereby mark
himself as an unpractical doctrinaire. Quite lately, however, a
change in this attitude is noticeable. After a long period in which
there was practically no questioning of the principle as such and
the discussions on the whole merely repeated the old arguments,
there is a new critical attitude noticeable in the occasional references to the problem; and there have already appeared some notable
major contributions to the discussion.[1] There is, however, still much

[1] See especially: Walter J. Blum and Harry Kalven, Jr., *The Uneasy Case for
Progressive Taxation*, The University of Chicago Press, Chicago, Ill. Compare also
A Tax Program for Economic Growth, issued by the National Association of Manu-
facturers, New York, January 1955.

need for a systematic re-examination of the whole complex of problems raised by progressive taxation of the kind which is now actually practiced. This can not be attempted in a single article and what the following paragraphs will undertake is merely to sketch a few considerations which do not yet seem to have received the attention which they deserve.

The main reason why the whole subject requires reconsideration is that the gradual increase in the rates of taxation over the past fifty years has, in its cumulative effect, made the problem different in kind and not merely in degree. With scales of progression approaching and even exceeding ninety per cent of income their significance is of an altogether different nature from what it was when the upper limits were in the region of ten or at most fifteen per cent. This seemed to be the extreme figures which had to be seriously considered when, around the beginning of this century, the whole issue was for the last time thoroughly discussed. It was then still possible to treat the whole issue as if it were a problem of allocating a given tax burden among the various classes of society; and though it did raise important issues of principle if the comparatively wealthy were made to contribute a few per cent more of their income, no important economic effects were expected from this. To suggest at that time that progression might ever be carried to the figures it has now reached would have been treated by its advocates as a malicious travesty of the principle showing a disreputable contempt for the wisdom of democracy.

With the change in scale has come a general recognition of the fact that the only ground on which progressive taxation could be rationally justified was a desire to change the distribution of incomes [2] and that this could not be based on any scientific argument but had to be recognized as frankly a political decision, an attempt to impose upon society a pattern of distribution determined by political choice. All the ingenious theories of just taxation which had been developed in the early days of the discussion and which can still be found in the textbooks on public finance [3] have lost their relevance in view of the no longer disputed fact that present policy is guided almost exclusively by the desire to produce an all-round reduction of income inequalities.

[2] See Henry C. Simons, *Personal Income Taxation*, The University of Chicago Press, 1938.

[3] For a survey of the more recent discussions see Elmer D. Fagan, "Recent and Contemporary Theories of Progressive Taxation," *Journal of Political Economy*, 46/4, August 1938.

There is only one among these older theories which needs some brief consideration because it is still often asserted that it provides something like a scientific foundation for policy. This is the use of the conception of decreasing marginal utility in support of a proportionally greater taxation of the larger incomes. In spite of its abstract character it has had great influence in making scientifically respectable what originally had been frankly based on arbitrary postulates. How important it seemed at the time may be gauged by such statements as that of the late Lord Stamp who in 1929 wrote that "it was not until the marginal theory was thoroughly worked out on its psychological side that progressive taxation obtained a really secure basis in principle." [4] Yet I do not believe it is overstating the case to say that modern developments within the realm of utility analysis itself have left no justification whatever for this use of marginal utility. Not only does it fall with the abandonment of interpersonal comparisons of utility—a conclusion which seems to me inescapable notwithstanding the ever-recurring objection that individually most of us have definite views about whether a particular need of A is greater than a certain need of B. But the fact that we may have views about this, of course, does not prove that if these views differ there is any objective basis for deciding between them; and this is the question which has been at issue and which must undoubtedly be answered in the negative. But what is more, it is exceedingly doubtful whether even the conception of decreasing marginal utility as such, applied to income as a whole, has any clear meaning if we count as income all the benefits derived by a person from his disposal over his resources. The recognition that utility has definite meaning only as a relative concept, i.e., that we can say only that a given object is more, equally, or less useful than some particular other object, and that it is meaningless to speak of the utility of a thing in isolation, implies that in order that we should be able to speak of the utility, or the marginal utility, of income we have to define income so as to leave out of it something which can serve as a standard of comparison. We can meaningfully speak of the utility of income in terms of effort or of some other such magnitude, say, leisure. But if we were seriously to follow up the consequences of the contention that the utility of income in terms of effort is decreasing, this would lead to very curious results in our context: it would in effect mean that as a person's income grows, the incentive in terms of additional income required to induce the same marginal effort would increase. This might lead

[4] Josiah Stamp, *The Fundamental Principles of Taxation*, London, 1929, p. 40.

to an argument in favor of degressive taxation but certainly not to one for progressive taxation. It is scarcely worth while to follow this line of thought further. In retrospect we must probably say that the whole episode of introducing utility analysis into this discussion was a regrettable mistake (in which some of the most distinguished economists of the time shared) and that the sooner we can undo the effects produced by the quasi-scientific sanction which economic theory gave to a dangerous instrument of policy, the better it will be.

For what follows we shall take it for granted that today the only grounds on which progressive taxation can be defended is the desire for a more equal distribution of income. This it attempts to achieve mainly by flattening the top of the income pyramid. It differs from other measures of more specific controls of income distribution in that it does not directly manipulate the income of specific groups but, as it were, alters the scale of incomes which can be earned. How far it succeeds in this, i.e., how far its effects are not counteracted by an adjustment of gross incomes and the burden thus partially shifted, is a question we will not consider here. It has recently been attempted to show, by an ingenious argument of the "Keynesian"[5] type, that so far as the aggregate amount of profits is concerned, the attempt to reduce them by taxation cannot succeed. This argument is based on rather special assumptions (especially the assumption that the volume of investment can, for the purpose of this argument, be treated as fixed) and I doubt whether under actually existing conditions there is any validity in the contention. At any rate, there seems to me little doubt possible that in actual fact progressive taxation does succeed in greatly reducing the net incomes in the higher brackets compared with what they would otherwise be, and the further discussion will proceed on the assumption that this is the case.

Progressive taxation is, of course, not the only method by which a redistribution of incomes can be brought about. It would be possible to effect a considerable amount of redistribution under a system of proportional taxation. To achieve this it would merely be necessary to devote a substantial part of tax revenue to finance services which benefit mainly the relatively poor—or to subsidize

[5] Carl Föhl, "Kritik der progressiven Einkommensbesteuerung," *Finanzarchiv* 14/1, 1953, pp. 88-109. The author had developed his general approach which has certain similarities to that of Lord Keynes independently of and before the work of the latter. A similar argument is also to be found in H. J. Rüstow, *Theorie der Vollbeschäftigung*, 1951.

them directly. Yet there are several limitations to the extent to which this could be carried. Not only is it doubtful how far the people in the lower income classes would be willing to have their freely spendable income reduced by taxation in return for services offered free. It is also particularly difficult to conceive how in this manner the differentials in the higher income classes could be substantially altered. There might well be brought about in this manner a considerable transfer of incomes from the rich as a class to the poor as a class; but it would not bring about that flattening of the top of the income pyramid which is the characteristic effect of progressive taxation. For the comparatively well-to-do it would presumably mean that they would all be taxed proportionately on their whole incomes and that the differences in the services they received would be negligible. It is in this class, however, that the changes in the income structure resulting from progressive taxation are most significant. The consequences for progress, for the allocation of resources, the effect on incentives, on social mobility, and on investment, operate mainly through the effect on this group (which, in the most advanced countries today includes, of course, many of the highly skilled manual workers). Whatever may be the possible developments in the future, for the present at any rate it seems beyond question that progressive taxation is the main tool available for effecting a redistribution of income and that without it the scope of such a policy would be very limited.

A distinction must, of course, be drawn between the progressive character of a particular tax, such as the income tax, and the progressive character of the burden which the tax system as a whole imposes upon incomes. It is well-known that the heavier incidence of indirect taxation on the lower incomes may make the effect of the tax system as a whole regressive in the lower brackets, even though the income tax is progressive, and that, on the other hand, a progressive income tax may be used to make the tax burden as a whole proportional to incomes by compensating for the degressive effects of indirect taxation. The argument for a progressive income tax which does no more than this is probably very strong and it seems to us the only valid argument in favor of a progressive tax, but, be it noted, only in favor of progressive scales for one particular tax, and not in favor of a progressive character of the tax system as a whole. The significance of this argument is today, however, somewhat diminished because it seems probable that the regressive character of taxation in the lowest income brackets is largely compensated for by the redistributive effects of government expenditure.

It is, however, still worth while to look a little more closely at the information we have on the distribution of the tax burden between the different income classes, since it throws an interesting light on the alleged inevitability of relieving the lowest incomes from the burden of taxation. The most detailed investigation of this kind known to me concerns the situation in Great Britain,[6] but similar studies for other countries, especially the United States,[7] suggest that the main results of the British investigation reveal a situation which also prevails elsewhere. It will be useful to reproduce here some of the results of that investigation. According to it the total burden of taxation on different fully "earned" incomes of a family with two children were as follows during the last pre-war year (1937/38) for which these figures were worked out: [8]

Income £	Per cent taken in taxation	Income £	Per cent taken in taxation
100	18	1,000	19
150	16	2,000	24
200	15	2,500	25
250	14	5,000	33
300	12	10,000	41
350	11	20,000	50
500	14	50,000	58

It will be noticed that the lowest rate of taxation occurs at an income of £350; other data given in the same work suggest that it may actually have been as high as £500 and that this situation had prevailed during the preceding twenty years, while during the first two decades of the century the income with the lowest taxation had gradually risen from £150 and was again somewhat reduced by the severe taxation of the Second World War.

In our immediate context these figures are significant in two respects. In the first instance they show that the argument that pro-

[6] G. Findlay Shirras and L. Rostas, *The Burden of British Taxation*, Cambridge, at the University Press, 1943. See also the earlier discussion in the *Report of the Committee on National Debt and Taxation*, London, His Majesty's Stationary Office, Cmd 2800, 1927; data from France are available in Hubert Brochier, *Finances Publiques et Redistribution des Revenues*, Paris, 1950.

[7] G. Colm and H. Tarasov, *Who Pays the Taxes?* Monograph No. 3 of the Temporary National Economic Committee, U. S. Government Printing Office, Washington, 1941. Compare also: H. Adler, "The Fiscal System. The Distribution of Income and Public Welfare" in *Fiscal Policies and the American Economy*, ed. by Kenyon E. Poole, New York, 1951, pp. 359-409.

[8] Shirras and Rostas, *loc. cit.*, p. 56.

gressive taxation is inevitable because the poorest must be relieved from bearing a proportional share of the tax burden is, so far as the effects of the tax system as a whole is concerned, just humbug. It may be questioned whether any tax system has been ever able to dispense with the individually small but so very numerous contributions from the smallest incomes. At any rate, this has not been the situation since progressive taxation has become an important feature and is not the position today. We have already conceded that the regressive character of indirect taxation may be a valid argument for compensating for it by making the income tax progressive. But in view of the actual practice of democratic countries in modern times the *necessity* of exempting the poorest from the tax burden can hardly be advanced as an argument for making the tax structure as a whole progressive. (Since this argument has usually been coupled with the contention that the prohibitive costs of a direct taxation of small incomes made the exemption a practical necessity and in consequence also a progressive structure of the income tax inevitable, it may be mentioned that the techniques for levying small contributions developed in connection with social insurance, etc., have deprived also this argument of most of its validity.)

The second interesting point arises if one compares these figures about the relative tax burden in the different income classes with the proportional numbers of taxpayers in each class, or, what amounts to much the same thing, their relative strength in the electorate. If the figures given above were plotted in a diagram together with a curve representing the relative frequency of the taxpayers in each class, it would be found that the two curves were approximately mirror images: this means that it was not the poorest but the most numerous and therefore politically most powerful classes which were left off relatively lightly, while not only those above them but also those below them were burdened more heavily —approximately in proportion to their smaller political strength. I am not suggesting, of course, that this is the deliberate result of a diabolic policy; it seems to be rather the unforeseen but almost inevitable result of the democratic process when it is not guided by at least the desire to apply the same uniform principle to all. Once it is admitted that a majority has a right to impose upon minorities burdens of a kind which the majority does not bear itself, there is little reason that this will be used only for discrimination against the rich.

There is one more consideration which ought to be kept in mind in this connection. There is clearly little justification for specially favoring those lower middle incomes which we have seen to be the actual gainers under the prevailing tax structures. But if we consider only that part of the scale of progression where it again exceeds the tax burden imposed on the very lowest incomes, it becomes clear that the part of revenue which depends on the progressive character of the tax system as a whole is negligible. If we remember that, e.g., in Great Britain, according to the latest information, "only about 10½ per cent of the total income over £155 a year lies in the slice above £1000" [9] while in the United States the sum of all incomes of $10,000 and more amounted in 1952 to only 17 per cent of the total of "adjusted gross income," [10] it becomes clear how relatively small the financial yield from the progressive taxation of these incomes is. It is almost certainly considerably smaller than the additional revenue which would be obtained if the lower middle groups just mentioned were taxed as heavily as the poorest.

This is important because it in effect disposes of the supposed fiscal necessity of making the tax system as a whole progressive. It just is not the case that the sums actually raised could not be raised without resort to progression; they could in fact, probably, be raised without increasing the burden on the very poorest at all and by merely bringing up the proportional burden on those lower middle groups to that actually borne by the poorest.

It seems that the conclusion we must draw from this is that rates of taxation in the upper part of the progressive scale have very little to do with the benefit the resulting redistribution of income confers on the lower income classes or the relief in the tax burden they actually obtain. They must be regarded as purely punitive rates, as an expression of the dislike of the majority of the idea that anybody should enjoy the command of such large incomes. It is in this region, however, where marginal tax rates rise in Great Britain and the United States more or less rapidly from the neighborhood

[9] *Second Report of the Royal Commission on the Taxation of Profits and Income,* London, Her Majesty's Stationary Office, Cmd 9105, 1954, paragraph 140. This important and characteristic document has come into my hands too late for the full use and comment which it deserves.

[10] *Statistics of Income for 1952, Preliminary Report,* issued by the U. S. Treasury Department, Internal Revenue Service, Part I, Washington, D.C., April 1955. According to the corresponding complete report for 1951, total adjusted gross incomes of $10,00C and more, amounting to 17.3 per cent of the total, contributed 39 per cent of total income tax liability. If, instead of an average of about 27 per cent, at which these incomes were taxed, they had been taxed at the rate at which income between $10,000 and $11,000 were taxed, namely, approximately 15.5 per cent, total income tax revenue would have been reduced by only 17 per cent.

of 20 per cent (for a married couple with two children) to 90 per cent or over, that the effect of progressive taxation is so very important. The percentage of the population directly affected by it is comparatively small; but it is probably the section of the population which in a free society predominantly decides on how efficiently the resources will be used. It will be for this reason that in what follows we shall be concerned mainly with the effect of progressive taxation on this group.

Before we go on to examine some of the specific effects of this kind of taxation we will pause for a moment to consider how it has come about that we have arrived at a scale of progression leading up to rates which a generation ago would have been regarded as thoroughly unreasonable. We have already been able to eliminate real financial necessity as an explanation—though this does not exclude the possibility that mistaken beliefs about the extent to which the burden might be shifted to the rich may not have had a determining influence. Indeed, it seems more than likely that the illusion that by means of progressive taxation the cost of additional expenditure can be raised from the rich has made such expenditure much more attractive and that as a result even the poor now have to give up a larger proportion of their income than they would have consented to do.

Another factor which has operated in a similar direction was, of course, inflation. It is now well understood how a general rise in money incomes tends to lift everybody into a higher tax bracket even though his real income may have remained the same. In this manner many members of the majority must have found themselves unexpectedly the victims of discriminatory rates for which they had readily voted in the belief that it would never affect them. This particular effect of progressive taxation is often represented as a special merit of the system because it tends to make inflation (and deflation) produced by unbalanced budgets to some extent self-correcting. If the source of inflation is a budget deficit, the tax revenue will tend to rise proportionately more than incomes and thus to close the gap; and if a budget surplus has produced deflation the resulting fall of incomes will soon bring an even greater reduction of revenue and wipe out the surplus. I doubt, however, whether with the ever-present bias in favor of inflation which at this time seems particularly strong, this is really an advantage. Even without this consideration the needs of government finance have been in the past the main source of recurrent inflations and only the knowledge that an inflation, once started, was difficult to stop has acted in some measure as a deterrent. With a tax system under which inflation produces a more than proportional increase in revenue by way of a disguised increase in taxes which needs no vote of the legislature, this device may become almost irresistibly tempting.

These special factors, however, had done no more than speed up further a process which is practically inevitable once the principle of progressive taxation has been accepted. From the very beginning it has been one of the main arguments against it that once the principle is adopted there is no stopping on the road to steeper and steeper scales. As early as the sixteenth century, as Professor Seligman pointed out, Guicciardini had argued that "it lies in the nature of things that the beginnings are slight, but unless great care is taken, the rates will multiply rapidly and finally reach a point that no one could have foreseen." [11] The nineteenth century literature, particularly in its discussions of democracy, is full of such warnings. The best-known statement of the fears is probably that of J. R. McCulloch: "The reasons that made the step taken in the first instance, backed as they are sure to be by agitation and clamor, will impel you forwards. Having once given way, having said that a man with 500£ a year shall pay 5 per cent, another with 1000£ 10 per cent, and another with 2000£ 20 per cent, on what pretence or principle can you stop in your ascending scale? Why not take 50 per cent from the man of 2000£ a year, and confiscate all the higher classes of income before you tax the lower? In such matters the maxim of *obsta principiis* should be firmly adhered to by every prudent and honest statesman. Graduation is not an evil to be paltered with. Adopt it and you will effectually paralyze industry and check accumulation; . . . The moment you abandon . . . the cardinal principle of exacting from all individuals alike the same proportion of their income of their property, you are at sea without rudder or compass, and there is no amount of injustice or folly you may not commit." [12]

The question why these pessimistic prognostications of the opponents of progressive taxation have come to be confirmed and not the confidence of its supporters that it would be used in moderation raises a problem of much wider application than merely in our field.

[11] F. Guicciardini, *Opere Inedite*, 1867, Vol. X, p. 337, translation quoted from E. R. A. Seligman, *Progressive Taxation in Theory and Practice*, Second edition, 1908, p. 295.
[12] J. R. McCulloch, *Taxation and the Funding System*, London, 1845, p. 142.

It is the problem why it is apparently necessary, in social no less than in private action, to abstain altogether from certain kinds of measures if we want to avoid consequences which would follow if we applied the principle underlying them as a general rule. The problem is very similar to that why in individual ethics, when a kind of action is held to be bad because bad consequences frequently spring from it, it is still held to be bad if in the particular instance no such bad consequences seem to follow. Yet while, on the whole, we still accept in private ethics the need of such hard and fast rules which prohibit certain classes of actions irrespective of whether we can see that they will have immediate bad effects, similar rules applied to social action are generally regarded as superstitions which should not be allowed to interfere with our freedom to experiment. Yet, if we want to avoid altogether undesired results of what we are doing, strict adherence to general rules, even in instances where their justification is not readily seen, is probably even more important here than in individual behavior. This might not be true if social organization was ever designed as a whole and if in designing it we could judge each individual feature in relation to all others. But a social structure is never really the result of design, not even in what is called a planned society. It rather results from the application to particular and partial decisions of general conceptions or ideals ruling that society. The arguments underlying these principles of action cannot and are not re-examined in every individual instance; the mere fact that a principle has been applied in other instances becomes the main ground for it being applied again. But the cumulative effect of it being applied separately in many different instances or in many successive decisions will, of course, be very different from what on any of these occasions has been foreseen. Though as an isolated measure, and applied to a limited degree, action of the kind may seem innocuous enough and any possible harm that could follow from it negligible compared with the importance of the immediate object, the joint effects of many measures of this type may be exceedingly harmful.

To any one who views the social process realistically it can offer little reassurance to be told that a principle which, if carried very far, is admittedly dangerous, will have only beneficial effects if used in moderation. It is, in fact, only the presumption against the principle as such which protects us against its abuse. This is particularly true where, as in the case of progressive taxation, every argument which can be advanced in favor of some progression is equally valid in favor of more progression. The idea merely points in a direction in which it is thought desirable to deviate from a standard. What at first limits it is no more than the unfamiliarity of it. But it always justifies a little more of the same than before. The principle itself indicates no halting point and the "good judgment" [13] of the people to which its defenders are usually driven to resort as the ultimate safeguard are merely the opinions shaped by past policy. In its cumulative effects the successive decisions on what is just in the light of the principle will always go far beyond what its initial sponsors thought desirable.

It is sometimes contended that taxation proportional to income is as arbitrary a principle as progressive taxation and that it has merely a greater apparent mathematical neatness but little else to commend itself. There are, however, fairly strong arguments in its favor. Not only is there still much in the old argument that, since almost all economic activity benefits from the basic services of government, these services form a more or less constant ingredient of all we consume and enjoy, and that, therefore, the more a person can command of the resources of society, the greater will also be his gain from what government has contributed to make these services possible. But more important is the fact that proportional taxation leaves the relation between the net remunerations of different kinds of work unchanged. This is not quite the same as the famous old maxim that "no tax is a good tax unless it leaves individuals in the same relative position as it finds them" [14] because it stresses the effect not on the relation between individuals but on the relation between the net remuneration for particular services performed, which is the economically relevant factor. It also does not, as might at first seem, beg the issue by simply postulating that the proportional size of the different incomes should be left unchanged.

While there might be a difference of opinion on the question whether the relation between two incomes is left unchanged if they are both reduced by the same proportion or if they are reduced by the same amount, there can be no difference on the question whether the net remuneration received for two services, of which the one was, before taxation, larger, equal or smaller than the second, stands after taxation still in the same relation to the second. This, however, is the crucial issue with regard to which the effects of progressive taxation are fundamentally different from that of

[13] *Second Report of the Royal Commission on the Taxation of Profits etc.*, paragraph 150.

[14] F. A. Walker, *Political Economy*, 2nd edition, New York, 1887, p. 491.

proportional taxation. It is, of course, the reward received for the use of particular resources which determines their allocation, and what is important is that taxation should leave these relative rewards unchanged. Progressive taxation, however, alters them very considerably by making the net reward received by the owner dependent on what else he has earned during some arbitrary period, such as a year. If, before taxation, a surgeon gets as much for an operation as an architect for planning a house, or a salesman selling ten refrigerators as much as a photographer for making forty portraits, this will still be true if equal proportional deductions are made from these payments. But with progressive taxation of incomes this relation may be violently changed. Not only will services which before taxation receive the same reward leave very different net rewards to those who rendered them; a much larger payment for one service may indeed leave less to him who rendered it than a smaller payment to another person.

This means in the first instance that progressive taxation inevitably offends against what seems to me the most basic principle of economic justice, that of "equal pay for equal work." If what two lawyers are allowed to retain from their fees for doing exactly the same work, or two surgeons from their fees for performing the same operations, depends on their other earning during the year, they will in fact, probably, derive very different profits from their efforts. The man who has worked very hard or who has for other reasons been particularly successful during the year will receive a much smaller remuneration for further effort than the one who has been idle or unlucky. And, indeed, the more the consumers value a man's services, the less worth while it is made for him to exert himself further.

The fact that the taxation of a given sum earned will vary with the time rate at which such earnings accrue to the recipient is the source of most of the injustices and the cause of the misdirection of resources which present taxation produces. There is no need to dwell here on the familiar and insoluble difficulties which, as a result of progressive taxation, arise in all instances where effort (or outlay) and reward are not approximately synchronized but where the former are expended in the expectation of a distant and uncertain result—in short, in all instances where human efforts take the form of long and risky investment. No practical scheme of averaging incomes can really do justice to the problems of the author or inventor, the artist or actor, who reap the reward of perhaps decades of effort in a few years. Nor will it be necessary to stress once again the discouraging effects progressive taxation must have on the willingness for the more risky type of capital investments. That such taxation discriminates against the risky ventures which are worth while only because in the case of success they will bring a return big enough to compensate for the great probability of total loss is so obvious that it should not need emphasis. But it may perhaps be said that what little truth there is in the alleged exhaustion of investment opportunities probably is very largely the result of a fiscal policy which in this manner directly eliminates a wide range of ventures from the field which can be undertaken by private enterprise.

That this sort of taxation is so generally approved is closely connected with the fact that our society has come to think of an appropriate *income* as the only legitimate and socially desirable form of reward, and further, to think of this income not as related to the value of the particular services rendered but as conferring what is regarded as an appropriate status in society. This comes out very clearly in such arguments, frequently used in support of progressive taxation, as that no individual can be worth more to society than, say, $20,000 a year.[15] That this contention lacks any foundation and appeals solely to unreflecting emotion and prejudice would at once become clear if it were stated in the form of saying that no act any individual can perform in a year, or for that matter in an hour, can be worth more to society than $20,000. Of course it can and sometimes will have many times that value. There is no necessary relation between the time an action takes and the benefit society may derive from it.

The whole attitude which regards large gains as unnecessary and socially undesirable springs from the psychology of people who are used to sell their time for a fixed salary or fixed wages and have come to think as a remuneration of so much per unit of time as the normal thing. But, while this method of remuneration has become the only practicable one in an increasing number of fields, it is reasonable only where people sell their time to use it at another man's direction. But it is senseless with respect to men whose task it is to administer resources and whose main aim is to increase the resources under their control from their earning. For them to control resources is a condition for practicing their vocation just as much as the acquisition of certain skills and knowledge is such a condition in the professions. Profits and losses are a way of redistributing capital among them more than merely a means of providing their

[15] L. T. Hobhouse, *Liberalism,* Home University Press, pp. 199-207.

current sustenance. The conception that current net receipts are normally intended for current consumption, though natural to the salaried man, is alien to the thinking of one whose aim is to build up a business. Even the conception of income is in his case largely an abstraction forced on him by the income tax. It is no more than an estimate of what, in view of his expectations and plans, he can afford to spend, rather than an objective fact. I doubt whether a society consisting mainly of "self-employed" individuals would ever have come to take the income concept for granted as we do, or would ever have thought of taxing differently a given amount earned according to the time rate at which such earnings accrue.

It must appear somewhat doubtful, however, whether in a society which will recognize no other rewards than what to its majority appears a very ample income and do not admit the acquisition of a fortune in a comparatively short time as a legitimate form of remuneration for certain kinds of services, it is possible in the long run to preserve a system of private enterprise. Though there may be no difficulty in widely dispersing the ownership in well established enterprises among a large number of small capitalists, the building up of a new enterprise still is and probably always will be bound up with the control of large resources by a few individuals. New developments will, as a rule, still have to be backed by a few persons intimately acquainted with the field, and it is certainly not to be wished that all further evolution should be dependent on the existing financial and industrial corporations.

I do not wish here to enter into the much discussed question of the effect of progressive taxation on the amount of new capital formation—not because this seems to me unimportant but because another influence on capital formation seems to be equally important and less generally appreciated. It is the effect on the *locus* of capital formation. It is one of the advantages of a competitive system that successful new ventures are likely for a short time to bring very large profits with the result that new capital is being formed in the hands of the very people who have the best opportunity of employing it. The large gains of the successful innovator meant in the past that the man who had shown the capacity of profitably employing capital in new ventures would soon be able to back his judgment with his own means. Much of the individual formation of new capital, since it is offset by similar capital losses of others, is in this connection more usefully regarded as part of a continuous process of redistribution of the capital of society than as a profit which constitutes part of the net income of society. The taxation of such profits at more or less confiscatory rates amounts therefore in effect to a heavy tax on this turnover of capital which is part of the driving force of a progressive society.

One of the consequences of the discouragement of individual capital formation at the points where there are temporary opportunities for very large profits is a serious restriction of competition. As the whole system tends to favor corporate as against individual saving it strengthens the position of the established corporation against newcomers and tends to create quasi-monopolistic positions. By making the rise of new entrepreneurs more difficult it unquestionably assists, presumably against the intention of its advocates, the concentration of industry.

An even more paradoxical and socially grave effect of progressive taxation in this field is that this instrument, intended to decrease inequality, in effect helps to perpetuate existing inequalities and eliminates one of the most important compensations for the kind of inequality which is inevitable in a private enterprise society. It does this by greatly reducing vertical mobility because it diminishes the chances of rising from one class to another.[16] That the rich were not a closed group but that the successful man might in a comparatively short time become the owner of large capital resources used to be the redeeming features which did most to mitigate the psychological effects of inequality. The chances of rising into the class of the wealthy are today, however, in some countries such as Great Britain, probably already smaller than they have been at any time since the rise of modern industrialism. One significant effect of this is that the administration of more and more of the world's capital is coming into the hands of men who, though they enjoy very large incomes and all the facilities they can wish for, have never on their own account and at their personal risk controlled substantial property. Whether this is altogether an advantage to society remains to be seen.

At the rates to which progressive taxation ascends in some countries it means in effect that greater equality is brought about by setting a ceiling to the net income anybody may have available for spending. (In Great Britain, during the war and immediate post-war years, the largest net income anyone could earn was approximately £500, or $14,000—though this was partly mitigated by the fact that capital gains were not treated as incomes.) We have

[16] David McCord Wright, *Democracy and Progress*, New York, 1948, pp. 95-100.

seen that in view of the insignificant contribution which progression in the higher brackets makes to revenue, this can be justified only on the ground that it is regarded as in some sense socially undesirable that anyone should command such a high income. But what is a large income in this sense depends, of course, on the views of the particular community and thus in the last resort on its average wealth. The consequence of this is that, on the whole, the poorer a country is, the lower it tends to set the limits on permissible incomes or the more difficult it will make it for any of its inhabitants to reach the levels which in wealthier countries are still only moderate incomes. Or, in other words, the poorer a country is, the more difficult it will make it for all its citizens to get rich. This fact stands out very clearly in any international comparison of income tax rates on different incomes expressed in a common unit, say, the dollar—though Great Britain with her exceptionally severe progression somewhat upsets the rule. A rough comparison of this sort shows, for instance, that an average income tax rate of 25 per cent and 50 per cent respectively was reached by a family with three children in the countries named at the following incomes (figures for 1951 or the year nearest to it for which they were available):

	25 per cent	50 per cent
United States	$36,000	$140,000
Canada	20,000	126,000
France	8,800	18,000
United Kingdom	4,300	13,000
Austria	1,840	(scale approaches 50 per cent asymptotically)

One need merely to conceive of the same principle being applied to the different regions of any one country to appreciate its implications. It certainly throws a curious light both on the moral basis of the belief that the view of the majority of a community should be entitled to set a limit on what are to be regarded as "excessive" incomes, and on the wisdom of those who believe that in this manner they will assist the increase of well-being of the masses. Can there be much doubt that poor countries, by preventing individuals from getting rich, will also slow down the general increase of wealth? And does what applies to poor countries apply any less to the rich ones?

Any discussion of the relation between rich and poor in our own environment is so strongly charged with emotional attitudes that it is generally useful to examine the principles involved with reference to differences between national groups. If we do this, can there be serious doubt that today the prospect of the relatively backward people of raising their standard of life is very much better because there exist more advanced people who have developed the techniques they can apply; and that their prospects would be very much poorer if progress of wealth in other parts of the world had, by some kind of international taxation, been kept to a level not too much ahead of their own? This is not the place to go into any systematic examination of the connections between inequality and progress. But the point which must be briefly mentioned is that a substantial part of the larger income of the more advanced people is spent on financing the cost of experimentation and that the results then become available to the others without all the losses due to the recurrent investment in blind alleys, etc. Is it not clear that not only the advanced but also the more backward people would be still at a much lower level if from the beginning the more successful had not been allowed to pull ahead but if any incomes far above the rest had at once been taxed away for redistribution among the poor? And is the role of the rich within any given nation in this respect really very different from that of the few wealthy nations in the world as a whole?

In the last resort the whole problem of progressive taxation is, of course, an ethical problem and the real question in a democracy is whether the support it now receives would continue if people fully understood how it acts. That in many respects it is based on principles which these people would not approve if they were put in the abstract is probably true. Neither that a majority should be free to impose a discriminatory tax burden on a minority, nor that as a result identical services are very differently remunerated, nor that for a whole class, merely because its incomes are out of line with those of the rest of the community, the normal incentives are practically removed, are principles which can be defended from the point of view of justice. If, in addition, one considers the waste of energy and effort to which progressive taxation induces in so many ways and only on a few of which we have here touched, it should not seem impossible to convince reasonable people of its undesirability. Yet experience shows how rapidly habit blunts in these fields the sense of justice and how the mere fact that a principle has once been applied for some time makes it easy to carry it to extremes.

It is indeed one of the strongest arguments against progressive taxation that it is so difficult again to abandon once it has been introduced. There would probably be no danger and no justified objection if a majority decided to grant an economically weak minority some relief in the form of proportionally lower taxation and the main principle at which one should probably aim is that the majority which determines the burden of taxation should also bear it at its maximum rate; because once it is admitted that it is right that a majority impose a heavier proportional burden on a minority, there seem to be no limits to the length to which this will be carried.

The problem of erecting a barrier which will stop this process of drift is greatly complicated by the fact that, as we have seen, so far as personal taxation only is concerned, some progression is probably both legitimate and desirable. But is there any principle which we can hope will be adopted and which will prevent that the opportunity thus opened will be abused? It is hardly to be expected that an attempt to limit the scale of progression to some particular maximum figure would, in this respect, be effective. Such a percentage figure would be as arbitrary as the principle of progression itself and would be as readily changed when there was need for additional revenue.

What would be needed is a principle which, while limiting the maximum rate of direct taxation in relation to the total burden of taxation, will keep the possible progression of total taxation within narrow limits. The most reasonable limit of this kind would seem to be that the maximum admissible (marginal) rate of direct taxation be fixed at the proportion of the national income which the government takes in taxation, so that, if the government took 30 per cent of the national income, 30 per cent would also be the maximum rate of direct taxation. If a national emergency raised this proportion, the maximum tax rate would also be raised and similarly be automatically reduced when the over-all tax burden was reduced. The application of this principle would still leave some progression of total taxation in existence, since those paying the maximum rate would also pay some indirect taxes which would bring their total taxation above the average for the community. The application of this principle would have the not inconsiderable advantage that every budget would have to be prefaced, as it were, by an estimate of the percentage of the national income which the government proposed to take in taxation. This percentage would provide a sort of standard rate which for the lower income classes would be reduced in proportion as they were taxed directly. The net result would probably be a slight over-all progression, in which the marginal taxation of the largest incomes could, however, never exceed the rate at which incomes were taxed on the average by more than the amount of indirect taxation and in fact (since the limit would apply to the marginal rate of direct taxation) by considerably less.

XIX

Is Further Intervention a Cure for Prior Intervention?

A study of the so-called "Right-to-Work" laws as a remedy for the current evils resulting from Union Shop practices in American industry.

by PERCY L. GREAVES, JR.

All varieties of (government) interference with the market phenomena not only fail to achieve the ends aimed at by their authors and supporters, but bring about a state of affairs which—from the point of view of the authors' and advocates' valuations—is less desirable than the previous state of affairs which they were designed to alter. If one wants to correct their manifest unsuitableness and preposterousness by supplementing the first acts of intervention with more and more of such acts, one must go farther and farther until the market economy has been entirely destroyed and socialism has been substituted for it.
—LUDWIG VON MISES, *Human Action,* Page 854.

THE mass myopia of our age has been a reactionary reverence for government intervention. When anything goes wrong, from a train wreck to a change in stock market prices, the craven crowds always clamor for just one more law. Throughout the world there is a spirit of egalitarianism and trust in government omnipotence that blinds people to the inevitable and undesirable consequences of the very intervention they currently advocate. There can be little question that the great majority of our fellow men believe that governmental action is the best answer to every economic problem of poverty or prosperity.

This general trend toward government intervention has been spurred on by the thought that majorities can continue to take by legal force from the rich and give to the poor to the perpetual benefit of society as a whole. Government intervention is therefore considered a moral and economic weapon to be used for the welfare of all the "have-nots." The crusade for creature comforts is no longer considered to be a struggle against the niggardliness of nature. Instead, it is dreamily idealized as a campaign for the political allotment of each group's "fair share" of the wealth produced by others.

The most astonishing phase of this development has been the rapidity with which more and more of the despoiled "haves" are joining the interventionists' cult, formed for the express purpose of leveling down their supposedly unearned wealth. Every day new groups of "haves" are joining the pressure groups who feel that "there ought to be a law" to end their troubles by protecting them from the operations of a free market. Seldom do they ask for a repeal of the laws which are so often the root of their troubles. In accordance with the religion of the day, they ask for new legal restrictions which they think will protect them from the ills produced by the interventional laws already on the statute books.

In the United States, an example of this trend is clearly seen in the demand arising from some employers and their associations for the individual States to enact so-called "right-to-work" laws. The proposed laws would outlaw all employment contracts which specify that all employees must pay dues to the union chosen by the majority of an employer's employees in a government supervised election. Such contracts, even though they represent the free and voluntary wishes of the employers and the employees concerned, would be declared to be against public policy and therefore illegal. A growing number of employers believe that such laws will bring about a better balance of the scales in the "class warfare" supposedly going on between "labor" and management. This would seem to indicate that many present-day employers have neither faith in freedom nor an understanding of the economic principles which reveal that a free market is the most efficient means that free, peaceful, and intelligent men can use for the advancement of individual men as well as the general welfare.

Those who advocate a legal ban on union shops seldom realize that they are sealing their own doom and placing their future fate in the hands of legislators who are only too eager to assume control of all economic activity. They fail to see that such laws are basically a surrender of their rights to employ whomever they might choose under free market conditions. They seem to believe that the intervention they support is good intervention because, in their opinion, it will strengthen their side against the common enemy "labor."

They believe it will increase their freedom and enchain their "opponents." Alas, employers, too, are victims of the current tendency to think of wealth production in terms of "class warfare," rather than in terms of social cooperation for mutual advantage in a free and peaceful market.

These employers, commonly considered as "haves," are actually advocating a program outlined by Karl Marx for the destruction of the very capitalistic system which has provided them with their present wealth and positions. They should know better. If they will not read, study and digest the 881 pages of *Human Action*, they should at least examine carefully the much shorter Communist Manifesto pamphlet written by Marx and Engels in 1848.

The Communist Manifesto tells us that "The immediate aim of the Communists is . . . a conquest of political power by the proletariat. . . . In this sense, the theory of the Communists may be summed up in the single sentence: Abolition of private property. . . . Property, in its present form, is based on the antagonism of capital and wage-labor. . . . The proletariat will use its political supremacy, to wrest, by degrees, all capital from the bourgeoisie, to centralize all instruments of production in the hands of the State, i.e., of the proletariat organized as the ruling class. . . .

"Of course, in the beginning, this cannot be effected except by means of despotic inroads on the rights of property, and on the conditions of bourgeois production; by means of measures, therefore, which appear economically insufficient and untenable, but which, in the course of the movement, outstrip themselves, necessitate further inroads upon the old social order, and are unavoidable as a means of entirely revolutionizing the mode of production."

This document, which represents the early thinking of Marx, provides a blueprint for all government intervention. It is in line with the Mises thesis that government intervention, that results in a successful demand for more and more government intervention, must finally lead to the elimination of the market economy and the establishment of a socialist dictatorship.

There are, of course, many methods for destroying wealth and setting up a dictatorship, but the original method of the Marxists, as mentioned above, was to propose crippling intervention which would be "economically insufficient and untenable." Then, when this original intervention made matters worse, they could easily create a demand for further "despotic inroads on the rights of property" until finally all economic activity was directed by the Socialist State as the sole owner or controller of the means of pro-

duction. Marx decreed that this program of government intervention would eventually lead to the abolition of private property and
the establishment of the Socialist State. Mises agrees. It was a
series of such "despotic inroads" upon private property that eventually converted the German economy into a National Socialist
dictatorship. Such step-by-step intervention, if followed to its
logical conclusion, will produce the same results in any country,
even in the United States.

The major mistake in the thinking of those who advocate the
so-called "right-to-work" laws is their thought that these laws will
remedy some of the sins of the Federal Labor Laws that now grant
special privileges to labor unions. By the sagacious use of these
privileges, labor unions extort higher than free market incomes for
their members at the expense of the general welfare. This situation
results from popular blindness to the fact that in a moral society
the only way anyone, including unions and their members, can
honestly earn more wealth is to create it and not take it from
others.

The advocates of such laws accept the fallacious idea, found in
many classical economic textbooks, that wealth is distributed after
it is produced. While much wealth is distributed, in the sense of
being transported geographically, it is not distributed in the popular
sense that the entrepreneur distributes or divides the proceeds of a
contemplated or completed business venture into rent, wages, and
interest, with the remainder labelled as profit or loss. Few, all too
few, even among those called economists, seem to realize that in a
free market economy the owner of every factor of production receives the full market value of its contribution, as it is freely evalu-
ated at the time the owner of that factor agrees to participate in
the joint venture. This must be true, if we believe that free men
only make and sign contracts which provide each signer with what
he considers the best terms available to him at that time.

All free market contracts or agreements seek a share of the benefits emanating from the increased division of labor and the resulting exchanges. In a free economy these exchanges take place at
prices set at the margin where supply and demand balance as the
result of the relative subjective values placed on all the offered
products by all those participants who both contribute to and share
in such market exchanges. These prices will be arrived at by a
mental process wherein each participant arranges his satisfiable
desires according to a scale of values. Each participant then exchanges his contributions for a mutually acceptable medium of

exchange to the point where further quantities of that medium would no longer, in his opinion, buy goods or services which the participant values higher than the pleasures of rest (disutility of further labor) or those things which he has produced or can produce without the cooperation of others.

Too many people fail to understand the underlying principles of voluntary exchange in a free market. This ignorance of economic principles leads many to believe that when labor unions use their government-granted privileges to take by force (steal) that wealth which belongs to others, they are registering "social gains" for all workers. This is part and parcel of the Marxian class warfare doctrine that wealth production is a battle between capitalists and workers and that any gain for some workers is a loss for capitalists and therefore a gain for all workers. Unfortunately many people tend to place themselves mentally in the position of those who get these so-called "gains," obtained by the legal looting of society by labor unions. The majority of people today do not realize that they are often the very ones who must pay for these so-called "social gains" in the form of higher prices, lower wages, and, all too frequently, chronic unemployment. They are not co-gainers. They are the losers. Popular acceptance of this fallacy permits labor unions to go on their merry way of extortion with encouragement from the very folks they are injuring.

Unless the popular thinking on this matter is corrected, these immoral and uneconomic activities of labor unions will eventually create a situation for which the popular solution may well be a socialist dictatorship. If this possibility is to be averted, those who are better informed must pierce the fog and show beyond any peradventure of doubt that the currently popular activities of labor unions are injurious to the general welfare and result in relatively lower living standards than would prevail in a free market economy.

The fact that many current labor union practices are injurious to the general welfare does not mean that all actions of all labor unions must of necessity be considered evil or uneconomic. There are many truly economic functions that labor unions can perform. In a free and moral society, unions would be solely voluntary groups organized to help their members by helping them to increase their production and thereby their contributions to society. Their chief purpose would be to raise the standards of workmanship and production. They would then be a force for the general economic good of society as well as their members.

In the last half century, popular and professional opinion has swept from one extreme to another. Fifty years ago, it was thought that unions could do no good. Today, there is a strong tendency to think that unions can do no wrong. Even their physical violence is accepted with complacency. They are a law unto themselves, free from legal liability for their lawlessness. It is both necessary and important that we distinguish between the activities of unions that are economically beneficial and those that are destructive of life, property, and social cooperation.

Because of the recent activities of most labor unions, there is a growing tendency for those who have some understanding of economics to associate all union activities, and thus unions themselves, with evil or uneconomic actions. We do not do this with those professional organizations that now set high standards of ability and performance for all their members and prospective members. At another time and clime, it is entirely possible that groups called unions might more closely resemble our best professional organizations in that they might set and maintain high standards of membership and performance. They might then attract all the better workers and, if such were the case, employers might find that union members were much better workers than non-union members. If memberships in such unions were open to all qualified workers, they would no longer represent a group that was seeking selfish privileges at the expense of the general welfare. They would be groups straining to increase the quantity and quality of production so that all market participants would receive higher returns for their contributions. If we can visualize such a situation, we will then be better able to understand why employers should be free to sign contracts to hire only such high type workers and why the so-called "right-to-work" laws would interfere with the main objective of social cooperation—the increased satisfactions of all the individual participants in the market.

What is the "right-to-work?"

Since the days of Adam and long before Adam Smith, man has been vitally concerned with his right to live. God so created man that he cannot live without continually refueling and refurbishing his body. Men must work in order that men may live. Men thus have an absolute need and, therefore, an inherent right to work. This is an elementary fact which very few question.

This inherent right-to-work, like the allied right to the pursuit of happiness, is God-given. If we assume that it is given equally to every man, and to be consistent we must, we must also assume that the rights of one man, properly understood, cannot conflict with the rights of another. It must then follow that the inherent right to work is merely the right of each individual man to use *his* mind, physical abilities, and accumulated capital to produce those things which he needs and wants in accordance with his own individual values,' abilities, and moral desires. It does not include any right for one man to impose his will on any other man. Nor does it compel any man to employ any other man, union member or non-union member.

Intelligent men know and understand the underlying economic principle of the division of labor, whereby men by mutual cooperation can increase their total production and thereby the satisfactions of all who voluntarily participate in such social cooperation. This system of cooperative specialized production and exchange, known as the free market economy, permits each participant to profit by his contribution to the increased satisfaction of other participants. If, at any time, any participant did not consider his market receipts more valuable to him than his contributions, he need merely refrain from market participation.

In a free market economy, every human act of social cooperation is undertaken with the expectation that the results will improve the condition or satisfactions of each participant. If this were not so, the individuals would not voluntarily participate. These principles of mutual advantage apply to all market transactions, including employment agreements freely negotiated between employers and employees. Agreement as to terms can be reached only when all parties thereto expect that the results will increase their satisfactions over what they would be, if they did not so agree.

Unfortunately, few people understand these economic principles. Confused by our modern complicated society, many people seem to think that one party to an agreement is in a position to impose his will upon the other. In the case of employment agreements, it is erroneously assumed that, left alone, employers can force their terms on employees. This fallacious belief leads to a demand that the government should intervene to "protect" employees by passing laws that limit and regulate the terms and conditions of private as well as public employment.

Some such laws seek to give certain men, usually union members, a legal "right-to-work" for employers who would prefer to hire other men, usually non-union members, willing to work for terms more satisfactory to the employers. Such coercive measures have led some men to believe that new laws should be passed which would give non-union men a legal "right-to-work" for employers who have agreed to hire only union members. These man-made legal "rights-to-work" for specified employers should not be confused with our God-given inherent right-to-work for ourselves or for others who voluntarily seek our services at terms that are mutually satisfactory. The one, government intervention, is a coercive unequal right that forcefully limits the equal rights of others; the other, God-given, is an equal right of free men that places no burden on any man.

The so-called "right-to-work" laws would outlaw "union shop" agreements, whereby employers contract to hire only those who agree to join the majority selected union within a specified time period. Proponents of such laws maintain that where union shops are legal, unions can and do stop the employment of those who will not join or pay tribute to the union. That, of course, is true. Such proponents then argue that union shop contracts prevent non-union men from earning a living in their chosen fields. This, they hold, is a violation of the inherent right-to-work of men who refuse to join or pay tribute to the union of the majority. Such logic assumes that men have an inherent right-to-work for a particular employer, whether he wants them or not.

Do men have such an inherent right? In this writer's opinion they do not.

We should keep our minds on the chief objective of a free society. This should always be the pursuit and maintenance of economic freedom with its two basic corollaries: (1) The right to own and enjoy all property rightfully earned or received; (2) the right to make and sign contracts with others for the mutual advantage of the participants, provided such contracts do not trespass on the property or equal rights of other free and moral men. This right, to make and sign contracts, includes the right of employers and employees to make and sign mutually agreeable contracts for moral employment.

In a free economy, all such mutually satisfactory employment agreements would be valid. On the other hand, all employment relations maintained by compulsion would be invalid. No employer or prospective employer has any right to employ any person who does not want such employment at the terms proffered. Likewise, no employee or prospective employee has any right to employment with any specific employer, if that employer does not desire him as an employee at the terms for which that person is willing to labor. In a free society, all employment must be mutually advantageous in the long run to employers, employees, and consumers. If, for any reason or lack of reason, either party to an employment agreement finds the agreement unsatisfactory or disadvantageous in any manner, he should be free to terminate that agreement and accept a more satisfactory one as soon as his contractual obligations have been fulfilled. In a free economy, this right to discontinue employment applies equally to employers and employees. In the absence of a prior voluntary agreement, no employer has any valid right to the services of any free man. Likewise, in the absence of a prior voluntary agreement, no man has any valid right to a job with any specific employer.

It is apparently difficult today for many people to understand that while people do have a right to work, they do not have a right to any specific job. When the late Calvin Coolidge was Governor of Massachusetts, he met the issue squarely at the time some Boston policemen went out on strike. He stated simply and clearly that no one had the right to be a policeman. Failure to grasp this principle is the crux of popular confusion about the Oppenheimer, Ladejinsky, and many other cases in current headlines.

In the absence of prior agreements, people do not have a right to a job with the government or any other specific employer. In a free economy all employment is agreed upon at mutually satisfactory terms. No employer has any right to employ an unwilling worker. Likewise, no job applicant has an inherent right to employment with any employer who does not want his services. A voluntarily signed union shop contract indicates that, under prevailing conditions, the employer prefers not to hire non-union workers. He has every right to sign such a contract and would only do so if he thought it would be economically advantageous.

One of the most valuable attributes of freedom is the right of free men to choose their associates, so long as that association is mutually satisfactory and not in conflict with the equal rights of others. This right of free association includes the right of men to reject association with those whom they consider objectionable. If these rights are exercised wisely and economically, individuals, and thus society, will benefit. If they are misused, those responsible and, to a lesser extent, all others will suffer.

In a free economy, men have a right to associate voluntarily in labor unions. Likewise men have a right to refuse to join any such unions. Unions, as organizations of free men, also have the right to accept or reject applications for membership and suffer the consequences. So long as all this is done voluntarily, without force or coercion or the threat thereof, no free man need complain except to point out the wisdom or lack of wisdom of any particular action.

In a free society, men will join unions and pay dues only when they consider it is to their advantage to do so. If the laws did not grant union members privileges over and above those of non-union members, few men would join unions unless those unions, operating in a free economy, could help them get and keep better paid positions. To do this, unions would have to help their members locate and fill more productive jobs. This and this alone would entitle union members to increased real wages. All union dues and fees would then represent only a fraction of this increased wealth production.

Thus, unions, if stripped of their special legal privileges, would only exist where they contributed to the increased satisfactions of society as well as of their members. No worker would voluntarily contribute to a union treasury, unless he believed that the benefits received, or expected to be received, would exceed the costs to him.

In a free society, employers also enjoy the right of free association. They are entitled to employ any applicant they wish, provided the contemplated type of activity is acceptable in a free and moral market society and the terms of employment are acceptable to the applicant. Employers also have a right to reject any or all applicants and suffer the consequences. They have a right to hire only union members or only non-union members, if they can find such applicants willing to accept their terms. If they refuse employment to the best available applicants because of personal antipathies, their economic losses may be considerable. If they seek the greatest economic advantages or profits, they must select their employees with economic efficiency and profits uppermost in their minds. If they are to survive in a highly competitive market for consumer dollars, they must employ only those who provide the most efficient service desired for the wages paid. In a free market, supply and demand will determine wage rates. If all men are employed at their market wage, that is the highest wage any employer believes he can profitably recover from customers for the product of that labor, then any employer or prospective employer, seeking a new employee, must offer applicants better terms than those previously prevailing and these new and higher terms must be paid to all doing similar work.

Both employers and labor unions have a right to sign and maintain any contract for moral employment, so long as the agreement is reached voluntarily without the use or threat of any force, coercion, or violence. Only the market compulsions of supply and demand should prevail. Once such a contract is signed, it becomes the private property of the respective parties. It is then the function of government to protect that private property from violence and assist in the peaceful adjudication of any differences which may arise.

Today there is an almost religious belief that the government should do more than maintain peace and umpire differences of opinion. Millions believe that government intervention can create "social gains" by interfering in the free market so as to force one group to grant another group certain terms, rights, or privileges that they could not obtain in a free market. Taking advantage of this popular lack of economic understanding, labor unions have sought and obtained the sanction of laws which permit them to dictate the terms under which their chosen branch of production is permitted to function. If the entrepreneurs cannot or will not agree, production ceases and accumulated capital lies idle, deteriorating without satisfying any of the admitted desires of consumers. Even when they permit industry to operate, unions have often acted so as to prevent the use of the most efficient methods of production. They utilize their legal right, to prevent others from taking the jobs they want, to insist on "featherbedding," whereby consumers, acting through employers, must pay for labors that are not needed or may not be performed.

These and many other current activities of labor unions act as a damper on production and the general welfare of all market participants. Such union activities also irk employers and all others who understand economics and seek increased production for the greater satisfaction of themselves and other consumers.

Many employers seem to feel that if they could only get State governments to step into the employment picture on their side and outlaw union shop contracts, such as they now sign largely under duress, they could then increase production, profits, and the general welfare without so much union interference. They fail to realize that the power of unions to exact uneconomic benefits for minority groups at the expense of society is the result of legal rights obtained under Federal Law, whereby majority selected unions are entitled to speak for all employees, whether or not they are members of the union and whether or not the employer desires to hire or fire any particular employee. This is the legal source of present-day uneconomic union power and until this legal right is withdrawn, the unions will continue to be able to extort privileges for those they represent at the expense of all others, including employers, consumers, and non-organized workers.

If these practices should become general, the losses of union members would exceed their gains. Those the unions represent would then suffer as consumers in a market that offered fewer consumer goods than would be found in a free market. If these decreases in production were not offset by increased capital accumulation and operating efficiency, a real, as well as a relative, decline in production would result. In such an event, the uneconomic effects of union policies would become evident to more people than they are today. Our continued increase in both capital accumulation and business efficiency has tended to hide the losses resulting from the depredations of unions. As a result, only a few people are now able to visualize and realize that our increasing living standards could be increased still further, if popular opinion would only oppose the uneconomic actions of unions.

All members of society, who desire to enjoy the advantage of social cooperation, must be willing to pay the price for such advantages. If we want to go to the opera, we must pay the price of admission. If a man is a member of any private organization and certain dues or fees are levied on its members, he must pay them or withdraw. If a worker wants a certain job, he must meet the terms acceptable to other applicants. If an employer wants an employee to report for work at seven o'clock in the morning and the employee refuses to report for work that early, the employer should be free to seek someone else willing to do so. No prior employee should have any right to stop the employer from employing such a willing applicant in his stead. No one questions the right of workers to change their jobs, if they can find others they like better. Likewise no one should question an employer's right to change his employees, if he can find new ones more suited to his needs or personal likes.

The same principle applies to the union shop. The right to contract is a basic part of economic freedom and private property. No laws should prohibit or limit the free right of contract unless the contemplated contract violates the equal rights of others. In a free economy, employers and employees would be permitted to sign union shop contracts. They would also be legally permitted to sign, if both parties so desired, what have been called "yellow dog" contracts (wherein employees voluntarily agree not to join a union). In order to get union shop contracts, unions would then have to offer employers something better than they could get from non-union workers. In order to get "yellow dog" contracts, employers would have to offer more attractive terms than unions could obtain for their members. A man has no inherent right to any specific job. The fact that an employer voluntarily signs a union shop contract merely shows that, under the prevailing circumstances, he prefers to hire union help. He does not violate the rights of any person, unless such person is a party to a contrary valid employment agreement that preceded the signing of the union shop contract.

Where the union shop contract is a voluntary agreement, it is similar in principle to any other voluntary employment contract signed for the purpose of increasing production. Employers should be free to employ whatever applicants they can persuade to accept their proffered terms. If they are foolish enough to want only workers who demand higher than free market wages, without providing higher than average output, either in quantity or quality, that is their right. However, in a free economy few employers would be that foolish. If they were, the consumers would not long allow them to remain employers in a free market. They would take their trade to those who could sell at lower prices because they paid lower wages.

No businessman voluntarily signs any contract unless he is convinced, at the time of signing, that its advantages outweigh its disadvantages. Whenever an employer signs a contract with a union, he expects that the net results will be lower business costs than if he did not sign that contract. He would not sign a union shop contract unless he thought that, all things considered, it would bring him the best workers at the lowest wages. If he did not think so, he would never voluntarily sign such a contract.

Under present laws and popular opinion, however, labor unions can call a strike and prevent men from working. Under existing circumstances, they can prevent not only the employment of their own members but also the employment of all applicants for the jobs they refuse to fill. Some of this power arises from popular acceptance of the union picket line, but part of it arises from the strength given unions by law, wherein employers are prevented from negotiating with non-union members or non-strikers. The law gives the union and its members a vested right in jobs once occupied by them and curtails the right of employers to discharge workers they no longer desire. Employers are often stopped from finding other workers willing to work at terms that strikers refuse. This, of course, is a violation of the free market principle of voluntary social cooperation.

Unions and their members frequently occupy key positions enabling them to close down an entire plant or industry by interrupting the flow of production at a vulnerable spot. They are thus able to interfere with the work of many jobs other than their own. The losses they can thus afflict on employers, fellow workers, and consumers often exceed the cost of their immediate demands. By the use of this form of coercion, they are often able to force employers to sign contracts, including union shop contracts, which they would not sign under free market conditions where the wishes of consumers would prevail instead of the legal privileges granted unions and their members.

In a free economy, men and groups of men would have the right to compete for all jobs. They would have no right to prevent unemployed or lower paid men from competing for their jobs, particularly when they refuse to work at them themselves. As the law now operates, unions and their members are able to force some employers to pay higher than market wages. They can also force some consumers to pay higher than market prices. This reduces consumer purchases and satisfactions. In addition, unions are often able to bar applicants from employment in their industry. This forces the rejected men to compete and drive wages still lower in other jobs, or else remain unemployed. This, in turn, has resulted in a demand for so-called minimum wage laws and then a further demand for unemployment insurance for those that unions and minimum wage laws make unemployable.

Our problem is to correct popular opinion and remove from the statute books all laws that are a result of the popular fallacy that it is a "social gain" for labor unions to be granted privileges to hold up production until they can extort whatever they want from the hides of all other participants in the market. Once this is done, unions will no longer be able to compel employers to sign union shop contracts under duress or fear of uneconomic losses.

The difficulty before us can be seen by a comparison of current newspaper stories with those of thirty-five or more years ago. Today, when union strikers threaten violence, injure peaceful citizens and damage property, most Governors refuse to call out the national guard or militia to protect the menaced populace and private property. Instead, they issue statements blaming both sides in the "dispute." They seek to compel mediation. They refuse to protect non-strikers who want to work. They thus permit small groups to terrorize the community for weeks and months on end with great losses of property and occasional loss of limbs and lives. Present-day politicians fear the power of the unions at the polls.

In 1919, when the police of Boston, Massachusetts, struck for the right to join the American Federation of Labor, things were different. Large numbers of policemen then went on a strike, hoping they could compel the city to grant them more favorable terms than they could obtain on a free market. The lives and property of Bostonians were suddenly left without police protection. Governor Calvin Coolidge immediately called out the State Guard and protected all those who desired to work as Boston policemen at the terms the city offered. The Governor was warned that organized labor would oppose him at any future election and thus prevent his advancement in the political world. His laconic reply was "It does not matter."

The important thing to note, however, is that the very next year the Governor was nominated and elected as Vice President of the United States. Five years later, he proved to be very popular at the polls as a candidate to succeed himself in the Presidency.

Today, there is no way of knowing whether a political candidate could be elected if he took such a stand in favor of a free market in labor management relations. Few, if any, candidates for public office will take such a stand because it is generally accepted that most people now believe that the present uneconomic actions of unions represent "social gains." The answer does not lie in enacting into law similar "social gains" for employers whereby the States become their champions in a "class warfare" with employees championed by the national government. Transferring economic decisions, from the economic dollar democracy of the market to the political democracy of an electorate without economic understanding, would not solve any problem. It would only create a demand for more "economically insufficient and untenable" measures which would further help to revolutionize "the mode of production," from a consumer-run economy into a socialized political dictatorship that would closely resemble the National Socialist regime of Hitler's Germany.

The philosophy behind the agitation for the so-called right-to-work laws is the philosophy that production is a form of "class warfare" between employers and employees. It then follows that if government gives one group too much power, it must in justice give the other group sufficient counter-balancing power. Government then attempts to maintain a balance in the arena where these battles are fought. Under such conditions, competition is maintained only

by bringing the most competent down to the level to which the
least competent can be boosted.

The purpose of business is production for the economic satisfaction of consumers. Success and profits are measured by the ability
of market suppliers to satisfy consumers. All production for market
exchange, based on the advantages obtained by the division of
labor, is a matter of social cooperation and not "social warfare."
Trying to equalize two groups by granting privileges now to one
and now to the other is like trying to make two opera singers equal,
by preventing each one from singing notes the other cannot dupli-
cate. The only way that such equality can possibly be attained
is by curtailing the satisfactions that each party can provide consumers. It is a matter of pulling down, not building up. The fact
that unions have been given certain privileges destructive of social
cooperation is not sufficient reason for giving other destructive privileges to employers. The net result can only be less social cooperation and a decrease in total production.

One of the great things that the agitators for "right-to-work" laws
forget is that the problem is basically one of getting the government
out of moral business transactions and not into them. If they now
seek State laws controlling employment contracts, they are inviting
State governments to participate in every employment situation. All
employment agreements and their terminations will then admittedly
become a function for political, rather than market, decision. It will
be a further delimiting of the free market area wherein individuals
and consumers remain free to register their wishes on economic
matters.

If these laws are enacted, they will tend to develop further a situation such as is now found in some states where labor-management
relations are supervised by Fair Employment Practices Commissions. In those states employers no longer feel free to employ those
applicants whom they consider the most capable to perform the
tasks at hand. They fear the ruling of some bureaucrat and must
pay strict attention to the whims and wishes of those who have
full power to penalize them or injure their public relations by threat
of a court suit.

The evils of much uneconomic intervention of government is apparent in the operation of the New York State FEPC law. This
writer was recently told of a situation concerning a girl who belonged to a particular religious sect. She desired a position in a
bank department which at that time was entirely composed of girls
belonging to the same particular religious sect. The bank wanted

to employ this applicant, but would not do so because it feared that some bureaucrat might rule that such employment would be evidence of bias in favor of that particular sect. The employer felt that he must employ a member of another sect, or better yet a member of a minority race, who might or might not fit into this particular job as well as the rejected applicant.

Many New York employers no longer hire people solely on the basis of their ability. Instead, they feel that their employment policies must be so conducted as to maintain the same racial and religious ratios that are found in the local population. The aptitudes and predilections of any particular group or individual must be forgotten. If they do not do so, they must waste time and energy in defending their decisions before bureaucratic commissions and in the public press.

Under "right-to-work" laws, non-union applicants would be given a legal standing in court and the employer might well be told whom he could employ and whom he could not employ, or be found guilty of bias against trouble making non-union members. The bureaucrats of the States would intervene more and more, telling employers how many union and non-union members they could employ as well as whom they could or could not fire, promote, or retire. The bureaucrat would be present at every hiring, firing, and promotion. Labor-management relations might well resemble those of Hitler's Germany where a man once hired could not be fired except for a crime against the State.

The problem is to stop the States from intervening in free market personnel relations and not to seek such intervention. Two wrongs never make a right. The economic answer is to repeal the bad intervention and not try to counterbalance it with another bad intervention. Such moves only provide the politicians with greater power over the entire economy.

Unfortunately, many businessmen seem to think that the evils of intervention began with the New Deal. Actually, the seeds were sown far, far earlier. They were in the Interstate Commerce Act, the Sherman Anti-Trust Law, and the Act creating the Labor Department to help a politically favored group, the Income Tax Amendment, and the Federal Reserve Act and many others of Pre-New Deal days. These earlier acts bore the fruit that led to the depression that started in 1929.

Each of these early laws was a government intervention which interfered with and hampered the operation of free markets. Each one granted privileges to one group at the expense of all others.

They were all a burden on consumers and the general welfare. They all created vested interests that now resist the removal of these privileges. They were the original "despotic inroads on the rights of property . . . which appear economically insufficient and untenable." The New Deal Acts were only the "further inroads upon the old social order . . . unavoidable as a means of entirely revolutionizing the mode of production."

Actually, if we stop to think of it, it is ridiculous for the government to grant counter-privileges to one group to offset the very privileges it has granted to other groups. All such privileges are a further obstruction to production and tend to reduce the satisfactions obtained from participation in the market.

The best example is probably the monopoly situation. First, the government grants monopoly privileges to certain firms or domestic industries. Then these firms or industries utilize these privileges to line their pockets at the expense of consumers. Isn't it then ridiculous to point to the results and demand that the injured groups be granted offsetting monopolies whereby they can recoup their losses? The logical solution is to take away the original privileges which caused the trouble in the first place.

The same solution is applicable to the labor-management situation. The cause of the present economic evils in labor-management relations is the club that Federal laws have furnished labor unions whereby they can bludgeon established employers with capital in the form of fixed production facilities. Such employers must continually surrender to the unions or lose the entire value of their established reputation and invested capital. They are not free to employ the unemployed or lower paid workers who might be very happy to work for them.

The unions should be stripped of this club, as most employers have been stripped of the privileges they had legally obtained during the latter part of the last century. Granting privileges to labor unions is no better or no worse than granting privileges to employers or groups of employers. A free market society requires that government be neutral, so far as it can be, and refuse to grant special unearned privileges to any group, because, in the end, all such privileges must be paid for in the sweat of all who labor and produce the wealth that consumers seek in the marketplace.

A perfect free market society is probably unattainable by fallible men. Nevertheless it should ever be the goal of all moral and intelligent men and particularly of those economists who try to educate and influence their fellow men. As Mises has so ably demonstrated

in all his writings, "There is no other means to attain full employment, rising real wage rates and a high standard of living for the
common man than private initiative and free enterprise." [1]

Every proposed measure should be weighed as to whether or not
it advances the economy toward "private initiative and free enterprise." Increased government intervention tends to direct the economy further away from a free market society.

Many call our economy a mixed economy. Actually it is, in the
terms of Mises, a "hampered market economy." It is constantly in
movement as every economy must be. It must move either toward
freedom or toward Statism. The better economic understanding our
leaders and people have, the more likely it is that present uneconomic measures will be repealed and that the trend will be toward
rising real wage rates and constantly higher living standards for all
participants in the market economy. Economists should, therefore,
oppose every proposed measure that moves in the other direction.
So long as American popular opinion approves of present-day union
shops and union activities, we are going to have them, but we shall
have to pay the price in terms of lower production and lower living
standards than a free economy would provide.

Everyone wants freedom, but probably no group wants it any
more than employers as a group. Unfortunately, too many employers have sought special privileges in the past. Actually, it was undoubtedly some of the early government-granted privileges for some
employers that produced the demand for the New and Fair Deal
intervention. Most such intervention was planned to help organized
"labor" and the other large groups that had suffered when employers were in the saddle and obtaining favorable intervention
for themselves.

So long as political groups can grant economic privileges, there
will always be attempts to buy their votes in one way or another.
The political problem is to so limit government that politicians
cannot grant economic privileges to any groups. We must remove
the temptations to greedy men who seek to gain their wealth at the
expense of others rather than through the economic principles of
voluntary social cooperation.

The aim of free people should always be a government that provides equal protection for all and favors for none. Men alone, or in
groups, should be permitted to choose their associates and that includes the right to choose those with whom they associate in their

[1] *Planning for Freedom,* p. 17.

employment. The right to make contracts, one man with another or a group, should be unlimited so long as other men have a similar right. Employers and employees should be free to sign mutually satisfactory employment contracts for closed shops, union shops, open shops, or anti-union shops. The only limitation should be that they are signed voluntarily.

The important thing is to work for basic principles whereby peaceful persons can pursue their personal satisfactions through the cooperation inherent in a free market. The place of government in the market is that of a policeman who arrests marauders, not that of a politician who bestows favors.

If the country is flooded with "right-to-work" laws, it will only serve to temporize for a time the evils now inherent in Federal Labor Laws. Such State laws will perhaps allay for a time the fears that many people have concerning the dire consequences we are now experiencing as a result of union activities. Actually, it might be both better economics and better expediency to let present laws go their limit, so that people might soon learn how bad they really are.

This writer now hates to admit that, as an "expert" for the House Committee on Education and Labor, he was one of the few who helped to write the first draft of the Hartley bill. This was the bill that was later amended and passed as the National Labor Management Relations Act of 1947, more popularly known as the Taft-Hartley Law. He is quick to add that he resigned from this Committee before it reported the bill in a different form to the House of Representatives. He has learned through personal experience that it does not pay to compromise either moral or economic principles for illusory short-term advantages. His 1947 political experience, as related below, substantiates his belief that even politicians, who place emphasis on winning the next election, would do well to advocate freedom ideas consistently and not seek favors for either employers or employees.

After the Republican Congressional victory in 1946, the late Senator Robert A. Taft, of Ohio, summoned this writer to his office to discuss the top position on the Senate Labor Committee which was then about to consider what later became the Taft-Hartley Law. This writer wanted as much freedom in the law as Congress would approve and was willing to make the financial sacrifice involved, if he could work toward that goal. But the Senator outlined his philosophy and stated that he wanted to change the law just to the extent that it could be passed over the veto of the then Democratic

President, Harry Truman. The Senator sincerely believed that with a Republican Presidential and Congressional victory in 1948, the law could subsequently be changed to the form in which he really desired it.

At that time, 1947, the country was thoroughly aroused against the union abuses practiced under the protection of the Wagner Act. The nation was ready for a change in its basic labor laws, but there were only a very few people who had any understanding of the specific changes that were needed to protect private initiative and free enterprise. The Senator proposed that the law be ameliorated toward freedom only so far as two-thirds of the Congress would approve over a Presidential veto. The Senator and others thought such an expedient move would improve the immediate situation and help elect a Republican slate in the ensuing national elections.

This writer opposed this thinking on the basis that it would be better not to have any new law at that time. His contention was that a successful veto of a better law would result in a growing public pressure for the repeal of the Wagner Act and the election of the party that espoused such a move. The Senator was not willing to go that far. He believed his policy was politically more realistic. It was this writer's contention that, if the Senator's plan were successful, the public would be persuaded that the then evident economic distress flowing from union activity had been remedied and the next tide of public opinion might well be in the other direction. The Senator demurred and so this writer accepted employment with the House, rather than the Senate, Committee.

The late great Senator from Ohio had his wish and skillfully drafted an ameliorating measure which passed over the Presidential veto. However, in the judgment of this writer, freedom and the Republican Party lost. The Republicans failed to carry on their fight to repeal the still obnoxious sections of our Federal Labor laws and public opinion, which once seemed against government intervention in labor-management relations, has apparently taken a turn in the opposite direction. In fact, the amendments, more recently proposed by the Republican leadership, have been in the direction desired by union leaders. In the words of their sponsors, they are "middle-of-the-road" in principle.

Somewhat the same situation is involved in the so-called "right-to-work" laws. If they are passed in a large number of States, they will temporarily relieve the present uneconomic evils that exist in Federal Labor Laws. They will allay the fear among those people who see and comprehend the dire results now flowing from present union activities. The organized labor union minority can then more easily organize its forces to lobby successfully for a Federal law which would at one stroke outlaw all the so-called "right-to-work" laws of the various States.

On occasion, this writer has watched with interest the actions of John L. Lewis, President of the United Mine Workers Union. This union leader has, more consistently than any other union leader, followed the policy of getting his members all the privileges the law permits them. He has obtained high wages for a few miners, while greatly reducing the number of jobs in coal mining. Young men, who might have become miners, are shut out and must compete for lower-paid jobs by driving those wages still lower or remain unemployed.

This is using the laws to the fullest extent. It also illustrates how economically foolish they are. A privileged few gain at the expense of the entire community and production is diverted into other lines whose products are not the ones consumers want most.

Neither labor leaders nor their members can be blamed for using privileges which the people have granted them by law. It has only been the prudent temporizing of most unions that has permitted their Marxian moves to become so generally accepted. Few people understand the underlying fallacies on which they are based. Economic education must be rescued from the political arena. The burden placed on economists, who are not dependent on political or public payrolls, is great and they have a public duty to speak out against all those who would expand political controls at the expense of a free people supported by the products of a free market.

We cannot blame those who take advantage of present uneconomic laws. These laws are wrong. The blame must fall on those who sanction them and permit them to continue on the statute books. Actually, if the unions had been less temperate in pushing their legal privileges to their ultimate and logical conclusion, they might well have lost their privileges to hamper the free market at will. It is by the very process of slow steps, each scarcely noticed, that unions have been able to persuade unsuspecting millions that the uneconomic gains of the legally privileged few are "social gains" for all.

The American public, as well as the world public, must be alerted to the dangers that flow from government economic intervention. By a process of gradualism, a politically privileged few have fastened on our economy this Marxian policy of ever-increasing "despotic inroads on the rights of property." If the New and Fair Deals had been enacted in toto, they might well have brought the people to their senses far quicker than our continued middle-of-the-road compromising with moral and economic principles.

The so-called "right-to-work" laws are just that, a proposed middle-of-the-road compromise with free market principles for expedient purposes, with the hope lurking in the back of the minds of those who advocate them that some day everything will clear up without employers or consumers ever having to face the issue or the price of meeting it. They forget that the laws of economics are the inexorable laws of cause and effect and that unsound actions will never produce desirable results.

If men want to enjoy ever higher living standards, they must act intelligently and oppose all man-made laws that limit the application of such intelligence to economic matters. Every government intervention is an interference with actions which would grant greater satisfactions to consumers. The only way to increase human satisfactions is to remove all such brakes on increased human happiness and not place any new ones on the statute books of either State or Federal governments.

Every legislative proposal should be weighed on the scales of economic understanding. Does it tip the balance toward a free economy or toward a socialist dictatorship with the politicians in control of the means of production? The so-called "right-to-work" laws are definitely a step in the direction toward Socialism. They limit the right of free men to negotiate contracts for morally acceptable purposes and attempt to substitute the decisions of politicians for those that consumers would like to express in the market place.

PART SIX

On Socialism

XX

French Socialism

by Louis Baudin

(translated from the French by Stephen DiBari)

Professor von Mises has defeated socialism after placing it on scientific ground. This is one of his titles to fame. And yet the name of socialism is still identified with deluded hopes and with memories distorted by time. We therefore propose to examine the so-called socialist doctrine that has survived in France and now serves as the party banner to the "French Section of the Workers' International." (S.F.I.O.)

Economists concur in the belief that there are two characteristics of socialism in its non-communist form: (1) its goal, i.e., the socialization of the means of production and redistribution according to effective services rendered; (2) its means applied, i.e., reforms attained through the manipulation of political forces. Communists, however, advocate the total socialization of production, with the distribution of goods according to need. They count upon the evolution of productive forces to obtain this result. Those who hold to the first doctrine would modify capitalism with graftings of statism, whereas the communists anticipate its spontaneous collapse.

In reality communism reveals a definite shape, whereas we have but a fleeting vision of socialism. A large segment of public opinion conceives the difference between the two doctrines to lie in the submission of the one to the orders of the Kremlin and the maintenance of an independence from Moscow by the other. Undoubtedly, in Stalinist terms, the sole criterion of the non-capitalist world is its conformity with society as organized in Russia—which in its evolution must theoretically evolve through socialism to reach communism. For this reason those socialists in France who refuse obedience to Moscow call themselves "French Socialists." Thus our

French socialism assumes a character contrary to tradition—for in the past it has always posed as a champion of internationalism—and contrary to its name: Section of the International.

To reinforce their position the French socialists attempt to provide their party with historical foundations. They endeavor to re-establish its connection with the predecessors of Marx. But they have not been too happy in this undertaking. For one of their most eminent spokesmen, the sociologist Bouglé, in his book entitled, *Socialismes français*,[1] reviews three nineteenth-century economists whose identification as socialists is very dubious: Saint-Simon, the industrialist who gave power to industrial managers; Fourier, the advocate of cooperatives who generously remunerated capital; Proudhon, the anarchist who reviled the socialists.

Bouglé belongs to the large group of French socialist writers who embrace a truly imperialist spirit: in tracing their socialist ancestry they annex those economists who are not patently liberal and who only may be called "socialists" if one defines the term very broadly and vaguely or, as is often the case, if one abstains from classifying them at all. For them, he who proclaims the supremacy of reason and justice is a socialist. This is the opinion of Léon Blum, for example.[2] But if this were the criterion, there would no longer be a problem, for forty million Frenchmen would all be socialists!

The same thing may be said of present-day writers who apply the term "socialist" to anyone who dedicates himself to the promotion of the common good. These authors disdain the use of classical definitions and even refrain from mentioning their hostility for individual property, which after all is the most distinct characteristic of socialism. Such is the case of Mr. A. Spire who in his *Inventaire des socialismes français contemporains* writes: "Socialism assumes that the purpose of economic activity must be in harmony with collective interests."[3] And thus socialism benefits from this ambiguous definition uniting Christian socialists and syndicalists. The confusion is complete!

Let us recognize that socialism in France has met with misfortune. Whereas liberalism is presently experiencing a magnificent revival through neo-liberalism, socialism has been arrested in its doctrinal evolution by the failure of the neo-socialists: Déat, Mar-

[1] First edition, 1932; third edition, 1941.
[2] *Revue de Paris*, 1 May 1924. Another socialist, M. L. Laurat, emphasizes reason rather than justice, demanding a rationalization of the system of social organization. (*Economie dirigée et socialisation*, Brussels, 1934; *Le manifeste communiste de 1848 et le monde d'aujourd'hui*, Paris, 1948.)
[3] Paris, 1945.

quet, Frossard and some others. These leaders recognized correctly that National Socialism indeed was socialism as its name indicates, and that Hitler "had realized true socialism in Europe." But they were mistaken in drawing from this the conclusion that they could collaborate with the invader. The French socialists not only reproached them for their "treason" but also denied that Nazism had been socialistic, which is so grave an error that one wonders whether it was not deliberate. Indeed, it was better to be injurious to socialism than to recognize it as the doctrine of the occupant. The German economy was certainly socialistic, but the followers of socialism were not motivated by this fact to place themselves under orders of the Nazi leaders.

Let us examine the two contemporary authors who are both theorists and men of action. Both have studied extensively the science of economics and have participated in contemporary politics: Messrs. André Philip and Jules Moch, both former cabinet members.

In 1952, André Philip expounded his ideas in an address to the *Société d'économie politique* [4] and in an article published in the *Revue socialiste*. [5] Indeed, he rejects the Marxian theories and recognizes that the doctrines of capitalist concentration and growing pauperization of the masses are fallacious. He is cognizant of the fact that the lot of the working class is improving, and that labor and management sometimes cooperate in the exploitation of the consumers. Thus he openly abandons Marx and finds another master in Keynes—an unexpected but understandable affinity, for this eminent British economist declared himself a defender of capitalism, but expounded the theory of full employment. André Philip lays little emphasis on doctrine, maintaining that those socialist countries which do not resort to any particular doctrine are better off than those that do, because there are no rigid principles which may hinder adaptation to changing conditions. According to Philip, socialism must conform to certain developments, that is to say, those developments concerning the working class. This is the key to many socialistic notions in France: the precedence of the worker. Everything must hinge upon him; he must be assured the maximum well-being.

We find the same ideas by A. Spire. The general interest is deliberately sacrificed to a collective interest, that of the laboring class. Thus, after having renounced Marx, André Philip reaffirms

[4] January 8, 1952.
[5] April 1952, p. 346.

one of his principle doctrines and makes it the very core of his system: the war of classes.

But in his entire presentation there is not a single attack against private property, nor capital, nor profit. Socialism has become hazy and elusive merely existing on its recognition of its servitude to one segment of the population.

With Mr. Moch we get an entirely different perspective. The latter part of his large volume entitled *Confrontations*[6] interestingly presents the plan of the future state. A central authority regulates the economy with the help of statistics, distributes the factors of production, manages investments, and redistributes the products according to needs. In the case of a shortage, consumption is limited through rationing for the sake of production; at other times the public officials set prices in order to modify demand. One trembles in the thought that the planners vested with so much power are human beings who may err and be led by their feelings and emotions.

Naturally, interest from capital is abolished. It is difficult to understand why the author at first poses as the defender of small savings, without further defining such savings, whereas he later condemns them severely. According to Mr. Moch, small savings must disappear but the victims of this expropriation will be indemnified with a lifetime annuity equal to the average income from the securities expropriated.[7]

It can be seen that this promised land closely resembles the communist paradise. Besides, the author revives the Marxian doctrine through his tacit approval. But he never stops chanting a hymn in praise of liberty, in spite of the authoritarian nature of the system he recommends.

After reading these basic texts, we are at a loss for a proper definition of French socialism. The leeway between the two authors whose works we have just examined is such that we could insert between them all the doctrines that run the gamut from communism to liberalism. Thus socialism is nothing more than a label affixed to a flask whose contents vary according to the whim of the shopkeeper.

How then can we explain the existence of such a socialism in France? First of all, its greatest strength is its vagueness: everybody

[6] Paris, 1952.

[7] In 1945, in a common manifesto, both communists and socialists demanded that the securities of those enterprises whose nationalization was recommended be transformed into lifetime annuities. The conditions of this transformation are those cited by Mr. Moch in his text.

believes what he wants to, adding to it some of his own ideals. Politically speaking, this doctrinal adaptability lends itself to very clever combinations. The problem consists of distributing the promises and benefits among the groups which compose the National Assembly in such a way that enough are satisfied to assure a majority. For example, Mr. Pineau, who was invited to become President of the Council of Ministers but was defeated in February 1955, presented an economic and social program that on many points was not in accord with socialist ideals, as, for example, on the organization of agricultural markets. He even failed to propose all the reforms demanded by the socialist party at the Congress of Suresnes in 1954, notably, in fiscal matters.

Furthermore, socialism in France benefits from two major noneconomic characteristics: its sentimental flavor and its mystic nature.

Socialism poses as the defender of the weak and the poor. Its spokesmen never fail to reiterate the sad conditions of the workers and, above all, of women and children at the beginning of the nineteenth century, for which they blame present-day capitalism. This sort of anachronism impresses the rank and file who are always easily moved. "Men of heart are socialists," says Mr. Moch. There is no doubt that capitalism, which serves as the whipping boy, is presented as monopolistic, Malthusian, instigator of unemployment, war, etc. Indeed one wonders how the readers or listeners can take such a dubious, if not ridiculous, picture seriously.

In reality, it is a one-way sentimentalism. A great number of socialists believe that only the workers are poor, which contradicts actual fact. In France the "economically weak," the small investors, pensioners and aged and sick, are all much more destitute than the workers. André Philip, Jules Moch, and others believe in Jaurès' prediction that "Socialism will come into its own with the growth of the proletariat."

Thus, the socialists are motivated by the interests of a single class and not by the general interest. They candidly acknowledge that governmental measures are accepted or rejected according to the advantages they promise to the workers. Everything else is sacrificed. This is why the socialists oppose any reform of nationalized enterprises and of social security, in spite of the abuses denounced by boards of enquiry. This is also the reason why they do not flinch before the budgetary deficit, inflation[8] or devaluations of the cur-

[8] The Socialist Congress at Suresnes demanded a general increase in the guaranteed minimum wage, without its counterpart in productivity, fully realizing they courted the danger of a formidable inflation.

rency, as we have seen in 1936 and 1937. In order quickly to bring about the hoped-for improvements, the socialists try to raise wages and social costs instead of seeking ways to lower prices, even at the risk of ruining other social classes. In other words, the socialists are apostles of "redistribution of income" through fiscal means. To sum up, we may say that they propose to combat misery—when they are not creating it!

This characteristic class sentimentality has a strong attraction for religious writers. In Catholic circles a campaign is being conducted in favor of an "economy of needs." Their reasoning is as follows: Present demand corresponds only to effective wants and not to genuine wants. The economic price mechanism is inhuman. Society must therefore renounce the play of the law of supply and demand and substitute a system based on the satisfaction of wants. According to these writers, these wants must correspond not only to the vital necessities but also to the amenities of existence and to the "higher values of civilization," which they call "needs of comfort" and of "elevation." [9]

This school of thought benefits from the prestige inherent in the word "humanism" which they make use of. Their opponents are cast in the role of those deprived of any humane feeling. But this is fallacious and confused. First of all, we may conclude from the remarks of these imprudent reformers, that the purchasing power which everybody possesses and which determines his demand, is attributable to chance. In reality, in an unhampered liberal society purchasing power is the outcome of an application of labor or sacrifice of saving. The price system is fair because it corresponds to merit. Next, the "humanitarians" want to distribute the products according to wants. They would thus destroy the tie between production and consumption. An even graver error is their confusion of needs with desires, thereby attributing to the latter the importance that should be reserved for the former. In a word, they arrive at the communist solution without even realizing it!

As to the mystic nature of socialism, people in France call it "leftist," which is a word without precise meaning but with popular appeal. Mr. Moch expressly emphasizes that socialism "is almost a secular religion." On such a ground logic is without force. The man in the street "votes to the left" because his leader wants him to. This reminds us of a parliamentary candidate of liberal leaning, who at the time when a district system of election existed, asked a good friend to run as a conservative—of course, without a chance of suc-

[9] *Economie et humanisme,* March-April 1954, p. 1.

cess. Now he could say at public rallies: "I'm to the left of this gentleman; he is the reactionary!" The words "right" and "left" are among the most effective of all irrational gimmicks of French politics.

Has this sliding towards empiricism and this doctrinal disintegration of socialism brought at least more fortunate results in practice? A poll by the French Institute of Public Opinion[10] has answered this question: the "United Socialist Party" (S.F.I.O.) in less than six years has lost a third of its supporters who turned either communist or moderate. They are growing old noticeably, for some 34 per cent of its voters have passed the fifty mark and, among their loyal supporters, the men far exceed the women in number. It is characteristic that this workers' party is supported at the polls by large numbers of civil servants but relatively few workers who mostly vote the communist ticket.

As the crowning disgrace, the socialist voters lack a militant spirit. That is to say, they are little inclined to work for their party, hardly try to convince their friends, and do not like to discuss politics nor to contribute money. Worse still, they lack full confidence in the party leaders. "One voter in five has confidence in Mr. Guy Mollet; one in ten in Mr. Moch."

The poll-taking concludes that the S.F.I.O. is a common meeting ground for "often contradictory aspirations, for doubts and uncertainties. It is not even a socialism which unites, but almost a group of different socialisms which assemble without a single direction designating the path which all may follow."

Recent events confirm these observations. In 1954-55 we were witness of the revolt of the parliamentary socialists against the central committee of the Party. The rebels went as far as to speak of their individual mental reservations in order to justify their insubordination at the time of the debates on the European Defense Community and the Paris Agreements. It is a party without a single leader who is able to assert himself.

The socialists themselves, in their newspapers and magazines, hardly fail to deplore the "decline," "defeat" and "dissipation" of their party and doctrine.[11] A shrewd observer, who is sympathetic towards socialism, already wrote in 1946: "The socialist idea has foundered and that's a fact."[12]

[10] Published in the revue, *Sondages,* number 3 of 1952.
[11] For numerous references see this author's work *L'aube d'un nouveau libéralisme,* Paris, 1953, p. 125.
[12] François Mauriac: "Le crépuscule du socialisme," *Le Figaro,* 28 August 1946.

Some socialists find consolation in the fact that their party maintains a strong position wherever personal issues retain their importance, in regional and local affairs, in the general councils and in municipalities. Or they find comfort in their central position in Parliament between communists and moderates, which makes them the arbitrators with opportunities to shift the balance of power.

Some good authors attempt to "rejuvenate the doctrine," as they call it. But they are clever enough to circumvent classic socialism. Such is the case of Professor Robert Mossé who writes: "Central planning does not require the collectivization of all the means of production; it is compatible with the existence of private property in certain important areas." He rejects authoritarian central planning; he wants it to be flexible or as "strategic supervision of the whole."[13] In order to avoid bureaucratic tyranny, he falls back on the price mechanism as the yardstick of measurement, allowing free choice to consumers and workers. And he explains that the price alone permits comparison between costs and utilities and allows economic calculation.[14]

Oscar Lange suggested that socialists erect a statue to Ludwig von Mises in gratitude for having made them elaborate their doctrine. Such elaboration seems to be a transformation. The proper inscription of the base of the monument should announce the destruction of socialism rather than its perfection, for this alleged elaboration of doctrine is nothing more than its substitution by vague planning.

The hopes of these advocates of control are varied. Certain of them cling to the conceptions of abundance, of technocracy or control over marginal prices. Their panacea is nationalization and redistribution of income through taxation. Others adhere to the ideas of improving the lot of the workers and of economic democracy through political or syndicalist action. Some latecomers are inspired by the utopians and moralizers of the last century, but they are rare in this age where morality is not held in high regard. A few believe in the virtue of the movement for itself without wanting to know the bank towards which the current is carrying them. In all these tendencies and aspirations we fail to see a single socialist contribution. The literature and particularly the *Revue socialiste* are curiously empty.[15]

[13] "L'évolution doctrinale du socialisme," *Revue de l'Institut de Sociologie de Bruxelles*, 1952, page 373.

[14] *Aux Ecoutes de la Finance*, August 27, 1953.

[15] The revue *Reconstruction*, organ of the French Confederation of Christian Workers, makes a genuine effort to enter the sphere of doctrine.

We do not know whether our present socialism will still be in vogue in the year 2000, as has been predicted by a reformer. We believe that it will remain democratic, although also this expression has become quite ambiguous since the birth of "people's democracies."[16] But we deny that it would be a "true" socialism.

Let us conclude that so-called French socialism is today a "socialism without doctrine."

[16] The word "democracy" vies with the word "socialism" for first place in the realm of ambiguity. (J. Monnerot: "Sur le déclin du socialisme," *Liberté de l'esprit*, November 1950.) Mr. Moch considers Saint Thomas to be a democratic socialist! It may be useful in this respect to recall that in the encyclical Quadragesimo Anno (par. 44 to 50), socialism clearly distinguished from communism is condemned.

Index

(Contributed by Vernelia Crawford)

321